The UK Spirits Industry

Profiles of the leading 1500 companies

John D Blackburn

Editor

dp

First Edition

Spring 2019

ISBN-13: 978-1-912736-13-3

ISBN-10: 1-912736-13-6

All rights reserved. No part of this publication may be reproduced, distributed, or transmitted in any form or by any means, including photocopying, recording, or other electronic or mechanical methods, without our prior written permission, except in the case of brief quotations embodied in critical reviews and certain other non-commercial uses permitted by copyright law. For permission requests, please write to us.

Copyright © 2019 Dellam Publishing Limited

Printed in 8pt Nimbus Sans L

Designed by URW++ Design and Development GmbH

Dellam Publishing Limited

2 Heath Drive, Sutton, Surrey, SM2 5RP

Fax: 020 8770 7478   email: enquiries@dellam.com

SAN: 0177881   EAN/GLN: 5030670177882

Table of Contents

1 Acknowledgements iv

2 Introduction v

3 Total Assets League Table 1
- As a measure of size, total assets is preferable to turnover which is influenced by profit margins and whether companies are capital or labour intensive.

4 Age of Companies 9
- Each company is ranked by its date of incorporation. Newcomers are defined as those registered since 2017.

5 Geographic Distribution 19
- Each company is classed by county.

6 Company Profiles 29
- Full company name, date incorporated, net worth, total assets, registered office, activities, shareholders and parent company, directors (with date of birth, nationality and occupation) and number of employees (if available).

7 Index of Directorships 125
- Alphabetical list of directors showing their directorships. If several directors have identical names then their date of birth is shown.

8 Standard Industrial Classification 161
- These codes are used to classify businesses by the type of economic activity in which they are engaged.

9 *finis* 167

Acknowledgements

This is a long and detailed publication containing thousands of facts and figures. It is only to be expected, despite continuous and repeated editing and checking, that errors may occur. In such cases, once we are aware of any, we publish a correction on our website.

Readers are encouraged to check regularly at www.dellam.com/books for any corrections and updates.

Although we take extreme care to ensure accuracy and being up-to-date, we cannot accept responsibility for any errors or omissions.

Contains public sector information licensed under Open Government Licence v3.0. from The Charity Commission (England and Wales) and The Charity Commission for Northern Ireland. © Crown Copyright and database right (2018).

Contains information from the Scottish Charity Register supplied by the Office of the Scottish Charity Regulator and licensed under the Open Government Licence v.2.0. © Crown Copyright and database right (2018).

Contains OS data © Crown copyright and database right (2018)

Contains Royal Mail data © Royal Mail copyright and database right (2018)

Contains National Statistics data © Crown copyright and database right (2018)

Contains Office for National Statistics © Crown copyright and database right (2018)

Maps based on those produced by the Office for National Statistics Geography GIS & Mapping Unit (2012 and 2018).

Contains HM Land Registry data © Crown copyright and database right (2018).

Contains Parliamentary information licensed under the Open Parliament Licence v3.0.

House of Commons Library Briefing Papers licensed under the Open Parliament Licence v3.0.

Contains Food Standards Agency data © Crown copyright and database right (2018).

Contains Eurostat data, 1995-2018, copyright European Commission by the Decision of 12 December 2011.

Maps based on produced by ONS Geography GIS & Mapping Unit.

Contains Companies House data supplied under section 47 and 50 of the Copyright, Designs and Patents Act 1988 and Schedule 1 of the Database Regulations (SI 1997/3032).

We appreciate your interest in our publications, and your comments and suggestions are always welcome. Please contact us at enquiries@dellam.com.

Introduction

This study looks at all companies registered in the United Kingdom where they identify themselves as distillers, rectifiers and blenders of spirits.

This study includes companies that are dormant or non-trading some of which might be latent while others may operate under their owners' names but are incorporated to protect the business name. In addition, all newly incorporated companies are included. The study will exclude those companies that do not specifically identify themselves as distillers, rectifiers and blenders of spirits.

The aim of this study is to provide an overview of the key movers and shakers in the UK distilling, rectifying and blending of spirits sector. Only key data has been isolated, particularly the company's net worth and total assets, but also its full name, date incorporated, registered office, other activities, shareholders, directors (with date of birth, occupation and nationality) and number of employees.

Two indicators of size are used: net worth and total assets. These are preferable to turnover which is influenced by profit margins and whether the companies are capital or labour intensive.

In the years 2016, 2017 and 2018, new company incorporations in this sector were 155, 273 and 456 respectively.

Whisky has 25% and gin has 7% share of the beverages market in the UK. EU production of whisky is dominated by the UK at £3.4 billion, comprising 81% of the total production, with Spain being second largest at only £74 million. UK manufacturers sales of gin have increased 267% since 2009 from £130 million to £461 million. UK sales represent 72% of the total EU production in 2017, followed by Spain at 11% (£71 million).

The Scotch Whisky Association is the whisky trade body. There are around 128 malt and grain distilleries in Scotland. In 2017, of every £100 of goods exported from the UK, £1.30 was Scotch whisky. Exports of whisky accounted for £4.5 billion worth, or 79%, of spirits exports, with £4.37 billion being Scotch whisky. The EU is main region for Scotch whisky exports and accounted for 32% of the total value of exports in 2017.

Before 2009, no distillery under 400 gallons would be granted a licence. After this policy changed, small, licensed distilleries soared from 113 in 2009 to the current 419.

The Wine and Spirit Trade Association represents the gin trade. Sales of gin at home and abroad has doubled in the last five years. Sales of gin in the UK is £1.5 billion. Gin exports are around £532 million. There are around 315 distilleries in the UK; more than double five years ago. 1.5 million more UK adults are drinking gin than 4 years ago.

More than 11,000 pubs have closed in the UK in the last decade, a fall of almost a quarter (23%). The number of UK pubs has fallen from around 50,000 in 2008 to some 39,000 in 2018. Although many pubs have closed, the total turnover of pubs and bars has held up, remaining flat since 2008, adjusting for inflation. Around 70% of workers in pubs and bars are paid less than the Living Wage Foundation's living wage.

Standard cataloguing guidelines for company names in the profile section have been used, but there will be occurrences when the name may not be strictly alphabetical. A certain licence was adopted where it was felt that strictly alphabetical could lead to improper cataloguing. Some company names have been shortened in the league tables for aesthetic reasons.

John D Blackburn
Editor

This page is intentionally left blank

Total Assets League Table

Chivas Brothers Limited	£6,831,062,016	Drambuie Liqueur Company Ltd. (The)	£15,869,000
Diageo Scotland Limited	£5,077,000,192	CES Whisky Limited	£15,000,296
Coates & Co. (Plymouth) Limited	£3,483,909,888	Kilchoman Distillery Company Ltd.	£13,973,451
Diageo Great Britain Limited	£3,436,999,936	The Welsh Whisky Company Limited	£12,221,553
Chivas Brothers Pernod Ricard	£2,548,134,912	Speyside Distillers Company Limited	£12,144,597
The Edrington Group Limited	£1,904,000,000	Annandale Distillery Company Limited	£10,949,549
William Grant & Sons Distillers Limited	£1,586,162,048	The Glenmorangie Company Limited	£10,889,000
Justerini & Brooks,Limited	£1,432,017,024	The Lakes Distillery Company PLC	£10,870,000
The Macallan Distillers Limited	£702,000,000	Sipsmith Limited	£10,079,000
Whyte and MacKay Limited	£619,561,024	Morrison Glasgow Distillers Limited	£9,972,933
Beam Suntory UK Limited	£573,376,000	Adelphi Distillery Limited	£9,967,888
John Dewar and Sons Limited	£537,265,024	Isle of Harris Distillers Limited	£9,860,436
William Grant & Sons Limited	£450,376,992	AJC Homes Scotland Limited	£9,717,623
Highland Distillers Limited	£374,300,000	Adelphi Distillery (1826) Limited	£9,545,149
MacDonald & Muir Limited	£273,318,016	The Three Stills Company Limited	£9,540,301
Loch Lomond Distillers Limited	£217,186,000	The Cotswold Distilling Company Limited	£9,455,019
Morrison Bowmore Distillers Limited	£176,492,992	Ben Nevis Distillery (Fort William) Limited	£9,320,196
The Old Bushmills Distillery Company Limited	£176,020,992	Wemyss Distillery Limited	£8,179,615
Distell International Limited	£171,064,992	R & B Distillers Limited	£8,173,131
Edrington Distillers Limited	£165,700,000	Greenwood Spirits Limited	£7,645,300
Inver House Distillers Limited	£158,866,000	Ardnahoe Distillery Company Limited	£7,384,944
Loch Lomond Distillery Company Limited	£154,226,000	The Kingsbarns Company of Distillers Ltd	£6,888,285
Glen Scotia Distillery Company Limited	£154,226,000	The Lindores Distilling Co. Ltd	£6,874,879
Highland Distillers Group Limited	£153,200,000	Mossburn Distillers Limited	£5,841,532
Ian MacLeod Distillers Limited	£145,944,992	Chase Distillery Limited	£5,499,464
The Benriach Distillery Company Limited	£141,497,376	True North Brew Co Limited	£5,119,779
The Littlemill Distillery Company Limited	£110,479,000	Ncn'ean Distillery Limited	£4,991,578
Brothers Drinks Co. Limited	£72,885,224	Caledonian Bottlers PLC	£4,929,933
CL World Brands Limited	£71,084,000	MacNab Distilleries Limited	£4,738,000
Adnams PLC	£64,708,000	Brockmans Gin Limited	£4,508,086
The North British Distillery Company Limited	£64,013,000	Campbell Meyer & Co Limited	£4,301,927
Tomatin Distillery Company Limited,(The)	£43,479,584	Aurora Brewing Limited	£4,269,322
Speymalt Whisky Distributors Limited	£43,225,660	Warner's Distillery Limited	£4,156,981
Tullibardine Limited	£42,996,404	Lochlea Distilling Company Limited	£4,154,356
G & J Distillers Ltd.	£26,892,000	Wm. Lundie & Company	£3,754,690
Giorgio's Continental Ltd.	£23,144,680	Echlinville Distillery Limited	£3,634,831
Bladnoch Distillery Limited	£22,376,304	Dr Scotch Whisky Ltd.	£3,594,184
Glasgow Whisky Limited	£22,168,110	Spirits Development & Management Company (SDMC)	£3,439,762
Hunter Laing & Company Limited	£20,675,920	Glasgow Distillery Company Limited	£3,287,564
The Artisanal Spirits Company Limited	£20,343,000	LLDR Alexandria Ltd	£3,200,073
J. & A. Mitchell and Company, Limited	£20,268,120	Glenrinnes Distillery Limited	£3,144,057
The Scotch Malt Whisky Society Limited	£19,495,000	Ramsbury Brewing and Distilling Company Limited	£3,085,206
Distell International Holdings Limited	£18,152,844	Joseph Mills (Denaturants) Limited	£2,964,848
Atom Supplies Limited	£18,093,900	Compass Box Delicious Whisky Ltd.	£2,688,070
Edradour Distillery Company Limited	£17,985,994	D & M Winchester Ltd.	£2,509,464
John Fergus & Co Limited	£17,824,424	Meadowside Blending Company Limited	£2,432,321
Alcohols Limited	£17,664,496	Mitchell's Glengyle Limited	£2,377,487
Broxburn Bottlers Limited	£16,314,073	The Glenglassaugh Distillery Company Limited	£2,351,101
Row & Company Limited	£16,136,183	Rademon Estate Distillery Limited	£2,342,651
MacDuff International (Scotch Whisky) Limited	£16,000,089	St Andrews Brewers Limited	£2,329,965

The UK Spirits Industry dellam

English Whisky Co. Limited	£2,327,734	Arbikie Distilling Limited	£678,686
Torabhaig Distillery Limited	£2,183,058	Doghouse Distillery Limited	£614,778
Demball Limited	£2,080,221	Orkney Distilling Limited	£592,350
Michel Couvreur (Scotch Whiskies) Limited	£2,077,092	Laurence Philippe Wines Limited	£590,043
Hinch Distillery Limited	£1,969,733	Trossachs Distillery Limited	£560,727
Spiritmen Limited	£1,956,913	Strathearn Distillery Ltd.	£538,754
The Peak District Distilling Company Limited	£1,921,380	Durham Gin Limited	£520,394
Spirit of Yorkshire Limited	£1,866,032	JW Distillers Limited	£516,809
Skinnybrands Ltd	£1,702,059	Branscombe Vale Brewery Limited	£507,271
The Bombay Spirits Company Limited	£1,699,000	Broughton Ales Limited	£502,688
U'Luvka Ltd	£1,679,686	The London Distillery Company Ltd	£490,926
London Alcohol Company Ltd	£1,591,884	Cambridge Distillery Ltd	£483,989
Kirklee Scotch Whisky Limited	£1,580,819	Strathleven Distillers Company Limited	£483,106
LDC Scotland Limited	£1,550,313	The Glenallachie Distillers Co Limited	£476,095
White Peak Distillery Limited	£1,547,363	Crafty Scottish Distillers Ltd	£471,299
Still on the Hill Limited	£1,490,932	Bimber Distillery Ltd	£468,935
East London Liquor Company Limited	£1,482,015	House of Elrick Gin Limited	£463,376
Summerhall Distillery Limited	£1,460,160	Drinks of Manchester Limited	£427,028
The Somerset Cider Brandy Company Limited	£1,439,011	Castleheather Facilities Management Ltd	£425,183
Renegade Spirits Grenada Limited	£1,347,563	180 East Limited	£422,677
Thames Distillers Limited	£1,204,068	Global Premium Spirits Ltd	£419,674
Liquid Vision Enterprise Limited	£1,202,885	Food Development Company Limited	£416,502
Bramley and Gage Limited	£1,145,977	Union Distillers Ltd	£378,551
Raer Scotch Whisky Ltd	£1,141,138	Dark Matter Distillers Limited	£377,564
Lone Wolf Spirits Limited	£1,141,000	The 8o8 Drinks Company Limited	£376,639
William Riddell & Sons Limited	£1,132,326	Isle of Wight Distillery Ltd	£367,523
RSM Solutions (NE) Limited	£1,128,360	45 West Distillers Limited	£366,733
Portavadie Distillery Limited	£1,110,483	The Beautiful Distillery Limited	£362,625
Matisse Spirits Company Limited	£1,067,537	Conker Spirit Limited	£359,920
Elephant Gin Ltd	£1,003,937	The Boatyard Distillery Ltd	£343,542
Our/London Vodka Limited	£998,494	Ulster Distilleries Limited	£337,801
Masons Yorkshire Gin Ltd	£990,712	EMS Corp Limited	£336,169
Dunnet Bay Distillers Ltd.	£987,089	Dartmoor Whisky Distillery Ltd	£320,302
Southwestern Distillery Limited	£954,224	Central Line Holdings Limited	£317,674
Foxdenton Estate Company Limited	£947,171	Dormont Distilling Limited	£308,555
3R Whisky Limited	£891,303	Langstane Liquor Company Limited	£289,319
Burnbrae Distillery Company Ltd	£874,890	Pure Wild Spirits Ltd	£276,864
Russell Distillers Limited	£872,949	Batch Brew Ltd	£276,600
Diageo Balkans Limited	£866,000	Dornoch Distillery Company Limited	£267,280
Matthew D'Arcy & Company Limited	£852,956	Colonsay Beverages Ltd.	£264,888
Salcombe Distilling Company Ltd	£816,737	Harrogate Distillery Ltd	£256,057
H. J. Neill Ltd	£807,000	Sweetdram Limited	£246,384
W & S Distillery Limited	£791,180	Moorland Spirit Company Limited	£245,883
Ginmeister Ltd	£766,861	Anno Distillers Limited	£244,081
Zymurgorium Ltd	£765,763	Stanley Morrison & Co. Ltd	£243,950
Princetown Distillers Ltd	£758,686	The Shetland Distillery Company Limited	£241,674
Spirit of Harrogate Limited	£751,580	Eccentric Gin Co Limited	£240,106
Broker's Gin Limited	£748,671	Alastair McIntosh Management Services Limited	£239,897
Patient Wolf Limited	£741,320	The High Street Trading Company Limited	£236,342
Kammerling's Investment Holdings Ltd	£721,544	The Orogin Distilling Co. Limited	£232,358

Company	Amount	Company	Amount
Scream Retail Limited	£226,147	Blackford Craft Distillery Ltd	£118,942
Gordon & Company (Distillers) Limited	£224,826	Forest Spirits Ltd	£118,825
Fanny's Distilling Company Limited	£223,099	Rockwood & Hines Limited	£116,539
The Bloomsbury Club UK Limited	£219,460	Peats Beast Limited	£116,214
Black Shuck Ltd	£211,625	Sibling Distillery Limited	£115,581
The Start-Up Drinks Lab Limited	£206,699	The East India Company Gin Limited	£114,618
Deya Brewing Company Limited	£205,995	Kinrara Distillery Limited	£112,360
Finnieston Distillery Company Limited	£205,776	Deerness Distillery Ltd	£106,849
LLDY Alexandria Ltd	£199,195	Crossbill Distilling Limited	£105,868
Tea Venture Limited	£197,442	NB Distillery Limited	£103,695
The Old Curiosity Distillery Ltd	£194,936	The Old Chapel Brendon Limited	£103,407
Bermondsey Distillery Limited	£191,576	New Adventure (Norfolk) Limited	£102,022
Devon Distillery Limited	£189,845	Chalk & Charcoal Limited	£101,676
Psychopomp Ltd	£187,351	Slamseys Drinks Limited	£101,425
Barford Imports Limited	£183,614	Griffiths Brothers Distillery Ltd	£100,445
Jose Reyes Bodega Ltd	£182,001	Leith Liqueur Company Limited	£96,268
Forest Distillery Ltd	£179,255	Trevethan Distillery Ltd	£96,234
Green Box Drinks Limited	£178,101	Soapbox Spirits Ltd	£93,507
Barcelona Spirit Brands UK Limited	£170,381	Isle of Skye Distillers Ltd	£86,353
Cooper King Distillery Ltd	£169,977	Langs Consulting Ltd.	£84,933
Liberty Orchards Limited	£169,754	Tipsy Fruit Gins Limited	£84,087
House of St Giles Ltd	£168,900	Loch Ness Spirits Limited	£81,895
Archangel Distilleries Ltd	£167,756	Pocketful of Stones Distillers Limited	£81,306
The Nodding Donkey Distillery Company Limited	£167,352	Sangobeg Ltd	£80,739
Copeland Spirits Ltd	£167,026	Tay Spirits Ltd.	£80,124
Knowcal Limited	£164,842	Ron de Mestizo Ltd	£80,000
Ogilvy Spirits Limited	£161,757	Round Wood Distillery Ltd	£79,588
Verdant Spirits Ltd.	£160,755	Fixed Axis Ltd	£79,012
Gin Foundry Limited	£160,727	Gibson Whisky Ltd	£78,818
Locksley Distilling Company Limited	£157,771	Todka Limited	£77,324
Story Brands Limited	£154,527	Capreolus Distillery Ltd	£77,124
Penton Park Brewery Limited	£153,757	Scots' Cheer Limited	£76,971
Beinn An Tuirc Distillers Limited	£152,922	Gun Dog Gin Limited	£75,401
Dyfi Distillery Ltd	£152,164	Spirit of The Lakes Limited	£74,064
Westmorland Spirits Limited	£144,894	Islay Spirits (No. 2) Limited	£73,741
Colwith Farm Distillery Limited	£138,957	4t's Brewery Ltd	£73,183
Brighton Spirits Company Ltd	£138,022	Snowdonia Distillery Ltd	£72,976
Willem Barentsz Limited	£137,830	Wight Spirits Ltd	£72,237
Henstone Distillery Limited	£136,999	Shakespeare Distillery Limited	£71,215
The Ely Gin Company Ltd.	£136,975	The Ginking Company Limited	£71,013
The Handmade Gin Company Ltd	£132,143	The Chilgrove Gin Company Ltd	£70,473
Black Cat Distillery Limited	£130,135	Wild Thyme Spirits Limited	£70,226
The Boutique Cellar Limited	£128,656	Newton Drinks Limited	£69,497
VS Distillers Limited	£128,277	The Islay Boys Limited	£68,227
Riverside Spirits Ltd	£127,183	Sloeberry Spirits Ltd.	£67,466
Pococello Ltd	£125,443	East Neuk Organic Brewing & Distilling Ltd	£64,209
The Bloomsbury Distillery Ltd	£123,031	Black Powder Gin Company Ltd	£64,042
Gin Bothy Limited	£122,361	Brennen & Brown Limited	£62,979
The Kendal Mint Cake Company Limited	£121,148	Broad Street Brands Limited	£62,949
Alnwick Rum Company Limited	£120,093	Ludlow Distillery Limited	£62,902

The UK Spirits Industry

R2 Distillers Ltd	£60,152	City of Aberdeen Distillery Ltd	£36,429
Escubac Limited	£59,933	Carrick Thomson Limited	£35,463
Mourne Dew Limited	£59,749	The Surrey Hills Distilling Company Ltd	£35,124
Dartmoor Distillery Limited	£58,638	A Little Luxury Ltd	£34,864
Lincoln Imp Drinks Company Limited	£58,326	MWBH Bottling Co. Limited	£33,563
Kirkwood Distillery Limited	£56,672	The Lickerish Tooth Ltd	£33,307
The Cornish Distilling Company Ltd	£56,377	HMS Spirits Company Limited	£32,855
Rainbow Chaser Limited	£55,869	Graveney Gin Limited	£32,652
Newcastle Gin Co. Limited	£55,660	Steampunk Ltd	£32,139
Pesvebi Ltd	£54,104	The Southey Brewing Company Limited	£30,692
Silverback Distillers Ltd	£54,043	Canebrake Ltd	£30,400
Bath Botanics Limited	£53,687	The Corrupt Drinks Company Limited	£30,296
Rare Bird Distillery Limited	£53,406	Etoh Studio Limited	£29,614
Dr Adam Elmegirabs Bitters Ltd	£52,683	Linlithgow Distillery Limited	£29,549
Benjamin & Blum Limited	£51,247	Tasty Beverages Limited	£29,530
Spirit of Manchester Distillery Limited	£50,140	Willimott House Limited	£29,010
Guilty Libations Limited	£49,384	New Dawn Traders Ltd	£28,844
Northumberland Spirit Company Ltd	£48,823	Flint & Hardings Limited	£28,472
Espensen Spirit Ltd	£48,818	The Garden Shed Drinks Company Limited	£28,326
Inshriach Distilling Limited	£48,520	Matugga Beverages Limited	£28,172
Kingston Distillers Ltd.	£48,291	Honey Spirits Co Ltd	£27,741
Tipsy Wight Ltd	£48,064	Jim & Tonic Limited	£27,379
Golden Measure Limited	£47,857	Gin Jar Drinks Company Ltd	£27,034
Founding Drinks Ltd	£47,806	HS (Distillers) Limited	£27,000
North Uist Distillery Ltd	£47,572	Shed 1 Distillery Ulverston. Limited	£25,806
Exmoor Distillers Ltd	£47,192	O'Hara's Spiced Rum Limited	£25,740
55 Above Ltd	£46,887	The Teasmith Spirit Company Limited	£25,574
Leeds Gin Limited	£46,884	Exeter Gin Ltd	£25,560
The Really Brilliant Company Limited	£46,406	Silhill Brewery Limited	£25,329
The Shropshire Gin Company Limited	£45,883	Lakeland Moon Limited	£24,758
Twisting Spirits Ltd	£45,546	Amber Glen Scotch Whisky Co., Ltd	£24,671
Libation Liberation Limited	£44,670	Tarbraxus Distillers Ltd	£24,301
The Whisky Cellar Limited	£43,998	El Gin Findrassie Ltd	£24,125
Kammerlings Limited	£43,302	Armadillo Spirits Limited	£23,887
The Tiny Tipple Company Limited	£42,939	Cheshire Distilleries Limited	£23,876
The Sipping Shed Limited	£42,485	Badvo Distillery Limited	£23,817
The Suffolk Distillery Limited	£42,172	Black Cat Brewery Limited	£23,795
Whitetail Spirits Limited	£42,150	Marron (Lincoln) Ltd	£23,794
Rhucello Limited	£42,096	Electric Spirit Company Ltd.	£23,569
Burning Barn Limited	£41,544	Royal Wootton Bassett Gin Company Ltd	£23,556
Family of Hounds Limited	£41,226	Wood Brothers Distilling Company Limited	£23,525
Nip from The Hip Limited	£40,667	Jo & Matt Ltd	£23,287
Lundin Distilling Company Limited	£40,462	Maxchater Ltd	£22,563
Moorland Distillery Limited	£39,428	Stonedean Limited	£22,004
YDC Ltd	£38,467	Morant Bay Distillery Co Limited	£21,740
Glass Jigsaw Ltd.	£37,955	Fruity Tipples Limited	£21,613
Martin-Wells Distillery Ltd.	£37,135	Manchester Still Ltd.	£21,477
York Gin Company Limited	£37,024	Artisan Brands Limited	£21,472
Bottomley Distillers Ltd	£36,976	Montoscar Enterprises Limited	£21,274
2H1O Limited	£36,470	Gin Tales Ltd	£21,148

Company	Amount	Company	Amount
Distillutions Ltd	£21,097	Whitley Neill Limited	£11,612
The Northumberland Gin Company Limited	£20,822	The Willow Tree Distilling Company Limited	£11,562
Asterley Bros, London Ltd	£20,780	Hilary Blackford Associates Limited	£11,335
Pixel Spirits Limited	£20,714	Cornish Spirit Company Limited	£11,167
Foxhole Spirits Limited	£20,333	Richie & Nikki Ltd	£11,048
Pure Distilled Spirit Company Limited	£20,225	Charlie Kaane Enterprises Ltd.	£10,933
Polo Gin Limited	£20,141	Granite North Spirits Limited	£10,646
Buxton Distillery Limited	£20,087	Mews Gin Company Limited	£10,505
Faith and Sons Limited	£20,074	Duck and Crutch Limited	£10,363
Esker Spirits Ltd	£19,972	Windfall Wood Group Limited	£10,361
Desire Drinks Limited	£19,932	Crafted Beverages Limited	£10,332
Heart of Suffolk Distillery Limited	£19,929	Strawhill Estate Distillery Ltd	£10,321
50 Degrees North Limited	£19,175	3 Lids Rum Ltd	£10,296
Greywood Distillery Limited	£18,753	Helford River Distillery Ltd	£10,003
Single Estate Spirits Ltd	£18,700	Label 5 First Blending Company Limited	£10,000
Sartorial Spirits Limited	£18,538	Waveney Valley Spirits Limited	£9,730
Tappers Artisan Spirits Ltd.	£18,525	Gaelic Pure Scotch Whisky Limited	£9,526
McCaigs Distillery Ltd	£18,520	The Beers Spirit Company Ltd	£9,423
Koolvibes Limited	£18,448	Deeside Distillers Ltd	£9,294
Corner Fifty Three Distilling Ltd	£18,034	The Rum Club Ltd	£8,515
Stirling Gin Ltd.	£17,831	Fatman and Friends Ltd.	£8,100
Kelso Gin Company Limited	£17,682	The Pentland Still Ltd	£7,722
Tors Vodka Limited	£17,640	Malt of the Earth Whisky Company Ltd.	£7,675
Tarsier Spirit Ltd	£17,515	Empire Bar Service Ltd	£7,648
Geordie-Gin Co Ltd	£17,343	Ten Bears Spirits Limited	£7,471
Originalsip Ltd	£17,260	3D Shapie Limited	£7,178
Loca Beverages Ltd	£17,037	Lindsay's Still Room Ltd	£7,038
Rebel Distillers Ltd	£16,610	Northern Spirits Partnership Ltd	£6,904
Gin Kitchen Limited	£16,198	Fort Glen Whisky Company Limited	£6,720
Fourfolk Gin Company Ltd	£16,103	Your Buddy Mary Limited	£6,460
Jacqson Limited	£15,989	Myatt's Fields Limited	£6,316
Cabin Pressure Spirits Ltd	£15,719	Ginomics Ltd	£5,970
Highland Boundary Ltd	£15,599	Parlay Drinks Ltd	£5,785
Duration Brewing Ltd	£15,542	The Ecclefechan Whisky Company Limited	£5,292
Rathlee Distilling Company Ltd.	£15,337	Redrosesforme Limited	£4,973
One Point Eight Bar Limited	£15,214	Montrose Scotch Whisky Ltd.	£4,938
Alderman's Drinks Ltd.	£15,207	Bluu Spirit Limited	£4,778
The Brixham Gin Company Ltd.	£14,813	Boho Drinks Ltd	£4,394
Spirits and Bubbles Limited	£14,706	Madame Jennifer Distillery Limited	£4,392
Hoggnorton Limited	£14,050	Little Rotters Limited	£4,370
The Spirits of Bronte Drinks Co. Ltd	£13,924	Red Squirrel Brands Ltd	£4,294
Dunville & Co. Limited	£13,882	Artisan Blending Limited	£4,284
Highland Whisky Limited	£13,548	Papillon Dartmoor Distillery Limited	£4,050
Buck and Birch Ltd	£13,534	For The Love of Limited	£4,041
V7 Enterprises Ltd	£13,309	Whisky and Cognac.Uk Limited	£3,866
Libaeration Limited	£12,393	Camden Distillers Limited	£3,846
Square Street Distillery Ltd	£12,258	Toulvaddie Distillery Limited	£3,765
K1 Beer PLC	£12,046	Scout and Sage Spirits Limited	£3,513
Hinton's of Bewdley Ltd	£11,827	Crossbill Gin Limited	£3,178
Ban Poitin Ltd	£11,730	Drink It Limited	£2,843

Dallinger Gin Limited	£2,833	Coyote Ventures Limited	£169
Dutch Courage Spirits Limited	£2,819	Distill8 Limited	£142
The Sin of Gin Ltd	£2,799	Skinny Russian Vodka Ltd	£100
Second Son Distillery Limited	£2,626	Inverroche International Limited	£100
Avalon Distillery Company Ltd	£2,545	Avinshaw Industries Limited	£100
The Pentone Family Limited	£2,269	Five Fathoms Spirit Limited	£100
Bishopsgate Distillery & Wine Company Limited	£2,166	Supermarine Vodka Distillers Limited	£100
The Hebridean Liqueur Company Limited	£2,149	London Spiced Dry Limited	£100
Fancy A Tipple Limited	£1,954	Port Charlotte Limited	£100
Knockeen Hills Spirits Ltd	£1,951	The Shieling Scotch Whisky Co Ltd	£100
The Lowestoft Distillery Company Limited	£1,945	Andrew Laing & Company Limited	£100
Isle of Barra Distillers Ltd	£1,914	Hunter Douglas Scotch Whisky Limited	£100
Londinio Liqueurs Ltd.	£1,795	Isle of Arran Gin Company Limited	£100
Tricort Limited	£1,778	Chileanspirit Ltd	£95
Loch Leven Distillery Limited	£1,745	Jedhart Distillery Limited	£80
Galleon Liqueurs UK Ltd	£1,645	Loch Earn Brewery Ltd	£69
American Beverage Marketers Limited	£1,517	William Craig & Company Limited	£66
London Spice Company Limited	£1,404	Block, Grey and Block Limited	£27
Sword of Spirit Distillery Limited	£1,397	Murphy, Black and Mills Limited	£21
Caribbean Drinks Ltd	£1,372	A.D.C. Halford & Company Limited	£8
Boozy Infusion Limited	£1,364	Irish Whiskey Company Limited	£5
Lochglen Whisky Company Ltd.	£1,300	The East India Company London Dry Gin Ltd	£2
Rebel Rabbet Ltd	£1,198	The Big Hill Distillery Limited	£2
Nightrep Limited	£1,197	Belfast Distillers Ltd	£2
Renaissance Drinks Ltd	£1,190	Glasgow Partners Ltd.	£2
Dark Art Gin Limited	£1,186	The Armagnac Company Limited	£2
Spirit of Glasgow Ltd	£1,036	Macmillan Scotch Whisky Company Limited	£2
Beerdsman Limited	£1,018	Malcolm Browne Distillery Company Limited	£1
Syndicate 58/6 Limited	£1,000	London Heaven Spirits Company UK Ltd	£1
Loch Ness Drinks Ltd	£977	Seduction Rum Punch UK Ltd	£1
Anstie Distillers International Limited	£915	Seven Deadly Sins Ltd	£1
Terrepure Spirits UK Ltd.	£757	Gaslight Distillery Limited	£1
Eoforwic Distilling Company Limited	£724	Whitby Gin Limited	£1
Beach Craft Spirits Limited	£656	Beachcomber Gin Ltd	£1
HI&PE Limited	£511	Curious Liquids Limited	£1
Black Arid Kegs Ltd	£354	Shire Gin Limited	£1
Calder Glen Ltd	£300	The Shropshire Distillery Limited	£1
McMillan MacRaild Ltd	£262	Glen Clyde Ltd.	£1
Saddleworth Distillery Ltd	£240	The Benromach Distillery Co Ltd	£1
Jewel Isle Global Productions Ltd	£200	The Whisky Club Ltd	£1
Gedrick Distilling Company Limited	£200	Glasgow Gin Company Limited	£1
Deshi Liqueur Ltd	£172		

This page is intentionally left blank

Age of Companies

1800s [5]
Adnams PLC
Diageo Scotland Limited
Highland Distillers Group Ltd
J. & A. Mitchell and Company, Ltd
North British Distillery Co Ltd

1900-1909
Justerini & Brooks, Limited

1910-1919 [5]
Ardbeg Distillery Limited
Bonding and Transport Company, Ltd
James Catto & Co Ltd
Diageo Distilling Limited
James Martin & Company, Ltd

1920-1929 [6]
Drambuie Liqueur Co Ltd.
Edrington Distillers Limited
Glendronach Distillery Co Ltd
Nicol Anderson & Co Ltd
Scottish Independent Distillers Co Ltd
Whyte and MacKay Limited

1930-1939 [10]
Foxdenton Estate Co Ltd
Glenmorangie Distillery Co Ltd, The
Matthew Gloag & Son Limited
Alistair Graham Limited
MacDonald & Muir Limited
MacNab Distilleries Limited
Douglas MacNiven & Co Ltd
Charles Muirhead & Son. Ltd
Old Bushmills Distillery Co Ltd
Row & Co Ltd

1940-1949 [5]
Ben Nevis Distillery (Fort William)
Glenmorangie Co Ltd
J. & G. Grant
Macallan Distillers Limited
Mason & Summers Limited

1950-1959 [6]
Alcohols Limited
R. Carmichael & Sons Limited
John Dewar and Sons Limited
Diageo Great Britain Limited
Hayman Distillers Limited
Ian MacLeod Distillers Ltd

1960-1969 [9]
Avonside Whisky Limited
Carillon U.K. Limited
Edrington Group Limited
Elgin Bonding Co Ltd
Inver House Distillers Limited
Ian MacLeod and Co Ltd
Port Charlotte Limited
Speymalt Whisky Distributors Ltd
Strathnairn Whisky Limited

1970-1979 [7]
Dunville & Co. Limited
Glen Calder Blenders Limited
Hankey Bannister & Co Ltd
Wm. Lundie & Company
J. MacArthur Jr. & Co. Ltd
Joseph Mills (Denaturants) Ltd
Montrose Scotch Whisky Ltd.

1980-1989 [30]
Barford Imports Limited
Blairmhor Limited
Broxburn Bottlers Limited
Campbell Meyer & Co Limited
Michel Couvreur (Scotch Whiskies)
Demball Limited
Diageo Balkans Limited
Distell International Limited
EB Alexandria Ltd
English Whisky Co. Limited
Giorgio's Continental Ltd.
Glen Gordon Whisky Co Ltd
Glenmorangie Spring Water Co Ltd
Glenturret Distillery Limited
Gordon Bonding Co Ltd
James Gordon Whisky Co Ltd
Irish Whiskey Co Ltd - The
Knockdhu Distillery Co Ltd
Light Spirit Co Ltd
Lombard Scotch Whisky Limited
Meadowside Blending Co Ltd
Morangie Mineral Water Co Ltd
Morangie Springs Limited
Morrison Bowmore Distillers Ltd
Laurence Philippe Wines Ltd
Scotch Malt Whisky Society Ltd
Somerset Cider Brandy Co Ltd
Tarlogie Springs Limited
Tomatin Distillery Co Ltd,(The)
Tricort Limited

1990-1994 [20]
Aberdeen Distillers Limited
Adelphi Distillery Limited
Ardbeg Limited
Blairmhor Distillers Limited
Brothers Drinks Co. Limited
CES Whisky Limited
Caledonian Bottlers PLC
William Grant & Sons Distillers Ltd
William Grant & Sons Limited
Hart Brothers Limited
High Street Trading Co Ltd
Hurlingham International Ltd
LLDY Alexandria Ltd
MacDuff & Co Ltd
MacDuff (Scotch Whisky) Ltd
MacDuff International (Scotch Whisky)
Wm Maxwell (Scotch Whisky) Ltd
Speyburn-Glenlivet Distillery Co.
United Distillers UK Limited
Wee Beastie Ltd.

1995 [10]
Broughton Ales Limited
Dun Eideann Scotch Whisky Co Ltd
Hawksburn Spirits International Ltd
Hebridean Liqueur Co Ltd
Highland Distillers Limited
MacDonald Martin Distilleries Ltd

Alastair McIntosh Management Services
Moffat & Towers Limited
Pulteney Distillery Co Ltd
Scream Retail Limited

1996 [5]
Atom Supplies Limited
Balblair Distillery Co Ltd
Coates & Co. (Plymouth) Ltd
HS (Distillers) Limited
Thames Distillers Limited

1997
Block, Grey and Block Limited
Fogcutter Limited

1998 [9]
AJC Homes Scotland Limited
Bombay Spirits Co Ltd
Broker's Gin Limited
Glasgow Partners Ltd.
A.D.C. Halford & Co Ltd
LLDR Alexandria Ltd
Perthshire Whisky Co Ltd
Scots' Cheer Limited
Welsh Whisky Co Ltd

1999
MWBH Bottling Co. Limited
New Welsh Whiskey Co Ltd
Speyside Distillers Co Ltd

2000 [8]
Armagnac Co Ltd
Burn Stewart (U.S. Holdings) Ltd
Chivas Brothers Pernod Ricard
Compass Box Delicious Whisky Ltd.
Ecclefechan Whisky Co Ltd
Mitchell's Glengyle Limited
Tullibardine Limited
Y Cwmni Chwisgi Cymraeg Newydd Cyf

2001
Glen Moray-Glenlivet Distillery Co Ltd
Kilchoman Distillery Co Ltd.
Rathlee Distilling Co Ltd.
Whisky Galore Limited

2002 [8]
Branscombe Vale Brewery Ltd
Edradour Distillery Co Ltd
Hendrick's Gin Distillery Ltd
Sailor Jerry Limited
True North Brew Co Limited
Ulster Distilleries Limited
Wilson & Morgan Limited
Wood and Co Ltd

2003 [11]
Alnwick Rum Co Ltd
Benriach Distillery Co Ltd
Malcolm Browne Distillery Co Ltd
Bunnahabhain Distillery Co Ltd
CL World Brands Limited
Gordon Graham & Co Ltd
Lang Brothers Limited
Loch Earn Brewery Ltd
Ludlow Vineyard Limited
Peter J Russell & Co Ltd.
St. James Distillery Limited

The UK Spirits Industry

2004 [9]
American Beverage Marketers Ltd
Chivas Brothers Limited
William Craig & Co Ltd
Echlinville Distillery Limited
Kirklee Scotch Whisky Limited
Matisse Spirits Co Ltd
Tipsy Fruit Gins Limited
Whitley Neill Limited
D & M Winchester Ltd.

2005 [15]
50 Degrees North Limited
Beam Suntory UK Limited
Bishopsgate Distillery & Wine Co Ltd
Spencer Collings & Co Limited
Deshi Liqueur Ltd
Drink It Limited
Guilty Drinks Limited
Highland Whisky Limited
C S James & Sons Limited
Leith Liqueur Co Ltd
Macmillan Scotch Whisky Co Ltd
Norfolk Whisky Co. Limited
Percy's T Limited
Spencerfield Spirit Co Ltd
Todka Limited

2006 [11]
Brockmans Gin Limited
Castleheather Facilities Management Ltd
Chase Distillery Limited
Corky's Brands Limited
Glenglassaugh Distillery Co Ltd
Knowcal Limited
Lochindaal Distillery Limited
Rockwood & Hines Limited
Sangobeg Ltd
Strathleven Distillers Co Ltd
V K Brands Limited

2007 [11]
Annandale Distillery Co Ltd
Bramley and Gage Limited
Glasgow Whisky Limited
Highlands Spirit Ltd.
Independent Spirits Limited
Isle of Harris Distillers Ltd
Portavadie Distillery Limited
Rainbow Chaser Limited
William Riddell & Sons Ltd
Rosebank Whisky Limited
Sipsmith Limited

2008 [6]
Islay Rum Co Ltd
Libaeration Limited
Ludlow Distillery Limited
RSM Solutions (NE) Limited
Spirit of The Lakes Limited
Square Street Distillery Ltd

2009 [12]
2H1O Limited
Caribbean Drinks Ltd
Chileanspirit Ltd
Damsons in Distress Limited
Distill8 Limited
EMS Corp Limited
Food Development Co Ltd
Global Premium Spirits Ltd
Kingsbarns Company of Distillers Ltd
Lochglen Whisky Co Ltd.
Stonedean Limited
Windfall Wood Group Limited

January-June 2010 [12]
4t's Brewery Ltd
Brennen & Brown Limited
Cornish Distillery Co Ltd
East India Company London Dry Gin Ltd
Fort Glen Whisky Co Ltd
Kammerlings Limited
Liberty Orchards Limited
London Alcohol Co Ltd
Old Chapel Brendon Limited
Silhill Brewery Limited
V7 Enterprises Ltd
Westmorland Spirits Limited

July-December 2010
Adelphi Distillery (1826) Ltd
Donnach Whisky Limited
Mannequin Ltd.

January-June 2011 [20]
1761 Limited
A Little Luxury Ltd
Bimber Distillery Ltd
Boozy Infusion Limited
Botanical Alchemy Ltd
Cambridge Distillery Ltd
John Fergus & Co Limited
G & J Distillers Ltd.
Gaelic Pure Scotch Whisky Ltd
Glass Jigsaw Ltd.
Glen Clyde Ltd.
Lakeland Moon Limited
Liquid Vision Enterprise Ltd
Liveras Limited
London Distillery Co Ltd
Marron (Lincoln) Ltd
Nip from The Hip Limited
Story Brands Limited
Ten Bears Spirits Limited
W & S Distillery Limited

July-December 2011 [15]
Anno Distillers Limited
Aurora Brewing Limited
Batch Brew Ltd
Black Cow Vodka Co Ltd
Broad Street Brands Limited
Camden Distillers Limited
Ely Gin Co Ltd.
Gilbert and John Greenall Ltd
Howards of Kent Limited
Kammerling's Investment Holdings Ltd
Lakes Distillery Company PLC
Marblehead Brand Development Ltd
Stanley Morrison & Co. Ltd
Riverside Spirits Ltd
Willimott House Limited

January-March 2012 [12]
Benjamin & Blum Limited
Botanist Limited
Gibson Whisky Ltd
Green Box Drinks Limited
Jewel Isle Global Productions Ltd
Ludlow Apple Brandy Distillery Ltd
O'Hara's Spiced Rum Limited
Peats Beast Limited
Slamseys Drinks Limited
Sloeberry Spirits Ltd.
St Andrews Brewers Limited
Union Distillers Ltd

April-June 2012 [15]
Boutique Cellar Limited
Caribbean Flaava Limited
Cornish Spirit Co Ltd
Dark Matter Distillers Limited
Galleon Liqueurs UK Ltd
Kendal Mint Cake Co Ltd
LDC Scotland Limited
Morrison Glasgow Distillers Ltd
Orbis Whiskey Limited
Oxford Distillery Limited
R2 Distillers Ltd
Rademon Estate Distillery Ltd
Raer Scotch Whisky Ltd
Terrepure Spirits UK Ltd.
Warner's Distillery Limited

July-September 2012 [12]
Armadillo Spirits Limited
Bermondsey Distillery Limited
Black Cat Brewery Limited
Calder Glen Ltd
Cognac Growers' Collective Ltd
Dr Scotch Whisky Ltd.
Elephant Gin Ltd
K1 Beer PLC
Pesvebi Ltd
Southwestern Distillery Ltd
Spirit of Yorkshire Limited
Syndicate 58/6 Limited

October-December 2012 [19]
3R Whisky Limited
Ban Poitin Ltd
Benromach Distillery Co Ltd
Hilary Blackford Associates Ltd
Compass Box Whisky Supply Ltd
Cu Dhub Distilling Co Ltd
Cwmni Distyllfa Llanberis Cyf
Devon Distillery Limited
Dr Adam Elmegirabs Bitters Ltd
Glasgow Distillery Co Ltd
Glens of Antrim Whiskey Co Ltd
Gordon & Company (Distillers) Ltd
Islay Boys Limited
Knockeen Hills Spirits Ltd
Malt Whisky Investment Co Ltd
Masons Yorkshire Gin Ltd
Rosebank Distillery Camelon Ltd
Strawhill Ltd
Wemyss Distillery Limited

January-March 2013 [23]
Amber Glen Scotch Whisky Co., Ltd
Chinn-Chinn Ginn Limited
Thomas Dakin Distiller Ltd
Thomas Dakin Limited
Dornoch Distillery Co Ltd
Durham Gin Limited
Ginmeister Ltd
Hereford & Ludlow Cider Brandy Co Ltd
Hunter Laing & Co Ltd
Lindores Distilling Co. Ltd
Locksley Distilling Co Ltd
London Heaven Spirits Company UK Ltd
Luxury Trading Co Ltd
NB Distillery Limited
Ncn'ean Distillery Limited
Premier Bonding Co Ltd
Ramsbury Brewing and Distilling Co Ltd
Still House Ltd
Strathearn Distillery Ltd.
Sword of Spirit Distillery Ltd
Three Stills Co Ltd
Tipsy Wight Ltd
U'Luvka Ltd

April-June 2013 [14]
Artisan Brands Limited
Boatyard Distillery Ltd
Cotswold Distilling Co Ltd
Duckenfield Ltd
East London Liquor Co Ltd
Edinburgh Whisky Ltd.
G & J Greenall Group Limited
G & J Limited
Garden Shed Drinks Co Ltd
Ludlow Whisky Limited
Malt of the Earth Whisky Co Ltd.
Russell Distillers Limited
Surrey Hills Distilling Co Ltd
Wicked Wolf Limited

July-September 2013 [27]
Berkshire Distillery Limited
Brighton Spirits Co Ltd
Chilgrove Gin Co Ltd
Darlington Brewing and Distilling Co Ltd
Duke's Distilling Co Ltd
Dunnet Bay Distillers Ltd.
Edinburgh Gin Limited
Fanny's Distilling Co Ltd
Finnieston Distillery Co Ltd
Glen Scotia Distillery Co Ltd
Half Cock Limited
Highland Toddy Ltd
Jedhart Distillery Limited
Littlemill Distillery Co Ltd
Loca Beverages Ltd
Loch Lomond Distillers Limited
Loch Lomond Distillery Co Ltd
Mossburn Distillers Limited
New Dawn Traders Ltd
Ogilvy Spirits Limited
Shetland Distillery Co Ltd
Spnet Ltd.
Summerhall Distillery Limited
Torabhaig Distillery Limited
Valt Vodka Co Ltd
Yorkshire Distillery Co Ltd
Yorkshire Whisky Co Ltd

October-December 2013 [11]
180 East Limited
Arbikie Distilling Limited
Dartmoor Distillery Limited
Faith and Sons Limited
Kelpies Whisky Limited
Kingston Distillers Ltd.
Label 5 First Blending Co Ltd
Langholm Distillery Limited
Sibling Distillery Limited
Spirits Development & Management Company (SDMC)
Trevethan Distillery Ltd

January-March 2014 [12]
Bath Botanics Limited
Beautiful Distillery Limited
Coleburn Distillery Limited
Conker Spirit Limited
Crossbill Distilling Limited
Dundee Distillery Co Ltd
Escubac Limited
Gin Foundry Limited
Harrogate Distillery Ltd
Sipping Shed Limited
Spiritmen Limited
Sweetdram Limited

April-June 2014 [21]
55 Above Ltd
8o8 Drinks Co Ltd
Carrick Thomson Limited
Dunbar Drinks Co Ltd
Eccentric Gin Co Limited
Isle of Wight Distillery Ltd
Lambeth Spirits Ltd
London Dry Gin Co Ltd
Moorland Spirit Co Ltd
Northumberland Distillery Co Ltd
Old Curiosity Distillery Ltd
Our/London Vodka Limited
Penton Park Brewery Limited
Psychopomp Ltd
Really Brilliant Co Ltd
Red Squirrel Brands Ltd
Silent Pool Distillers Limited
Skinny Russian Vodka Ltd
Soho Shebeen Co Ltd
South Side Spirit Limited
Steampunk Ltd

July-September 2014 [25]
Artisan Blending Limited
Willem Barentsz Limited
Buxton Distillery Limited
Capreolus Distillery Ltd
Thomas Dakin Artisan Distillers Ltd
Thomas Dakin Craft Distillers Ltd
Doggy John Distillery Limited
Edinburgh Distillery Co Ltd.
Fatman and Friends Ltd.
Jawbox Spirits Co Ltd
Lindsay's Still Room Ltd
London Vodka Ltd
Morant Bay Distillery Co Ltd
Pococello Ltd
R & B Distillers Limited
Renaissance Drinks Ltd
Saffron Gin Co Ltd
Saffron Spirit Co Ltd
Saffron Spirits Limited
Salcombe Distilling Co Ltd
Spirit of Harrogate Limited
Surrey Hills EBT Limited
Verdant Spirits Ltd.
Waveney Valley Spirits Limited
Wimbledon Distillery Co Ltd

October-December 2014 [16]
Artisanal Spirits Co Ltd
Asterley Bros, London Ltd
Bladnoch Distillery Limited
Distillery Process Ltd
Electric Spirit Co Ltd.
Fablas Limited
Garej Spirits Co Ltd
Gedrick Distilling Co Ltd
Geordie-Gin Co Ltd
Lickerish Tooth Ltd
Loch Ness Distilling Co. Ltd.
Mews Gin Co Ltd
New Adventure (Norfolk) Ltd
Pentone Family Limited
Sin of Gin Ltd
Spirit of The Shires Limited

January 2015 [5]
3D Shapie Limited
Avalon Distillery Co Ltd
Crafty Scottish Distillers Ltd
Forest Spirits Ltd
JW Distillers Limited

February 2015 [6]
Colonsay Beverages Ltd.
Dartmoor Whisky Distillery Ltd
Deya Brewing Co Ltd
Gin Tales Ltd
McCaigs Distillery Ltd
Montoscar Enterprises Limited

March 2015 [16]
Black Shuck Ltd
Chalk & Charcoal Limited
Cygnet Spirits Limited
Matthew D'Arcy & Co Ltd
Gin Bothy Limited
Hunter Douglas Scotch Whisky Ltd
Idle Saint Spirits Limited
Jo & Matt Ltd
James Johnstone Distillers Ltd.
Andrew Laing & Co Ltd
London Craft Distillers Ltd
Norfolk Distillery Ltd
Princetown Distillers Ltd
Shieling Scotch Whisky Co Ltd
Soapbox Spirits Ltd
Wight Spirits Ltd

April 2015 [7]
&Spirit Limited
Borders Distillers Limited
Burnbrae Distillery Co Ltd
Desire Drinks Limited
Forest Distillery Ltd
Langs Consulting Ltd.
Matugga Beverages Limited

May 2015 [8]
Black Cat Distillery Limited
Deerstalker Whisky Co Ltd
HG Family Enterprise Ltd
Privacy Domains Limited
Rebel Distillers Ltd
Rebel Rabbet Ltd
Strawhill Estate Distillery Ltd
Tors Vodka Limited

June 2015 [17]
Ardnahoe Distillery Co Ltd
Canebrake Ltd
Crossbill Gin Limited
Drimnin Estate Trading Limited
Espensen Spirit Ltd
Fruity Tipples Limited
Graveney Gin Limited
Jesmond Distilling Co Ltd
Kozuba & Sons Limited
Langstane Liquor Co Ltd
Lundin Distilling Co Ltd
McMillan MacRaild Ltd
Newcastle Gin Co. Limited
One Point Eight Bar Limited
Shakespeare Distillery Limited
Whisky and Cognac.Uk Limited
YDC Ltd

July 2015 [7]
Borders Distillery Co Ltd
El Gin Findrassie Ltd
Gin Jar Drinks Co Ltd
Henstone Distillery Limited
KSSM International Limited
Seduction Rum Punch UK Ltd
Trossachs Distillery Limited

August 2015 [10]
Bloomsbury Club UK Limited
Central Line Holdings Limited
Cheshire Distilleries Limited
Coyote Ventures Limited
Dyfi Distillery Ltd
East India Company Gin Limited
Loch Shiel Whisky Limited
Spirits and Bubbles Limited
Stirling Gin Ltd.
Whisky Club Ltd

September 2015 [11]
Bloomsbury Distillery Ltd
Buck and Birch Ltd
Clydeside Distillery Limited
Ferintosh Whisky Limited
Greenwood Spirits Limited
Libation Liberation Limited
Maxchater Ltd
Rum Club Ltd
Sartorial Spirits Limited
Skinnybrands Ltd
Snowdonia Distillery Ltd

October 2015 [10]
Esker Spirits Ltd
Fixed Axis Ltd
For The Love of Limited
Loch Ness Spirits Limited
Orogin Distilling Co. Limited
Rhucello Limited
Seven Deadly Sins Ltd
Shropshire Gin Co Ltd
Still on the Hill Limited
Tap End Brands Ltd

November 2015 [9]
Barcelona Spirit Brands UK Ltd
Big Hill Distillery Limited
Colwith Farm Distillery Ltd
Greywood Distillery Limited
HI&PE Limited
Pure Wild Spirits Ltd
St.Andrews Gin Co Ltd
St.Andrews Whisky Co Ltd
Toulvaddie Distillery Limited

December 2015 [11]
Anstie Distillers International Ltd
Copeland Spirits Ltd
Doghouse Distillery Limited
Drinks of Manchester Limited
Etrusca Brewery & Distillery in St. Andrews
Hoggnorton Limited
JDB Spirits Ltd
Leeds Gin Limited
Little Gin Shop Limited
H. J. Neill Ltd
Somerset Drinks Ltd

January 2016 [16]
Cornish Distilling Co Ltd
Corrupt Drinks Co Ltd
Great Yorkshire Spirit Co Ltd
Highland Boundary Ltd
Lincoln Gin Ltd
Newton Drinks Limited
Parlay Drinks Ltd
Pigeon Fisher Gin Co Limited
Redrosesforme Limited
Saddleworth Distillery Ltd
Scout and Sage Spirits Limited
Spirit Stories Ltd
Suffolk Distillery Limited
Tea Venture Limited
Twisting Spirits Ltd
Underground Brewing Co Ltd

February 2016 [14]
1725 Limited
Beinn An Tuirc Distillers Ltd
Deeside Distillers Ltd
Foxhole Spirits Limited
Martin-Wells Distillery Ltd.
Orkney Distilling Limited
Pocketful of Stones Distillers Ltd
Rare Bird Distillery Limited
Renegade Spirits Grenada Ltd
Stokers Spirits Ltd
Swallow London Ltd
Tivoli's Gin Limited
Wild and Spirited Limited
York Gin Co Ltd

March 2016 [12]
Archangel Distilleries Ltd
Belfast Distillers Ltd
Dallinger Gin Limited
Gun Dog Gin Limited
Isle of Skye Distillers Ltd
Jim & Tonic Limited
Jose Reyes Bodega Ltd
Koolvibes Limited
Pixel Spirits Limited
Speyside Vodka Co Ltd
St Faiths Distillery Limited
Your Buddy Mary Limited

April 2016 [18]
Beerdsman Limited
Cabin Pressure Spirits Ltd
Cooper King Distillery Ltd
Deerness Distillery Ltd
Distell International Holdings Ltd
Gin Kitchen Limited
Hebridean Distillers Limited
Holyrood Distillery Ltd
House of Elrick Gin Limited
House of St Giles Ltd
Lochlea Distilling Co Ltd
Lytham Distillers Limited
Moorland Distillery Limited
Peak District Distilling Co Ltd
Polo Gin Limited
Ron de Mestizo Ltd
Tappers Artisan Spirits Ltd.
White Peak Distillery Limited

May 2016 [17]
Avinshaw Industries Limited
Beach Craft Spirits Limited
Fancy A Tipple Limited
Farkin Distillery Limited
Griffiths Brothers Distillery Ltd
Handmade Gin Co Ltd
Helford River Distillery Ltd
Inshriach Distilling Limited
Inverroche International Ltd
London Society of Mixologists
Lone Wolf Spirits Limited
Manchester Still Ltd.
Mastropasqua & Brothers Ltd.
Mint Drinks Co Ltd
Shed 1 Distillery Ulverston. Ltd
Spirit of Glasgow Ltd
VS Distillers Limited

June 2016 [7]
Bluu Spirit Limited
Bottomley Distillers Ltd
Mr Bonds Tonic Limited
Northern Spirits Partnership Ltd
Northumberland Spirit Co Ltd
Spirits of Bronte Drinks Co. Ltd
Willow Tree Distilling Co Ltd

July 2016 [9]
45 West Distillers Limited
Crafted Beverages Limited
Glastonbury Distillery Limited
Golden Measure Limited
Kelso Gin Co Ltd
Pell and Co Spirits Limited
Still Shining Distillers Ltd
Stockholm Distillers and Vintners
Teasmith Spirit Co Ltd

August 2016 [18]
Corner Fifty Three Distilling Ltd
Dutch Courage Spirits Limited
Flint & Hardings Limited
Glenrinnes Distillery Limited
William Grant & Sons Distinction
Guilty Libations Limited
High Road Rum Co Ltd
Hinch Distillery Limited
Hukleys Limited
Charlie Kaane Enterprises Ltd.
Little Rotters Limited
Newbury Gin Limited
Nodding Donkey Distillery Co Ltd
Southey Brewing Co Ltd
Speakeasy Spirits UK Ltd
Taunton Distiller's Ltd
Twisted Roots Distillery Ltd
Wild Thyme Spirits Limited

September 2016 [8]
Azure Distilleries Limited
Beware Gin Brands Ltd.
Distillers of Surrey Limited
Ginomics Ltd
Jacqson Limited
Round Wood Distillery Ltd
Whitetail Spirits Limited
Zymurgorium Ltd

October 2016 [14]
Blackford Craft Distillery Ltd
City of Aberdeen Distillery Ltd
Empire Bar Service Ltd
Gaslight Distillery Limited
Glasgow Gin Co Ltd
Granite North Spirits Limited
Kettlesing Gin Limited
London Distillery - Battersea Ltd
London Spice Co Ltd
Newcastle Whisky Distillery Co Ltd
Poetic License Distillery Ltd
Pure Cornish Limited
Richie & Nikki Ltd
Second Son Distillery Limited

November 2016 [7]
Family of Hounds Limited
Mezcal Reina Limited
New Forest Distillery Ltd
Newcastle Distilling Ltd
Starling & Wasp Ltd
Tay Spirits Ltd.
Whisky Cellar Limited

December 2016 [15]
Arisaig Distillers Ltd
Black Powder Gin Co Ltd
Eoforwic Distilling Co Ltd
Goldy Gin Limited
HMS Spirits Co Ltd
Honey Spirits Co Ltd
Isle of Arran Gin Co Ltd
Murphy, Black and Mills Ltd
Nightrep Limited
Pink Gin Co Ltd
Potion Universe Ltd
Salcombe Cider Co Ltd
Single Estate Spirits Ltd
South Causey Distillery Ltd
Whitby Gin Limited

January 2017 [20]
Alderman's Drinks Ltd.
Badvo Distillery Limited
Balno Distillery Limited
Belfast Gin and Spirits School Ltd
Belfast Whiskey School Limited
Bristol Spirit Collective Ltd
East Neuk Organic Brewing & Distilling
Edinburgh Rum Co Ltd
Exeter Gin Ltd
Exmoor Distillers Ltd
Isle of Barra Distillers Ltd
Kelpie Whisky Limited
Kingston upon Hull Liqour Co Ltd
Lost Roots Limited
W. P. Lowrie & Co Ltd
Mr & Mrs Gin Ltd
Oktogin Ltd
Royal Wootton Bassett Gin Co Ltd
Tempus Gin Limited
Yorkshire Rum Co Ltd

February 2017 [18]
Belvoir Gin Distillery Limited
Boho Drinks Ltd
Broken Wings Limited
Craft Scottish Spirits Co Ltd
Dr Eamers Emporium Limited
Fourfolk Gin Co Ltd
Gordon & MacPhail Limited
Hinton's of Bewdley Ltd
Islay Spirits Co Ltd
Kinrara Distillery Limited
Mayfield Distilling Co Ltd
Mourne Dew Limited
Myatt's Fields Limited
Papillon Dartmoor Distillery Ltd
Pure Distilled Spirit Co Ltd
Salcombe Moonshine Ltd
Simple Sips International Ltd
UK Distillers Limited

March 2017 [26]
Burning Barn Limited
Craft Distilling Expo Limited
Csatrina Holdings Ltd
Dark Art Gin Limited
Dartmouth Distillery Co Ltd
Dormont Distilling Limited
Five Fathoms Spirit Limited
Glenallachie Distillers Co Ltd
Hayter Divisions Limited
Hidden Gem - Urban Artisan Spirit Ltd
Kirkwood Distillery Limited
Linlithgow Distillery Limited
Liverpool Gin Distillery Ltd
Loch Ewe Spirits Limited
Loch Ness Drinks Ltd
Luxury Spirit Co Limited
Madame Jennifer Distillery Ltd
North Uist Distillery Ltd
Pronto Cocktails Limited
Raw Distilling Ltd
Sheffield Distillery Limited
Silverback Distillers Ltd
Supermarine Vodka Distillers Ltd
Tasty Beverages Limited
Telser & Pauli Ltd
Winchester Distillery Limited

April 2017 [23]
Angola Beverages Holding Co Ltd
Ayrshire Craft Distillers Ltd
Beaufort Spirit Ltd
Company of Dark Spirits Ltd
Curio Spirits Co Ltd
Dark Spirits Co Ltd
Dirty Drinks Collective Ltd
Duck and Crutch Limited
Duration Brewing Ltd
Durham Distillery Limited
Etoh Studio Limited
Islay Spirits (No. 2) Limited
Lime Street Distillery Limited
Lincoln Imp Drinks Co Ltd
Liquid Revolution Ltd
Manchester Liquor Co. Limited
Northumberland Gin Co Ltd
Originalsip Ltd
Tarbraxus Distillers Ltd
Tarsier Spirit Ltd
J.G. Thomson & Co. Limited
Towiemore Distillery and Warehousing
Wood Brothers Distilling Co Ltd

May 2017 [18]
Atlantic Distillery Ltd
Beachcomber Gin Ltd
Brixham Gin Co Ltd.
Copper Frog Distilling Limited
Distinctively Orkney Drinks Ltd
Founding Drinks Ltd
Jackson Distillers Limited
Lincoln Distillery Limited
Loch Leven Distillery Limited
New Comber Distillery Ltd
New Galloway Inspired Ltd
Old Tom Gin Company in St Andrews Ltd
Shanty Spirit Ltd
Silvertown Brewery and Distillery Co Ltd
Sloosh Limited
Steel River Drinks Ltd
Swift Half Collective Ltd
UK Dorset Ltd

June 2017 [15]
Aber Falls Distillery Limited
Artificer Spirit Limited
Beers Spirit Co Ltd
Boho Drinks Brands Ltd
Brentingby Gin Ltd
Cornish Gin Mine Ltd
Glen Monarch Distillery Ltd
H & S Distillers Ltd
Lochaber Craft Brewing and Distilling
Patient Wolf Limited
Peakys Distillery Ltd
Snowdonia Spirit Co Ltd
Start-Up Drinks Lab Limited
Surrey Copper Distillery Ltd
Tea Rocks Ltd

July 2017 [26]
Bitter Union Limited
Deco Spirits Limited
Drinkology Limited
Fowey River Gin Ltd
Harley House Craft Distillery Ltd
Harley House Distillery Ltd
Honey Gin Co Ltd
Horseguards London Dry Gin Ltd
Illicit Spirits Ltd
Jervis Trading Limited
Juniper Street Gin Co Ltd
Killowen Distillery Ltd
Lazy Drinks Ltd.
Legendary Distillers Ltd
Lonburg 449 Limited
Lowestoft Distillery Co Ltd
Lymm Gin Limited
Myperfectgin Ltd
Patterson and Clarke Distillery Ltd
Pentric Distillery Ltd
Pure Sussex Distillery Ltd
Ramsbottom Gin Co Ltd
Spirit of Leith Ltd
Spirit of Manchester Distillery Ltd
Stolowa Ltd
Sweet Afton Scotch Whisky Ltd

August 2017 [34]
Bitter Salvation Ltd
Blendworks Ltd
Brew House Yorkshire Limited
Cantails Limited
Chalgrove Artisan Distillery Ltd
Clock Tower Distilleries Ltd
Country Garden Drinks Co Ltd
Distillutions Ltd
Elstead Village Distillers Ltd
Exeter Distillery Ltd
Fen Spirits Limited
Forgan Distillery Ltd
Four Sisters Distillery Ltd
Ginking Co Ltd
Incognito Ltd
Kimbland Distillery Ltd
Lincolnshire Gin Ltd
London Rum Limited
Long Gin Ltd
Maeden Group Ltd
Neat Distillery Ltd
Nele Drinks Limited
Raw Distiller Ltd
Revolution Rum Ltd
Rhum Liquor Limited
Rosemullion Distillery Ltd
Ryhall Distillery Limited
Sunderland Gin Limited
Surendran & Bownes Ltd.
Tewkesbury Distillery Ltd
Twenty Oaks, Ltd
Ulverston Gin Limited
Yarm Gin Ltd
Yarm Spirits Co Ltd

September 2017 [28]
3 Lids Rum Ltd
Azenja Limited
Black Arid Kegs Ltd
Burnsland Distillery Co Ltd
Collards Distillery Limited
Dark Sky Spirits Ltd
Doctor Bird Rum Ltd
Downton Distillery Limited
Dram in a Can Limited
Empirical Trading Co. Limited
Fire Beard Spirits Limited
Folklore Distillery Ltd
Galldachd Na H-Alba Brewing Ltd
Ginglish Limited
Glenmaster Distillers Limited
Henley Gin Co Ltd
Kendal Brewery Ltd
LDN Spirits Limited
Mourne Mountains Whiskey Co Ltd
Oxford Gin Co Ltd
Pure Spirit in Wales Limited
SOS Gin Ltd
Sacred Spirits Holdings Ltd
Unit Thirteen Limited
Ursus Americanus Limited
Wessex Distillery Limited
Whitby Distillery Limited
Wilson's Henley Gin Co Ltd

October 2017 [24]
Beets Incorporated Ltd
Black Cat Drinks Ltd
Bootleg Club Limited
Bowland Distillery Ltd
Brindle Distillery Limited
Checkers Gin Ltd
Curious Liquids Limited
Flavour Traders Limited
Gateway Spirit Co Ltd
Heart of Suffolk Distillery Ltd
Hussingtree Blends Limited
Little Red Berry Co Ltd.
London Spiced Dry Limited
Luxbev Limited
Moores of Warwick Limited
Nene Distillery Limited
New Forest Spirits Ltd
Nitrogin Ltd.
Oxfordshire Gin Co Ltd
Penrhos Spirits Ltd
Pilgrim Spirit Ltd
Strawhill Estate Spirits Co Ltd
Sweetwater Distillery Limited
Weatheralls Distillery Limited

November 2017 [19]
Angels Share (MCR) Limited
Conglomerate Spirits Ltd.
Cross Distillery Limited
Demon Vodka Limited
H.B. Evelyo Ltd.
Gin Hub Limited
Jivana Spirits Ltd.
Liquid Lounge Drinks Co. Ltd
Orkney Spirits Limited
Pentland Still Ltd
Raven Spirits Limited
Renaissance Vodka Limited
Rumbustian Limited
Spirit of Captain Cook Limited
Tiny Tipple Co Ltd
Two Fathoms Distillery Ltd.
White Smoke Distillery Ltd
Woodlab Distillery Limited
Yorkshire Spirit Limited

December 2017 [22]
Afallon Mon Cyf
Bashiba Gin Ltd
Batch88 Ltd
Borders Distilling Limited
Churchill Distillery Limited
Clyde Bottlers Ltd
Cornish Spiritsmith Ltd
Fal River Distillery Limited
Gin Ting Limited
Good Life Gin Co Ltd
Ian Hart Distilling Limited
Holler Brewery Limited
Holme Gin Limited
Mudlark Investments Ltd
Puddlebrook Distillery Limited
Q & S Distilling Co Ltd
Queen Cleo Rum Ltd
River Test Distillery Limited
Smart Brewing and Distilling Solutions
Tres Amigos Limited
Turncoat Distillery Limited
Whisky Works Ltd

January 2018 [42]
AM Distilling Ltd
Afterthought Spirits Co Ltd
Atom Distillery Ltd
Badachro Distillery Ltd
Barclay Distillery Limited
Blessed Skye Limited
Bloodline Spirits Ltd
Cask Coin Ltd
Cloughmor Consulting Ltd
Distinctly Different Spirits Co Ltd
Equilibrium Food & Drink Ltd
Falkirk Gin Ltd
Falmouth Gin Limited
Fenney Street Distillery Ltd
Formby Spirits Limited
Goldman Distillery Ltd
Goosnargh Gin Ltd
Great Don Ltd
Great White Gin Limited
Hackney Distillery Limited
Hothams Limited
Hurricane Rum Co Ltd
In The Welsh Wind Distillery Ltd
Isle of Bute Gin Co Ltd
Kafecal Global Co Ltd
Loaded Spirits Ltd
Lucent Drinks Ltd
Margate Distillery Ltd
McLean's Gin Ltd
Mull Gin Co Ltd
Mull Gin Distillery Ltd
Rivington Distillery Ltd
Otten Schmidt Ltd.
Scouse Girls Gin Ltd
Shire Gin Limited
Shropshire Distillery Limited
Sovereign Spirits Ltd.
Tipo Loco Drinks Co. Limited
Tres Bombarderos Gin Limited
Undaunted Limited
Verset Vodka Holdings Limited
Warwickshire Spirits Limited

February 2018 [50]
Arbikie X Limited
Atlantis Gin Ltd
Belfast Titanic Whiskey Distillery Ltd
Blue Sky Drinking Ltd
Caskcoin Holdings Limited
DWD Whiskey Co Ltd
Derbyshire Distillery Limited
Doncaster Dry Gin Limited
Dr Junipers Ltd.
Dunnford Craft Distillers Ltd
Forth Bridge Brewery and Distillery
W.C. Fowler & Sons Limited
Geordie-Gin Corporation Ltd
Gin Dobry Gin Co Ltd
Gin-Ger Gin Limited
Ginkhana Limited
Godka Ltd
Gorgeous Gin Limited
Gower Distillery Ltd
Hazell & Hazell Distillers Ltd
Hinch Distillery Holdings Ltd
Hinch Whiskey Co Ltd
Isle of Mull Gin Distillery Ltd
Isle of Mull Gin Limited
Italian Gin Co Ltd
Londinio Liqueurs Ltd.
Longtooth Gin Limited
McCallums Liqueurs Ltd
Molotov Brand Limited
New Found Spirit Scotland Ltd
Old Smiths Distillery Ltd
One Swan Ltd
Penningtons Spirits and Liqueurs Ltd
Penny Lane Gin Ltd
Perth Distillery Co Ltd
Ribble Valley Gin Co Ltd.
Saint Patricks Ltd
Soul Vodka Ltd
Spirit of Malt House Limited
Stonehenge Distillery Limited
Suffolk Smugglers Limited
TCBP Holdings Limited
Tickle Drinks Limited
Titanic Gin Ltd
Titanic Vodka Ltd
Tudor Court Distillers Limited
UK McLouis Liquor Co Ltd
Uncle Nearest Ltd.
Waters of Deugh Limited
Wrekin Spirit Limited

March 2018 [40]
Amber Valley Gin Ltd
Atom Brands Limited
Atom Cask Holdings Limited
Atom Drinks Limited
Atom Group Limited
Atom Scotland Limited
Bearded Lion Drinks Co Ltd
Crosskeys Whiskey Co Ltd
Docked Distillery International Ltd
Eden Mill Distillers Ltd
Halton Turner Brewing Co Ltd
Hawkshead Gin and Spirit Co Ltd
JKM Spirits Limited
Lamson Wine Co Ltd
London Botanical Drinks Ltd
London Fortifiers Limited
Lujo Distilling Co Ltd
Lumber Distillers Limited

Luxco Drinks Limited
Lytham Gin Co Ltd
Mackintosh Gin Limited
Master of Malt Limited
Masters of Malt Limited
Maverick Brands Limited
Maverick Drinks Limited
Maverick Spirits Limited
Mill House Distillery Limited
Mousehole Brewery Limited
Neptune SA Ltd
Nero Drinks Co Ltd
Orkney Mead Ltd
RWB Drinks Ltd
Redcastle Spirits Limited
Rutland Distillery Co Ltd
Shotgun Limited
Soul of The Spirit Limited
Touch Lucky Limited
Wells Gin Limited
Wilmington Spirits Limited
Yarm Brewing and Distilling Co Ltd

April 2018 [41]
Alko Vintages UK Ltd
Anglesey Distillery Ltd
Arundo Limited
Barti Rum Ltd
Beaumonde Desserts Limited
Bottlers & Distillers (Wales) Ltd
Copper Drinks Limited
Copper Tree Partnership Ltd
Edale Gin Co Ltd
Edinburgh Distillers Limited
Farman & Son Ltd
Hawkridge Distillers Ltd
Hebden Bridge Spirit Co Ltd
Hibernian Beverage Group Ltd
Holy Grail Beverages Limited
Hooting Owl Distillery Ltd
Hoyle Bottom Spirits Ltd
Incharvie Group Limited
Irish Gin Co Ltd
Isledon Gin Ltd
LighthouseVodka Ltd
Liqueur Manufactory Limited
Masham Distillery Co Ltd
Matugga Distillers Limited
Nibbs Spirits Limited
Ninth Wave Gin Co Ltd
North Tyne Ventures Ltd
Otter Distillery Limited
Peedie Sea Distilling Limited
Portsmouth Gin Co Ltd
Pryzm Cocktails Limited
Red Door Gin Co Ltd
Shannon & Thomas Limited
Sip Antics Limited
Smithies Gin Co Ltd
Staffordshire Gin Co Ltd
Steel City Craft Spirits Boutique Ltd
Stirling Distillery Co Ltd
Tweed Valley Distilling Co Ltd
Wayfinder Distillery Limited
Whiskymen Limited

May 2018 [31]
Belfast Artisan Distillery Ltd
Blue Marble Distillery Ltd
Bothy Trading Limited
Bright Spirits Limited

Bros Distilling Ltd
Club Rum Limited
Clwydian Range Distillery Ltd
Delicious Drinks Limited
Devon Coast Distillery Limited
Ely's Cocktails Ltd
Frensham Distillery Limited
Gaymens Gin Ltd
Good Spirits Ltd
Horsforth Distillery Ltd
Isle of Lewis Distillers Ltd
Jones Gin Ltd
KO Gin Limited
Loch Lomond Liquor Co Ltd
Neat Spirits Limited
Pembrokeshire Comestibles Co Ltd
Seaway Royale Limited
Solway Spirits Ltd
Spice Island Gin Co Ltd
Spirit of Unicorn Ltd
Sunfire Spirits Ltd
Tolsta Europe Ltd
Twisted Melon Scotland Limited
Two Drifters Distillery Ltd
Universal Robo Innovations Ltd
Vijobar Ltd
Weymouth and Portland Distillery Co Ltd

June 2018 [41]
20trees Gin Ltd
Basil's Botanicals Limited
Be Rude Not To Ltd
Beaucroft Beverages Ltd
Bitter Lemons Gin Ltd
Blend Experts Limited
Bournemouth Distillers Limited
CP Infusions Ltd
Cartmel Gin Ltd
Clifden Arms Property Ltd
Clifden Arms Trading Ltd
Cool Brew Dept Ltd
Cox & Mall Ltd
Cragside Spirit Co Ltd
Cupids Bow 35 Limited
Dilly Dilly Limited
Dimbandit Ltd
Distilled Experience Ltd
Drops of Juniper Limited
Duchy Beverages Ltd
Ethereal Cut Limited
GNR Distillery Limited
Grain Artisan Ltd
Hamilton Rose Gin Ltd
JustaGinCo Ltd
LWD Holdings Limited
Liverpool Spring Gin Limited
Llanfairpwll Distillery Ltd
Long Walk Spirits Limited
Mezky Ltd
Millom Distillery Limited
Mulberry Distillery Limited
Musicspeller Ltd
Norfolk Gin Limited
Old Brenin Distillery Ltd
Sendivogius Limited
Shropshire Hills Distillery Ltd
Skye Vodka Co Ltd
Somerset Distillery Ltd
Vonlevers Limited
Whittaker's Distillery Limited

July 2018 [42]
Abbey Distillery Ltd
Adventure Brands Ltd
Amethystcave Ltd
Aztec Spirits Ltd
Banideep Ltd
Bethera Ltd
Botan Grey Ltd
Botanical Jack's Limited
Cherry Drop Gin Ltd
Crystaldrifter Ltd
De Facto Spirits Limited
Edge Gin Ltd
Engin Yard Beverage Co Ltd
Fairfields Liqueurs Ltd
Gentlemen Distillers Ltd
Glaswegin Distilling Co. Ltd
Jonomade Limited
Juggling King Rum Co Ltd
Kiko Mezcal Ltd
Lianorin Ltd
Liquid Spirit Ltd
London Brewery Limited
Madrise Ltd
Moody Rum Ltd
Nectardigger Ltd
Nestwonder Ltd
Norcabis Ltd
Northern Fried Drinks Limited
Northlew Distillery Ltd
Pipeline Drinks Ltd
Polaris Spirits Limited
Polestar Spirits Limited
Portsmouth Distillery Co Ltd
Purdy Distillers Limited
Rock Hill Cider Co Ltd
SB Gin Limited
Shorts Boy Distillery Ltd
Soulmate Gin Ltd
Staffordshire Distillery Ltd
Tuerto Tequila Ltd
Unthank Distillery Limited
Village Spirit Collective Ltd

August 2018 [39]
78 Dbar Limited
Black Label Spirits Ltd
Braefoot Distillery Ltd
Bristol Rum Co Ltd
Buidheann Beag Distillery Ltd
Conwy Distillery Limited
Corglass Wild Spirit Ltd
Dowdeswell Distillery Limited
Drumeland Distillery Ltd
Esq Vodka Limited
F.W Exports Ltd
Forsaken Limited
Fox Gins Ltd
Ground Inn Ltd
High Water Distilling Co Ltd
Kac70 Limited
London Rum Company Holdings Ltd
Lytham Distillery Co Ltd
Maiden Batch Ltd
Maidstone Distillery Ltd
N.Gin Distillery Ltd
NineTailsDistillery Ltd
Northumberland Whisky Ltd
Perfidious Albion Limited
R & T Stills Limited
Rabakkan Ltd
Royton Gin Ltd
Seadwealths Ltd
Slains Castle Spirit Co Ltd
Soak Engineering Ltd
Still Wild Limited
Taplin & Mageean Ltd
Three Graces Distillery Ltd
Tippling Tonic Limited
Titanic Distillers Limited
Urban Vodka Limited
Wally Wonka Ltd
White House Distillery Limited
White House Gin Limited

September 2018 [34]
Artisan Distillery (Staffordshire)
Blackingstone Ltd
Boutique Distillery Ltd
British and Colonial Merchants of Jamaica
Carse of Stirling Distillers Ltd
Cross Stream Distillery Ltd
Cuba Trading Co Ltd
Dallas Dhu Ltd
Devine Distillates Group (Manufacturing)
Distillery 96 Limited
Ditchling Spirits Limited
Dockers Spirit Co Ltd
Dr Gin Limited
Droylsden Craft Limited
Dulwich Gin Limited
Edinburgh and Leith Distillery Ltd
Faiers Distillery Ltd
Forager Drinks Limited
Fords of Wakefield Ltd
Gibraltar Gin Co Ltd
Gyffordes Distillers Ltd
Harbour Gin Co Ltd
Harrison Distillery Ltd
Hatters Distillery Limited
Jacob's Gin Limited
Little Brown Dog Spirits Ltd
Lonberg Limited
McKerr Farming Ltd
Mr Kegz Ltd
Prentice Spirits Ltd
Revelry Brewing & Distilling Ltd
Sky Pirate Ltd
South London Urban Gin Co Ltd
St Andrews Botanics Limited

October 2018 [29]
4607 Distillery Limited
Animal Spirits Ltd
Antibio UK Ltd
Beeble Liquor Limited
Berwick Brewrey Co Ltd
Bombini Ltd
Copeland Distillery Company (NI) Ltd
Crawford's Rock Ltd
Daisy Distillery Limited
Ealing Distillery Ltd
Ginsecco Ltd
Herbert's Distillery & Co Ltd
Kindred Gin Ltd
Kinelarty Limited
Last Drop Spirit Co Ltd
MK Drinks Co Ltd
Pant y Foel Gin Ltd
R & R Distillery Ireland Ltd
Somerset Craft Distillery Ltd
Somerset Craft Spirit Co Ltd
Surrey Hills Whisky Co Ltd
Topsham Gin Ltd
Tready's Ltd
Treganna Gin Ltd
Warwickshire Gin Co Ltd
West Spirits MCR Ltd
Wild Foragin Ltd
Wolftown Distillery Limited
Zero Gravity Spirits Ltd

November 2018 [44]
Alkemista Limited
Ataxirola Ltd
Bonny Gin Ltd
Brewhouse Spirits Limited
Brittains Beverages Ltd
Commonwealth Gin Ltd
Croft Distillery Ltd
Crosstown Cocktail Co Ltd
Dalrymples Distillery Ltd
Druid's Distillery Ltd
Eastwater Gin Ltd
Edmunds Cocktails Ltd
Eight Vodka Limited
WJ Evans a'i Gwmni (Ynys Enlli) Cyf
Evolution Brewing Ltd
Falkirk Whisky Ltd
Flavour Premium Brands Limited
Glencoe Distilleries Ltd
Harlequin Distillery Ltd
Hawkshead Distillery Ltd
Hendre Distillery Ltd
Ilkley Gin Co Ltd
Invoke Distillery Ltd
Invoke Distilling Co. Ltd
Jackson's Gin Ltd
Landeavour Distillery Ltd
Lanty Slee Liquor Co Ltd
Lough Neagh Distillers - 1837 Ltd
Mooshine Ltd
Murphy's Gin Ltd
Oxford Distillers Limited
Paradise Cocktails Ltd
Pickering's Gin Limited
Revelry Spirits Ltd
Maurice Richard Ltd
Rum To You Ltd
Russian Doll Vodka Limited
SV Distilleries Limited
Seada Distillery Limited
Silver Circle Distillery Ltd
Skylark Distillery Ltd
Stockport Gin Ltd
Unconventional Distillery Co. Ltd
Vape Pure Ltd

December 2018 [23]
Blinders Pubs & Clubs Ltd
Brain Brew UK Limited
Butlers Cross Limited
Clandestine Distillery Limited
Contract Bottlers Glasgow Ltd
Exploration Distillation Ltd
Field Distillers Ltd
Fifty-Nine Spirits Co Ltd
Gleneagles Distillery Limited
Glenturret Limited
Hin Ltd
Jefferson & Bennett Distillers Ltd
Lillington Distillation Ltd
Linden and Lime Limited

Mersey Gin Co Ltd
Shetland Whisky Co Ltd
South Loch Ltd
Spirit of Coalpit - Ysbryd y Pwll Glo
Spirit of Leeds Ltd
TBD Tipples Ltd
Twisted Gin Ltd
Wee Hemp Spirits Ltd
Yorkshire Gin Limited

January 2019 [38]
A Little Luxury Distillery Ltd
Anura Drinks Ltd
Back Bar Spirits Limited
Break Line Brewing & Distilling Ltd
Caperdonich Whisky Limited
El Pulpo Loco Ltd
Gest Spirits Limited
Goldings Distillery Ltd
Grey Dog of Meoble Limited
Hawkshead Spirit Co Ltd
Inspirited Ltd
Ironbridge Gorge Gin Co Ltd
Jacobite Spirit Co Ltd

Jorvik Distillery Limited
Klerck Distillery Ltd
Land's End Gin Limited
Mahiki Trading Limited
New Union Brewing Co Ltd
Norfolk Rum Co Ltd
Paradise Rum Limited
Porthilly Spirit Distillery Ltd
Precision Spirits Ltd
Red Distillery Limited
Scotch Malt Distillers Ltd
Sleepy Hollow Spirits Ltd
Solent Spirits Co Ltd
South Devon Liqueur Co Ltd
Southampton Distillery Ltd
St Davids Gin Limited
Strontium Gin Co Ltd
Taunton Gin Limited
Tubeoptics. Ltd
WL Distillery Ltd
Wallhouse Distillery Limited
Wave'n Ltd
Whitstable Distillery Ltd
York Distillery Limited

Zero-Moo Ltd

February 2019 [21]
Am Byth Distillery Ltd
Askival Rum Ltd
Conscious Collaborative Ltd
Deer Island Distillery Limited
Distillers of St.Andrews Ltd
Ellon Spirit Co Ltd
Flagg Ltd
Ginwimmin Ltd
Isle of Iona Gin Limited
Krupnikoz Ltd
Mavarac UK Limited
Modern Botanicals Limited
My Nan's Favourite Ltd
Pin Fold Distillery Ltd
Riktig Limited
Ruskin Spirit Co Ltd
Stargazey Spirits Ltd
Three Wrens Gin Limited
West Highland Distillers Ltd
West Midlands Distillery Ltd
Wild Atlantic Distillery Ltd

Geographic Distribution by County

Co Antrim [19]
Belfast Artisan Distillery Ltd
Belfast Distillers Ltd
Beware Gin Brands Ltd.
Cross Distillery Limited
Crosskeys Whiskey Co Ltd
DWD Whiskey Co Ltd
Dunville & Co. Limited
Glens of Antrim Whiskey Co Ltd
Hinch Distillery Holdings Ltd
Hinch Distillery Limited
Hinch Whiskey Co Ltd
Jawbox Spirits Co Ltd
LWD Holdings Limited
Nele Drinks Limited
New Comber Distillery Ltd
Ninth Wave Gin Co Ltd
Old Bushmills Distillery Co Ltd
TCBP Holdings Limited
Titanic Distillers Limited

Co Armagh [7]
Black Arid Kegs Ltd
Matthew D'Arcy & Co Ltd
Drumeland Distillery Ltd
Lough Neagh Distillers - 1837 Ltd
Purdy Distillers Limited
Strawhill Estate Distillery Ltd
Strawhill Estate Spirits Co Ltd

Co Down [18]
Belfast Gin and Spirits School Ltd
Belfast Titanic Whiskey Distillery Ltd
Belfast Whiskey School Limited
Cloughmor Consulting Ltd
Copeland Distillery Company (NI) Ltd
Copeland Spirits Ltd
Echlinville Distillery Limited
Irish Whiskey Co Ltd - The
Killowen Distillery Ltd
Kinelarty Limited
Mourne Dew Limited
Mourne Mountains Whiskey Co Ltd
R & R Distillery Ireland Ltd
Rademon Estate Distillery Ltd
Strawhill Ltd
Titanic Gin Ltd
Titanic Vodka Ltd
Ulster Distilleries Limited

Co Londonderry
One Swan Ltd

Co Tyrone
Irish Gin Co Ltd
Wild Atlantic Distillery Ltd
Woodlab Distillery Limited

Aberdeenshire [27]
Blackford Craft Distillery Ltd
City of Aberdeen Distillery Ltd
Michel Couvreur (Scotch Whiskies)
Dallinger Gin Limited
De Facto Spirits Limited
Deeside Distillers Ltd
Dr Adam Elmegirabs Bitters Ltd
Dunnford Craft Distillers Ltd
Dutch Courage Spirits Limited
Ellon Spirit Co Ltd
Esker Spirits Ltd
Ginkhana Limited
Granite North Spirits Limited
House of Elrick Gin Limited
Inspirited Ltd
Langstane Liquor Co Ltd
Little Brown Dog Spirits Ltd
Lone Wolf Spirits Limited
Raven Spirits Limited
Single Estate Spirits Ltd
Slains Castle Spirit Co Ltd
Still Shining Distillers Ltd
Teasmith Spirit Co Ltd
Tipo Loco Drinks Co. Limited
Twisted Melon Scotland Limited
Wee Hemp Spirits Ltd
Whisky Galore Limited

Angus [14]
Arbikie Distilling Limited
Bothy Trading Limited
Club Rum Limited
Dallas Dhu Ltd
Distillutions Ltd
Dundee Distillery Co Ltd
Gedrick Distilling Co Ltd
Gin Bothy Limited
Lochglen Whisky Co Ltd.
Mackintosh Gin Limited
Ogilvy Spirits Limited
Redcastle Spirits Limited
Sangobeg Ltd
Smithies Gin Co Ltd

Argyll [12]
Adelphi Distillery (1826) Ltd
Adelphi Distillery Limited
Botanist Limited
Colonsay Beverages Ltd.
Farkin Distillery Limited
High Road Rum Co Ltd
Islay Boys Limited
Kilchoman Distillery Co. Ltd.
Lochindaal Distillery Limited
J. & A. Mitchell and Company, Ltd
Mitchell's Glengyle Limited
Port Charlotte Limited

Argyll & Bute [6]
Beinn An Tuirc Distillers Ltd
Drimnin Estate Trading Limited
Hebridean Liqueur Co Ltd
Ncn'ean Distillery Limited
Portavadie Distillery Limited
Wild Thyme Spirits Limited

Ayrshire [8]
Ayrshire Craft Distillers Ltd
EB Alexandria Ltd
Hendrick's Gin Distillery Ltd
LDC Scotland Limited
LLDR Alexandria Ltd
LLDY Alexandria Ltd
Macmillan Scotch Whisky Co Ltd
Stanley Morrison & Co. Ltd

Banffshire
Glenallachie Distillers Co Ltd
J. & G. Grant
Macallan Distillers Limited

Dumfries-shire
Annandale Distillery Co Ltd

Dumfries & Galloway [7]
Dark Sky Spirits Ltd
Dormont Distilling Limited
Galldachd Na H-Alba Brewing Ltd
Langholm Distillery Limited
New Galloway Inspired Ltd
Solway Spirits Ltd
Waters of Deugh Limited

Dunbartonshire [5]
Arisaig Distillers Ltd
Hazell & Hazell Distillers Ltd
Loch Lomond Liquor Co Ltd
Malt of the Earth Whisky Co Ltd.
Pink Gin Co Ltd

Fife [17]
1725 Limited
Blendworks Ltd
Distillers of St.Andrews Ltd
East Neuk Organic Brewing & Distilling
Etrusca Brewery & Distillery in St. Andrews
John Fergus & Co Limited
Gorgeous Gin Limited
Incharvie Group Limited
Lindores Distilling Co. Ltd
Lundin Distilling Co Ltd
Old Tom Gin Company in St Andrews Ltd
Red Squirrel Brands Ltd
St Andrews Brewers Limited
St.Andrews Gin Co Ltd
St.Andrews Whisky Co Ltd
Tay Spirits Ltd.
Tres Bombarderos Gin Limited

Highland [7]
Badachro Distillery Ltd
Balno Distillery Limited
Ben Nevis Distillery (Fort William)
Dornoch Distillery Co Ltd
Grey Dog of Meoble Limited
Inshriach Distilling Limited
Lochaber Craft Brewing and Distilling

Inverness-shire [6]
Castleheather Facilities Management Ltd
Loch Ness Distilling Co Ltd.
Loch Ness Spirits Limited
Pixel Spirits Limited
Strathnairn Whisky Limited
Tomatin Distillery Co Ltd,(The)

Isle of Arran
Isle of Arran Gin Co Ltd

Isle of Harris
Isle of Harris Distillers Ltd

Isle of Iona
Isle of Iona Gin Limited

Isle of Jura
Deer Island Distillery Limited

Isle of Lewis
Isle of Lewis Distillers Ltd

The UK Spirits Industry

Isle of Mull
Whitetail Spirits Limited

Isle of Skye
Blessed Skye Limited
Isle of Skye Distillers Ltd
Skye Vodka Co Ltd

Kincardineshire
Dark Matter Distillers Limited

Kinross-shire
Blinders Pubs & Clubs Ltd
Loch Leven Distillery Limited

Kirkcudbrightshire
Crafty Scottish Distillers Ltd

Lanarkshire [114]
Aberdeen Distillers Limited
Ardnahoe Distillery Co Ltd
Armagnac Co Ltd
Askival Rum Ltd
Balblair Distillery Co Ltd
Blairmhor Distillers Limited
Blairmhor Limited
Block, Grey and Block Limited
Bonny Gin Ltd
Broken Wings Limited
Broughton Ales Limited
Buidheann Beag Distillery Ltd
Bunnahabhain Distillery Co Ltd
Burn Stewart (U.S. Holdings) Ltd
Burnbrae Distillery Co Ltd
Burnsland Distillery Co Ltd
CES Whisky Limited
CL World Brands Limited
Calder Glen Ltd
Campbell Meyer & Co Limited
R. Carmichael & Sons Limited
James Catto & Co Ltd
Clyde Bottlers Ltd
Clydeside Distillery Limited
Conglomerate Spirits Ltd.
Contract Bottlers Glasgow Ltd
William Craig & Co Ltd
Crossbill Distilling Limited
Cu Dhub Distilling Co Ltd
Deerstalker Whisky Co Ltd
Delicious Drinks Limited
Distell International Limited
Dr Scotch Whisky Ltd.
Drambuie Liqueur Co Ltd.
Eden Mill Distillers Ltd
Edrington Distillers Limited
Edrington Group Limited
F.W Exports Ltd
Finnieston Distillery Co Ltd
Flagg Ltd
Garden Shed Drinks Co Ltd
Gaymens Gin Ltd
Gibson Whisky Ltd
Ginsecco Ltd
Glasgow Distillery Co Ltd
Glasgow Gin Co Ltd
Glasgow Partners Ltd.
Glasgow Whisky Limited
Glen Calder Blenders Limited
Glen Clyde Ltd.

Glencoe Distilleries Ltd
Glenturret Limited
Matthew Gloag & Son Limited
Goldman Distillery Ltd
Gordon & Company (Distillers) Ltd
Gordon Graham & Co Ltd
HS (Distillers) Limited
Hankey Bannister & Co Ltd
High Street Trading Co Ltd
Highland Distillers Group Ltd
Highland Distillers Limited
Highland Whisky Limited
Hunter Douglas Scotch Whisky Ltd
Illicit Spirits Ltd
Incognito Ltd
Inver House Distillers Limited
Islay Spirits (No. 2) Limited
Islay Spirits Co Ltd
Isle of Barra Distillers Ltd
Isle of Bute Gin Co Ltd
Jacobite Spirit Co Ltd
C S James & Sons Limited
James Johnstone Distillers Ltd.
Kirklee Scotch Whisky Limited
Knockdhu Distillery Co Ltd
Andrew Laing & Co Ltd
Hunter Laing & Co Ltd
Leith Liqueur Co Ltd
Loch Earn Brewery Ltd
Luxury Spirit Co Limited
J. MacArthur Jr. & Co. Ltd
MacDuff & Co Ltd
MacDuff (Scotch Whisky) Ltd
MacDuff International (Scotch Whisky)
Maiden Batch Ltd
Malt Whisky Investment Co Ltd
McKerr Farming Ltd
McLean's Gin Ltd
Meadowside Blending Co Ltd
Moffat & Towers Limited
Morrison Bowmore Distillers Ltd
Morrison Glasgow Distillers Ltd
Nero Drinks Co Ltd
Old Curiosity Distillery Ltd
Premier Bonding Co Ltd
Privacy Domains Limited
Pulteney Distillery Co Ltd
Raw Distiller Ltd
Renaissance Vodka Limited
William Riddell & Sons Ltd
Row & Co Ltd
SB Gin Limited
Shieling Scotch Whisky Co Ltd
Speyburn-Glenlivet Distillery Co.
Speyside Distillers Co Ltd
Spirit of Glasgow Ltd
Starling & Wasp Ltd
Sweet Afton Scotch Whisky Ltd
Tolsta Europe Ltd
Wee Beastie Ltd.
Whisky Club Ltd
Whisky Works Ltd
Whisky and Cognac.Uk Limited
Whyte and MacKay Limited

Moray [23]
Avonside Whisky Limited
Beach Craft Spirits Limited
Benromach Distillery Co Ltd
Braefoot Distillery Ltd
Coleburn Distillery Limited
Corglass Wild Spirit Ltd

El Gin Findrassie Ltd
Elgin Bonding Co Ltd
Field Distillers Ltd
Glen Gordon Whisky Co Ltd
Glenrinnes Distillery Limited
Gordon & MacPhail Limited
Gordon Bonding Co Ltd
James Gordon Whisky Co Ltd
William Grant & Sons Distillers Ltd
William Grant & Sons Limited
Kinrara Distillery Limited
Wm. Lundie & Company
Red Door Gin Co Ltd
Speymalt Whisky Distributors Ltd
Speyside Vodka Co Ltd
Towiemore Distillery and Warehousing
D & M Winchester Ltd.

North Uist
North Uist Distillery Ltd

Orkney [7]
Deerness Distillery Ltd
Distinctively Orkney Drinks Ltd
Orkney Distilling Limited
Orkney Mead Ltd
Orkney Spirits Limited
Peedie Sea Distilling Limited
VS Distillers Limited

Peebles-shire
Bloodline Spirits Ltd
Distilled Experience Ltd
McMillan MacRaild Ltd
Tweed Valley Distilling Co Ltd

Perthshire [18]
Badvo Distillery Limited
Bright Spirits Limited
Dun Eideann Scotch Whisky Co Ltd
Edradour Distillery Co Ltd
Gleneagles Distillery Limited
Glenturret Distillery Limited
Highland Boundary Ltd
Highlands Spirit Ltd.
Langs Consulting Ltd.
Nightrep Limited
Perth Distillery Co Ltd
Perthshire Whisky Co Ltd
Shetland Whisky Co Ltd
Strathearn Distillery Ltd.
Trossachs Distillery Limited
Undaunted Limited
Verdant Spirits Ltd.
Wally Wonka Ltd

Perth & Kinross
Craft Scottish Spirits Co Ltd
W. P. Lowrie & Co Ltd
Scotch Malt Distillers Ltd
St Andrews Botanics Limited

Renfrewshire [16]
Cask Coin Ltd
Caskcoin Holdings Limited
Chivas Brothers Limited
Chivas Brothers Pernod Ricard
Ferintosh Whisky Limited
Glaswegin Distilling Co. Ltd
Isle of Mull Gin Distillery Ltd
Isle of Mull Gin Limited
Legendary Distillers Ltd
Lochlea Distilling Co Ltd
Mull Gin Co Ltd
Mull Gin Distillery Ltd
Rhum Liquor Limited
Start-Up Drinks Lab Limited
Strathleven Distillers Co Ltd
Valt Vodka Co Ltd

Ross & Cromarty
Dram in a Can Limited
Loch Ness Drinks Ltd

Ross-shire
Highland Toddy Ltd
Toulvaddie Distillery Limited

Roxburghshire [10]
Borders Distillers Limited
Borders Distillery Co Ltd
Borders Distilling Limited
Golden Measure Limited
Jackson Distillers Limited
Jedhart Distillery Limited
Kelso Gin Co Ltd
Mossburn Distillers Limited
Three Stills Co Ltd
Torabhaig Distillery Limited

Shetland
Shetland Distillery Co Ltd

Stirlingshire [11]
Caperdonich Whisky Limited
Carse of Stirling Distillers Ltd
Distillery Process Ltd
Falkirk Gin Ltd
Falkirk Whisky Ltd
Kelpies Whisky Limited
New Found Spirit Scotland Ltd
Rosebank Distillery Camelon Ltd
Rosebank Whisky Limited
Stirling Distillery Co Ltd
Stirling Gin Ltd.

Sutherland
Dunnet Bay Distillers Ltd.

Anglesey
Afallon Mon Cyf
Anglesey Distillery Ltd
Llanfairpwll Distillery Ltd

Avon
Bath Botanics Limited

Bedfordshire [5]
Anura Drinks Ltd
Bombini Ltd
Botan Grey Ltd
Jim & Tonic Limited
New Forest Distillery Ltd

Berkshire [16]
&Spirit Limited
Brain Brew UK Limited
Cross Stream Distillery Ltd
Ditchling Spirits Limited
Exploration Distillation Ltd
Griffiths Brothers Distillery Ltd
Hawkridge Distillers Ltd
Jorvik Distillery Limited
Kozuba & Sons Limited
Lumber Distillers Limited
Masham Distillery Co Ltd
Newbury Gin Limited
Polaris Spirits Limited
Polestar Spirits Limited
Whitley Neill Limited
York Distillery Limited

Buckinghamshire [6]
Atlantis Gin Ltd
Bishopsgate Distillery & Wine Co Ltd
HG Family Enterprise Ltd
MK Drinks Co Ltd
Pronto Cocktails Limited
Salcombe Moonshine Ltd

Cambridgeshire [14]
Blue Marble Distillery Ltd
Cambridge Distillery Ltd
Ely Gin Co Ltd.
Fen Spirits Limited
Holme Gin Limited
Landeavour Distillery Ltd
Linden and Lime Limited
Little Rotters Limited
Oxford Distillery Limited
Round Wood Distillery Ltd
Saffron Gin Co Ltd
Saffron Spirit Co Ltd
Saffron Spirits Limited
Terrepure Spirits UK Ltd.

Cardiganshire
In The Welsh Wind Distillery Ltd
Pembrokeshire Comestibles Co Ltd

Carmarthenshire
Garej Spirits Co Ltd
R & T Stills Limited
Spirit of Coalpit - Ysbryd y Pwll Glo

Cheshire [36]
1761 Limited
4t's Brewery Ltd
Big Hill Distillery Limited
Caribbean Flaava Limited
Cheshire Distilleries Limited
Copper Tree Partnership Ltd
Coyote Ventures Limited
Thomas Dakin Artisan Distillers Ltd
Thomas Dakin Craft Distillers Ltd
Thomas Dakin Distiller Ltd
Thomas Dakin Limited
Forest Distillery Ltd
G & J Distillers Ltd.
G & J Greenall Group Limited
G & J Limited
Gilbert and John Greenall Ltd
Harbour Gin Co Ltd
Hatters Distillery Limited
Jackson's Gin Ltd
Jervis Trading Limited
Jones Gin Ltd
Kelpie Whisky Limited
Lazy Drinks Ltd.
London Dry Gin Co Ltd
Lymm Gin Limited
Marblehead Brand Development Ltd
Mersey Gin Co Ltd
O'Hara's Spiced Rum Limited
Riverside Spirits Ltd
Second Son Distillery Limited
Silverback Distillers Ltd
Soho Shebeen Co Ltd
Still House Ltd
Stockport Gin Ltd
Telser & Pauli Ltd
Three Wrens Gin Limited

Cleveland [8]
78 Dbar Limited
Lickerish Tooth Ltd
RSM Solutions (NE) Limited
Revelry Spirits Ltd
Sleepy Hollow Spirits Ltd
Spirit of Captain Cook Limited
Steel River Drinks Ltd
Yarm Brewing and Distilling Co Ltd

Clwyd
Conwy Distillery Limited
Snowdonia Distillery Ltd

Co Durham [12]
Break Line Brewing & Distilling Ltd
Commonwealth Gin Ltd
Durham Distillery Limited
Durham Gin Limited
Engin Yard Beverage Co Ltd
A.D.C. Halford & Co Ltd
Hart Brothers Limited
Montrose Scotch Whisky Ltd.
Northumberland Gin Co Ltd
WL Distillery Ltd
Yarm Gin Ltd
Yarm Spirits Co Ltd

Cornwall [26]
Atlantic Distillery Ltd
Beets Incorporated Ltd
Colwith Farm Distillery Ltd
Cornish Distillery Co Ltd
Cornish Distilling Co Ltd
Cornish Spiritsmith Ltd
Curio Spirits Co Ltd
Duchy Beverages Ltd
Fal River Distillery Limited
Fowey River Gin Ltd
Helford River Distillery Ltd
High Water Distilling Co Ltd
Land's End Gin Limited
Liquid Lounge Drinks Co. Ltd

Liquid Revolution Ltd
Moorland Distillery Limited
Mousehole Brewery Limited
Paradise Cocktails Ltd
Pure Cornish Limited
Rathlee Distilling Co Ltd.
Rosemullion Distillery Ltd
Shannon & Thomas Limited
Southwestern Distillery Ltd
Stargazey Spirits Ltd
Todka Limited
Trevethan Distillery Ltd

Cumbria [19]
Cartmel Gin Ltd
Cragside Spirit Co Ltd
Ecclefechan Whisky Co Ltd
Hawkshead Distillery Ltd
Hawkshead Gin and Spirit Co Ltd
Hawkshead Spirit Co Ltd
Kendal Brewery Ltd
Kendal Mint Cake Co Ltd
Lakeland Moon Limited
MWBH Bottling Co. Limited
Millom Distillery Limited
Mint Drinks Co Ltd
New Union Brewing Co Ltd
Penningtons Spirits and Liqueurs Ltd
Ruskin Spirit Co Ltd
Shed 1 Distillery Ulverston. Ltd
Spirit of The Lakes Limited
Ulverston Gin Limited
Wolftown Distillery Limited

Denbighshire
Cwmni Distyllfa Llanberis Cyf
Pant y Foel Gin Ltd

Derbyshire [16]
20trees Gin Ltd
Amber Valley Gin Ltd
Buxton Distillery Limited
Corky's Brands Limited
Derbyshire Distillery Limited
Edale Gin Co Ltd
Grain Artisan Ltd
Hoggnorton Limited
Honey Spirits Co Ltd
Lindsay's Still Room Ltd
Peak District Distilling Co Ltd
Peakys Distillery Ltd
Pigeon Fisher Gin Co Limited
V K Brands Limited
White Peak Distillery Limited
Zero Gravity Spirits Ltd

Devon [37]
Bermondsey Distillery Limited
Blackingstone Ltd
Botanical Jack's Limited
Branscombe Vale Brewery Ltd
Brixham Gin Co Ltd.
Coates & Co. (Plymouth) Ltd
Dartmoor Distillery Limited
Dartmoor Whisky Distillery Ltd
Dartmouth Distillery Co Ltd
Devon Coast Distillery Limited
Devon Distillery Limited
Distinctly Different Spirits Co Ltd
H.B. Evelyo Ltd.

Exeter Distillery Ltd
Exeter Gin Ltd
Exmoor Distillers Ltd
Falmouth Gin Limited
Forsaken Limited
Horseguards London Dry Gin Ltd
Knockeen Hills Spirits Ltd
Krupnikoz Ltd
Newton Drinks Limited
Nitrogin Ltd.
Northlew Distillery Ltd
Old Chapel Brendon Limited
Otter Distillery Limited
Papillon Dartmoor Distillery Ltd
Q & S Distilling Co Ltd
Salcombe Cider Co Ltd
Salcombe Distilling Co Ltd
Seaway Royale Limited
Seven Deadly Sins Ltd
Skylark Distillery Ltd
Topsham Gin Ltd
Tors Vodka Limited
Two Drifters Distillery Ltd
Wicked Wolf Limited

Dorset [13]
Avalon Distillery Co Ltd
Beaucroft Beverages Ltd
Black Cow Vodka Co Ltd
Clifden Arms Property Ltd
Clifden Arms Trading Ltd
Liberty Orchards Limited
Pentric Distillery Ltd
Shanty Spirit Ltd
Soapbox Spirits Ltd
Twisted Gin Ltd
UK Distillers Limited
Ursus Americanus Limited
Zero-Moo Ltd

Essex [21]
55 Above Ltd
Aurora Brewing Limited
Boho Drinks Brands Ltd
Boho Drinks Ltd
Central Line Holdings Limited
Cuba Trading Co Ltd
Demon Vodka Limited
GNR Distillery Limited
Gibraltar Gin Co Ltd
Glass Jigsaw Ltd.
Hayter Divisions Limited
Herbert's Distillery & Co Ltd
JW Distillers Limited
Loca Beverages Ltd
Neptune SA Ltd
Orbis Whiskey Limited
Laurence Philippe Wines Ltd
Pocketful of Stones Distillers Ltd
Slamseys Drinks Limited
St. James Distillery Limited
Two Fathoms Distillery Ltd.

Flintshire
Clwydian Range Distillery Ltd

Glamorgan [11]
Aztec Spirits Ltd
Bottlers & Distillers (Wales) Ltd
Cherry Drop Gin Ltd
Cygnet Spirits Limited
Eccentric Gin Co Limited
Godka Ltd
Gower Distillery Ltd
Moody Rum Ltd
NineTailsDistillery Ltd
Treganna Gin Ltd
Y Cwmni Chwisgi Cymraeg Newydd Cyf

Gloucestershire [20]
Hilary Blackford Associates Ltd
Boutique Distillery Ltd
Bramley and Gage Limited
Brennen & Brown Limited
Capreolus Distillery Ltd
Copper Frog Distilling Limited
Deya Brewing Co Ltd
Dowdeswell Distillery Limited
W.C. Fowler & Sons Limited
Mr Bonds Tonic Limited
Neat Spirits Limited
Polo Gin Limited
Puddlebrook Distillery Limited
Sibling Distillery Limited
Stokers Spirits Ltd
Sweetwater Distillery Limited
Tewkesbury Distillery Ltd
Tivoli's Gin Limited
Twisting Spirits Ltd
Weatheralls Distillery Limited

Gwent
Old Brenin Distillery Ltd

Gwynedd
WJ Evans a'i Gwmni (Ynys Enlli) Cyf

Hampshire [28]
Beachcomber Gin Ltd
Blend Experts Limited
Bombay Spirits Co Ltd
Bournemouth Distillers Limited
Checkers Gin Ltd
Conker Spirit Limited
Corner Fifty Three Distilling Ltd
Cornish Spirit Co Ltd
Dalrymples Distillery Ltd
John Dewar and Sons Limited
Etoh Studio Limited
Fairfields Liqueurs Ltd
HI&PE Limited
HMS Spirits Co Ltd
Knowcal Limited
Lillington Distillation Ltd
Maeden Group Ltd
New Forest Spirits Ltd
Penton Park Brewery Limited
Portsmouth Distillery Co Ltd
Portsmouth Gin Co Ltd
River Test Distillery Limited
Rum Club Ltd
Silver Circle Distillery Ltd
Solent Spirits Co Ltd
Spice Island Gin Co Ltd
Strontium Gin Co Ltd
Winchester Distillery Limited

Herefordshire [7]
Chase Distillery Limited
Gun Dog Gin Limited
Mooshine Ltd
Peats Beast Limited
Penrhos Spirits Ltd
Shropshire Hills Distillery Ltd
Wild Foragin Ltd

Hertfordshire [14]
Alcohols Limited
Alkemista Limited
Chalk & Charcoal Limited
Clock Tower Distilleries Ltd
Gaelic Pure Scotch Whisky Ltd
Ginmeister Ltd
Great Don Ltd
Gyffordes Distillers Ltd
Kimbland Distillery Ltd
Liveras Limited
Norcabis Ltd
Pesvebi Ltd
South Devon Liqueur Co Ltd
Southey Brewing Co Ltd

Humberside
Holy Grail Beverages Limited

Isle of Wight
Isle of Wight Distillery Ltd
Southampton Distillery Ltd
Tipsy Wight Ltd
Wight Spirits Ltd

Kent [34]
Anno Distillers Limited
Archangel Distilleries Ltd
Armadillo Spirits Limited
Atom Brands Limited
Atom Cask Holdings Limited
Atom Drinks Limited
Atom Group Limited
Atom Supplies Limited
Basil's Botanicals Limited
Brewhouse Spirits Limited
Chileanspirit Ltd
Elephant Gin Ltd
Gin Dobry Gin Co Ltd
Howards of Kent Limited
Invoke Distillery Ltd
Invoke Distilling Co. Ltd
Jonomade Limited
KSSM International Limited
Lambeth Spirits Ltd
Liquid Vision Enterprise Ltd
London Craft Distillers Ltd
Maidstone Distillery Ltd
Margate Distillery Ltd
Master of Malt Limited
Masters of Malt Limited
Maverick Brands Limited
Maverick Drinks Limited
Maverick Spirits Limited
Maxchater Ltd
Nip from The Hip Limited
Revelry Brewing & Distilling Ltd
Spirit of Malt House Limited
Tea Rocks Ltd
Whitstable Distillery Ltd

Lancashire [56]
2H1O Limited
Alderman's Drinks Ltd.
Atom Distillery Ltd
Batch Brew Ltd
Beaumonde Desserts Limited
Black Powder Gin Co Ltd
Bowland Distillery Ltd
Brindle Distillery Limited
Curious Liquids Limited
Dimbandit Ltd
Distillery 96 Limited
Drinks of Manchester Limited
Droylsden Craft Limited
Edge Gin Ltd
Faith and Sons Limited
Farman & Son Ltd
Fenney Street Distillery Ltd
Flavour Premium Brands Limited
Flavour Traders Limited
Four Sisters Distillery Ltd
Foxdenton Estate Co Ltd
Ginwimmin Ltd
Goosnargh Gin Ltd
Ground Inn Ltd
Hidden Gem - Urban Artisan Spirit Ltd
Hoyle Bottom Spirits Ltd
JustaGinCo Ltd
Luxury Trading Co Ltd
Lytham Distillers Limited
Lytham Distillery Co Ltd
Lytham Gin Co Ltd
Manchester Liquor Co. Limited
Manchester Still Ltd.
Nestwonder Ltd
Northern Spirits Partnership Ltd
Pentone Family Limited
Pin Fold Distillery Ltd
Pure Wild Spirits Ltd
Ramsbottom Gin Co Ltd
Ribble Valley Gin Co Ltd.
Richie & Nikki Ltd
Rivington Distillery Ltd
Royton Gin Ltd
Saddleworth Distillery Ltd
Skinnybrands Ltd
Soulmate Gin Ltd
Speakeasy Spirits UK Ltd
Spirit of Manchester Distillery Ltd
Square Street Distillery Ltd
Supermarine Vodka Distillers Ltd
Tarsier Spirit Ltd
Touch Lucky Limited
Twenty Oaks, Ltd
West Spirits MCR Ltd
Your Buddy Mary Limited
Zymurgorium Ltd

Leicestershire [6]
45 West Distillers Limited
Brentingby Gin Ltd
Honey Gin Co Ltd
Raw Distilling Ltd
Union Distillers Ltd
Urban Vodka Limited

Lincolnshire [17]
A Little Luxury Ltd
Bottomley Distillers Ltd
Country Garden Drinks Co Ltd
Damsons in Distress Limited
Deco Spirits Limited
Drink It Limited
Gentlemen Distillers Ltd
Hin Ltd
Libaeration Limited
Lincoln Distillery Limited
Lincoln Gin Ltd
Lincoln Imp Drinks Co Ltd
Lincolnshire Gin Ltd
Marron (Lincoln) Ltd
Percy's T Limited
Ryhall Distillery Limited
Unconventional Distillery Co. Ltd

London [206]
180 East Limited
808 Drinks Co Ltd
A Little Luxury Distillery Ltd
AJC Homes Scotland Limited
AM Distilling Ltd
Alko Vintages UK Ltd
American Beverage Marketers Ltd
Animal Spirits Ltd
Anstie Distillers International Ltd
Arundo Limited
Asterley Bros, London Ltd
Avinshaw Industries Limited
Ban Poitin Ltd
Barclay Distillery Limited
Willem Barentsz Limited
Bashiba Gin Ltd
Batch88 Ltd
Beerdsman Limited
Benjamin & Blum Limited
Berkshire Distillery Limited
Bimber Distillery Ltd
Bitter Salvation Ltd
Black Label Spirits Ltd
Bladnoch Distillery Limited
Bloomsbury Club UK Limited
Bloomsbury Distillery Ltd
Bootleg Club Limited
Botanical Alchemy Ltd
Broad Street Brands Limited
Brockmans Gin Limited
Malcolm Browne Distillery Co Ltd
Butlers Cross Limited
Camden Distillers Limited
Canebrake Ltd
Cantails Limited
Churchill Distillery Limited
Spencer Collings & Co Limited
Compass Box Whisky Supply Ltd
Copper Drinks Limited
Craft Distilling Expo Limited
Crafted Beverages Limited
Crawford's Rock Ltd
Demball Limited
Devine Distillates Group (Manufacturing)
Diageo Balkans Limited
Diageo Great Britain Limited
Dirty Drinks Collective Ltd
Dockers Spirit Co Ltd
Doctor Bird Rum Ltd
Doggy John Distillery Limited
Doghouse Distillery Limited
Dr Gin Limited
Druid's Distillery Ltd
Dulwich Gin Limited
EMS Corp Limited
Ealing Distillery Ltd
East India Company Gin Limited

East India Company London Dry Gin Ltd
East London Liquor Co Ltd
Eight Vodka Limited
Ely's Cocktails Ltd
Empire Bar Service Ltd
Empirical Trading Co. Limited
Escubac Limited
Fatman and Friends Ltd.
Fixed Axis Ltd
For The Love of Limited
Forgan Distillery Ltd
Gaslight Distillery Limited
Gest Spirits Limited
Gin Foundry Limited
Gin Hub Limited
Gin Tales Ltd
Ginomics Ltd
Glen Monarch Distillery Ltd
Glen Scotia Distillery Co Ltd
Global Premium Spirits Ltd
Goldings Distillery Ltd
Goldy Gin Limited
Good Spirits Ltd
Graveney Gin Limited
Green Box Drinks Limited
Greenwood Spirits Limited
Guilty Drinks Limited
Hackney Distillery Limited
Half Cock Limited
Hamilton Rose Gin Ltd
Ian Hart Distilling Limited
Hayman Distillers Limited
Henley Gin Co Ltd
Hurricane Rum Co Ltd
Idle Saint Spirits Limited
Independent Spirits Limited
Inverroche International Ltd
Isledon Gin Ltd
Italian Gin Co Ltd
JDB Spirits Ltd
Jacob's Gin Limited
Jefferson & Bennett Distillers Ltd
Jewel Isle Global Productions Ltd
Jivana Spirits Ltd.
Jo & Matt Ltd
Juggling King Rum Co Ltd
Justerini & Brooks, Limited
K1 Beer PLC
KO Gin Limited
Charlie Kaane Enterprises Ltd.
Kac70 Limited
Kammerling's Investment Holdings Ltd
Kammerlings Limited
Kiko Mezcal Ltd
Kindred Gin Ltd
Klerck Distillery Ltd
Koolvibes Limited
LDN Spirits Limited
Lanty Slee Liquor Co Ltd
Littlemill Distillery Co Ltd
Loaded Spirits Ltd
Loch Lomond Distillers Limited
Loch Lomond Distillery Co Ltd
Lonberg Limited
Lonburg 449 Limited
Londinio Liqueurs Ltd.
London Alcohol Co Ltd
London Botanical Drinks Ltd
London Brewery Limited
London Distillery - Battersea Ltd
London Distillery Co Ltd
London Fortifiers Limited

London Rum Company Holdings Ltd
London Society of Mixologists
London Spiced Dry Limited
London Vodka Ltd
Long Walk Spirits Limited
Lost Roots Limited
Lucent Drinks Ltd
Luxbev Limited
MacNab Distilleries Limited
Mahiki Trading Limited
Mason & Summers Limited
Matugga Beverages Limited
Mavarac UK Limited
Mezcal Reina Limited
Modern Botanicals Limited
Mr & Mrs Gin Ltd
Mulberry Distillery Limited
Myatt's Fields Limited
Newcastle Whisky Distillery Co Ltd
Norfolk Rum Co Ltd
Northumberland Distillery Co Ltd
One Point Eight Bar Limited
Originalsip Ltd
Our/London Vodka Limited
Patient Wolf Limited
Patterson and Clarke Distillery Ltd
Perfidious Albion Limited
Pipeline Drinks Ltd
Pococello Ltd
Porthilly Spirit Distillery Ltd
Potion Universe Ltd
RWB Drinks Ltd
Renaissance Drinks Ltd
Renegade Spirits Grenada Ltd
Maurice Richard Ltd
Riktig Limited
Rock Hill Cider Co Ltd
Russian Doll Vodka Limited
Sacred Spirits Holdings Ltd
Saint Patricks Ltd
Otten Schmidt Ltd.
Seduction Rum Punch UK Ltd
Sendivogius Limited
Shorts Boy Distillery Ltd
Silvertown Brewery and Distillery Co Ltd
Sipsmith Limited
Sky Pirate Ltd
Sloosh Limited
Soak Engineering Ltd
Spirit Stories Ltd
Spirit of Unicorn Ltd
Spirits and Bubbles Limited
Stockholm Distillers and Vintners
Stolowa Ltd
Surendran & Bownes Ltd.
Swallow London Ltd
Sweetdram Limited
Tasty Beverages Limited
Thames Distillers Limited
Tippling Tonic Limited
Tready's Ltd
Tres Amigos Limited
U'Luvka Ltd
UK Dorset Ltd
UK McLouis Liquor Co Ltd
Uncle Nearest Ltd.
Unit Thirteen Limited
Universal Robo Innovations Ltd
Vape Pure Ltd
Verset Vodka Holdings Limited
W & S Distillery Limited
Wave'n Ltd

Wayfinder Distillery Limited
Wessex Distillery Limited
Westmorland Spirits Limited
Wilson's Henley Gin Co Ltd
Wimbledon Distillery Co Ltd

Lothian [21]
Broxburn Bottlers Limited
Buck and Birch Ltd
Dunbar Drinks Co Ltd
Edinburgh Gin Limited
Glen Moray-Glenlivet Distillery Co Ltd
Label 5 First Blending Co Ltd
Lang Brothers Limited
Linlithgow Distillery Limited
Ian MacLeod Distillers Ltd
Ian MacLeod and Co Ltd
Matugga Distillers Limited
Wm Maxwell (Scotch Whisky) Ltd
Alastair McIntosh Management Services
NB Distillery Limited
Peter J Russell & Co Ltd.
Scots' Cheer Limited
Scottish Independent Distillers Co Ltd
Spencerfield Spirit Co Ltd
Syndicate 58/6 Limited
Tarbraxus Distillers Ltd
Wallhouse Distillery Limited

Merseyside [26]
3 Lids Rum Ltd
Aber Falls Distillery Limited
Bearded Lion Drinks Co Ltd
Dr Junipers Ltd.
Formby Spirits Limited
Fox Gins Ltd
Great White Gin Limited
Handmade Gin Co Ltd
Juniper Street Gin Co Ltd
Lime Street Distillery Limited
Liverpool Gin Distillery Ltd
Liverpool Spring Gin Limited
Joseph Mills (Denaturants) Ltd
Mudlark Investments Ltd
Murphy's Gin Ltd
Murphy, Black and Mills Ltd
N.Gin Distillery Ltd
H. J. Neill Ltd
Penny Lane Gin Ltd
Rabakken Ltd
Redrosesforme Limited
Scouse Girls Gin Ltd
Seadwealths Ltd
Swift Half Collective Ltd
Tappers Artisan Spirits Ltd.
Turncoat Distillery Limited

Middlesex [13]
3D Shapie Limited
Angels Share (MCR) Limited
Back Bar Spirits Limited
Beam Suntory UK Limited
Beautiful Distillery Limited
Boatyard Distillery Ltd
Family of Hounds Limited
London Spice Co Ltd
Neat Distillery Ltd
Paradise Rum Limited
Soul Vodka Ltd
Soul of The Spirit Limited
Tubeoptics. Ltd

Midlothian [74]
3R Whisky Limited
Amber Glen Scotch Whisky Co., Ltd
Arbikie X Limited
Ardbeg Distillery Limited
Ardbeg Limited
Artisanal Spirits Co Ltd
Atom Scotland Limited
Benriach Distillery Co Ltd
Bonding and Transport Company, Ltd
Caledonian Bottlers PLC
Carillon U.K. Limited
Company of Dark Spirits Ltd
Compass Box Delicious Whisky Ltd.
Dark Art Gin Limited
Dark Spirits Co Ltd
Diageo Distilling Limited
Diageo Scotland Limited
Donnach Whisky Limited
Edinburgh Distillers Limited
Edinburgh Distillery Co Ltd.
Edinburgh Rum Co Ltd
Edinburgh Whisky Ltd.
Edinburgh and Leith Distillery Ltd
Electric Spirit Co Ltd.
Forest Spirits Ltd
Fort Glen Whisky Co Ltd
Forth Bridge Brewery and Distillery
Glendronach Distillery Co Ltd
Glenglassaugh Distillery Co Ltd
Glenmaster Distillers Limited
Glenmorangie Co Ltd
Glenmorangie Distillery Co Ltd, The
Glenmorangie Spring Water Co Ltd
Alistair Graham Limited
Hebridean Distillers Limited
Holyrood Distillery Ltd
Islay Rum Co Ltd
Kingsbarns Company of Distillers Ltd
Loch Ewe Spirits Limited
MacDonald & Muir Limited
MacDonald Martin Distilleries Ltd
Douglas MacNiven & Co Ltd
James Martin & Company, Ltd
Mastropasqua & Brothers Ltd.
Matisse Spirits Co Ltd
McCaigs Distillery Ltd
Morangie Mineral Water Co Ltd
Morangie Springs Limited
Charles Muirhead & Son. Ltd
Myperfectgin Ltd
Nicol Anderson & Co Ltd
North British Distillery Co Ltd
Pentland Still Ltd
Pickering's Gin Limited
Precision Spirits Ltd
R & B Distillers Limited
Russell Distillers Limited
SOS Gin Ltd
Scotch Malt Whisky Society Ltd
Sip Antics Limited
South Loch Ltd
South Side Spirit Limited
Spirit of Leith Ltd
Spirits Development & Management Company (SDMC)
Stonedean Limited
Summerhall Distillery Limited
Tarlogie Springs Limited
J.G. Thomson & Co. Limited
Tullibardine Limited
United Distillers UK Limited
Wemyss Distillery Limited
West Highland Distillers Ltd
Whisky Cellar Limited
Wilson & Morgan Limited

Monmouthshire
Boutique Cellar Limited
Clandestine Distillery Limited
Hendre Distillery Ltd
Windfall Wood Group Limited

Norfolk [16]
Black Shuck Ltd
Duration Brewing Ltd
English Whisky Co. Limited
Evolution Brewing Ltd
Founding Drinks Ltd
New Adventure (Norfolk) Ltd
Norfolk Distillery Ltd
Norfolk Gin Limited
Norfolk Whisky Co. Limited
Pell and Co Spirits Limited
Sartorial Spirits Limited
St Faiths Distillery Limited
Sunfire Spirits Ltd
TBD Tipples Ltd
Unthank Distillery Limited
Waveney Valley Spirits Limited

Northamptonshire [15]
Amethystcave Ltd
Artisan Blending Limited
Banideep Ltd
Bethera Ltd
Black Cat Distillery Limited
Black Cat Drinks Ltd
Crystaldrifter Ltd
Distill8 Limited
Duck and Crutch Limited
Galleon Liqueurs UK Ltd
Lianorin Ltd
Long Gin Ltd
Madrise Ltd
Old Smiths Distillery Ltd
Warner's Distillery Limited

Northumberland [5]
Alnwick Rum Co Ltd
Berwick Brewrey Co Ltd
North Tyne Ventures Ltd
Northumberland Spirit Co Ltd
Pilgrim Spirit Ltd

Nottinghamshire [14]
Belvoir Gin Distillery Limited
Carrick Thomson Limited
Croft Distillery Ltd
Dilly Dilly Limited
Drops of Juniper Limited
Giorgio's Continental Ltd.
House of St Giles Ltd
Jose Reyes Bodega Ltd
Loch Shiel Whisky Limited
Northumberland Whisky Ltd
Ron de Mestizo Ltd
Snowdonia Spirit Co Ltd
Sovereign Spirits Ltd.
Spnet Ltd.

Oxfordshire [16]
CP Infusions Ltd
Chalgrove Artisan Distillery Ltd
Cornish Gin Mine Ltd
Drinkology Limited
Espensen Spirit Ltd
Fifty-Nine Spirits Co Ltd
Food Development Co Ltd
Ginglish Limited
Oxford Distillers Limited
Oxford Gin Co Ltd
Oxfordshire Gin Co Ltd
Pure Distilled Spirit Co Ltd
Still on the Hill Limited
Ten Bears Spirits Limited
Weymouth and Portland Distillery Co Ltd
Wood Brothers Distilling Co Ltd

Pembrokeshire
Barti Rum Ltd
St Davids Gin Limited
Still Wild Limited

Powys
Am Byth Distillery Ltd
Collards Distillery Limited
Dyfi Distillery Ltd
Fablas Limited

Rhondda Cynon Taf
New Welsh Whiskey Co Ltd
Pure Spirit in Wales Limited
Welsh Whisky Co Ltd

Rutland
Rutland Distillery Co Ltd
Sloeberry Spirits Ltd.

Shropshire [15]
Blue Sky Drinking Ltd
Forager Drinks Limited
Henstone Distillery Limited
Hereford & Ludlow Cider Brandy Co Ltd
Ironbridge Gorge Gin Co Ltd
Kirkwood Distillery Limited
Ludlow Apple Brandy Distillery Ltd
Ludlow Distillery Limited
Ludlow Vineyard Limited
Ludlow Whisky Limited
Seada Distillery Limited
Shire Gin Limited
Shropshire Distillery Limited
Shropshire Gin Co Ltd
Wrekin Spirit Limited

Somerset [23]
4607 Distillery Limited
Artificer Spirit Limited
Bristol Rum Co Ltd
Bristol Spirit Collective Ltd
Brothers Drinks Co. Limited
Crosstown Cocktail Co Ltd
Gateway Spirit Co Ltd
Gin Jar Drinks Co Ltd
Glastonbury Distillery Limited
Last Drop Spirit Co Ltd
Mezky Ltd
New Dawn Traders Ltd
Princetown Distillers Ltd

Psychopomp Ltd
Somerset Cider Brandy Co Ltd
Somerset Craft Distillery Ltd
Somerset Craft Spirit Co Ltd
Somerset Distillery Ltd
Somerset Drinks Ltd
Taunton Distiller's Ltd
Taunton Gin Limited
Underground Brewing Co Ltd
Wild and Spirited Limited

Staffordshire [9]
Artisan Distillery (Staffordshire)
Beers Spirit Co Ltd
Bros Distilling Ltd
Greywood Distillery Limited
Halton Turner Brewing Co Ltd
Parlay Drinks Ltd
Spirit of The Shires Limited
Staffordshire Distillery Ltd
Staffordshire Gin Co Ltd

Suffolk [14]
Abbey Distillery Ltd
Adnams PLC
British and Colonial Merchants of Jamaica
Edmunds Cocktails Ltd
Faiers Distillery Ltd
Flint & Hardings Limited
Heart of Suffolk Distillery Ltd
Libation Liberation Limited
Longtooth Gin Limited
Lowestoft Distillery Co Ltd
Suffolk Distillery Limited
Suffolk Smugglers Limited
Tiny Tipple Co Ltd
White Smoke Distillery Ltd

Surrey [51]
Angola Beverages Holding Co Ltd
Azure Distilleries Limited
Bitter Union Limited
Broker's Gin Limited
Caribbean Drinks Ltd
Cox & Mall Ltd
Csatrina Holdings Ltd
Cupids Bow 35 Limited
Deshi Liqueur Ltd
Distell International Holdings Ltd
Distillers of Surrey Limited
Duckenfield Ltd
Eastwater Gin Ltd
Elstead Village Distillers Ltd
Ethereal Cut Limited
Fire Beard Spirits Limited
Fogcutter Limited
Frensham Distillery Limited
Gin Kitchen Limited
Ginking Co Ltd
Good Life Gin Co Ltd
William Grant & Sons Distinction
Hurlingham International Ltd
Kingston Distillers Ltd.
Light Spirit Co Ltd
Mannequin Ltd.
Mews Gin Co Ltd
Morant Bay Distillery Co Ltd
My Nan's Favourite Ltd
Nibbs Spirits Limited
Rebel Distillers Ltd
Rebel Rabbet Ltd

Red Distillery Limited
Revolution Rum Ltd
Sailor Jerry Limited
Silent Pool Distillers Limited
Simple Sips International Ltd
Smart Brewing and Distilling Solutions
South London Urban Gin Co Ltd
Spiritmen Limited
Surrey Copper Distillery Ltd
Surrey Hills Distilling Co Ltd
Surrey Hills EBT Limited
Surrey Hills Whisky Co Ltd
Tricort Limited
Vijobar Ltd
Village Spirit Collective Ltd
Vonlevers Limited
Whiskymen Limited
Willimott House Limited
Wood and Co Ltd

Sussex [27]
Afterthought Spirits Co Ltd
Antibio UK Ltd
Azenja Limited
Black Cat Brewery Limited
Brighton Spirits Co Ltd
Cabin Pressure Spirits Ltd
Chilgrove Gin Co Ltd
Foxhole Spirits Limited
Guilty Libations Limited
H & S Distillers Ltd
Harlequin Distillery Ltd
Harley House Craft Distillery Ltd
Harley House Distillery Ltd
Hawksburn Spirits International Ltd
Holler Brewery Limited
Liquid Spirit Ltd
Madame Jennifer Distillery Ltd
Martin-Wells Distillery Ltd.
Mayfield Distilling Co Ltd
Nodding Donkey Distillery Co Ltd
Pure Sussex Distillery Ltd
Rainbow Chaser Limited
Really Brilliant Co Ltd
Rockwood & Hines Limited
Rumbustian Limited
Scream Retail Limited
Wilmington Spirits Limited

Tyne & Wear [18]
El Pulpo Loco Ltd
Geordie-Gin Co Ltd
Geordie-Gin Corporation Ltd
Jesmond Distilling Co Ltd
Lakes Distillery Company PLC
LighthouseVodka Ltd
London Rum Limited
Moorland Spirit Co Ltd
Nene Distillery Limited
Newcastle Distilling Ltd
Newcastle Gin Co. Limited
Northern Fried Drinks Limited
Poetic License Distillery Ltd
South Causey Distillery Ltd
Steampunk Ltd
Sunderland Gin Limited
Tea Venture Limited
V7 Enterprises Ltd

Warwickshire [11]
Beaufort Spirit Ltd
Cotswold Distilling Co Ltd
Hukleys Limited
Kafecal Global Co Ltd
Moores of Warwick Limited
Orogin Distilling Co. Limited
Queen Cleo Rum Ltd
Shakespeare Distillery Limited
Three Graces Distillery Ltd
Warwickshire Spirits Limited
Willow Tree Distilling Co Ltd

West Midlands [20]
Artisan Brands Limited
Ataxirola Ltd
Bitter Lemons Gin Ltd
Bluu Spirit Limited
Burning Barn Limited
Corrupt Drinks Co Ltd
Dr Eamers Emporium Limited
Duke's Distilling Co Ltd
Gin Ting Limited
Liqueur Manufactory Limited
London Heaven Spirits Company UK Ltd
Mr Kegz Ltd
Oktogin Ltd
Silhill Brewery Limited
Sin of Gin Ltd
Story Brands Limited
Tap End Brands Ltd
Tempus Gin Limited
Warwickshire Gin Co Ltd
West Midlands Distillery Ltd

Wiltshire [11]
Beeble Liquor Limited
Cognac Growers' Collective Ltd
Docked Distillery International Ltd
Downton Distillery Limited
Lombard Scotch Whisky Limited
Montoscar Enterprises Limited
Ramsbury Brewing and Distilling Co Ltd
Royal Wootton Bassett Gin Co Ltd
Scout and Sage Spirits Limited
Stonehenge Distillery Limited
Tickle Drinks Limited

Worcestershire [10]
Chinn-Chinn Ginn Limited
Esq Vodka Limited
Gin-Ger Gin Limited
Hinton's of Bewdley Ltd
Hussingtree Blends Limited
Prentice Spirits Ltd
Pryzm Cocktails Limited
Raer Scotch Whisky Ltd
Tipsy Fruit Gins Limited
Tudor Court Distillers Limited

Yorkshire [83]

50 Degrees North Limited
Adventure Brands Ltd
Barcelona Spirit Brands UK Ltd
Barford Imports Limited
Be Rude Not To Ltd
Boozy Infusion Limited
Brew House Yorkshire Limited
Brittains Beverages Ltd
Conscious Collaborative Ltd
Cool Brew Dept Ltd
Cooper King Distillery Ltd
Crossbill Gin Limited
Daisy Distillery Limited
Darlington Brewing and Distilling Co Ltd
Desire Drinks Limited
Doncaster Dry Gin Limited
Eoforwic Distilling Co Ltd
Equilibrium Food & Drink Ltd
Fancy A Tipple Limited
Fanny's Distilling Co Ltd
Five Fathoms Spirit Limited
Folklore Distillery Ltd
Fords of Wakefield Ltd
Fourfolk Gin Co Ltd
Fruity Tipples Limited
Great Yorkshire Spirit Co Ltd
Harrison Distillery Ltd
Harrogate Distillery Ltd
Hebden Bridge Spirit Co Ltd
Hibernian Beverage Group Ltd
Hooting Owl Distillery Ltd
Horsforth Distillery Ltd
Hothams Limited
Ilkley Gin Co Ltd
JKM Spirits Limited
Jacqson Limited
Kettlesing Gin Limited
Kingston upon Hull Liqour Co Ltd
Lamson Wine Co Ltd
Leeds Gin Limited
Little Gin Shop Limited
Little Red Berry Co Ltd.
Locksley Distilling Co Ltd
Lujo Distilling Co Ltd
Luxco Drinks Limited
Masons Yorkshire Gin Ltd
McCallums Liqueurs Ltd
Mill House Distillery Limited
Molotov Brand Limited
Musicspeller Ltd
Nectardigger Ltd
R2 Distillers Ltd
Rare Bird Distillery Limited
Rhucello Limited
Rum To You Ltd
SV Distilleries Limited
Sheffield Distillery Limited
Shotgun Limited
Sipping Shed Limited
Skinny Russian Vodka Ltd
Spirit of Harrogate Limited
Spirit of Leeds Ltd
Spirit of Yorkshire Limited
Spirits of Bronte Drinks Co. Ltd
Steel City Craft Spirits Boutique Ltd
Sword of Spirit Distillery Ltd
Taplin & Mageean Ltd
True North Brew Co Limited
Tuerto Tequila Ltd
Twisted Roots Distillery Ltd
Wells Gin Limited
Whitby Distillery Limited
Whitby Gin Limited
White House Distillery Limited
White House Gin Limited
Whittaker's Distillery Limited
YDC Ltd
York Gin Co Ltd
Yorkshine Spirit Limited
Yorkshire Distillery Co Ltd
Yorkshire Gin Limited
Yorkshire Rum Co Ltd
Yorkshire Whisky Co Ltd

Company Profiles

&Spirit Limited
Incorporated: 20 April 2015
Previous: Antillia Drinks Company Limited
Registered Office: 3 Laychequers Meadow, Taplow, Maidenhead, Berks, SL6 0BF
Major Shareholder: Jon Robert Jenkins
Officers: Jon Robert Jenkins [1987] Director/Accountant

1725 Limited
Incorporated: 18 February 2016
Registered Office: Spencerfield Farmhouse, Hillend, Dunfermline, Fife, KY11 9LA
Shareholders: Finlay James Gowl Nicol; Harriet Mary Alexandra Nicol; Hannah Felicity Nicol
Officers: Hannah Felicity Nicol, Secretary; Finlay James Gowl Nicol [1985] Director/Distiller; Harriet Mary Alexandra Nicol [1987] Director/Events Manager

1761 Limited
Incorporated: 15 February 2011
Registered Office: Distribution Point, Melbury Park, Clayton, Birchwood, Warrington, Cheshire, WA3 6PH
Shareholders: Vincenzo Visone; Warren Michael Scott
Officers: Michael Clifford, Secretary; Warren Michael Scott [1963] Director/Businessman; Vincenzo Visone [1955] Director/Businessman [Italian]

180 East Limited
Incorporated: 10 December 2013
Net Worth: £298,180 *Total Assets:* £422,677
Registered Office: 85 Great Portland Street, London, W1W 7LT
Major Shareholder: William Jeremy Turnage
Officers: Nicholas James Whishaw Masters [1978] Director; James Geoffrey Bethune Taylor [1979] Director; William Turnage [1978] Director

20trees Gin Ltd
Incorporated: 25 June 2018
Registered Office: 123 Kinder Road, Hayfield, High Peak, Derbys, SK22 2LE
Shareholders: Jonathan David Young; Lorna Ann Young
Officers: Jonathan David Young [1964] Director; Lorna Ann Young [1968] Director

2H1O Limited
Incorporated: 19 August 2009
Net Worth: £8,003 *Total Assets:* £36,470
Registered Office: Croft House, Station Road, Barnoldswick, Lancs, BB18 5NA
Shareholders: Guido Pietro Mastrantuono; Alessandro Mastrantuono
Officers: Alessandro Mastrantuono [1954] Director/Retailer [Italian]; Guido Pietro Mastrantuono [1956] Director/Retailer [Italian]

3 Lids Rum Ltd
Incorporated: 29 September 2017
Net Worth: £900 *Total Assets:* £10,296
Registered Office: 1 Beechurst Road, Liverpool, L25 3PX
Shareholders: Andrew Robert John Laird; Andrew Robert John Laird
Officers: Andrew Robert John Laird [1985] Director

3D Shapie Limited
Incorporated: 5 January 2015
Net Worth Deficit: £49,465 *Total Assets:* £7,178
Registered Office: 428 Chertsey Road, Twickenham, Middlesex, TW2 6LP
Major Shareholder: Geoffrey Peter Malvisi
Officers: Geoffrey Peter Malvisi [1954] Director

3R Whisky Limited
Incorporated: 8 October 2012
Net Worth: £251,861 *Total Assets:* £891,303
Registered Office: Edinburgh Park, 5 Lochside Way, Edinburgh, EH12 9DT
Officers: James Matthew Crayden Edmunds [1974] Director; Gabor Kovacs [1980] Director [Hungarian]; Kara Elizabeth Major [1977] Director/Lawyer [American]

45 West Distillers Limited
Incorporated: 12 July 2016 *Employees:* 8
Net Worth Deficit: £317,354 *Total Assets:* £366,733
Registered Office: The Collection Yard, Bawdon Lodge Farm, Charley Road, Nanpantan, Loughborough, Leics, LE12 9YE
Parent: Autarky Ventures Limited
Officers: Matthew Edward Charles Payne [1972] Director; Graham Peter Veitch [1968] Director

4607 Distillery Limited
Incorporated: 2 October 2018
Registered Office: 213 High Street, Street, Somerset, BA16 0NE
Major Shareholder: Simon Harvey
Officers: Simon Harvey, Secretary; Simon Harvey [1968] Director

4t's Brewery Ltd
Incorporated: 14 April 2010
Net Worth Deficit: £117,536 *Total Assets:* £73,183
Registered Office: Suite 11, Station House, Central Way, Winwick Street, Warrington, Cheshire, WA2 7TT
Major Shareholder: John Michael Wilkinson
Officers: John Michael Wilkinson [1968] Director

50 Degrees North Limited
Incorporated: 28 June 2005
Net Worth Deficit: £235,796 *Total Assets:* £19,175
Registered Office: 14-15 Harelands Court Yard Office, Moor Road, Melsonby, Richmond, N Yorks, DL10 5NY
Shareholders: Dan Hiza; Ritu Manocha Hiza
Officers: Ritu Manocha Hiza, Secretary/Director; Daniel Paul Hiza [1965] Director; Ritu Manocha Hiza [1963] Director

55 Above Ltd
Incorporated: 25 April 2014
Net Worth Deficit: £90,586 *Total Assets:* £46,887
Registered Office: 4 Langford Court, Ongar Road, Kelvedon Hatch, Brentwood, Essex, CM15 0LB
Major Shareholder: Alan Colin Gilchrist
Officers: Alan Colin Gilchrist [1971] Director/IT Consultant

78 Dbar Limited
Incorporated: 29 August 2018
Registered Office: 16 Hartburn Mews, Stockton on Tees, Cleveland, TS18 5HZ
Shareholders: Jack Oliver Hammersley; Alan Ronald Hammersley
Officers: Alan Ronald Hammersley [1963] Director; Jack Oliver Hammersley [1995] Director

The 8o8 Drinks Company Limited
Incorporated: 29 May 2014
Net Worth: £276,624 *Total Assets:* £376,639
Registered Office: 55 Drury Lane, London, WC2B 5RZ
Shareholders: Thomas Asher Danvers; Paul Stephen Pullinger
Officers: Thomas Asher Danvers [1965] Director/Music Producer; Jonathan Paul Norman Driver [1961] Director; Harry Francis Drnec [1946] Director/Consultant [American]; John Justin Delany Hicklin [1960] Director/Consultant; Paul Stephen Pullinger [1963] Director/Entrepreneur; William David Rae [1953] Director/Consultant

A Little Luxury Distillery Ltd
Incorporated: 23 January 2019
Registered Office: 20-22 Wenlock Road, London, N1 7GU
Shareholders: Barbara Ann Daughtrey; Laura Elizabeth Daughtrey
Officers: Barbara Ann Daughtrey, Secretary; Barbara Ann Daughtrey [1953] Director; Laura Elizabeth Daughtrey [1981] Director

A Little Luxury Ltd
Incorporated: 9 February 2011
Net Worth Deficit: £47,635 *Total Assets:* £34,864
Registered Office: 15 Barnes Close, Sleaford, Lincs, NG34 8BF
Major Shareholder: Barbara Ann Daughtrey
Officers: Barbara Ann Daughtrey [1953] Director/Teacher; Laura Elizabeth Daughtrey [1981] Director/Self Employed

Abbey Distillery Ltd
Incorporated: 13 July 2018
Registered Office: 14 Mustow Street, Bury St Edmunds, Suffolk, IP33 1XU
Major Shareholder: Steven Minns
Officers: Steven Minns, Secretary; Peter Beadle [1953] Director; Steven Minns [1959] Director

Aber Falls Distillery Limited
Incorporated: 29 June 2017
Registered Office: The Sovereign Distillery, Wilson Road, Huyton, Knowsley, Merseyside, L36 6AD
Parent: Halewood International Holdings (UK) Limited
Officers: Stewart Andrew Hainsworth [1969] Director/Chief Executive Officer; Alan William Robinson [1965] Finance Director; Christopher James Wright [1975] Director

Aberdeen Distillers Limited
Incorporated: 21 January 1993
Registered Office: Unit F14 Festival Business Centre, 150 Brand Street, Glasgow, G51 1DH
Officers: Hannah Eveline Tucek, Secretary; Hannah Eveline Tucek [1982] Director; Robin Michael Tucek [1948] Director

Adelphi Distillery (1826) Limited
Incorporated: 31 August 2010 *Employees:* 5
Net Worth Deficit: £721,235 *Total Assets:* £9,545,149
Registered Office: The Ardnamurchan Distillery, Glenbeg, Ardnamurchan, Acharacle, Argyll, PH36 4JG
Parent: Adelphi Distillery Limited
Officers: Elizabeth Jean MacDonald, Secretary; Alexander Victor Bruce [1971] Director/Whisky Sales; Alistair Carnegie Campbell [1954] Director/Writer to The Signet; James Keith Ross Falconer [1955] Director; Gordon James Hamilton [1964] Operations Director; Elizabeth Jean MacDonald [1950] Director/Farmer

Adelphi Distillery Limited
Incorporated: 18 December 1992 *Employees:* 15
Net Worth: £2,528,072 *Total Assets:* £9,967,888
Registered Office: The Ardnamurchan Distillery, Glenbeg, Ardnamurchan, Acharacle, Argyll, PH36 4JG
Shareholders: Keith Falconer; Donald Francis Irwin-Houston
Officers: Elizabeth Jean MacDonald, Secretary; Alexander Victor Bruce [1971] Managing Director; Alistair Carnegie Campbell [1954] Director/Writer to The Signet; James Keith Ross Falconer [1955] Director; Gordon James Hamilton [1964] Operations Director; Elizabeth Jean MacDonald [1950] Director

Adnams PLC
Incorporated: 24 March 1890 *Employees:* 203
Net Worth: £28,642,000 *Total Assets:* £64,708,000
Registered Office: East Green, Southwold, Suffolk, IP18 6JW
Officers: Elizabeth Sarah Cantwell, Secretary; Jonathan Adnams [1956] Director; Nicola Joy Dulieu [1963] Director; Michael Guy Hilliard Heald [1950] Director; Karen Hester [1962] Director; Bridget Fiona McIntyre [1961] Director; Stephen Crommelin Pugh [1958] Director; Dr Steven Michael Sharp [1950] Marketing Director; Andrew Charles Wood [1960] Director

Adventure Brands Ltd
Incorporated: 27 July 2018
Registered Office: Corner House, Luton Street, Keighley, W Yorks, BD21 2LE
Shareholders: Jayne Margaret Watmough; George Watmough
Officers: George Watmough [1948] Director; Jayne Margaret Watmough [1958] Director/Company Secretary

Afallon Mon Cyf
Incorporated: 7 December 2017
Registered Office: Bedo, Llanfachraeth, Sir Ynys Mon, LL65 4DH
Shareholder: Owen Arwyn Owen
Officers: Emyr Wyn Gibson [1977] Director; Owen Arwyn Owen [1977] Director; Owen Gethin Owen [1971] Director

Afterthought Spirits Company Ltd
Incorporated: 30 January 2018
Registered Office: Unit 43 Henfield Business Park, Henfield, W Sussex, BN5 9SL
Parent: Afterthought Group Ltd
Officers: Douglas Walford [1977] Director/Engineer

AJC Homes Scotland Limited
Incorporated: 18 March 1998 *Employees:* 11
Net Worth: £2,674,521 *Total Assets:* £9,717,623
Registered Office: 4th Floor, Swan House, 17-19 Stratford Place, London, W1C 1BQ
Major Shareholder: The Earl of Aboyne Alistair Granville Gordon
Officers: Alistair Granville Gordon, Secretary; Brian Pirie [1961] Director/Business Development

Alcohols Limited
Incorporated: 5 April 1955 *Employees:* 54
Net Worth: £12,355,989 *Total Assets:* £17,664,496
Registered Office: Charringtons House, The Causeway, Bishop's Stortford, Herts, CM23 2ER
Parent: W.H.Palmer & Co. (Industries) Limited
Officers: Richard Charles Evans [1964] Director/Chartered Accountant; Robert Harry Ling [1952] Director/Accountant; Adam John Wallis [1960] Director

Alderman's Drinks Ltd.
Incorporated: 31 January 2017
Net Worth Deficit: £6,839 *Total Assets:* £15,207
Registered Office: Wework, Number 1 Spinningfields, Quay Street, Manchester, M3 3JE
Shareholders: Liam Manton; Mark Smallwood
Officers: Liam Manton [1987] Director; Mark Smallwood [1978] Director

Alkemista Limited
Incorporated: 21 November 2018
Registered Office: Willow Lodge, Feathers Hill, Hatfield Broad Oak, Bishop's Stortford, Herts, CM22 7HB
Major Shareholder: Anthony Joseph Wilson
Officers: Danielle Elizabeth Wilson, Secretary; Anthony Joseph Wilson [1980] Technical Director

Alko Vintages UK Ltd
Incorporated: 19 April 2018
Registered Office: 71-75 Shelton Street, Covent Garden, London, WC2H 9JQ
Shareholders: Archard Lwihula Kati; Elkanah Ondieki Oenga
Officers: Archard Lwihula Kato [1960] Director [New Zealander]; Elkanah Ondieki Oenga [1984] Director [Kenyan]

Alnwick Rum Company Limited
Incorporated: 18 February 2003 *Employees:* 3
Net Worth Deficit: £102,321 *Total Assets:* £120,093
Registered Office: 6 Market Place, Alnwick, Northumberland, NE66 1HS
Parent: Spirit of Northumberland Limited
Officers: Ian Booth Robinson [1947] Director/Manager; Keith Caville Stephenson [1954] Director/Retired; Christopher Darryl Walwyn-James [1952] Director/Manager

Am Byth Distillery Ltd
Incorporated: 27 February 2019
Registered Office: 5 High Street, New Radnor, Presteigne, Powys, LD8 2SL
Major Shareholder: James Alexander Baxter
Officers: James Alexander Baxter [1962] Director

AM Distilling Ltd
Incorporated: 8 January 2018
Registered Office: 20-22 Wenlock Road, London, N1 7GU
Major Shareholder: Ashley McCallum
Officers: Stacey Amanda Lindley, Secretary; Stacey Amanda Lindley [1988] Director/H&S Coordinator; Ashley McCallum [1985] Director/Royal Naval Engineer

Amber Glen Scotch Whisky Co., Ltd
Incorporated: 21 February 2013
Net Worth Deficit: £90,361 *Total Assets:* £24,671
Registered Office: Summit House, 4-5 Mitchell Street, Edinburgh, EH6 7BD
Major Shareholder: Samuel Minionis
Officers: Samuel Minionis, Secretary; Nathan Nicholas Lowry [1972] Director; Donald Maclaren of Maclaren [1954] Director/Consultant; Samuel Minionis [1954] Director/Entrepreneur; Bhai Raja Thapa [1974] Director/Accountant

Amber Valley Gin Ltd
Incorporated: 20 March 2018
Registered Office: The Knoll, Vicarage Lane, Duffield, Derbys, DE56 4EB
Major Shareholder: Simon Hayward
Officers: Simon Hayward, Secretary; Simon Hayward [1978] Director

American Beverage Marketers Limited
Incorporated: 7 May 2004
Net Worth Deficit: £24,955 *Total Assets:* £1,517
Registered Office: Regina House, 124 Finchley Road, London, NW3 5JS
Parent: Clark Foods, Inc.
Officers: Thomas Bradshaw Clark, Secretary/Director [American]; Thomas Bradshaw Clark [1946] Director [American]; William Andrew Hinkebein [1964] Director [American]; George Jacob Wagner [1968] Director [American]

Amethystcave Ltd
Incorporated: 18 July 2018
Registered Office: 214a Kettering Road, Northampton, NN1 4BN
Shareholders: Rosalyn Salaya; Mark Skevy
Officers: Rosalyn Salaya [1992] Director [Filipino]

Angels Share (MCR) Limited
Incorporated: 8 November 2017
Registered Office: 8 Peterborough Road, Harrow, Middlesex, HA1 2BQ
Major Shareholder: Stephanie Amanda Buttery
Officers: Stephanie Amanda Buttery [1991] Director

The Anglesey Distillery Ltd
Incorporated: 30 April 2018
Registered Office: 6 Plas Britannia, Church Road, Llanfairpwllgwyngyll, Anglesey, LL61 6AD
Major Shareholder: Robert Clayton Laming
Officers: Robert Clayton Laming [1981] Director

Angola Beverages Holding Company Limited
Incorporated: 12 April 2017
Registered Office: Avalon House, 72 Lower Mortlake Road, Richmond, Surrey, TW9 2JY
Parent: Distell International Holdings Limited
Officers: Karen Spy, Secretary; Werner Nolte [1976] Director/Head of Finance [South African]

Animal Spirits Ltd
Incorporated: 19 October 2018
Registered Office: Kemp House, 160 City Road, London, EC1V 2NX
Major Shareholder: Lukas Radosa
Officers: Dr Lukas Radosa, Secretary; Dr Lukas Radosa [1986] Director/Scientist [Slovak]

Annandale Distillery Company Limited
Incorporated: 12 February 2007 *Employees:* 22
Net Worth Deficit: £2,992,641 *Total Assets:* £10,949,549
Registered Office: Annandale Distillery, Northfield, Annan, Dumfries-shire, DG12 5LL
Major Shareholder: Professor David Marshall Thomson
Officers: Christopher Rogers, Secretary; Teresa Carol Church [1959] Director; Christopher Rogers [1966] Group Operations Director; Seshagiri Sondur [1982] Finance Director; Prof David Marshall Hall Thomson [1954] Director/Company Chairman

Anno Distillers Limited
Incorporated: 4 August 2011 *Employees:* 6
Net Worth Deficit: £72,594 *Total Assets:* £244,081
Registered Office: Unit 4 Crest Industrial Estate, Pattenden Lane, Marden, Kent, TN12 9QJ
Officers: Dr Norman John Lewis [1954] Director; Michael Garrick Pearce [1962] Director [Irish]; Daniel Brett Radice [1967] Director; Dr Andrew John Reason [1955] Director

Anstie Distillers International Limited
Incorporated: 9 December 2015
Net Worth: £915 *Total Assets:* £915
Registered Office: Kemp House, 160 City Road, London, EC1V 2NX
Major Shareholder: Richard John Leonard
Officers: Richard Leonard [1941] Director

Antibio UK Ltd
Incorporated: 10 October 2018
Registered Office: Laurel Cottage, London Road, Uckfield, E Sussex, TN22 2EA
Major Shareholder: Roger John Hayward
Officers: Benjamin Hayward [1994] Director/Sales Manager; Roger John Hayward [1947] Director

Anura Drinks Ltd
Incorporated: 30 January 2019
Registered Office: 6 Swallowfield, Wyboston, Bedford, MK44 3AE
Officers: Bernadette Kylie Hall [1976] Director; Graham Howard Hall [1972] Director; Ivor West Myburgh [1968] Director [Zimbabwean]; Renee Monique Myburgh [1970] Director [Zimbabwean]

Arbikie Distilling Limited
Incorporated: 19 November 2013 *Employees:* 5
Net Worth: £88,670 *Total Assets:* £678,686
Registered Office: Arbikie, Arbroath, Angus, DD11 4UZ
Shareholder: John Alexander Stirling
Officers: David William Stirling [1970] Director/Consultant; Iain Anderson Stirling [1966] Director/Consultant; John Alexander Stirling [1964] Director/Consultant

Arbikie X Limited
Incorporated: 22 February 2018
Registered Office: Exchange Tower, 19 Canning Street, Edinburgh, EH3 8EH
Officers: Iain Anderson Stirling [1966] Director; John Alexander Stirling [1964] Director/Consultant

Archangel Distilleries Ltd
Incorporated: 2 March 2016
Net Worth Deficit: £3,226 *Total Assets:* £167,756
Registered Office: Camburgh House, 27 New Dover Road, Canterbury, Kent, CT1 3DN
Shareholders: Peter David de Grey Allingham; Jude Christopher de Souza
Officers: Peter David de Grey Allingham, Secretary; Peter David de Grey Allingham [1963] Director; Jude Christopher de Souza [1961] Director

Ardbeg Distillery Limited
Incorporated: 6 June 1918
Registered Office: The Cube, 45 Leith Street, Edinburgh, EH1 3AT
Parent: The Glenmorangie Company Limited
Officers: Jean-Marc Rene Boulan [1972] Director [French]; Dr Peter Jonathon Nelson [1959] Director

Ardbeg Limited
Incorporated: 14 October 1993
Registered Office: The Cube, 45 Leith Street, Edinburgh, EH1 3AT
Parent: MacDonald & Muir Limited
Officers: Jean-Marc Rene Boulan [1972] Director [French]; Dr Peter Jonathon Nelson [1959] Director

Ardnahoe Distillery Company Limited
Incorporated: 4 June 2015 *Employees:* 2
Net Worth Deficit: £563,633 *Total Assets:* £7,384,944
Registered Office: 16 Park Circus, Glasgow, G3 6AX
Parent: Hunter Laing Holdings Limited
Officers: Andrew William Douglas Laing [1982] Director; Scott Hepburn Laing [1979] Director

Arisaig Distillers Ltd
Incorporated: 20 December 2016
Registered Office: Arisaig Gartocharn, Alexandria, W Dunbartonshire, G83 8ND
Major Shareholder: Sharon Newall
Officers: Sharon Newall, Secretary; Sharon Newall [1961] Director

Armadillo Spirits Limited
Incorporated: 17 August 2012
Net Worth Deficit: £13,489 *Total Assets:* £23,887
Registered Office: The White House, Clifton Marine Parade, Gravesend, Kent, DA11 0DY
Shareholders: Douglas Brougham Cunningham; Jonathan David Welch; Nicholas Shaun Woodward
Officers: Douglas Brougham Cunningham [1968] Director; Jonathan David Welch [1968] Director; Nicholas Shaun Woodward [1970] Director

The Armagnac Company Limited
Incorporated: 7 February 2000
Net Worth: £2 *Total Assets:* £2
Registered Office: 27 Dunkeld Court, Balfron, Glasgow, G63 0TL
Major Shareholder: William Charles Henry Phillips
Officers: William Charles Henry Phillips, Secretary; William Charles Henry Phillips [1939] Director

Artificer Spirit Limited
Incorporated: 8 June 2017
Registered Office: Moon End, Higher Street, Norton Sub Hamdon, Stoke-Sub-Hamdon, Somerset, TA14 6SN
Officers: David Richard John Batstone [1978] Director/Farmer; Gordon White McBain [1972] Director/Engineer

Artisan Blending Limited
Incorporated: 23 July 2014 *Employees:* 2
Net Worth: £1,215 *Total Assets:* £4,284
Registered Office: Milton House, 75 Harrington Road, Loddington, Kettering, Northants, NN14 1JZ
Shareholders: Quentin John Neville; Sara Jane Neville
Officers: Sara Jane Neville, Secretary; Quentin John Neville [1963] Director/Consultant

Artisan Brands Limited
Incorporated: 12 April 2013
Net Worth: £10,519 *Total Assets:* £21,472
Registered Office: Unit 10 Silver End Business Park, Brettell Lane, Brierley Hill, W Midlands, DY5 3LG
Major Shareholder: Dominic Michael John Carter
Officers: Dominic Michael John Carter [1966] Director

Artisan Distillery (Staffordshire) Limited
Incorporated: 4 September 2018
Registered Office: 4 Station Court, Girton Road, Cannock, Staffs, WS11 0EJ
Shareholders: John Robinson; Amanda Louise Robinson
Officers: Amanda Louise Robinson [1971] Director; John Robinson [1954] Director

The Artisanal Spirits Company Limited
Incorporated: 3 November 2014 *Employees:* 72
Net Worth: £12,413,000 *Total Assets:* £20,343,000
Registered Office: The Vaults, 87 Giles Street, Edinburgh, EH6 6BZ
Officers: William Alexander Bremner, Secretary; Mark Francis Bedingham [1955] Director; Kai Ivalo [1965] Director; David John Ridley [1969] Director [Australian]; Mehdi Shalfrooshan [1950] Director; Paul Henry Skipworth [1968] Director; Benjamin John Paget Thomson [1963] Director

Arundo Limited
Incorporated: 24 April 2018
Registered Office: 70 Castellain Mansions, Castellain Road, London, W9 1HA
Major Shareholder: Archie Patrick Finton Reed
Officers: Archie Patrick Finton Reed [1994] Director

Askival Rum Ltd
Incorporated: 18 February 2019
Registered Office: 2/2, 89 Dinart Street, Glasgow, G33 2DW
Officers: Iona MacLeod [1994] Director/Brewer; Skye MacLeod [1994] Director/Bar Staff; Sorcha Scott [1993] Director/Bar Staff

Asterley Bros, London Ltd
Incorporated: 5 November 2014 *Employees:* 1
Net Worth Deficit: £34,982 *Total Assets:* £20,780
Registered Office: 62-72 Keynote Studios, Dalmain Road, London, SE23 1AT
Major Shareholder: Robert Berry
Officers: Robert Berry [1977] Director/Sales Manager

Ataxirola Ltd
Incorporated: 7 November 2018
Registered Office: Suite 16, Haldon House, Brettell Lane, Brierley Hill, W Midlands, DY5 3LQ
Major Shareholder: Claire Lomas
Officers: Toni Rose Reyes [1992] Director [Filipino]

Atlantic Distillery Ltd
Incorporated: 22 May 2017
Registered Office: Bryndon House, 5-7 Berry Road, Newquay, Cornwall, TR7 1AD
Major Shareholder: Stuart Drysdale Thomson
Officers: David Ernest Carbis [1951] Director/Retired; Stuart Drysdale Thomson [1968] Director/Brewery Owner

Atlantis Gin Ltd
Incorporated: 26 February 2018
Registered Office: Manor Farm, Church End, Leckhampstead, Buckingham, MK18 5NU
Major Shareholder: James Blackham
Officers: James Blackham [1992] Director

Atom Brands Limited
Incorporated: 13 March 2018
Registered Office: Unit 1 Ton Business Park, 2-8 Morley Road, Tonbridge, Kent, TN9 1RA
Parent: Atom Supplies Limited
Officers: Joel John Kelly [1980] Director/Solicitor

Atom Cask Holdings Limited
Incorporated: 13 March 2018
Registered Office: Unit 1 Ton Business Park, 2-8 Morley Road, Tonbridge, Kent, TN9 1RA
Parent: Atom Supplies Limited
Officers: Joel John Kelly [1980] Director/Solicitor

Atom Distillery Ltd
Incorporated: 29 January 2018
Registered Office: 82 Wordsworth Road, Swinton, Manchester, M27 9SE
Officers: Matthew James Coakley [1987] Director/Property Consultant

Atom Drinks Limited
Incorporated: 13 March 2018
Registered Office: Unit 1 Ton Business Park, 2-8 Morley Road, Tonbridge, Kent, TN9 1RA
Parent: Atom Supplies Limited
Officers: Joel John Kelly [1980] Director/Solicitor

Atom Group Limited
Incorporated: 13 March 2018
Registered Office: Unit 1 Ton Business Park, 2-8 Morley Road, Tonbridge, Kent, TN9 1RA
Parent: Atom Supplies Limited
Officers: Joel John Kelly [1980] Director/Solicitor

Atom Scotland Limited
Incorporated: 14 March 2018
Registered Office: Unit 9 A1 Industrial Estate, Sir Harry Lauder Road, Edinburgh, EH15 2QA
Parent: Atom Supplies Limited
Officers: Joel John Kelly [1980] Director/Solicitor

Atom Supplies Limited
Incorporated: 1 May 1996 *Employees:* 221
Net Worth: £4,185,871 *Total Assets:* £18,093,900
Registered Office: Unit 1 Ton Business Park, 2-8 Morley Road, Tonbridge, Kent, TN9 1RA
Parent: Pioneer Brewing Company Limited
Officers: Terri Francis, Secretary; Benedict James Olaf Ellefsen [1981] Director; Terri Nicole Francis [1986] Director/Lawyer [Australian]; Joel John Kelly [1980] Director/Solicitor; Andrew Kenneith Logan [1985] Ecommerce Director; Thomas Stanley McGuinness [1980] Director; Justin Toby Petszaft [1981] Managing Director

Aurora Brewing Limited
Incorporated: 14 December 2011
Net Worth Deficit: £1,530,823 *Total Assets:* £4,269,322
Registered Office: 15 King Edward Avenue, Rainham, Essex, RM13 9RH
Parent: Aurora International Holdings Limited
Officers: David Kenneth Hill [1966] Director

Avalon Distillery Company Ltd
Incorporated: 13 January 2015 *Employees:* 2
Net Worth Deficit: £52,339 *Total Assets:* £2,545
Registered Office: 8 Gainsborough Drive, Sherborne, Dorset, DT9 6DR
Major Shareholder: Carl Hankey
Officers: Carl Hankey [1982] Director

Avinshaw Industries Limited
Incorporated: 25 May 2016
Net Worth: £100 *Total Assets:* £100
Registered Office: 27 Old Gloucester Street, London, WC1N 3AX
Officers: Leonora Scott [1955] Director; Michael James Scott [1967] Director

Avonside Whisky Limited
Incorporated: 8 May 1964
Registered Office: George House, Boroughbriggs Road, Elgin, Moray, IV30 1JY
Parent: Speymalt Whisky Distributors Ltd
Officers: Norman Ross, Secretary; Ewen Cameron Mackintosh [1968] Whisky Supply Director; Stephen Alexander Masson Rankin [1971] UK Sales Director; Neil Edward Urquhart [1975] Logistics & Facilities Director

Ayrshire Craft Distillers Ltd
Incorporated: 13 April 2017
Registered Office: 29 Portland Road, Kilmarnock, E Ayrshire, KA1 2BY
Officers: Scott McMurray Watson [1972] Director; Brian David Woods [1974] Director

Azenja Limited
Incorporated: 6 September 2017
Registered Office: 168 Church Road, Hove, E Sussex, BN3 2DL
Shareholders: James Allen Spears; Jeffrey Scott Morrison
Officers: Jeffrey Scott Morrison [1962] Director [American]; James Allen Spears [1974] Director [American]

Aztec Spirits Ltd
Incorporated: 23 July 2018
Registered Office: 17 Glyndwr Street, Port Talbot, SA13 1YH
Shareholders: Ritchie Lee Care; Owen Jones
Officers: Ritchie Lee Care [1983] Director/Laboratory Technician; Owen Jones [1991] Director/Analyst

Azure Distilleries Limited
Incorporated: 26 September 2016
Registered Office: Union House, Walton Lodge, Bridge Street, Walton on Thames, Surrey, KT12 1BT
Shareholder: Panayiotis Panayiotou
Officers: Nicholas Stephen Kelly [1961] Director; Iain Christian Thompson [1972] Director

Back Bar Spirits Limited
Incorporated: 22 January 2019
Registered Office: Suite 510, Hyde Park Hayes 3, 11 Millington Road, Hayes, Middlesex, UB3 4AZ
Major Shareholder: Dhruv Luthra
Officers: Dhruv Luthra [1977] Director

Badachro Distillery Ltd
Incorporated: 19 January 2018
Registered Office: Aird Hill, Badachro, Gairloch, Highland, IV21 2AB
Shareholders: Vanessa Quinn; Gordon Rodger Quinn
Officers: Gordon Rodger Quinn [1963] Director/Distiller; Vanessa Quinn [1971] Director

Badvo Distillery Limited
Incorporated: 6 January 2017 *Employees:* 1
Net Worth Deficit: £7,229 *Total Assets:* £23,817
Registered Office: Knockbarry Farm, Moulin, Pitlochry, Perthshire, PH16 5JN
Officers: Helen Avril Stewart [1995] Director/Student

The Balblair Distillery Company Limited
Incorporated: 1 February 1996
Registered Office: Moffat Distillery, Airdrie, N Lanarks, ML6 8PL
Shareholders: Charoen Sirivadhanabhakdi; Khunying Wanna Sirivadhanabhakdi
Officers: Man Kong Lee [1968] Director/Accountant [Chinese]; Dr Martin John Leonard [1961] Managing Director; Prapakon Thongtheppairot [1971] Director [Thai]

The Balno Distillery Limited
Incorporated: 23 January 2017
Registered Office: Orrinside View, Balno, Muir of Ord, Highland, IV6 7XB
Officers: Christopher Robert Corsie Hyde [1973] Commercial Director; Fiona Hyde [1975] Operations Director; Claire Matheson [1982] Director/Child Health Records Assistant; Donald John Marshall Matheson [1983] Director/Senior Designer

Ban Poitin Ltd
Incorporated: 10 December 2012
Net Worth: £11,093 *Total Assets:* £11,730
Registered Office: 34 Statham Court, Tollington Way, London, N7 6FP
Shareholder: David Mulligan
Officers: David Mulligan [1983] Director/Sales Executive [Irish]

Banideep Ltd
Incorporated: 20 July 2018
Registered Office: Unit 3 Trinity Centre, Park Farm Industrial Estate, Wellingborough, Northants, NN8 6ZB
Major Shareholder: Adele Watton
Officers: Liza Blanco [1997] Director [Filipino]

Barcelona Spirit Brands UK Limited
Incorporated: 23 November 2015
Net Worth: £14,450 *Total Assets:* £170,381
Registered Office: Unit A11, A19 Business Park, Selby Road, Riccall, York, YO19 6QR
Officers: Raimundo Balaguer [1970] Director [Spanish]; Thomas Francis Williams [1977] Director/Sales Agent

The Barclay Distillery Limited
Incorporated: 11 January 2018
Registered Office: Acre House, 11-15 William Road, London, NW1 3ER
Major Shareholder: Alistair James Barclay
Officers: Alistair James Barclay [1989] Director

Willem Barentsz Limited
Incorporated: 11 July 2014
Net Worth Deficit: £412,829 *Total Assets:* £137,830
Registered Office: 51 Welbeck Street, London, W1G 9HL
Major Shareholder: Michael Joseph Francis Claessens
Officers: Michael Joseph Francis Claessens [1993] Director [Dutch]

Barford Imports Limited
Incorporated: 11 November 1985 *Employees:* 3
Net Worth: £100,010 *Total Assets:* £183,614
Registered Office: Church Fold, Leathley Lane, Leathley, Otley, W Yorks, LS21 2JX
Shareholders: Jurgen Kaiser; Nicholas John Shagouri
Officers: Jurgen Kaiser, Secretary; Christian James Kaiser [1979] Director/Account Manager; Jurgen Kaiser [1939] Director/Wine Merchant [German]; Marcus Jurgen Kaiser [1975] Director/Surveyor

Barti Rum Ltd
Incorporated: 3 April 2018
Registered Office: 24 Merlins Cross, Pembroke, SA71 4AG
Major Shareholder: Jonathan Williams
Officers: Jonathan Williams [1979] Director/Entrepreneur

Bashiba Gin Ltd
Incorporated: 21 December 2017
Registered Office: 82 Wandsworth Bridge Road, London, SW6 2TF
Major Shareholder: Mark Philip Parsley
Officers: Mark Philip Parsley [1967] Director/Banking

Basil's Botanicals Limited
Incorporated: 8 June 2018
Registered Office: 123 Cross Lane East, Gravesend, Kent, DA12 5HA
Major Shareholder: Nicholas William Stephens
Officers: Nicholas William Stephens [1962] Director

Batch Brew Ltd
Incorporated: 7 November 2011 *Employees:* 6
Net Worth: £110,013 *Total Assets:* £276,600
Registered Office: Batch Brew, Coal Clough Lane, Unit 10 Habgerham Mill, Burnley, Lancs, BB11 5BS
Shareholders: Philip Whitwell; Philip Whitwell
Officers: Paul Anthony Hancock, Secretary; Philip Whitwell [1971] Director of Product Strategy

Batch88 Ltd
Incorporated: 14 December 2017
Registered Office: 91 Philbeach Gardens, London, SW5 9EU
Major Shareholder: Jordan Karl Swinscoe
Officers: Samantha Jane Swinscoe, Secretary; Jordan Karl Swinscoe [1968] Managing Director

Bath Botanics Limited
Incorporated: 6 January 2014 *Employees:* 2
Net Worth: £7,498 *Total Assets:* £53,687
Registered Office: Fair View, Steway Lane, Batheaston, Avon, BA1 8EH
Shareholder: Susan Rosemary Mullett
Officers: Susan Rosemary Mullett [1957] Director/Micro Distillery

Be Rude Not To Ltd
Incorporated: 11 June 2018
Registered Office: 4 Downe Close, East Cowick, Goole, E Yorks, DN14 9EY
Major Shareholder: David McIvor
Officers: David McIvor [1962] Director/Entrepreneur

Beach Craft Spirits Limited
Incorporated: 11 May 2016 *Employees:* 2
Net Worth Deficit: £17,620 *Total Assets:* £656
Registered Office: Gowen Bank, 9 Coal Row, Hopeman, Elgin, Moray, IV30 5TJ
Shareholders: David William John Beach; Lara Helene Beach
Officers: David William John Beach [1977] Director/Distiller; Lara Helene Beach [1981] Director/Distillery Administration

Beachcomber Gin Ltd
Incorporated: 26 May 2017
Net Worth: £1 *Total Assets:* £1
Registered Office: South Barn, Efford Park, Milford Road, Lymington, Hants, SO41 0JD
Major Shareholder: Karen Marie Bass
Officers: Stuart Russell Paton, Secretary; Karen Marie Bass [1968] Director/Gin Distiller

Beam Suntory UK Limited
Incorporated: 13 October 2005 *Employees:* 186
Previous: Beam Inc UK Limited
Net Worth: £474,952,000 *Total Assets:* £573,376,000
Registered Office: 2 Longwalk Road, Stockley Park, Uxbridge, Middlesex, UB11 1BA
Parent: Beam Suntory UK Holdings Limited
Officers: Nadim Assi [1967] Director/CFO International [Canadian]; Madame Del Pino Bermudez de La Puente Sanchez-Aguilera [1974] Director/Associate General Counsel [Spanish]; Pryce William David Greenow [1970] Director/President International; Jose Padilla Munoz [1959] Senior Director International Supply Chain Finance [Spanish]; David William James Wilson [1964] Director/MD Global Travel Retail

Bearded Lion Drinks Company Ltd
Incorporated: 23 March 2018
Registered Office: 170 Hereford Drive, Bootle, Merseyside, L30 1QZ
Major Shareholder: Johnathan Charles Stewart
Officers: Johnathan Charles Stewart [1987] Director/Manager

Beaucroft Beverages Ltd
Incorporated: 27 June 2018
Registered Office: 14 Beaucroft Road, Wimborne, Dorset, BH21 2QW
Shareholders: Adan Anthony Trimmer; Michelle Trimmer
Officers: Adan Anthony Trimmer [1973] Director

Beaufort Spirit Ltd
Incorporated: 3 April 2017
Registered Office: 13 The Courtyard, Timothys Bridge Road, Stratford upon Avon, Warwicks, CV37 9NP
Major Shareholder: Leo Crabtree
Officers: Leo Crabtree [1982] Director

Beaumonde Desserts Limited
Incorporated: 30 April 2018
Registered Office: 8 Cravenwood, Ashton under Lyne, Lancs, OL6 8AX
Major Shareholder: Kenna Ngoma
Officers: Aaron Longden [1994] Director/Analyst; Kenna Ngoma [1994] Director/Analyst

The Beautiful Distillery Limited
Incorporated: 30 January 2014
Net Worth: £261,424 *Total Assets:* £362,625
Registered Office: Wickham House, 464 Lincoln Road, Enfield, Middlesex, EN3 4AH
Major Shareholder: Anthony William David Osmond-Evans
Officers: Donald McGregor, Secretary; Anthony William David Osmond-Evans [1943] Director/Publisher

Beeble Liquor Limited
Incorporated: 23 October 2018
Registered Office: Eastcourt House, Eastcourt, Malmesbury, Wilts, SN16 9HP
Shareholders: Matthew Campbell Brauer; Nicola Jane Reed
Officers: Matthew Campbell Brauer [1991] Director/Accountant; Nicola Jane Reed [1965] Director/Artist

Beerdsman Limited
Incorporated: 5 April 2016
Net Worth Deficit: £19 *Total Assets:* £1,018
Registered Office: Charter House, 8-10 Station Road, London, E12 5BT
Officers: Avtar Singh Sandhu [1965] Director; Balwinder Kaur Sandhu [1976] Director; Ragbhir Singh Sandhu [1972] Director; Sukhwinder Kaur Sandhu [1965] Director

The Beers Spirit Company Ltd
Incorporated: 8 June 2017
Net Worth Deficit: £13,187 *Total Assets:* £9,423
Registered Office: 30 Biddulph Road, Mow Cop, Stoke on Trent, Staffs, ST7 3PU
Shareholders: Robert Anthony Beer; Rhian Elen Beer
Officers: Rhian Elen Beer [1979] Director/Housewife; Robert Anthony Beer [1983] Director/Contractor

Beets Incorporated Ltd
Incorporated: 4 October 2017
Registered Office: 22 St Nicholas Street, Bodmin, Cornwall, PL31 1AD
Major Shareholder: Jolyon Alexander Donald Ferrier
Officers: Jolyon Alexander Donald Ferrier [1988] Director

Beinn An Tuirc Distillers Limited
Incorporated: 11 February 2016
Net Worth: £6,391 *Total Assets:* £152,922
Registered Office: Ainsley Smith & Co Ltd, 21 Argyll Square, Oban, Argyll & Bute, PA34 4AT
Major Shareholder: Niall Donald Andrew MacAlister Hall
Officers: Emma MacAlister Hall [1974] Director/Marketing Manager; Kenneth Arthur MacAlister Hall [1978] Director/Designer; Niall Donald Andrew MacAlister Hall [1972] Director/Surveyor

The Belfast Artisan Distillery Ltd
Incorporated: 24 May 2018
Registered Office: 85 University Street, Belfast, BT7 1HP
Major Shareholder: Alex Fleck
Officers: Alex Fleck [1981] Director

Belfast Distillers Ltd
Incorporated: 24 March 2016
Net Worth: £1 *Total Assets:* £2
Registered Office: c/o Elliott Duffy Garrett, 40 Linenhall Street, Belfast, BT2 8BA
Parent: Belfast Distillery Holdings Limited
Officers: Mark Benton Fuller [1953] Director/Consultant [American]

The Belfast Gin and Spirits School Limited
Incorporated: 9 January 2017
Previous: The Belfast Gin School Limited
Registered Office: 7 The Strand, Portaferry, Newtownards, Co Down, BT22 1PE
Shareholder: Samuel John Ian Killen
Officers: Gillian Killen, Secretary; Anthony Farrell [1980] Director/Businessman [Irish]; Gillian Killen [1961] Director/Businesswoman; Samuel John Ian Killen [1949] Director/Sales & Marketing Consultant

Belfast Titanic Whiskey Distillery Ltd
Incorporated: 9 February 2018
Registered Office: 8 Station Road, Holywood, Co Down, BT18 0BP
Major Shareholder: Peter Martin Lavery
Officers: Peter Martin Lavery [1961] Director [Irish]

The Belfast Whiskey School Limited
Incorporated: 10 January 2017
Registered Office: 7 The Strand, Portaferry, Newtownards, Co Down, BT22 1PE
Shareholder: Samuel John Ian Killen
Officers: Gillian Killen, Secretary; Samuel John Ian Killen [1949] Director/Sales & Marketing Consultant

The Belvoir Gin Distillery Limited
Incorporated: 22 February 2017
Registered Office: 7 St John Street, Mansfield, Notts, NG18 1QH
Shareholders: Ian David Leivers; Laura Elizabeth Leivers
Officers: Ian David Leivers [1963] Director; Laura Elizabeth Leivers [1987] Director

Ben Nevis Distillery (Fort William) Limited
Incorporated: 5 February 1944 *Employees:* 26
Net Worth: £5,506,785 *Total Assets:* £9,320,196
Registered Office: Ben Nevis Distillery, Lochy Bridge, Fort William, Highland, PH33 6TJ
Parent: Demball Limited
Officers: Tetsuji Hisamitsu [1958] Director [Japanese]; Yoshisuke Motojima [1964] Director [Japanese]; Alexander Walter Ross [1948] Managing Director

Benjamin & Blum Limited
Incorporated: 27 February 2012
Net Worth: £34,701 *Total Assets:* £51,247
Registered Office: 17 Hanover Square, London, W1S 1BN
Shareholders: Paul Andrew Benjamin; Marta Magdalena Lejkowski
Officers: Paul Andrew Benjamin [1974] Director; Marta Magdalena Lejkowski [1975] Director [Polish]

The Benriach Distillery Company Limited
Incorporated: 30 October 2003 *Employees:* 115
Net Worth: £132,076,160 *Total Assets:* £141,497,376
Registered Office: 50 Lothian Road, Festival Square, Edinburgh, EH3 9WJ
Parent: Brown-Forman Scotland Limited
Officers: Mary Elizabeth Barrazotto [1960] Director/Senior Vice President General Counsel [American]; Michael Carr Jr [1979] Director/Attorney [American]; Leanne Dean Cunningham [1970] Director/General Manager [American]; Edward Wayne Mayrose [1973] VP, Global Director External Manufacturing [American]; Fiona Colette Michelle West [1968] Director/Marketing

The Benromach Distillery Co Ltd
Incorporated: 22 November 2012
Net Worth: £1 *Total Assets:* £1
Registered Office: Benromach Distillery, Invererne Road, Forres, Moray, IV36 3EB
Parent: Speymalt Whisky Distributors Ltd
Officers: Norman Ross, Secretary; Ewen Cameron Mackintosh [1968] Director; Stephen Alexander Masson Rankin [1971] Director; Neil Edward Urquhart [1975] Director

The Berkshire Distillery Limited
Incorporated: 18 September 2013
Registered Office: 4 Prince Albert Road, London, NW1 7SN
Shareholders: Tobin Jones; Eric Satya Darshan Srikandan
Officers: Tobin Jones [1965] Director/Accountant; Eric Satya Darshan Srikandan [1973] Director

Bermondsey Distillery Limited
Incorporated: 23 August 2012
Net Worth Deficit: £23,890 *Total Assets:* £191,576
Registered Office: 75 Multey Plain, Plymouth, PL4 6JJ
Major Shareholder: Christian Erboe Jensen
Officers: Christian Erboe Jensen [1964] Director/Hedge Fund Manager [Danish]

Berwick Brewrey Company Ltd
Incorporated: 23 October 2018
Registered Office: 76 Shielfield Terrace, Tweedmouth, Berwick upon Tweed, Northumberland, TD15 2EE
Shareholder: Sarah Carmichael
Officers: Robert Kingsley [1969] Director; Sarah Louise Kingsley [1970] Director

Bethera Ltd
Incorporated: 18 July 2018
Registered Office: 214a Kettering Road, Northampton, NN1 4BN
Shareholders: Edilon Gobres; Aimee Heenan
Officers: Edilon Gobres [1980] Director [Filipino]

Beware Gin Brands Ltd.
Incorporated: 6 September 2016
Registered Office: 131 Upper Road, Greenisland, Carrickfergus, Co Antrim, BT38 8RR
Officers: Simon Peter Smith, Secretary; Alanna Naoimh Smith [1992] Director/Entrepreneur; Matthew Stephen Smith [1994] Director/Entrepreneur; Owen Oliver Smith [1992] Director/Entrepreneur; Dr Stephen Patrick Smith [1966] Director/Entrepreneur

The Big Hill Distillery Limited
Incorporated: 30 November 2015
Net Worth Deficit: £11 *Total Assets:* £2
Registered Office: Meadowside, Hall Lane, Mobberley, Knutsford, Cheshire, WA16 7AE
Officers: David James Clayton [1973] Director; Benjamin Andrew Kaberry [1976] Director

Bimber Distillery Ltd
Incorporated: 3 February 2011
Previous: CH Design London Ltd
Net Worth: £120,053 *Total Assets:* £468,935
Registered Office: 56-58 Sunbeam Road, London, NW10 6JQ
Shareholders: Dariusz Plazewski; Ewelina Chruszczyk
Officers: Ewelina Chruszczyk [1984] Director/Manager [Polish]; Dariusz Plazewski [1977] Director/MD [Polish]

Bishopsgate Distillery & Wine Company Limited
Incorporated: 19 July 2005
Net Worth: £1 *Total Assets:* £2,166
Registered Office: 5 Clarks Cottages, Kiln Road, Prestwood, Great Missenden, Bucks, HP16 9DG
Major Shareholder: Andrew Graham Harvey
Officers: Andrew Graham Harvey, Secretary/Director; Andrew Graham Harvey [1971] Director

Bitter Lemons Gin Ltd
Incorporated: 14 June 2018
Registered Office: BSEEN, Aston University Innovation, Birmingham Campus, Faraday Wharf, Holt Street, Birmingham, B7 4BB
Major Shareholder: Luke Anthony Warren
Officers: Luke Anthony Warren [1996] Director/Student

Bitter Salvation Ltd
Incorporated: 16 August 2017
Registered Office: 190 New Kings Road, London, SW6 4NF
Shareholders: Alexandra Lynette Dover; Alexander Thomas Dover
Officers: Alexander Thomas Dover [1975] Director; Alexandra Lynette Dover [1988] Director

Bitter Union Limited
Incorporated: 14 July 2017
Registered Office: 1 Avenue Cottages, Bentley, Farnham, Surrey, GU10 5JA
Officers: Dr Lucy Catriona Moore [1984] Director/Founder; Thomas Samuel Moore [1985] Director/Founder

Black Arid Kegs Ltd
Incorporated: 12 September 2017
Net Worth Deficit: £2,551 *Total Assets:* £354
Registered Office: Quaker Buildings, High Street, Lurgan, Craigavon, Co Armagh, BT66 8BB
Major Shareholder: Iain George Dakers-Black
Officers: Iain George Dakers-Black [1972] Director

Black Cat Brewery Limited
Incorporated: 11 July 2012
Net Worth Deficit: £55,830 *Total Assets:* £23,795
Registered Office: Twitten Cottage, Southview Road, Crowborough, E Sussex, TN6 1HF
Shareholders: Kathryn Margaret Mary Wratten; Paul Wratten
Officers: Kathryn Margaret Mary Wratten [1962] Director/Brewery Owner; Paul Wratten [1964] Director/Brewery Owner

Black Cat Distillery Limited
Incorporated: 29 May 2015 *Employees:* 3
Net Worth Deficit: £137,270 *Total Assets:* £130,135
Registered Office: Artisans' House, 7 Queensbridge, Northampton, NN4 7BF
Major Shareholder: Serhat Sula
Officers: Serhat Sula [1971] Director

Black Cat Drinks Ltd
Incorporated: 3 October 2017
Registered Office: 21 Nether Lane, Flore, Northampton, NN7 4LR
Shareholders: Mark Vincent Curley; Vincent John Curley
Officers: Carol Jane Curley [1957] Director/Company Manager; Mark Vincent Curley [1982] Director/Compliance Consultant; Vincent John Curley [1956] Director/Indirect Tax Consultant

The Black Cow Vodka Company Limited
Incorporated: 20 July 2011
Registered Office: Black Cow, Unit 1 Childhay Manor, Beaminster, Dorset, DT8 3LQ
Shareholder: Paul Archard
Officers: Paul Archard [1964] Director/Sculptor; Jason Richard Barber [1967] Director/Farmer

Black Label Spirits Ltd
Incorporated: 24 August 2018
Registered Office: Kemp House, 160 City Road, London, EC1V 2NX
Major Shareholder: Michael Baptiste
Officers: Dean Edgar, Secretary; Michael Baptiste [1982] Director/Sales; Dean Philip Edgar [1985] Director/Recruitment Consultant; Moses Omarkongolo [1987] Director/Security

Black Powder Gin Company Ltd
Incorporated: 13 December 2016 *Employees:* 2
Net Worth Deficit: £31,510 *Total Assets:* £64,042
Registered Office: Preese Hall, Weeton, Preston, Lancs, PR4 3HT
Shareholders: John Loftus; Anthony George Dalnas
Officers: Anthony George Dalnas [1974] Director; Ronald John Loftus [1949] Director

Black Shuck Ltd
Incorporated: 13 March 2015 *Employees:* 1
Net Worth: £75,127 *Total Assets:* £211,625
Registered Office: Drayton Old Lodge, 146 Drayton High Road, Norwich, NR8 6AN
Shareholders: Patrick James Saunders; Sarah Elizabeth Saunders
Officers: Patrick James Saunders [1965] Director/Trails Officer; Sarah Elizabeth Saunders [1968] Director/Teacher

Hilary Blackford Associates Limited
Incorporated: 31 October 2012
Net Worth Deficit: £8,182 *Total Assets:* £11,335
Registered Office: Mill Cottage, The Street, Cerney Wick, Glos, GL7 5QJ
Shareholder: Paul Anthony Blackford
Officers: Hilary Ann Susan Blackford [1955] Director/Country Food and Drink; Paul Anthony Blackford [1948] Director/Country Food and Drink

Blackford Craft Distillery Ltd
Incorporated: 18 October 2016
Net Worth Deficit: £23,877 *Total Assets:* £118,942
Registered Office: Maryfield of Blackford, Rothienorman, Inverurie, Aberdeenshire, AB51 8YL
Shareholders: Neil Andrew Sime; Katie Elizabeth Sime
Officers: Kathryn Blanche Sime [1958] Director; Katie Elizabeth Sime [1979] Director; Keith Maurice Sime [1958] Director; Neil Andrew Sime [1978] Managing Director

Blackingstone Ltd
Incorporated: 18 September 2018
Registered Office: 3 Woolacombe Rise, Woolacombe, Devon, EX34 7AS
Shareholders: Kerry Carter; Thomas Matthew Foster
Officers: Kerry Carter [1979] Director/Physiotherapist; Thomas Matthew Foster [1991] Director/HM Forces

Bladnoch Distillery Limited
Incorporated: 9 December 2014
Net Worth Deficit: £7,318,033 *Total Assets:* £22,376,304
Registered Office: 20 Fenchurch Street, London, EC3M 3AG
Major Shareholder: David Neil Prior
Officers: David Neil Prior [1970] Director [Australian]

Blairmhor Distillers Limited
Incorporated: 4 September 1992
Registered Office: Moffat Distillery, Airdrie, N Lanarks, ML6 8PL
Shareholders: Chareon Sirivadhanabhakdi; Khunying Wanna Sirivadhanabhakdi
Officers: Sithichai Chaikriangkrai [1954] Director [Thai]; Dr Martin John Leonard [1961] Managing Director; Panote Sirivadhanabhakdi [1977] Director/Chairman [Thai]; Thapana Sirivadhanabhakdi [1975] Director/Chairman [Thai]; Ueychai Tantha-Obhas [1949] Director/Executive [Thai]; Prapakon Thongtheppairot [1971] Director [Thai]

Blairmhor Limited
Incorporated: 13 May 1986
Registered Office: Moffat Distillery, Airdrie, N Lanarks, ML6 8PL
Shareholders: Charoen Sirivadhanabhakdi; Khunying Wanna Sirivadhanabhakdi
Officers: Sithichai Chaikriangkrai [1954] Director [Thai]; Dr Martin John Leonard [1961] Managing Director; Panote Sirivadhanabhakdi [1977] Director/Company Executive [Thai]; Thapana Sirivadhanabhakdi [1975] Director/Company Executive [Thai]; Ueychai Tantha-Obhas [1949] Director/Executive [Thai]; Prapakon Thongtheppairot [1971] Director [Thai]

Blend Experts Limited
Incorporated: 19 June 2018
Registered Office: 40 Upper Brook Street, Winchester, Hants, SO23 8DG
Major Shareholder: Stephen Paul Bowler
Officers: Stephen Paul Bowler [1971] Director/Entrepreneur

Blendworks Ltd
Incorporated: 29 August 2017
Registered Office: Eden Mill Retail Outlet, Pilmour Links, St Andrews, Fife, KY16 9JQ
Major Shareholder: Anthony Kelly
Officers: Anthony Gerard Kelly, Secretary; Anthony Kelly [1963] Director [Irish]; Anthony Gerard Kelly [1991] Director; Paul Miller [1961] Director

Blessed Skye Limited
Incorporated: 23 January 2018
Registered Office: F C Manse, Lower Harrapool, Broadford, Isle of Skye, IV49 9AE
Major Shareholder: Michael Dawson
Officers: Michael Dawson [1981] Director

Blinders Pubs & Clubs Ltd
Incorporated: 12 December 2018
Registered Office: 10 Burnsbegg Street, Kinross, KY13 8DS
Parent: The Mackie Group Scotland Limited
Officers: William Mackie [1986] Director

Block, Grey and Block Limited
Incorporated: 12 February 1997
Net Worth: £27 *Total Assets:* £27
Registered Office: 3 Peel Park Place, East Kilbride, S Lanarks, G74 5LW
Parent: JG Distillers Ltd
Officers: Colin Shields Barclay [1958] Director/Merchant [Canadian]; Gerrard McSherry [1956] Director

Bloodline Spirits Ltd
Incorporated: 10 January 2018
Registered Office: 19 Standalane View, Peebles, EH45 8LS
Shareholders: Julie McLean; Colin McLean
Officers: Colin McLean [1982] Director; Julie McLean [1988] Director

The Bloomsbury Club UK Limited
Incorporated: 12 August 2015
Net Worth: £74,410 *Total Assets:* £219,460
Registered Office: c/o Gallaghers, Titchfield House, 69-85 Tabernacle Street, London, EC2A 4BD
Shareholders: Carl Louis Stephenson; Geoff Michael Curley
Officers: Carl Louis Stephenson [1970] Director

The Bloomsbury Distillery Ltd
Incorporated: 11 September 2015
Net Worth: £71,826 *Total Assets:* £123,031
Registered Office: 44 Emerald Street, London, WC1N 3QH
Major Shareholder: Alan McQuillan
Officers: Benjamin Peter Harriman [1986] Commercial Director; Alan McQuillan [1982] Director [Irish]; Paul Nigel Wickman [1955] Director

Blue Marble Distillery Ltd
Incorporated: 14 May 2018
Registered Office: 10 Granville Avenue, Northborough, Peterborough, Cambs, PE6 9DB
Major Shareholder: Robert Edward Barnes
Officers: Robert Barnes, Secretary; Robert Edward Barnes [1960] Director/Business Analyst

Blue Sky Drinking Ltd
Incorporated: 5 February 2018
Registered Office: c/o Columb & Gosling Accountants Ltd, Blount House, Hall Court, Hall Park Way, Telford, Salop, TF3 4NQ
Major Shareholder: Antony Nicholas Hobbs
Officers: Antony Nicholas Hobbs [1953] Director

Bluu Spirit Limited
Incorporated: 8 June 2016
Net Worth Deficit: £3,939 *Total Assets:* £4,778
Registered Office: Unit 2a Bannerley Road, Garretts Green, Birmingham, B33 0SL
Major Shareholder: David Jonathan Allbut
Officers: David Jonathan Allbut [1954] Director

The Boatyard Distillery Ltd
Incorporated: 18 June 2013 *Employees:* 4
Net Worth: £116,620 *Total Assets:* £343,542
Registered Office: 131 Nelson Road, Twickenham, Middlesex, TW2 7BB
Major Shareholder: Joe McGirr
Officers: Joseph Michael McGirr [1982] Director/Whisky Sales

Boho Drinks Brands Ltd
Incorporated: 23 June 2017
Registered Office: Central Chambers, 227 London Road, Hadleigh, Benfleet, Essex, SS7 2RF
Major Shareholder: Joanne Claire Birkitt
Officers: Joanne Claire Birkitt [1976] Director

Boho Drinks Ltd
Incorporated: 21 February 2017 *Employees:* 2
Net Worth Deficit: £9,053 *Total Assets:* £4,394
Registered Office: Central Chambers, 227 London Road, Hadleigh, Benfleet, Essex, SS7 2RF
Major Shareholder: Joanne Claire Birkitt
Officers: Joanne Claire Birkitt [1976] Director

The Bombay Spirits Company Limited
Incorporated: 8 June 1998 *Employees:* 15
Net Worth: £1,699,000 *Total Assets:* £1,699,000
Registered Office: Laverstoke Mill, London Road, Laverstoke, Whitchurch, Hants, RG28 7NR
Parent: Bacardi U.K. Limited
Officers: John Michael Burke [1965] Marketing Director; Iain MacGregor Lochhead [1962] Director; Matthew James Phillips [1983] Finance Director

Bombini Ltd
Incorporated: 5 October 2018
Registered Office: Apartment 3, 29 Goldington Road, Bedford, MK40 3LH
Major Shareholder: Ryan Michael Clifford
Officers: Ryan Michael Clifford [1994] Director

Bonding and Transport Company, Limited
Incorporated: 17 November 1917
Registered Office: The Cube, 45 Leith Street, Edinburgh, EH1 3AT
Parent: MacDonald & Muir Limited
Officers: Jean-Marc Rene Boulan [1972] Director [French]; Dr Peter Jonathon Nelson [1959] Director

Bonny Gin Ltd
Incorporated: 6 November 2018
Registered Office: 22 Moorhouse Avenue, Glasgow, G13 4RB
Major Shareholder: Patrick Gahagan
Officers: Patrick Gahagan [1994] Director/Supply Chain Manager

The Bootleg Club Limited
Incorporated: 18 October 2017
Registered Office: 34a Western Avenue, London, W3 7TZ
Officers: Samuel Livingstone Aird [1985] Director

Boozy Infusion Limited
Incorporated: 5 April 2011
Net Worth: £711 *Total Assets:* £1,364
Registered Office: 36-40 Doncaster Road, Barnsley, S Yorks, S70 1TL
Shareholders: Andrew Gardiner; Anita Michelle Gardiner
Officers: Andrew Gardiner [1962] Director/Restaurateur; Anita Michelle Gardiner [1967] Director/Restaurateur

Borders Distillers Limited
Incorporated: 23 April 2015
Registered Office: The Borders Distillery, Commercial Road, Hawick, Roxburghshire, TD9 7AQ
Parent: The Three Stills Company Limited
Officers: Timothy Ado Carton [1959] Director [Irish]; Laurence John Fordyce [1962] Director; Anthony Brian Roberts [1965] Director

The Borders Distillery Company Limited
Incorporated: 29 July 2015
Registered Office: The Borders Distillery, Commercial Road, Hawick, Roxburghshire, TD9 7AQ
Parent: The Three Stills Company Limited
Officers: Timothy Ado Carton [1959] Director/International Drinks Industry Executive [Irish]; Laurence John Fordyce [1962] Director; Anthony Brian Roberts [1965] Director

Borders Distilling Limited
Incorporated: 20 December 2017
Registered Office: The Borders Distillery, Commercial Road, Hawick, Roxburghshire, TD9 7AQ
Parent: The Three Stills Company Limited
Officers: Timothy Ado Carton [1959] Director [Irish]; Laurence John Fordyce [1962] Director; Anthony Brian Roberts [1965] Director

Botan Grey Ltd
Incorporated: 4 July 2018
Registered Office: 110 Wigmore Lane, Luton, Beds, LU2 8AD
Major Shareholder: Princess Serwah Adu-Gyamfi
Officers: Princess Serwah Adu-Gyamfi [1991] Director/Businesswoman

Botanical Alchemy Ltd
Incorporated: 17 March 2011
Registered Office: 47 Deodar Road, London, SW15 2NU
Major Shareholder: Susan Claire Lettice
Officers: Claire Lettice [1961] Director/Consultant

Botanical Jack's Limited
Incorporated: 19 July 2018
Registered Office: Taw Valley Brewery, Westacott Lane, North Tawton, Devon, EX20 2BS
Officers: Marc Whiteside, Secretary; Marc Andrew Whiteside [1975] Director/Brewer

The Botanist Limited
Incorporated: 31 January 2012
Registered Office: The Bruichladdich Distillery, Bruichladdich, Islay, Argyll, PA49 7UN
Officers: Simon Patrick Coughlin, Secretary; Madame Valerie Marie Anne Chapoulaud-Floquet [1962] Director/Chief Executive Officer [French]; Simon Patrick Coughlin [1961] Director; Douglas Adamson Taylor [1976] Director/Chief Executive Officer

Bothy Trading Limited
Incorporated: 2 May 2018
Registered Office: Garlowbank Smiddy, Kinnordy, Kirriemuir, Angus, DD8 4LH
Major Shareholder: Kim Margaret Cameron
Officers: Scott Campbell, Secretary; Kim Margaret Cameron [1976] Director/Producer of Beverages

Bottlers & Distillers (Wales) Limited
Incorporated: 12 April 2018
Registered Office: 2 The Paddock, Cowbridge, Vale of Glamorgan, CF71 7EJ
Officers: Rhys Andrew Mallows, Secretary; Andrew Bernard Mallows [1965] Managing Director; Rhys Andrew Mallows [1995] Managing Director

Bottomley Distillers Ltd
Incorporated: 3 June 2016 *Employees:* 2
Net Worth: £7,653 *Total Assets:* £36,976
Registered Office: Unit 6 Bolingbroke Court, Bolingbroke Road, Louth, Lincs, LN11 0ZW
Major Shareholder: Alan James Bottomley
Officers: Alan James Bottomley [1984] Director/Mechanical Engineer; Amy Jane Conyard [1988] Director/Customer Manager

Bournemouth Distillers Limited
Incorporated: 27 June 2018
Registered Office: 1a Uplands Gardens, Bournemouth, BH8 9SU
Shareholders: Lewis James Spendlove; Przemyslaw Piotr Seczkowski
Officers: Przemyslaw Piotr Seczkowski [1977] Director [Polish]; Lewis James Spendlove [1989] Director

The Boutique Cellar Limited
Incorporated: 7 June 2012
Net Worth Deficit: £30,394 *Total Assets:* £128,656
Registered Office: Low Barn, Gwehelog, Usk, Monmouthshire, NP15 1HY
Officers: Sarah Thompson [1976] Director

The UK Spirits Industry

The Boutique Distillery Ltd
Incorporated: 12 September 2018
Registered Office: 12 Sandhurst Road, Kingsholm, Gloucester, GL1 2SE
Major Shareholder: Jonathan Edward Harper
Officers: Jonathan Edward Harper [1970] Director/Rectifier and Compounder

Bowland Distillery Ltd
Incorporated: 19 October 2017
Registered Office: 53 George Street, Clitheroe, Lancs, BB7 1BU
Major Shareholder: Andrew Breckell
Officers: Andrew Breckell [1967] Director/Distiller; Donna Seed [1973] Director/Cook

Braefoot Distillery Ltd
Incorporated: 9 August 2018
Registered Office: Rockdale, 43 Green Street, Rothes, Aberlour, Moray, AB38 7BD
Shareholders: April Ashley Fair; Jennie Margaret Whitlock
Officers: April Ashley Fair [1989] Director/Housewife; Jennie Margaret Whitlock [1979] Director

Brain Brew UK Limited
Incorporated: 20 December 2018
Registered Office: Unit 1 Vansittart Estate, Duke Street, Windsor, Berks, SL4 1SE
Major Shareholder: Robert Morrison
Officers: Robert Morrison [1962] Director

Bramley and Gage Limited
Incorporated: 14 March 2007
Net Worth: £440,571 *Total Assets:* £1,145,977
Registered Office: C6 Ashville Park, Short Way, Thornbury, Glos, BS35 3UU
Shareholders: Michael Colin Kain; Felicity Eleanor Hall
Officers: Felicity Eleanor Hall, Secretary/IT Consultant; Felicity Eleanor Hall [1968] Director/IT Consultant; Timothy Giles Hall [1966] Director/Consultant; Edward Bramley Kain [1942] Director/Liqueur Maker; Michael Colin Kain [1971] Director/Liqueur Maker

Branscombe Vale Brewery Limited
Incorporated: 25 November 2002
Net Worth: £438,958 *Total Assets:* £507,271
Registered Office: Branscombe Vale Brewery, Great Seaside Farm, Branscombe, Seaton, Devon, EX12 3DP
Major Shareholder: Paul Christopher Dimond
Officers: Paul Christopher Dimond, Secretary/Chairman; Paul Christopher Dimond [1965] Director/Chairman

Break Line Brewing & Distilling Ltd
Incorporated: 31 January 2019
Registered Office: Capital Accounts, 17 Whessoe Road, Darlington, Co Durham, DL3 0QP
Major Shareholder: Matthew David Brown
Officers: Matthew David Brown [1981] Director/Manager

Brennen & Brown Limited
Incorporated: 9 February 2010
Net Worth Deficit: £91,258 *Total Assets:* £62,979
Registered Office: Unit 2C, The Bramery, Alstone Lane, Cheltenham, Glos, GL51 8HE
Shareholders: Richard Bamber; Richard Bamber
Officers: Rich Bamber, Secretary; Rich Bamber [1971] Director/Consultant; Joanna Hazlett [1975] Director/Chocolatier

Brentingby Gin Ltd
Incorporated: 16 June 2017
Registered Office: Brentingby Chapelry, Main Street, Brentingby, Melton Mowbray, Leics, LE14 4RX
Major Shareholder: Bruce Christopher Midgley
Officers: Bruce Christopher Midgley [1984] Director

Brew House Yorkshire Limited
Incorporated: 16 August 2017
Registered Office: c/o Wilkinson and Partners, 6a Millfield Road, Cottingley Business Park, Bingley, W Yorks, BD16 1PY
Major Shareholder: Mark Anthony Kelly
Officers: Mark Anthony Kelly [1964] Managing Director

Brewhouse Spirits Limited
Incorporated: 19 November 2018
Registered Office: 32-40 The Workshop, Folkestone, Kent, CT20 1JU
Shareholders: Benjamin Thomas de Haan; Tamara Jill de Haan
Officers: Benjamin Thomas de Haan [1976] Director; Tamara Jill de Haan [1978] Director

Bright Spirits Limited
Incorporated: 18 May 2018
Registered Office: 66 Tay Street, Perth, PH2 8RA
Parent: Vintage Saga Ltd
Officers: Iain McClune [1986] Director; Sean McGlone [1982] Director

Brighton Spirits Company Ltd
Incorporated: 31 July 2013 *Employees:* 11
Net Worth: £72,813 *Total Assets:* £138,022
Registered Office: The Old Casino, 28 Fourth Avenue, Hove, E Sussex, BN3 2PJ
Shareholder: Nigel Peter Lambe
Officers: Ian Eric Barry [1972] Director/Operations Manager [Irish]; Kathryn Melanie Kiele Caton [1974] Director/Radio Producer; Jonathan Cleeve Ray [1960] Director/Writer

Brindle Distillery Limited
Incorporated: 25 October 2017
Registered Office: Ollerton Fold Farm, Ollerton Lane, Withnell, Chorley, Lancs, PR6 8BW
Parent: Brindle Holdings Limited
Officers: Mark William Long [1987] Director/Manager; Catherine Singleton [1965] Director; Gerard Edmund John Singleton [1962] Director

The Bristol Rum Company Ltd
Incorporated: 22 August 2018
Registered Office: 425 Grace Apartments, College Road, Bishopston, Bristol, BS7 9LU
Major Shareholder: Daniel Charles Hughes
Officers: Daniel Charles Hughes [1990] Director

The Bristol Spirit Collective Limited
Incorporated: 4 January 2017
Registered Office: The Rummer Hotel, All Saints Lane, Bristol, BS1 1JH
Shareholders: Brett Hirt; David Blatch
Officers: David Blatch [1985] Director; Brett Hirt [1978] Director

British and Colonial Merchants of Jamaica Limited
Incorporated: 11 September 2018
Registered Office: AS8389, Alfasent Sortation, Falconer Road, Haverhill, Suffolk, CB9 7BG
Parent: British & Colonial Merchants Company Limited
Officers: Eamon O'Brien [1976] Director [Irish]

Brittains Beverages Ltd
Incorporated: 15 November 2018
Registered Office: Brittains, Sandall Stones Road, Kirk Sandall Industrial Estate, Doncaster, S Yorks, DN3 1QR
Major Shareholder: John Charles Raper
Officers: Mark Appleyard [1962] Director/Solicitor; John Charles Raper [1951] Director

The Brixham Gin Company Ltd.
Incorporated: 30 May 2017
Net Worth Deficit: £4,123 *Total Assets:* £14,813
Registered Office: 3 Doctors Road, Brixham, Devon, TQ5 9HR
Shareholders: Katrina Wade; Elizabeth Bernadette Edwards
Officers: Elizabeth Bernadette Edwards [1962] Director/Senior Business Advisor; Katrina Wade [1963] Director

Broad Street Brands Limited
Incorporated: 13 December 2011 *Employees:* 4
Previous: Broad Street Brands Public Limited Company
Net Worth: £32,220 *Total Assets:* £62,949
Registered Office: Level 17, Dashwood House, 69 Old Broad Street, London, EC2M 1QS
Officers: David Keith Papworth, Secretary; Richard Charles Quintin Ambler [1955] Director; Andrew William Burrows [1945] Director; Timothy Harold Garnett Lyle [1951] Director/Chartered Accountant; David Keith Papworth [1963] Director/Corporate Financier

Brockmans Gin Limited
Incorporated: 3 November 2006 *Employees:* 10
Net Worth Deficit: £2,866,239 *Total Assets:* £4,508,086
Registered Office: 40 Queen Anne Street, London, W1G 9EL
Shareholders: Kevin George Taylor; Lauren Cherie Willis; Graeme Walter Briggs
Officers: Marc Brownstein [1960] Director/President & Chief Executive Officer [American]; Anastasios Economou [1977] Director [Greek]; Neil John Everitt [1961] Director; Robert Andrew Fowkes [1957] Director; Alexandra Lesley Hincks [1967] Director/Consultant

Broken Wings Limited
Incorporated: 22 February 2017
Registered Office: 5 Newton Place, Glasgow, G3 7PR
Officers: Christopher Black [1989] Director/Marketing and Sales Manager; Matthew Burns [1985] Director/Graphic Designer [Australian]; Neil Paterson [1983] Director/Lawyer

Broker's Gin Limited
Incorporated: 27 May 1998 *Employees:* 8
Net Worth: £474,293 *Total Assets:* £748,671
Registered Office: 1st Floor, Suite Bridge House, 11 Creek Road, East Molesey, Surrey, KT8 9BE
Officers: Ronald Shults, Secretary; Michael Harris [1966] Director/Executive - Beverage Alcohol Company [American]; Richard Hillsman [1960] Director/Banking (Retired) [American]; Edward Pechar [1941] Director/Executive - Beverage Alcohol Company [American]

Bros Distilling Ltd
Incorporated: 24 May 2018
Registered Office: Unit 3 Reeds Row, Reads Road, Fenton Industrial Estate, Stoke on Trent, Staffs, ST4 2RL
Officers: Aleksandrs Rackovs [1991] Director/Self Employed [Latvian]; Vitalijs Rackovs [1980] Director [Latvian]

Brothers Drinks Co. Limited
Incorporated: 30 April 1992 *Employees:* 185
Net Worth: £56,965,680 *Total Assets:* £72,885,224
Registered Office: 4th Floor, St Catherines Court, Berkeley Place, Clifton, Bristol, BS8 1BQ
Officers: Iain David Glen, Secretary; Christopher John Courage [1962] Director; Iain David Glen [1969] Director/Accountant; Jonathan Showering [1962] Director/Financial Advisor; Matthew Herbert Showering [1964] Director/Marketing Advisor

Broughton Ales Limited
Incorporated: 14 August 1995 *Employees:* 9
Net Worth: £269,366 *Total Assets:* £502,688
Registered Office: Main Street, Broughton Village, Biggar, S Lanarks, ML12 6HQ
Shareholders: Stephen Lawrence McCarney; David Andrew McGowan; John Simon Hunt
Officers: John Simon Hunt [1963] Director; Stephen Lawrence McCarney [1961] Director; David Andrew McGowan [1963] Director

Malcolm Browne Distillery Company Limited
Incorporated: 18 November 2003
Net Worth: £1 *Total Assets:* £1
Registered Office: Suite 1, 3rd Floor, 11-12 St James's Square, London, SW1Y 4LB
Major Shareholder: James Finn
Officers: James Michael Finn, Secretary; James Michael Finn [1958] Director; John James Teeling [1946] Director [Irish]

Broxburn Bottlers Limited
Incorporated: 23 May 1984 *Employees:* 134
Net Worth: £11,532,073 *Total Assets:* £16,314,073
Registered Office: 5 Drovers Road, East Mains Industrial Estate, Broxburn, W Lothian, EH52 5ND
Shareholders: Ian MacLeod Distillers Limited; J & G Grant
Officers: Michael James Younger, Secretary; John Lynburn Scott Grant [1951] Director; David John Harris [1960] Plant Director; Leonard Stuart Russell [1961] Director

Buck and Birch Ltd
Incorporated: 30 September 2015
Net Worth Deficit: £2,907 *Total Assets:* £13,534
Registered Office: The Archive, Unit 9 Macmerry Industrial Estate, Tranent, E Lothian, EH33 1ET
Shareholders: Rupert Waites; Thomas Chisholm
Officers: Thomas Chisholm [1978] Director/Marketing; Rupert Waites [1976] Director/Food and Beverage Manufacturer

Buidheann Beag Distillery Limited
Incorporated: 24 August 2018
Registered Office: Pavilion 1, Finnieston Business Park, Minerva Way, Glasgow, G3 8AU
Major Shareholder: Douglas Gordon Wheatley

The Bunnahabhain Distillery Company Limited
Incorporated: 7 January 2003
Registered Office: 8 Milton Road, College Milton North, East Kilbride, S Lanarks, G74 5BU
Parent: Distell International Limited
Officers: Karen Spy, Secretary; Fraser John Thornton [1969] Director

Burn Stewart (U.S. Holdings) Limited
Incorporated: 12 July 2000
Registered Office: 8 Milton Road, College Milton North, East Kilbride, S Lanarks, G74 5BU
Shareholders: Distell International Limited; Distell Internatiional Limited
Officers: Karen Spy, Secretary; Nardus Oosthuizen [1968] Director/Accountant [South African]; Fraser John Thornton [1969] UK Sales Director

Burnbrae Distillery Company Ltd
Incorporated: 28 April 2015
Net Worth: £41,702 *Total Assets:* £874,890
Registered Office: 3 Peel Park Place, East Kilbride, S Lanarks, G74 5LW
Officers: Stephen James Ball [1954] Director; Colin Shields Barclay [1958] Director/Merchant [Canadian]; Michael Brian Julian Lulham [1955] Director; Gerrard McSherry [1956] Director

Burning Barn Limited
Incorporated: 20 March 2017 *Employees:* 2
Net Worth Deficit: £4,042 *Total Assets:* £41,544
Registered Office: The Orchards, Walsal End Lane, Hampton in Arden, Solihull, W Midlands, B92 0HU
Shareholders: Harry Jenner; Katherine Jenner
Officers: Harry Jenner [1986] Director; Katherine Jenner [1988] Commercial Director

The Burnsland Distillery Company Ltd
Incorporated: 29 September 2017
Registered Office: 4 Whitehill Grove, Newton Mearns, Glasgow, G77 5DH
Major Shareholder: Andrew Duncan Gray
Officers: Andrew Duncan Gray [1955] Director/Management Consultant

Butlers Cross Limited
Incorporated: 7 December 2018
Registered Office: 1st Floor, Gallery Court, 28 Arcadia Avenue, London, N3 2FG
Shareholders: David Julian Massey; Catherine Massey
Officers: Catherine Massey [1974] Director [Irish]; David Julian Massey [1971] Director

Buxton Distillery Limited
Incorporated: 11 July 2014
Net Worth Deficit: £9,093 *Total Assets:* £20,087
Registered Office: Unit 25A, Harpur Hill Industrial Estate, Buxton, Derbys, SK17 9JL
Shareholders: Ian Stefanuti; Paul James Carberry; Geoff Quinn
Officers: Paul James Carberry [1972] Director/Tour Operator; Geoff Quinn [1971] Director; Ian Stefanuti [1975] Director

Cabin Pressure Spirits Ltd
Incorporated: 11 April 2016
Net Worth: £5,014 *Total Assets:* £15,719
Registered Office: 70 St Leonards Road, Horsham, W Sussex, RH13 6AR
Major Shareholder: David Howard
Officers: David Howard [1983] Director/Software Developer

Calder Glen Ltd
Incorporated: 4 September 2012
Net Worth Deficit: £17,614 *Total Assets:* £300
Registered Office: 34 Milton Road, College Milton Industrial Estate, East Kilbride, S Lanarks, G74 5BU
Major Shareholder: William Hernon
Officers: William Hernon [1961] Director

Caledonian Bottlers PLC
Incorporated: 23 August 1993 *Employees:* 46
Net Worth: £3,784,607 *Total Assets:* £4,929,933
Registered Office: 4th Floor, 115 George Street, Edinburgh, EH2 4JN
Parent: Beverage Brands (UK) Ltd
Officers: Arthur Richmond, Secretary; Elaine Birchall [1966] Director [Irish]; Arthur William Richmond [1966] Director

Cambridge Distillery Ltd
Incorporated: 30 June 2011 *Employees:* 6
Net Worth: £450,400 *Total Assets:* £483,989
Registered Office: Cambridge Distillery 20 High Street, Grantchester, Cambridge, CB3 9NF
Parent: Diageo DV Limited
Officers: Lucy Nadine Lowe [1984] Director; William John Lowe [1979] Director

Camden Distillers Limited
Incorporated: 7 July 2011
Net Worth Deficit: £3,659 *Total Assets:* £3,846
Registered Office: 36 Chalcot Road, London, NW1 8LP
Major Shareholder: Philip Stuart Mills
Officers: Philip Stuart Mills [1956] Director/Alchemist

Campbell Meyer & Co Limited
Incorporated: 10 February 1989 *Employees:* 33
Net Worth: £1,758,425 *Total Assets:* £4,301,927
Registered Office: 3 Peel Park Place, East Kilbride, S Lanarks, G74 5LW
Parent: JG Distillers Ltd
Officers: Gerrard McSherry, Secretary/Director; Colin Shields Barclay [1958] Director/Merchant [Canadian]; Gerrard McSherry [1956] Director; Caroline Amy Purdie [1983] Director

Canebrake Ltd
Incorporated: 8 June 2015
Net Worth: £30,400 *Total Assets:* £30,400
Registered Office: 4 Maude Road, London, E17 7DF
Shareholders: Douglas Robert Miller; James Henry Kelshaw Conway
Officers: James Henry Kelshaw Conway [1987] Director/Management; Douglas Robert Miller [1987] Director/Consultant

Cantails Limited
Incorporated: 30 August 2017
Registered Office: Cantails Limited, 12b Lewisham Hill, Blackheath, London, SE13 7EJ
Officers: Christopher Donneky [1994] Director; Myles Donneky [1991] Director

Caperdonich Whisky Limited
Incorporated: 21 January 2019
Registered Office: Atrium House, Callendar Business Park, Falkirk, FK1 1XR
Major Shareholder: George Danskin Stewart
Officers: George Danskin Stewart [1945] Director/General Manager

Capreolus Distillery Ltd
Incorporated: 23 September 2014
Net Worth: £24,041 *Total Assets:* £77,124
Registered Office: The Mount, Park View, Stratton, Cirencester, Glos, GL7 2JG
Major Shareholder: Barney Michael Wilczak
Officers: Stefan Wilczak, Secretary; Barnaby Michael Wilczak [1984] Director

Caribbean Drinks Ltd
Incorporated: 8 December 2009
Net Worth Deficit: £85,607 *Total Assets:* £1,372
Registered Office: 12 Partridge Road, Hampton, Surrey, TW12 3SB
Major Shareholder: Atash Afzal Rafeeq
Officers: Atash Afzal Rafeeq [1971] Director/Chartered Accountant; Marina Wirkner [1978] Director/Development Trainer [German]

Caribbean Flaava Limited
Incorporated: 16 May 2012
Registered Office: 33 Bolesworth Road, Chester, CH2 1SQ
Major Shareholder: Servel Miller
Officers: Dr Servel Miller [1970] Director/Lecturer, Food Distribution and Catering

Carillon U.K. Limited
Incorporated: 20 January 1961
Registered Office: Edinburgh Park, 5 Lochside Way, Edinburgh, EH12 9DT
Parent: Anyslam Investments
Officers: James Matthew Crayden Edmunds [1974] Director/Solicitor; Gabor Kovacs [1980] Director [Hungarian]; Kara Elizabeth Major [1977] Director [American]

R. Carmichael & Sons Limited
Incorporated: 27 March 1952
Registered Office: Moffat Distillery, Airdrie, N Lanarks, ML6 8PL
Shareholders: Charoen Sirivadhanabhakdi; Khunying Wanna Sirivadhanabhakdi
Officers: Man Kong Lee [1968] Director/Accountant [Chinese]; Dr Martin John Leonard [1961] Managing Director; Prapakon Thongtheppairot [1971] Director [Thai]

Carrick Thomson Limited
Incorporated: 27 May 2014 *Employees:* 2
Net Worth Deficit: £23,543 *Total Assets:* £35,463
Registered Office: 64-66 Outram Street, Sutton in Ashfield, Notts, NG17 4FS
Shareholders: Wayne Asher; Tracey Margaret Asher
Officers: Tracy Margaret Asher [1980] Director; Wayne Asher [1967] Director

Carse of Stirling Distillers Ltd
Incorporated: 24 September 2018
Registered Office: Fordhead Farm, Kippen, Stirling, FK8 3JQ
Shareholders: Richard John Watson Lamb; Fiona Isobel Lamb
Officers: Fiona Isobel Lamb [1960] Director; Matthew David Cheyne Lamb [1993] Director; Richard John Watson Lamb [1960] Director/Farmer; Ian Anderson MacKay [1978] Business Development Director

Cartmel Gin Ltd
Incorporated: 11 June 2018
Registered Office: 4 Unsworths Yard, Ford Road, Cartmel, Grange-Over-Sands, Cumbria, LA11 6PG
Major Shareholder: Claire Elaine Unsworth
Officers: Claire Elaine Unsworth [1970] Director/Teacher

Cask Coin Ltd
Incorporated: 3 January 2018
Registered Office: 21 Forbes Place, Paisley, Renfrewshire, PA1 1UT
Major Shareholder: Roderick George Christie
Officers: Roderick George Christie [1952] Director/Whisky Consultant

Caskcoin Holdings Limited
Incorporated: 9 February 2018
Registered Office: 21 Forbes Place, Paisley, Renfrewshire, PA1 1UT
Officers: Roderick George Christie [1952] Director/Distiller; Walter James Russell [1966] Director

Castleheather Facilities Management Ltd
Incorporated: 10 March 2006
Net Worth Deficit: £16,031 *Total Assets:* £425,183
Registered Office: Castleheather House, Druid Temple Road, Inverness, IV2 6AA
Major Shareholder: Amelia Ann MacKenzie
Officers: Torquil Farquhar MacLeod, Secretary; Daniel Manuel MacAngus [1991] Director/General Manager; Amelia Ann MacKenzie [1963] Director

James Catto & Company Limited
Incorporated: 1 April 1918
Registered Office: Moffat Distillery, Airdrie, N Lanarks, ML6 8PL
Shareholders: Charoen Sirivadhanabhakdi; Khunying Wanna Sirivadhanabhakdi
Officers: Man Kong Lee [1968] Director/Accountant [Chinese]; Dr Martin John Leonard [1961] Managing Director; Prapakon Thongtheppairot [1971] Director [Thai]

Central Line Holdings Limited
Incorporated: 20 August 2015 *Employees:* 5
Net Worth: £147,294 *Total Assets:* £317,674
Registered Office: Ground Floor, Swift House, 18 Hoffmanns Way, Chelmsford, Essex, CM1 6YF
Officers: Michael Hughes [1980] Commercial Director; David James Rigby [1981] Director

CES Whisky Limited
Incorporated: 4 December 1991
Net Worth: £9,892,614 *Total Assets:* £15,000,296
Registered Office: 6 Newton Place, Glasgow, G3 7PR
Officers: David Alexander Sloan, Secretary; Per Steen Molin Heinze [1946] Director [Danish]; Thomas Just Karberg [1964] Director [Danish]; David Alexander Sloan [1962] Director/Accountant; Erik Pederson Thomsen [1967] Director [Danish]

Chalgrove Artisan Distillery Limited
Incorporated: 8 August 2017
Registered Office: 2 Marley Lane, Chalgrove, Oxford, OX44 7TF
Shareholders: Robert Stanley Clark; Jennifer Anne Clark
Officers: Jennifer Anne Clark [1960] Director/Accountant; Robert Stanley Clark [1956] Director/Teacher

Chalk & Charcoal Limited
Incorporated: 17 March 2015
Net Worth: £306 *Total Assets:* £101,676
Registered Office: Audley House, Northbridge Road, Berkhamsted, Herts, HP4 1EH
Shareholders: Kate Marston; Benedict John Marston
Officers: Benedict John Marston [1972] Director/Marketing/Production; Kate Marston [1975] Director/Marketing/Production

Chase Distillery Limited
Incorporated: 20 October 2006
Net Worth: £744,816 *Total Assets:* £5,499,464
Registered Office: Rosemaund Farm, Preston Wynne, Hereford, HR1 3PG
Parent: Chase Distillery (Holdings) Limited
Officers: Judith Penny Adcock, Secretary; Andrew James Carter [1968] Director; James Matthew Chase [1990] Director; William Leonard Chase [1960] Director; Adrian Lee Jones [1973] Managing Director

Checkers Gin Ltd
Incorporated: 3 October 2017
Registered Office: 22 Junction Road, Andover, Hants, SP10 3QU
Officers: Jason Karl Cooper [1967] Director/Distiller; Robert Peter Cubitt [1983] Director/Distiller

Cherry Drop Gin Ltd
Incorporated: 19 July 2018
Registered Office: Axis 8, Mallard Way, Swansea Vale, Swansea, SA7 0AJ
Shareholders: David Sidney Wakely; David Robert Bellis
Officers: David Robert Bellis [1984] Director; David Sidney Wakely [1985] Director

Cheshire Distilleries Limited
Incorporated: 28 August 2015
Net Worth: £1,437 *Total Assets:* £23,876
Registered Office: Unit 9 Mollington Grange, Parkgate Road, Mollington, Chester, CH1 6NP
Officers: Wayne Rose [1969] Director; Mark Arrowsmith Stanley [1981] Director

Chileanspirit Ltd
Incorporated: 12 March 2009
Net Worth Deficit: £23,839 *Total Assets:* £95
Registered Office: Accounting Freedom, Westhill House, 2a Devonshire Road, Bexleyheath, Kent, DA6 8DS
Shareholder: George Gino Heidke Bibiano
Officers: Richard Michael Bayles [1973] Director/Business Manager

The Chilgrove Gin Company Ltd
Incorporated: 9 September 2013
Net Worth Deficit: £52,992 *Total Assets:* £70,473
Registered Office: The Chilgrove Gin Company Ltd, P O Box 761, Chichester, W Sussex, PO19 9RJ
Shareholders: Celia Elizabeth Beaumont-Hutchings; Christopher Edward Beaumont-Hutchings
Officers: Dr Celia Elizabeth Beaumont-Hutchings [1985] Director/General Practitioner; Christopher Edward Beaumont-Hutchings [1986] Director

Chinn-Chinn Ginn Limited
Incorporated: 4 February 2013
Registered Office: 23 Harvington Road, Bromsgrove, Worcs, B60 2BA
Major Shareholder: Steven Gregory Chinn
Officers: Steven Gregory Chinn [1958] Director

Chivas Brothers Limited
Incorporated: 3 June 2004 *Employees:* 1,698
Net Worth: £3,331,140,096 *Total Assets:* £6,831,062,016
Registered Office: 111-113 Renfrew Road, Paisley, Renfrewshire, PA3 4DY
Parent: Allied Domecq Spirits & Wine Holdings Limited
Officers: Stuart MacNab, Secretary; Gordon William Buist [1964] Technical Director; Jean-Christophe Coutures [1966] Director [French]; Scott Livingstone [1968] HR Director; Alister Douglas McIntosh [1961] Manufacturing Director; Catherine Louise Thompson [1971] Director/General Counsel [Australian]; Vincent Turpin [1978] Director/Chief Financial Officer [French]

Chivas Brothers Pernod Ricard
Incorporated: 1 February 2000 *Employees:* 1
Net Worth: £2,372,194,048 *Total Assets:* £2,548,134,912
Registered Office: 111-113 Renfrew Road, Paisley, Renfrewshire, PA3 4DY
Parent: Chivas Brothers (Holdings) Limited
Officers: Stuart MacNab [1964] Director/Accountant; Vincent Turpin [1978] Director/Chief Financial Officer [French]

The Churchill Distillery Limited
Incorporated: 8 December 2017
Registered Office: 18 Normanton Avenue, London, SW19 8BB
Officers: Luke Dampier [1990] Director/Founder; Alex Stephens [1991] Director/Founder

City of Aberdeen Distillery Ltd
Incorporated: 7 October 2016
Net Worth Deficit: £6,759 *Total Assets:* £36,429
Registered Office: 3 Prospect Place, Westhill, Aberdeenshire, AB32 6SY
Shareholders: Alan David Milne; Daniel James Barnett
Officers: Daniel James Barnett [1982] Director; Alan David Milne [1975] Director

CL World Brands Limited
Incorporated: 9 January 2003
Net Worth: £70,180,000 *Total Assets:* £71,084,000
Registered Office: 110 Queen Street, Glasgow, G1 3BX
Officers: Dr Rolph Balgobin [1970] Director/Businessman [Trinidadian]; Kirby Anthony Hosang [1960] Director/Businessman [Trinidadian]; Albert George Tom Yew [1940] Chairman/Director [Trinidadian]

The Clandestine Distillery Limited
Incorporated: 21 December 2018
Registered Office: Low Barn, Llancayo Business Park, Usk, Monmouthshire, NP15 1HY
Shareholders: Nathan Edward Thompson; Sarah Thompson
Officers: Nathan Edward Thompson [1978] Director

Clifden Arms Property Ltd
Incorporated: 28 June 2018
Registered Office: Unit 3 Vista Place, Ingworth Road, Poole, Dorset, BH12 1JY
Parent: Cliften Arms Holding Co Ltd
Officers: Michael Berthet [1955] Director; Robert Alan Porter-Smith [1956] Director; Alex Pykett [1977] Director; Roy Frederick Pykett [1955] Director

Clifden Arms Trading Ltd
Incorporated: 28 June 2018
Registered Office: Unit 3 Vista Place, Ingworth Road, Poole, Dorset, BH12 1JY
Parent: Cliften Arms Holding Co Ltd
Officers: Michael Berthet [1955] Director; Robert Alan Porter-Smith [1956] Director; Alex Pykett [1977] Director; Roy Frederick Pykett [1955] Director

Clock Tower Distilleries Limited
Incorporated: 7 August 2017
Registered Office: Arquen House, 4-6 Spicer Street, St Albans, Herts, AL3 4PQ
Shareholders: Paul Anthony Marsh; Charlotte Trudy Carroll
Officers: Charlotte Trudy Carroll [1978] Director/Business Professional; Paul Anthony Marsh [1968] Business Consultant & Director

Cloughmor Consulting Ltd
Incorporated: 23 January 2018
Registered Office: 2 Seafields Avenue, Warrenpoint, Co Down, BT34 3XA
Shareholders: Ruairi O'Donnell; Catrina O'Donnell
Officers: Catrina O'Donnell [1963] Director [Irish]; Ruairi O'Donnell [1962] Director/Consultant Engineer [Irish]

Club Rum Limited
Incorporated: 25 May 2018
Registered Office: Whitehall House, 33 Yeaman Shore, Dundee, DD1 4BJ
Major Shareholder: Laura Greig Conway
Officers: Laura Greig Conway [1966] Director

Clwydian Range Distillery Limited
Incorporated: 25 May 2018
Registered Office: Delcroft, Ffordd Y Graig, Lixwm, Holywell, Flintshire, CH8 8LY
Major Shareholder: Fiona Lewis
Officers: Fiona Lewis [1974] Director/Administration Manager; Simon Keith Ollman [1971] Director/Retired Civil Engineer

Clyde Bottlers Ltd
Incorporated: 19 December 2017
Registered Office: 18 Lynedoch Crescent, Glasgow, G3 6EQ
Major Shareholder: Frederick Hamilton Laing
Officers: Frederick Hamilton Laing [1950] Managing Director; Danny MacLennan [1975] Finance Director

Clydeside Distillery Limited
Incorporated: 3 September 2015
Registered Office: Paxton House, 11 Woodside Crescent, Glasgow, G3 7UL
Major Shareholder: Andrew Morrison
Officers: Andrew Morrison [1977] Director

Coates & Co. (Plymouth) Limited
Incorporated: 8 March 1996
Previous: V & S Plymouth Limited
Net Worth: £3,483,100,928 *Total Assets:* £3,483,909,888
Registered Office: Blackfriars Distillery, 60 Southside, Plymouth, PL1 2LQ
Parent: Chivas Atlantic Holdings Limited
Officers: Ailsa Mary Robertson Mapplebeck, Secretary; Sean Jessop Harrison [1965] Director/Distiller; MacNab Stuart [1964] Director/Chartered Accountant; Vincent Turpin [1978] Director/Chief Financial Officer [French]

The Cognac Growers' Collective Limited
Incorporated: 3 August 2012
Registered Office: The Barn, Lotmead Business Village, Wanborough, Swindon, Wilts, SN4 0UY
Shareholder: Penelope Margaret Jackson
Officers: Peter Bowyer [1954] Director; Penelope Margaret Jackson [1963] Director

Coleburn Distillery Limited
Incorporated: 20 March 2014
Registered Office: Coleburn Distillery, Rothes, Elgin, Moray, IV30 8SN
Major Shareholder: Edward Odim
Officers: Edward Odim [1958] Director/Whisky Distilling & Warehousing

Collards Distillery Limited
Incorporated: 19 September 2017
Registered Office: The Lindens, Spa Road, Llandrindod Wells, Powys, LD1 5EQ
Major Shareholder: Thomas James Collard
Officers: Alice Jane Collard [1998] Director/Hotel Assistant; Penelope Jane Collard [1959] Director/Manager; Thomas James Collard [1994] Director/Driver; William James Nimrod Collard [1959] Director/Farmer

Spencer Collings & Co Limited
Incorporated: 15 December 2005
Registered Office: 1 Lumley Street, Mayfair, London, W1K 6TT
Major Shareholder: Michael George Spencer Collings
Officers: Michael George Spencer Collings [1949] Director

Colonsay Beverages Ltd.
Incorporated: 13 February 2015 *Employees:* 6
Net Worth: £91,704 *Total Assets:* £264,888
Registered Office: The Brew House, Dun Oran Park, Scalasaig, Isle of Colonsay, Argyll, PA61 7YW
Officers: Keith Bonnington [1976] Director/Senior Brand Manager; Allan Robert Erskine [1979] Director/Chartered Accountant; David Melville Steele Johnston [1954] Director; Christopher William Nisbet [1958] Director/Self Employed

Colwith Farm Distillery Limited
Incorporated: 20 November 2015 *Employees:* 1
Net Worth Deficit: £1,045 *Total Assets:* £138,957
Registered Office: Colwith Farm, Treesmill, Par, Cornwall, PL24 2TU
Major Shareholder: Steven Michael Dustow
Officers: Steven Michael Dustow [1982] Director

Commonwealth Gin Ltd
Incorporated: 19 November 2018
Registered Office: 8 Everson Way, Spennymoor, Co Durham, DL16 7BX
Shareholders: Connor Jack Smith; Jack Adam Hull; Asher Lewis Galley
Officers: Asher Lewis Galley [1997] Director; Jack Adam Hull [1997] Director; Connor Jack Smith [1998] Director

Company of Dark Spirits Limited
Incorporated: 3 April 2017
Registered Office: 31 Argyle Place, Edinburgh, EH9 1JT
Major Shareholder: Iain Ritchie Bell
Officers: Iain Ritchie Bell [1967] Director/Beverage Consultant; Jamie John MacDonald [1978] Director/Hospitality Consultant

Compass Box Delicious Whisky Ltd.
Incorporated: 17 March 2000 *Employees:* 10
Net Worth: £1,166,648 *Total Assets:* £2,688,070
Registered Office: 4th Floor, 115 George Street, Edinburgh, EH2 4JN
Shareholder: Bacardi UK Limited
Officers: Inga Hutchison, Secretary; Jonathan Paul Norman Driver [1961] Director/Consultant; John Reppert Glaser [1963] Director [American]; Jean Marc Lambert [1965] Supply Chain & Manufacturing Director [French]; Hector Ortiz [1968] Director/VP - Business Development [American]; Dr Alan Gray Rutherford [1942] Director

Compass Box Whisky Supply Ltd
Incorporated: 22 November 2012
Registered Office: Chiswick Studios, 9 Power Road, London, W4 5PY
Parent: Compass Box Delicious Whisky Ltd
Officers: John Reppert Glaser [1963] Director/Whisky Maker [American]

Conglomerate Spirits Ltd.
Incorporated: 21 November 2017
Registered Office: Blue Square Offices, 272 Bath Street, Glasgow, G2 4JR
Officers: Venkata Sainath Soora [1975] Director/Entrepreneur [Indian]

Conker Spirit Limited
Incorporated: 25 February 2014 *Employees:* 6
Net Worth: £180,911 *Total Assets:* £359,920
Registered Office: 5 Poole Road, Bournemouth, BH2 5QL
Major Shareholder: Rupert Vere Holloway
Officers: Emily Etherton, Secretary; Fred Gamper, Secretary; Rupert Vere Holloway [1984] Director

Conscious Collaborative Ltd
Incorporated: 13 February 2019
Registered Office: Balne Hall, Balne Hall Road, Goole, E Yorks, DN14 0EA
Shareholders: Phillip David White; Matthew Wood; Sam Weller
Officers: Sam Weller [1985] Director/Operations Manager; Phillip David White [1984] Managing Director; Matthew Wood [1990] Director/Chairman

Contract Bottlers Glasgow Ltd
Incorporated: 11 December 2018
Registered Office: 21 Southbrae Gardens, Glasgow, G13 1UB
Major Shareholder: Ronald William Grandison Young
Officers: Adrian Ross Louden [1971] Director; Ronald William Grandison Young [1968] Director

Conwy Distillery Limited
Incorporated: 17 August 2018
Registered Office: 13 Bangor Road, Conwy, LL32 8NG
Major Shareholder: Mark William Baravelli
Officers: Mark William Baravelli [1965] Director

Cool Brew Dept Ltd
Incorporated: 26 June 2018
Registered Office: Flat 2, 134 Valley Drive, Harrogate, N Yorks, HG2 0JS
Major Shareholder: Matthew Leonard Edgar
Officers: Matthew Leonard Edgar [1984] Director

Cooper King Distillery Ltd
Incorporated: 20 April 2016
Net Worth: £94,261 *Total Assets:* £169,977
Registered Office: The Old Stables, Stillington Road, Sutton-on-the-Forest, N Yorks, YO61 1EH
Shareholders: Abbie Louise Neilson; Christopher Mark Jaume
Officers: Christopher Mark Jaume [1986] Director; Dr Abbie Louise Neilson [1986] Director

Copeland Distillery Company (NI) Ltd
Incorporated: 26 October 2018
Registered Office: Unit 4 Windmill Business Park, Windmill Road, Saintfield, Ballynahinch, Co Down, BT24 7DX
Major Shareholder: Gareth James Irvine
Officers: Gareth James Irvine [1992] Director

Copeland Spirits Ltd
Incorporated: 7 December 2015
Net Worth: £24,713 *Total Assets:* £167,026
Registered Office: Unit 4 Windmill Business Park, Windmill Road, Saintfield, Ballynahinch, Co Down, BT24 7DX
Major Shareholder: Gareth James Irvine
Officers: Gareth James Irvine [1992] Managing Director; John Mark Prentice [1970] Director

Copper Drinks Limited
Incorporated: 10 April 2018
Registered Office: 18 Walton Street, London, SW3 1RE
Major Shareholder: James Henry Richards
Officers: James Henry Richards [1982] Director/Sales

Copper Frog Distilling Limited
Incorporated: 24 May 2017
Registered Office: The Stables, Manor Farm, Chavenage, Tetbury, Glos, GL8 8XW
Major Shareholder: Simon Grant Jason Hughes
Officers: Simon Grant Jason Hughes [1965] Director/Senior Network Technician

The Copper Tree Partnership Ltd
Incorporated: 27 April 2018
Registered Office: 5 Gawsworth Close, Poynton, Stockport, Cheshire, SK12 1XB
Officers: Adrian Booth [1967] Director

Corglass Wild Spirit Ltd
Incorporated: 7 August 2018
Registered Office: Corglass Lodge, Blacksboat, Ballindalloch, Moray, AB37 9BS
Shareholders: Joerg Thomas Gustav Bondzio; Fiona Jane Bondzio
Officers: Joerg Thomas Gustav Bondzio [1958] Managing Director [German]

Corky's Brands Limited
Incorporated: 23 February 2006
Registered Office: 5th Floor, Casa, Lockoford Lane, Chesterfield, Derbys, S41 7JB
Officers: Shaun Bacon, Secretary/Accountant; Steven James Garcia Perez [1956] Director; Mark Peter James [1971] Director

Corner Fifty Three Distilling Ltd
Incorporated: 5 August 2016 *Employees:* 2
Net Worth Deficit: £8,469 *Total Assets:* £18,034
Registered Office: 53 Green Lane, Clanfield, Waterlooville, Hants, PO8 0JX
Major Shareholder: Thomas Rudman
Officers: Elizabeth Rudman [1964] Director/Home Maker; Thomas Rudman [1995] Director/Bar Manager

The Cornish Distillery Company Limited
Incorporated: 9 April 2010
Registered Office: Condolden Farm, Tintagel, Cornwall, PL34 0HJ
Shareholders: John Reford Heard; Dylan Henry Simpson
Officers: Jane Louise Simpson, Secretary; John Reford Heard [1962] Director/Farmer; Dylan Henry Simpson [1976] Director/Engineer

The Cornish Distilling Company Ltd
Incorporated: 14 January 2016
Net Worth Deficit: £7,774 *Total Assets:* £56,377
Registered Office: Norton Barton, Launcells, Bude, Cornwall, EX23 9LG
Officers: Richard William Harding [1962] Director/Distilling; Dr Thomas Read [1986] Director/Distiller

The Cornish Gin Mine Ltd
Incorporated: 15 June 2017
Registered Office: 42 Corbett Road, Carterton, Oxon, OX18 3LE
Major Shareholder: David Richard Mayfield
Officers: David Richard Mayfield [1967] Director/Management

Cornish Spirit Company Limited
Incorporated: 25 June 2012 *Employees:* 1
Previous: Leiworthy Limited
Net Worth: £8,384 *Total Assets:* £11,167
Registered Office: 9 North Close, Lymington, Hants, SO41 9BT
Major Shareholder: Sophia Emma Fenton
Officers: Sophia Emma Fenton [1966] Director

Cornish Spiritsmith Ltd
Incorporated: 15 December 2017
Registered Office: The Marine Store, The Quay, East Looe, Looe, Cornwall, PL13 1DX
Shareholder: William Richard Martin
Officers: William Richard Martin [1964] Director/Publican

The Corrupt Drinks Company Limited
Incorporated: 7 January 2016
Net Worth Deficit: £27,915 *Total Assets:* £30,296
Registered Office: West Midlands House, Gipsy Lane, Willenhall, W Midlands, WV13 2HA
Shareholders: Matthew Haynes; Stephen Paul Haynes; Stuart Haynes
Officers: Stephen Paul Haynes [1964] Director

The Cotswold Distilling Company Limited
Incorporated: 7 June 2013 *Employees:* 33
Net Worth: £5,569,517 *Total Assets:* £9,455,019
Registered Office: Phillip's Field, Whichford Road, Stourton, Shipston on Stour, Warwicks, CV36 5HG
Officers: Paul Beckwith [1957] Investor and Director [Australian]; Sir Dominic Cadbury [1940] Director; Dr Katia Cikurel [1967] Director/Neurologist/Doctor; Leon Daniel Szor [1962] Director/Business Executive [American/British]; Richard Neil Watling [1948] Director

The Country Garden Drinks Company Limited
Incorporated: 30 August 2017
Registered Office: Chestnut House, Stewton Lane, Louth, Lincs, LN11 8SB
Shareholders: Matthew James Hamilton; Emma Hamilton
Officers: Emma Hamilton [1986] Director; Matthew James Hamilton [1991] Director

Michel Couvreur (Scotch Whiskies) Limited
Incorporated: 22 April 1988 *Employees:* 6
Net Worth: £1,514,178 *Total Assets:* £2,077,092
Registered Office: Meldrum House, Old Meldrum, Aberdeenshire, AB5 0AE
Parent: Al Spirit
Officers: Marthe Georgette Andree Couvreur [1932] Director [French]; Alexandra Marie Elisabeth Deschamps [1972] Director/Housewife [French]; Cyril Deschamps [1973] Director [French]; Jean Arnaud Frantzen [1973] Director [French]

Cox & Mall Ltd
Incorporated: 11 June 2018
Registered Office: Unit 1 Watchmoor Park Trading Estate, Watchmoor Road, Camberley, Surrey, GU15 3AQ
Shareholders: Thomas Matthew Cox; Ashim Mall
Officers: Thomas Matthew Cox [1988] Managing Director; Ashim Mall [1994] Director

Coyote Ventures Limited
Incorporated: 6 August 2015
Net Worth Deficit: £1,660 *Total Assets:* £169
Registered Office: 5 Brooklands Place, Brooklands Road, Sale, Cheshire, M33 3SD
Shareholders: Daniel Britt Glaister; Alison Jane Kayley
Officers: Daniel Britt Glaister [1962] Director; Ali Jane Kayley [1967] Director

CP Infusions Ltd
Incorporated: 4 June 2018
Registered Office: 24 Combe Road, Stonesfield, Witney, Oxon, OX29 8QD
Shareholders: Claire Renshaw; Paul Renshaw
Officers: Claire Renshaw, Secretary; Claire Renshaw [1972] Director; Paul Renshaw [1976] Director

Craft Distilling Expo Limited
Incorporated: 27 March 2017
Registered Office: Building 6, 30 Friern Park, London, N12 9DA
Major Shareholder: Daniel Newburg
Officers: Daniel Newburg [1959] Director [American]

The Craft Scottish Spirits Company Limited
Incorporated: 14 February 2017
Registered Office: Ruthven Villa, Montrose Road, Auchterarder, Perth & Kinross, PH3 1BZ
Major Shareholder: Robert Daniel Fergus Hartley
Officers: Robert Daniel Fergus Hartley [1965] Director

Crafted Beverages Limited
Incorporated: 8 July 2016
Net Worth Deficit: £10,700 *Total Assets:* £10,332
Registered Office: 27 Old Gloucester Street, London, WC1N 3AX
Shareholders: Emma Whiting; Andrew Whiting
Officers: Andrew George Whiting [1982] Director; Emma Whiting [1983] Director

Crafty Scottish Distillers Ltd
Incorporated: 22 January 2015 *Employees:* 6
Net Worth Deficit: £57,520 *Total Assets:* £471,299
Registered Office: Drumfoot, The Stell, Kirkcudbright, DG6 4SA
Major Shareholder: Graham Taylor
Officers: Graham Taylor [1978] Creative Director

Cragside Spirit Company Ltd
Incorporated: 21 June 2018
Registered Office: Unit 4 Aldby Farm, Dacre, Penrith, Cumbria, CA11 0HN
Major Shareholder: James Matthew McIntyre
Officers: James Matthew McIntyre [1973] Director/Self Employed

William Craig & Company Limited
Incorporated: 21 January 2004
Net Worth Deficit: £13,983 *Total Assets:* £66
Registered Office: Caledonia House, 89 Seaward Street, Glasgow, G41 1HJ
Major Shareholder: Doreen Craig
Officers: Doreen Craig, Secretary [Malaysian]; Doreen Craig [1969] Director

Crawford's Rock Ltd
Incorporated: 29 October 2018
Registered Office: 20-22 Wenlock Road, London, N1 7GU
Shareholders: Gareth Malcolm Wilson; Michelle Wilson
Officers: Gareth Malcolm Wilson [1963] Director/Driver; Michelle Wilson [1965] Director/Social Care Worker; Ronald William Henry Wilson [1992] Director/Fisherman; Tessa Desanne Wilson [1997] Director/Student

Croft Distillery Ltd
Incorporated: 7 November 2018
Registered Office: White House, Wollaton Street, Nottingham, NG1 5GF
Shareholders: Dennis Troy Denier; Croft TNG Ltd
Officers: Ashley James Beeden [1968] Director/Engineer; Dennis Troy Denier [1965] Director/Sales

Cross Distillery Limited
Incorporated: 17 November 2017
Registered Office: Killaney Lodge, 19 Carryduff Road, Lisburn, Co Antrim, BT27 6TZ
Major Shareholder: Terence Martin Cross
Officers: Terence Martin Cross [1950] Director

Cross Stream Distillery Ltd
Incorporated: 17 September 2018
Registered Office: Flat 2, Hazelwood Court, 31 Lower Cookham Road, Maidenhead, Berks, SL6 8JS
Shareholders: Charles Patrick Purcell White; Chloe Elizabeth White
Officers: Charles Patrick Purcell White [1987] Managing Director; Chloe Elizabeth White [1990] Managing Director

Crossbill Distilling Limited
Incorporated: 24 March 2014
Net Worth Deficit: £135,830 *Total Assets:* £105,868
Registered Office: 89 Seaward Street, Glasgow, G41 1HJ
Officers: John Roddison, Secretary; Thor Hvid Hansen [1967] Director [Danish]; Martin Niclasen [1970] Director [Danish]; Adam Dominic Bradley Shaw [1969] Director

Crossbill Gin Limited
Incorporated: 24 June 2015
Net Worth: £1 *Total Assets:* £3,178
Registered Office: 51 Clarkegrove Road, Sheffield, S10 2NH
Officers: John Roddison, Secretary; Adam Dominic Bradley Shaw [1969] Director

Crosskeys Whiskey Company Ltd
Incorporated: 12 March 2018
Registered Office: 40 Grange Road, Toomebridge, Co Antrim, BT41 3QB
Officers: Vincent Hurl [1971] Director/Publican [Irish]

The Crosstown Cocktail Company Ltd
Incorporated: 16 November 2018
Registered Office: 44 Victoria Avenue, Bristol, BS5 9NG
Shareholders: Lowri Thomas Clarke; Andrew Robert Ellis
Officers: Lowri Thomas Clarke [1981] Director/Writer; Andrew Robert Ellis [1980] Director/Set Designer

Crystaldrifter Ltd
Incorporated: 19 July 2018
Registered Office: Unit 3 Trinity Centre, Park Farm Industrial Estate, Wellingborough, Northants, NN8 6ZB
Major Shareholder: Claire Samantha Lomas
Officers: Marilyn Del Mundo [1987] Director [Filipino]

Csatrina Holdings Ltd
Incorporated: 10 March 2017
Registered Office: Somerton & Co, Challenge House, 616 Mitcham Road, Croydon, Surrey, CR0 3AA
Officers: Vikrant Sham Chougule [1971] Director; Vishal Ghanshyam Patel [1974] Director; Nitzan Podoswa Marrun [1995] Director [Mexican]; Jagdeep Singh Shonpal [1974] Director

Cu Dhub Distilling Co Ltd
Incorporated: 4 October 2012
Registered Office: Regent Court, 70 West Regent Street, Glasgow, G2 2QZ
Major Shareholder: Soren Norgaard
Officers: Soren Norgaard [1963] Director [Danish]

The Cuba Trading Company Ltd
Incorporated: 10 September 2018
Registered Office: Haydens Farm, High Easter, Chelmsford, Essex, CM1 4QU
Shareholders: William Richard Knight; Mark Ubsdell
Officers: William Richard Knight [1961] Film Director/Producer; Mark Ubsdell [1960] Film Director/Producer

Cupids Bow 35 Limited
Incorporated: 14 June 2018
Registered Office: Old Printers Yard, 156 South Street, Dorking, Surrey, RH4 2HF
Shareholders: Nicholas Charles Read; Claire Angela Read
Officers: Claire Angela Read [1965] Director/Highways Engineer; Nicholas Charles Read [1967] Director/IT Consultant

Curio Spirits Company Limited
Incorporated: 5 April 2017
Registered Office: Trenance Farm, Mullion, Helston, Cornwall, TR12 7HB
Officers: Rubina Khan Tyler-Street [1967] Director; William Gannel Tyler-Street [1965] Director/Entrepreneur

Curious Liquids Limited
Incorporated: 18 October 2017
Net Worth: £1 *Total Assets:* £1
Registered Office: 78b Temperance Street, Manchester, M12 6HU
Shareholders: Jennie Louise Wiggins; Sebastian Richard John Heeley; James Peter Stimson
Officers: Sebastian Richard John Heeley [1986] Director/Company Owner; James Peter Stimson [1984] Director; Jennie Louise Wiggins [1983] Director/Company Owner

Cwmni Distyllfa Llanberis Cyf
Incorporated: 17 October 2012
Registered Office: Roe Sion Philip, Mount Road, St Asaph, Denbighshire, LL17 0DH
Shareholders: David Nathaniel Walker; Barrie Mason Jackson
Officers: Barrie Mason Jackson [1955] Director; William Anthony Latham [1948] Director/Chartered Accountant; David Nathaniel Walker [1973] Director/Businessman

Cygnet Spirits Limited
Incorporated: 30 March 2015
Registered Office: 8 Axis Court, Mallard Way, Riverside Business Park, Swansea, SA7 0AJ
Shareholders: David Robert Bellis; David Wakely
Officers: David Robert Bellis [1984] Director; David Wakely [1985] Director

Matthew D'Arcy & Company Limited
Incorporated: 23 March 2015
Net Worth Deficit: £114,055   *Total Assets:* £852,956
Registered Office: 31 St Marys Street, Newry, Co Armagh, BT34 2AA
Major Shareholder: Michael McKeown
Officers: Michael McKeown, Secretary; Andrew Leo Cowan [1973] Director [Irish]; Sinead Elizabeth McAllister [1978] Finance Director [Irish]; Michael Anthony McKeown [1946] Director [Irish]

Daisy Distillery Limited
Incorporated: 1 October 2018
Registered Office: Unit 11 Bhive Business Centre, Skelton Industrial Estate, Skelton in Cleveland, Saltburn-by-the-Sea, N Yorks, TS12 2LQ
Officers: Gail Davidson [1972] Director; Stephen Robert Davidson [1972] Director/Marine Engineer

Thomas Dakin Artisan Distillers Limited
Incorporated: 30 September 2014
Registered Office: Distribution Point, Melbury Park, Clayton Road, Birchwood, Warrington, Cheshire, WA3 6PH
Shareholders: Vincenzo Visone; Warren Michael Scott
Officers: Michael Clifford, Secretary; Warren Michael Scott [1963] Director/Businessman; Vincenzo Visone [1955] Director/Businessman [Italian]

Thomas Dakin Craft Distillers Limited
Incorporated: 30 September 2014
Registered Office: Distribution Point, Melbury Park, Clayton Road, Birchwood, Warrington, Cheshire, WA3 6PH
Shareholders: Vincenzo Visone; Warren Michael Scott
Officers: Michael Clifford, Secretary; Warren Michael Scott [1963] Director/Businessman; Vincenzo Visone [1955] Director/Businessman [Italian]

Thomas Dakin Distiller Limited
Incorporated: 12 March 2013
Registered Office: Distribution Point, Clayton Road, Birchwood, Warrington, Cheshire, WA3 6PH
Shareholders: Warren Michael Scott; Vincenzo Visone
Officers: Michael Clifford, Secretary; Warren Michael Scott [1963] Director/Businessman; Vincenzo Visone [1955] Director/Businessman [Italian]

Thomas Dakin Limited
Incorporated: 12 March 2013
Registered Office: Distribution Point, Clayton Road, Birchwood, Warrington, Cheshire, WA3 6PH
Shareholders: Warren Michael Scott; Vincenzo Visone
Officers: Michael Clifford, Secretary; Warren Michael Scott [1963] Director/Businessman; Vincenzo Visone [1955] Director/Businessman [Italian]

Dallas Dhu Ltd
Incorporated: 19 September 2018
Registered Office: 56 Torridon Road, Broughty Ferry, Dundee, DD5 3JH
Officers: David Donald Corbett Morrison [1944] Director

Dallinger Gin Limited
Incorporated: 10 March 2016   *Employees:* 1
Net Worth Deficit: £3,237   *Total Assets:* £2,833
Registered Office: 19a Craigton Road, Aberdeen, AB15 7US
Major Shareholder: David Howatson
Officers: David Howatson [1986] Director/Process Engineer

Dalrymples Distillery Ltd
Incorporated: 7 November 2018
Registered Office: 51 Cleveland Drive, Fareham, Hants, PO14 1SW
Major Shareholder: Michael Norman Dalrymple
Officers: Michael Norman Dalrymple [1989] Director/Marine

Damsons in Distress Limited
Incorporated: 20 February 2009
Registered Office: Binbrook Hill Farm, Binbrook Hill, Binbrook, Market Rasen, Lincs, LN8 6BL
Major Shareholder: Phillipa Nickerson Gloeckner
Officers: Phillipa Nickerson Gloeckner [1980] Director/Solicitor

Dark Art Gin Limited
Incorporated: 7 March 2017   *Employees:* 1
Net Worth: £100   *Total Assets:* £1,186
Registered Office: 6 Redhall House Close, Edinburgh, EH14 1JN
Major Shareholder: Andrew Ronald Clark Hutchison
Officers: Andrew Ronald Clark Hutchison [1965] Director

Dark Matter Distillers Limited
Incorporated: 7 June 2012
Net Worth: £153,340   *Total Assets:* £377,564
Registered Office: Site 5 Burn O'Bennie Road, Banchory, Kincardineshire, AB31 5NN
Major Shareholder: James Ewen
Officers: John Michael Brett [1966] Director; Stephen Christopher Alexander Docherty [1970] Director; James Ewen [1968] Managing Director; Andrew Arthur Laing [1952] Director; Hugh Wilson McIntosh Little [1957] Director; William John Rattray [1958] Director

Dark Sky Spirits Ltd
Incorporated: 13 September 2017
Registered Office: Strathview, Well Road, Moffat, Dumfries & Galloway, DG10 9BH
Major Shareholder: Nicholas Ian Bullard
Officers: Nicholas Ian Bullard [1966] Director

Dark Spirits Company Limited
Incorporated: 3 April 2017
Registered Office: 31 Argyle Place, Edinburgh, EH9 1JT
Major Shareholder: Iain Ritchie Bell
Officers: Iain Ritchie Bell [1967] Director/Beverage Consultant; Jamie John MacDonald [1978] Director/Hospitality Consultant

Darlington Brewing and Distilling Company Ltd
Incorporated: 26 July 2013
Registered Office: 2 Park View, Middleton Tyas, Richmond, N Yorks, DL10 6SG
Shareholder: Ralph English Wilkinson
Officers: Gillian Margaret Wilkinson [1969] Director/Designer; Ralph English Wilkinson [1955] Director

Dartmoor Distillery Limited
Incorporated: 24 October 2013
Net Worth Deficit: £12,985 *Total Assets:* £58,638
Registered Office: Sigma House, Oak View Close, Edginswell Park, Torquay, Devon, TQ2 7FF
Officers: Ruth Coe, Secretary; Albyn Rodney Bolt [1962] Director/Businessman; Ruth Coe [1946] Company Secretary/Director; John Gregory Lawton [1964] Director; Timothy John Whitley [1950] Director/Farmer

Dartmoor Whisky Distillery Ltd
Incorporated: 16 February 2015
Net Worth: £83,388 *Total Assets:* £320,302
Registered Office: The Old Town Hall, Town Hall Place, Bovey Tracey, Newton Abbot, Devon, TQ13 9EG
Shareholders: Simon David Crow; Gregory Leslie Millar
Officers: Andrew Martin Clough, Secretary; Alison Mary Arnold [1965] Director/Property Manager; Guy Rory Arnold [1964] Director/Business Consultant; Simon David Crow [1963] Director; Gregory Leslie Millar [1965] Director

The Dartmouth Distillery Company Limited
Incorporated: 24 March 2017
Registered Office: Calancombe, Modbury, Ivybridge, Devon, PL21 0TU
Shareholders: Caroline Mary Whitehead; Lance James Whitehead
Officers: Martin Elliott Ranwell, Secretary; Caroline Mary Whitehead [1961] Director; Lance James Whitehead [1956] Director

De Facto Spirits Limited
Incorporated: 24 July 2018
Registered Office: Anderson House, 24 Rose Street, Aberdeen, AB10 1UA
Major Shareholder: Stuart Beange Duncan
Officers: Stuart Beange Duncan [1949] Director/Property Developer

Deco Spirits Limited
Incorporated: 26 July 2017
Registered Office: 55-57 High Street, Metheringham, Lincoln, LN4 3DZ
Shareholders: Samantha Ann Jones; Amy Jayne Havenhand
Officers: Amy Jayne Havenhand [1982] Director; Samantha Ann Jones [1985] Director

Deer Island Distillery Limited
Incorporated: 7 February 2019
Registered Office: Corran House, Craighouse, Isle of Jura, PA60 7XZ
Shareholders: Charlotte Gillett; Michael Walton
Officers: Charlotte Gillett [1986] Commercial Director; Michael Walton [1986] Director/Distiller

Deerness Distillery Ltd
Incorporated: 6 April 2016 *Employees:* 2
Net Worth Deficit: £3,578 *Total Assets:* £106,849
Registered Office: Newhall, Deerness, Orkney, KW17 2QJ
Major Shareholder: Stuart William Brown
Officers: Stuart William Brown [1974] Director/Distillery [British/Australian]

Deerstalker Whisky Company Limited
Incorporated: 7 May 2015
Registered Office: 16 Cairns Drive, Milngavie, Glasgow, G62 8AJ
Major Shareholder: Paul Michael Aston
Officers: Paul Michael Aston [1959] Director

Deeside Distillers Ltd
Incorporated: 25 February 2016
Net Worth Deficit: £18,850 *Total Assets:* £9,294
Registered Office: 58 Queens Road, Aberdeen, AB15 4YE
Major Shareholder: Paul Masterson
Officers: Paul Masterson [1978] Director/Engineering Consultant [Irish]

Delicious Drinks Limited
Incorporated: 16 May 2018
Registered Office: 18 Lynedoch Crescent, Glasgow, G3 6EQ
Shareholders: Christopher George Leggat; Caraline Sara Leggat
Officers: Caraline Sara Leggat [1982] Director; Christopher George Leggat [1981] Director

Demball Limited
Incorporated: 6 October 1988 *Employees:* 2
Net Worth: £2,078,421 *Total Assets:* £2,080,221
Registered Office: c/o Finance Associates, 65 London Wall, London, EC2M 5TU
Parent: The Nikka Whisky Distilling Co., Ltd.
Officers: Taketoshi Kishimoto [1959] Managing Director [Japanese]; Yoshisuke Motojima [1964] Director/Office Worker [Japanese]

Demon Vodka Limited
Incorporated: 28 November 2017
Registered Office: 16 Radford Crescent, Billericay, Essex, CM12 0DG
Major Shareholder: Philip Andrew Notley
Officers: Philip Andrew Notley [1967] Managing Director

Derbyshire Distillery Limited
Incorporated: 12 February 2018
Registered Office: Unit 2 Silver House, Adelphi Way, Staveley, Chesterfield, Derbys, S43 3LS
Shareholders: Philip Meakin; Anthony Carl Altman
Officers: Antony Carl Altman [1951] Director/Property Developer

Deshi Liqueur Ltd
Incorporated: 8 March 2005
Net Worth Deficit: £18,886 *Total Assets:* £172
Registered Office: 10 Kooringa, Warlingham, Surrey, CR6 9JP
Major Shareholder: John Anthony Francis Hugh Coulter
Officers: Rosalind Sylvia Ann Coulter, Secretary; Emma Margaret Coulter [1983] Director/Recruitment Consultant; John Anthony Francis Hugh Coulter [1943] Director; Rosalind Sylvia Ann Coulter [1946] Director/Secretary

Desire Drinks Limited
Incorporated: 27 April 2015
Net Worth Deficit: £4,482 *Total Assets:* £19,932
Registered Office: 228 Dewsbury Road, Leeds, LS11 6ER
Major Shareholder: Ian Edward Williams
Officers: Ian Edward Williams [1972] Director

Devine Distillates Group (Manufacturing) Ltd
Incorporated: 14 September 2018
Registered Office: 71-75 Shelton Street, Covent Garden, London, WC2H 9JQ
Shareholders: Peter Joseph Robson; Loch Shiel Whisky Ltd
Officers: Peter Joseph Robson, Secretary; Peter Joseph Robson [1959] Director

Devon Coast Distillery Limited
Incorporated: 16 May 2018
Registered Office: 8 King Street, Brixham, Devon, TQ5 9TW
Shareholders: Matthew Simon Collins; Andrew Graham Penrose
Officers: Matthew Simon Collins [1972] Director/Businessman; Andrew Graham Penrose [1970] Director/Businessman

Devon Distillery Limited
Incorporated: 20 December 2012 *Employees:* 2
Net Worth Deficit: £201,278 *Total Assets:* £189,845
Registered Office: Sigma House, Oak View Close, Edginswell Park, Torquay, Devon, TQ2 7FF
Major Shareholder: Cosmo Edward Caddy
Officers: Cosmo Edward Caddy [1982] Director

John Dewar and Sons Limited
Incorporated: 24 October 1958 *Employees:* 356
Net Worth: £188,070,000 *Total Assets:* £537,265,024
Registered Office: c/o Bacardi-Martini Limited, Bacardi Brown-Forman House, Kings Worthy, Winchester, Hants, SO23 7TW
Parent: Bacardi U.K. Limited
Officers: Jean Marc Lambert [1965] Director, Supply Chain and Manufacturing [French]; Iain MacGregor Lochhead [1962] Director/Executive; Ian Stuart Lowthian [1959] Chairman/Global Technical Director; Matthew James Phillips [1983] Finance Director; Paolo Camillo Tucci [1963] Finance Director

Deya Brewing Company Limited
Incorporated: 25 February 2015 *Employees:* 5
Net Worth: £2,444 *Total Assets:* £205,995
Registered Office: Preston Place, Preston, Cirencester, Glos, GL7 5PR
Shareholders: Aidan Patrick Bernard Freyne; Theodore Robert Sean Freyne
Officers: Aidan Patrick Bernard Freyne [1957] Director; Regine Patricia Freyne [1959] Director; Theodore Robert Sean Freyne [1990] Director

Diageo Balkans Limited
Incorporated: 14 July 1986 *Employees:* 7
Net Worth Deficit: £2,789,000 *Total Assets:* £866,000
Registered Office: Lakeside Drive, Park Royal, London, NW10 7HQ
Parent: Diageo Great Britain Limited
Officers: James Matthew Crayden Edmunds [1974] Director/Solicitor; Gabor Kovacs [1980] Director [Hungarian]; Kara Elizabeth Major [1977] Director [American]

Diageo Distilling Limited
Incorporated: 28 July 1914
Registered Office: Edinburgh Park, 5 Lochside Way, Edinburgh, EH12 9DT
Parent: Diageo Scotland Limited
Officers: James Matthew Crayden Edmunds [1974] Director/Solicitor; Gabor Kovacs [1980] Director [Hungarian]; Kara Elizabeth Major [1977] Director [American]

Diageo Great Britain Limited
Incorporated: 5 May 1952 *Employees:* 1,238
Net Worth: £2,988,000,000 *Total Assets:* £3,436,999,936
Registered Office: Lakeside Drive, Park Royal, London, NW10 7HQ
Parent: Grand Metropolitan Limited
Officers: Gavin Paul Crickmore [1958] Director/Chartered Accountant; James Matthew Crayden Edmunds [1974] Director/Solicitor; Sharon Lynnette Fennessy [1967] Director/Group Treasurer [Irish]; Kerryn Louise Haynes [1970] Director/Accountant; David Heginbottom [1970] Director/Group Treasurer; Hina Patel [1979] Director/Company Secretary Senior Assistant; Gabor Zeisler [1973] Director/General Manager [Hungarian]

Diageo Scotland Limited
Incorporated: 24 April 1877 *Employees:* 3,236
Net Worth: £2,122,000,000 *Total Assets:* £5,077,000,192
Registered Office: Edinburgh Park, 5 Lochside Way, Edinburgh, EH12 9DT
Parent: Diageo Great Britain Limited
Officers: Eduardo Peroni Barp [1968] Managing Director [Italian]; Gavin Paul Crickmore [1958] Director/Chartered Accountant; James Matthew Crayden Edmunds [1974] Director/Solicitor; Yvonne Elliott [1980] Director; Sharon Lynnette Fennessy [1967] Director/Group Treasurer [Irish]; Keith James Miller [1968] Director; Hina Patel [1979] Director/Company Secretary Senior Assistant; Gabor Zeisler [1973] Director/General Manager [Hungarian]

Dilly Dilly Limited
Incorporated: 7 June 2018
Registered Office: Hallgarth View, Middlefield Road, North Wheatley, Retford, Notts, DN22 9DA
Major Shareholder: David Anderson
Officers: David Anderson [1964] Commercial Director

Dimbandit Ltd
Incorporated: 4 June 2018
Registered Office: Office 3, 146-148 Bury Old Road, Whitefield, Manchester, M45 6AT
Shareholders: Gerson Alura; Josh Garcia
Officers: Gerson Alura [1990] Director [Filipino]

The Dirty Drinks Collective Limited
Incorporated: 12 April 2017
Registered Office: Unit 3, 33 North Cross Road, London, SE22 9ET
Shareholders: Magnum Brands Limited; Thirteen Innovation Holdings Ltd
Officers: Katherine Victoria Mafi [1977] Director

Distell International Holdings Limited
Incorporated: 8 April 2016
Net Worth: £16,970,308 *Total Assets:* £18,152,844
Registered Office: Avalon House, 72 Lower Mortlake Road, Richmond, Surrey, TW9 2JY
Parent: Distell Group Limited
Officers: Nwavudu Constance Ekebuisi, Secretary; Christopher John Blandford-Newson [1964] Director/Asset Management [British/South African]; Steven Jeffrey Nathan [1962] Director [South African]; Werner Nolte [1976] Finance Director [South African]; Fraser John Thornton [1969] Managing Director; Leonard Jacobus Volschenk [1971] Managing Director [South African]

Distell International Limited
Incorporated: 16 March 1988 *Employees:* 291
Previous: Burn Stewart Distillers Limited
Net Worth: £87,354,000 *Total Assets:* £171,064,992
Registered Office: 8 Milton Road, College Milton North, East Kilbride, S Lanarks, G74 5BU
Parent: Distell Group Limited
Officers: Nwavudu Constance Ekebuisi, Secretary; Werner Nolte [1976] Finance Director [South African]; Fraser John Thornton [1969] Director; Johan Van Zyl [1971] Supply Chain Director [South African]

Distill8 Limited
Incorporated: 18 June 2009
Net Worth Deficit: £40,640 *Total Assets:* £142
Registered Office: 30 Falcon View, Greens Norton, Towcester, Northants, NN12 8BT
Major Shareholder: Chris Smith
Officers: Christopher Stephen Smith [1959] Director/Marketeer

The UK Spirits Industry

Distilled Experience Ltd
Incorporated: 18 June 2018
Registered Office: 44 The Smithy, West Linton, Peebles-shire, EH46 7EZ
Major Shareholder: Ian Evans
Officers: Ian Evans [1953] Director

The Distillers of St.Andrews Limited
Incorporated: 6 February 2019
Registered Office: Unit 9 Bassaguard Estate, Bassaguard Business Park, St Andrews, Fife, KY16 8AL
Officers: Timothy George Edward Butler [1972] Director; Patrick Philip Mackey [1974] Director

Distillers of Surrey Limited
Incorporated: 22 September 2016
Registered Office: Chancery House, 30 St Johns Road, Woking, Surrey, GU21 7SA
Major Shareholder: Simon David Sherlock
Officers: Lianne Mary Sherlock, Secretary; Lianne Sherlock [1982] Director/Knowledge Manager; Simon David Sherlock [1980] Director/Distiller

Distillery 96 Limited
Incorporated: 28 September 2018
Registered Office: Heather Lea, Tockholes Road, Tockholes, Darwen, Lancs, BB3 0NR
Major Shareholder: Regan Toner
Officers: Regan Toner [1996] Director

Distillery Process Ltd
Incorporated: 28 November 2014
Registered Office: Unit 7 Alpha Centre, Stirling University, Innovation Park, Stirling, FK9 4NF
Shareholders: Ewen McDonald; Scott Duncan Allen
Officers: Ewen McDonald, Secretary; Scott Duncan Allen [1972] Director/Chemical Engineer

Distillutions Ltd
Incorporated: 31 August 2017 *Employees:* 2
Net Worth Deficit: £36,712 *Total Assets:* £21,097
Registered Office: 12 Traill Drive, Montrose, Angus, DD10 8SW
Major Shareholder: Paul Scothern
Officers: Lewis Scothern [1988] Director; Paul Scothern [1959] Director

Distinctively Orkney Drinks Ltd
Incorporated: 23 May 2017
Registered Office: Avari, 11 Moar Drive, Kirkwall, Orkney, KW15 1FS
Shareholders: Robert Scott Smith; Ingrid Noel Smith
Officers: Ingrid Noel Smith [1982] Director/Human Resources; Robert Scott Smith [1982] Director/Compliance

The Distinctly Different Spirits Company Ltd
Incorporated: 29 January 2018
Registered Office: 55 Dartmouth Road, Paignton, Devon, TQ4 5AE
Shareholder: Laurance Traverso
Officers: Laurance Traverso [1975] Director/Marketeer [Italian]

Ditchling Spirits Limited
Incorporated: 27 September 2018
Registered Office: Belmont Place, Belmont Road, Maidenhead, Berks, SL6 6TB
Major Shareholder: Crispin John Mair
Officers: Crispin John Mair [1970] Director

Docked Distillery International Limited
Incorporated: 26 March 2018
Registered Office: Basepoint Business Centre, Rivermead Drive, Swindon, Wilts, SN5 7EX
Shareholders: Andrea Susanne Bauder Fujarczuk; Cesar Vincent Remi Lefebvre
Officers: Andrea Susanne Bauder Fujarczuk [1986] Director [Canadian/Polish]; Cesar Vincent Remi Lefebvre [1986] Director [French]

Dockers Spirit Company Limited
Incorporated: 25 September 2018
Registered Office: 130 Old Street, London, EC1V 9BD
Officers: Robert Cowell [1983] Director/Train Driver (Present)

Doctor Bird Rum Ltd
Incorporated: 29 September 2017
Registered Office: 31b Grove Hill Road, London, SE5 8DF
Major Shareholder: Archibald Robert Burden
Officers: Archibald Robert Burden [1990] Director

Doggy John Distillery Limited
Incorporated: 30 September 2014
Registered Office: 55a Moore Park Road, London, SW6 2HH
Shareholder: Pavel Anastassov Marinov
Officers: Pavel Marinov [1990] Director/Consultant

Doghouse Distillery Limited
Incorporated: 9 December 2015 *Employees:* 3
Net Worth: £334,090 *Total Assets:* £614,778
Registered Office: Unit L, London Stone Business Estate, London, SW8 3QR
Major Shareholder: Braden Edward Saunders
Officers: Braden Edward Saunders [1976] Director [Australian]

Doncaster Dry Gin Limited
Incorporated: 27 February 2018
Registered Office: Unit 9 Armstrong House, First Avenue, Finningley, Doncaster, S Yorks, DN9 3GA
Major Shareholder: Michael Bennett
Officers: Michael Bennett [1956] Director/Accountant

Donnach Whisky Limited
Incorporated: 9 July 2010
Registered Office: Summit House, 4-5 Mitchell Street, Edinburgh, EH6 7BD
Major Shareholder: Nikolas Felix Prehn
Officers: Nikolas Felix Prehn [1980] Director [German]

Dormont Distilling Limited
Incorporated: 3 March 2017 *Employees:* 1
Net Worth: £273,279 *Total Assets:* £308,555
Registered Office: Dormont, Dalton, Lockerbie, Dumfries & Galloway, DG11 1DJ
Major Shareholder: Kit Carruthers
Officers: Dr. Kit Carruthers [1980] Director/Distiller

Dornoch Distillery Company Limited
Incorporated: 11 February 2013 *Employees:* 4
Previous: Black Isle Whisky Company Limited
Net Worth Deficit: £57,702 *Total Assets:* £267,280
Registered Office: Burn Farm Steading, Killen, Avoch, Highland, IV9 8RQ
Shareholders: Philip Duncan Thompson; Simon Lowthian Thompson
Officers: Philip Duncan Thompson, Secretary; Philip Duncan Thompson [1986] Director/Hotel Manager; Simon Lowthian Thompson [1984] Director/Hotel Manager

Dowdeswell Distillery Limited
Incorporated: 21 August 2018
Registered Office: 93 London Road, Cheltenham, Glos, GL52 6HL
Officers: Clarice Bijou Elliott-Berry [1993] Director

Downton Distillery Limited
Incorporated: 5 September 2017
Registered Office: The Manor House Cottage, Barford Lane, Downton, Salisbury, Wilts, SP5 3PU
Officers: Hugh Anderson, Secretary; Hugh Anderson [1972] Director/Programme Management; Charles Andrews [1970] Director/Self Employed

Dr Adam Elmegirabs Bitters Ltd
Incorporated: 15 November 2012
Net Worth Deficit: £2,631 *Total Assets:* £52,683
Registered Office: The House of Botanicals, Arch 4 Palmerston Road, Aberdeen, AB11 5RE
Major Shareholder: Adam Abdulrahim Elmegirab
Officers: Adam Abdulrahim Elmegirab [1982] Director/Spirit Compounder

Dr Eamers Emporium Limited
Incorporated: 21 February 2017
Registered Office: 24 Bryan Budd Close, Rowley Regis, W Midlands, B65 9BB
Officers: Jordan Lunn [1985] Director/Consultant; Lorna Lunn [1984] Director/Teacher

Dr Gin Limited
Incorporated: 24 September 2018
Registered Office: Flat 134, 14 Rossetti Road, London, SE16 3EZ
Major Shareholder: Martin John Law
Officers: Dr Martin John Law [1986] Commercial Director

Dr Junipers Ltd.
Incorporated: 23 February 2018
Registered Office: 4 Maryland House, Georgia Close, Bootle, Merseyside, L20 4FE
Officers: Dan John Duggan Edwards [1992] Director; Carly Riley [1986] Director

Dr Scotch Whisky Ltd.
Incorporated: 6 September 2012 *Employees:* 2
Net Worth Deficit: £32,068 *Total Assets:* £3,594,184
Registered Office: 4 Royal Crescent, Glasgow, G3 7SL
Shareholders: Christine Barnes; Douglas Charles Ross
Officers: Christine Barnes [1964] Director/Accountant; Douglas Charles Ross [1962] Director

Dram in a Can Limited
Incorporated: 4 September 2017
Registered Office: 3 Hillpark Brae, Munlochy, Ross & Cromarty, IV8 8PL
Officers: Dawn Louise MacLeod [1977] Director/Founder

Drambuie Liqueur Company Ltd. (The)
Incorporated: 29 June 1927
Net Worth: £15,792,000 *Total Assets:* £15,869,000
Registered Office: Phoenix Crescent, Strathclyde Business Park, Bellshill, N Lanarks, ML4 3AN
Parent: Drambuie Limited
Officers: Ewan John Henderson [1968] Director/Accountant; Michael Lamont [1960] Director

Drimnin Estate Trading Limited
Incorporated: 29 June 2015
Registered Office: Drimnin House, Drimnin, Oban, Argyll & Bute, PA80 5XZ
Major Shareholder: Derek Compton Lewis
Officers: Derek Compton Lewis [1946] Director; Louise Lewis [1949] Director/Counsellor

Drink It Limited
Incorporated: 23 February 2005 *Employees:* 1
Net Worth Deficit: £15,348 *Total Assets:* £2,843
Registered Office: 75 High Street, Boston, Lincs, PE21 8SX
Major Shareholder: Claire Louisa Hall
Officers: Jessica Ruth Hall, Secretary; Claire Louisa Hall [1982] Director/Project Manager

Drinkology Limited
Incorporated: 3 July 2017
Registered Office: 65 Cherwell Drive, Marston, Oxford, OX3 0ND
Shareholders: Sukhveer Singh Mattu; Amandeep Kaur Vig
Officers: Sukhveer Singh Mattu [1990] Director/Accountant; Amandeep Kaur Vig [1985] Director/Accountant

Drinks of Manchester Limited
Incorporated: 14 December 2015 *Employees:* 7
Net Worth: £173,344 *Total Assets:* £427,028
Registered Office: 125 Buckingham Road, Manchester, M21 0RG
Parent: Spirit of Manchester Distilley Ltd
Officers: Sebastian Richard John Heeley [1986] Director; Jennie Louise Wiggins [1983] Director

Drops of Juniper Limited
Incorporated: 7 June 2018
Registered Office: Hallgarth View, Middlefield Road, North Wheatley, Retford, Notts, DN22 9DA
Major Shareholder: David Anderson
Officers: David Anderson [1964] Director

Droylsden Craft Limited
Incorporated: 3 September 2018
Registered Office: 50 Clough Road, Droylsden, Manchester, M43 7NG
Major Shareholder: Anthony Thomas Conway
Officers: Anthony Thomas Conway [1990] Director/Manager

Druid's Distillery Ltd
Incorporated: 13 November 2018
Registered Office: 176 Franciscan Road, Tooting, London, SW17 8HH
Shareholders: Jamie Edwards; Lucie Signolet
Officers: Jamie Edwards [1987] Director; Lucie Signolet [1989] Director [French]

Drumeland Distillery Ltd
Incorporated: 9 August 2018
Registered Office: 69 Fergort Road, Derrynoose, Keady, Co Armagh, BT60 3DN
Major Shareholder: Enda McGrane
Officers: Dr Enda McGrane [1968] Director/Dental Surgeon

Duchy Beverages Ltd
Incorporated: 11 June 2018
Registered Office: 1 Elm Cottages, Park Bottom, Redruth, Cornwall, TR15 3XJ
Major Shareholder: Dean Apollo Bungay
Officers: Dean Apollo Bungay [1988] Director

Duck and Crutch Limited
Incorporated: 20 April 2017
Net Worth Deficit: £2,898 *Total Assets:* £10,363
Registered Office: 11b Boundary Road, Buckingham Road Industrial Estate, Brackley, Northants, NN13 7ES
Officers: George Brooker [1992] Director; Hollie Freestone [1989] Director/Marketing Consultant

Duckenfield Ltd
Incorporated: 18 June 2013
Net Worth Deficit: £1,100
Registered Office: Annecy Court, Ferry Works, Summer Road, Thames Ditton, Surrey, KT7 0QJ
Major Shareholder: Jane Caroline Duckenfield
Officers: Jane Caroline Duckenfield, Secretary; James Jeffrey Duckenfield [1973] Director; Jane Caroline Duckenfield [1976] Director/Doctor

The Duke's Distilling Company Limited
Incorporated: 29 July 2013
Registered Office: Unit 10 Silver End Business Park, Brettell Lane, Brierley Hill, W Midlands, DY5 3LG
Major Shareholder: Dominic Michael John Carter
Officers: Dominic Michael John Carter [1966] Director

Dulwich Gin Limited
Incorporated: 11 September 2018
Registered Office: 59 Calton Avenue, London, SE21 7DF
Major Shareholder: Morven Fiona Shaw
Officers: Morven Fiona Shaw [1976] Director

Dun Eideann Scotch Whisky Company Limited
Incorporated: 12 July 1995
Registered Office: Edradour Distillery, Pitlochry, Perthshire, PH16 5JP
Major Shareholder: Andrew William Symington
Officers: Graham Keith Cox, Secretary; Andrew William Symington [1963] Managing Director

Dunbar Drinks Company Limited
Incorporated: 5 June 2014
Registered Office: 1 Roxburghe Terrace, Dunbar, E Lothian, EH42 1LW
Officers: George James Thompson, Secretary; George James Thompson [1957] Director

The Dundee Distillery Company Limited
Incorporated: 24 February 2014
Registered Office: 138 Nethergate, Dundee, DD1 4ED
Major Shareholder: John Neil McHattie
Officers: Iain John McHattie, Secretary; John McHattie [1950] Director

Dunnet Bay Distillers Ltd.
Incorporated: 15 July 2013 *Employees:* 11
Net Worth: £624,758 *Total Assets:* £987,089
Registered Office: Ribbon House, Dunnet, Thurso, Caithness, Sutherland, KW14 8YD
Shareholders: Martin John Murray; Claire Margaret Murray
Officers: Claire Margaret Murray [1981] Director/Events Organiser; Martin John Murray [1981] Director/Process Engineer

Dunnford Craft Distillers Ltd
Incorporated: 26 February 2018
Registered Office: 50 Murray Street, Chapelton, Stonehaven, Aberdeenshire, AB39 8AJ
Officers: Kevin Dunn [1988] Director/Master Distiller

Dunville & Co. Limited
Incorporated: 8 August 1975
Net Worth: £1,960 *Total Assets:* £13,882
Registered Office: Eurocables, 1 West Bank Road, Belfast Harbour Estate, Belfast, BT3 9JL
Officers: Jarlath Francis Watson, Secretary; Shane Joseph Braniff [1963] Director; Jarlath Francis Watson [1972] Director/Accountant [Irish]

Duration Brewing Ltd
Incorporated: 5 April 2017 *Employees:* 2
Net Worth Deficit: £62,283 *Total Assets:* £15,542
Registered Office: Westacre Estate Office, Church Green, West Acre, King's Lynn, Norfolk, PE32 1TS
Officers: Derek Seth Bates [1981] Director [American]; Miranda Lilian Hudson [1975] Director; Lewis Benedict Sinclair Marten [1976] Director/Business Executive

Durham Distillery Limited
Incorporated: 27 April 2017
Registered Office: Unit 2F & 2G Riverside Industrial Estate, Langley Park, Co Durham, DH7 9TT
Major Shareholder: Jonathan David Chadwick
Officers: Jonathan David Chadwick [1968] Director

Durham Gin Limited
Incorporated: 12 February 2013
Net Worth: £35,032 *Total Assets:* £520,394
Registered Office: High Carr House, High Carr Road, Durham, DH1 5AT
Major Shareholder: Jonathan David Chadwick
Officers: Jonathan David Chadwick [1968] Director; Jessica Louise Tomlinson [1988] Director/Distiller

Dutch Courage Spirits Limited
Incorporated: 17 August 2016
Net Worth: £1,108 *Total Assets:* £2,819
Registered Office: Leschangie House, Leschangie, Kemnay, Inverurie, Aberdeenshire, AB51 5PP
Officers: Scott Rose [1969] Managing Director

DWD Whiskey Company Ltd
Incorporated: 9 February 2018
Registered Office: 12-15 Donegall Square West, Belfast, BT1 6JH
Major Shareholder: Raymond McLaughlin
Officers: Raymond McLaughlin [1980] Director [Irish]

Dyfi Distillery Ltd
Incorporated: 5 August 2015 *Employees:* 3
Net Worth: £66,735 *Total Assets:* £152,164
Registered Office: Gallteinion, Commins Coch, Machynlleth, Powys, SY20 8LS
Shareholders: Peter Douglas Cameron; Daniel Malcolm Cameron
Officers: Daniel Malcolm Cameron [1966] Director; Peter Douglas Cameron [1963] Director

Ealing Distillery Ltd
Incorporated: 8 October 2018
Registered Office: 50 Webster Gardens, Ealing, London, W5 5ND
Shareholders: Amanda Jane Duncan; Simon Francis Anson Duncan
Officers: Amanda Jane Duncan [1967] Director; Simon Francis Anson Duncan [1967] Director

The East India Company Gin Limited
Incorporated: 26 August 2015
Net Worth Deficit: £1,546 *Total Assets:* £114,618
Registered Office: 7-8 Conduit Street, London, W1S 2XF
Officers: Abhijit Banerjee [1963] Director/Service Employed; Zhooben Dossabhay Bhiwandiwala [1959] Director [Indian]; Sanjiv Mahendra Mehta [1961] Director; Samrat Ashok Navale [1976] Director [Indian]

The East India Company London Dry Gin Ltd
Incorporated: 17 June 2010
Net Worth: £2 *Total Assets:* £2
Registered Office: 39 St James's Street, London, SW1A 1JD
Major Shareholder: Robin Chapman
Officers: Robin Chapman, Secretary; Robin Chapman [1947] Director/Lawyer

East London Liquor Company Limited
Incorporated: 24 May 2013 *Employees:* 32
Net Worth Deficit: £853,232 *Total Assets:* £1,482,015
Registered Office: 23 Exmouth Market, London, EC1R 4QL
Shareholder: Alexander Michael Wolpert
Officers: Jon Andreas Akerlund [1971] Director [Swedish]; Scott Chillery [1970] Finance Director; Marc Francis-Baum [1971] Director; Patrik Ulf Mattias Franzen [1971] Director [Swedish]; Alexander Michael Ramin Wolpert [1982] Director

East Neuk Organic Brewing & Distilling Ltd
Incorporated: 16 January 2017
Net Worth Deficit: £20,242 *Total Assets:* £64,209
Registered Office: Unit 2 The Bowhouse, St Monans, Fife, KY10 2FB
Shareholders: Stephen Joseph Marshall; Lucy Catherine Hine
Officers: Lucy Catherine Hine [1983] Director; Stephen Joseph Marshall [1976] Director

Eastwater Gin Ltd
Incorporated: 27 November 2018
Registered Office: Eastwater House, Snowdenham Lane, Bramley, Surrey, GU5 0DB
Major Shareholder: Nicholas David Harry Beevers
Officers: Nicholas David Harry Beevers [1979] Director/Founder; Rosanna Charlotte Phillips [1995] Director/Founder

EB Alexandria Ltd
Incorporated: 22 March 1988
Registered Office: 1 Anthony Road, Largs, N Ayrshire, KA30 8EQ
Parent: LLDY Alexandria Ltd
Officers: Henry John Jagielko, Secretary/Accountant; Alexander Bulloch [1927] Director; Henry John Jagielko [1952] Director/Accountant

Eccentric Gin Co Limited
Incorporated: 29 April 2014
Net Worth Deficit: £62,344 *Total Assets:* £240,106
Registered Office: Tyn Y Cae Cottage, Groes Faen Road, Peterston-Super-Ely, Cardiff, CF5 6NE
Shareholder: Robert William Higgins
Officers: Robert William Higgins [1956] Director

The Ecclefechan Whisky Company Limited
Incorporated: 4 July 2000
Net Worth Deficit: £495 *Total Assets:* £5,292
Registered Office: 87 Kingstown Broadway, Kingstown Industrial Estate, Carlisle, Cumbria, CA3 0HA
Officers: Steven Cremin [1976] Director/Paramedic; Bryan Graham [1943] Director/Joiner; John Malcolm Hogg [1950] Director/Farmer; William Fredrick Horsburgh [1942] Director; Ian Edward Park [1958] Director; Robert Alfred Park [1964] Director/Electrical Engineer; William Reid [1943] Director/Consultant Obstetrician & Gynaecologist; Steven John Tyler [1957] Director/Builder; Derek Scott Wallace [1946] Director/Oil Distributor

Echlinville Distillery Limited
Incorporated: 2 December 2004 *Employees:* 18
Net Worth: £538,720 *Total Assets:* £3,634,831
Registered Office: 62 Gransha Road, Kircubbin, Newtownards, Co Down, BT22 1AJ
Shareholders: Shane Joseph Braniff; Lynn Braniff
Officers: Jarlath Francis Watson, Secretary; Carolynn Braniff [1962] Director; Shane Joseph Braniff [1963] Director; Jarlath Francis Watson [1972] Director/Accountant [Irish]

The Edale Gin Company Limited
Incorporated: 3 April 2018
Registered Office: Western House, Grindsbrook Booth, Edale, Hope Valley, Derbys, S33 7ZD
Major Shareholder: Alice Dammery-Quigley
Officers: Alice Dammery-Quigley [1991] Director

Eden Mill Distillers Ltd
Incorporated: 23 March 2018
Registered Office: Eden Mill, Glasgow Business Park, Glasgow, G69 6GA
Major Shareholder: Anthony Kelly
Officers: Anthony Gerard Kelly, Secretary; Anthony Kelly [1963] Director [Irish]; Anthony Gerard Kelly [1991] Director; Paul Miller [1961] Director

The Edge Gin Ltd
Incorporated: 4 July 2018
Registered Office: Cloth Hall, 150 Drake Street, Rochdale, Lancs, OL16 1PX
Shareholders: Michael Kevin Ryan; Clare Louise Ryan
Officers: Clare Louise Ryan [1977] Director; Michael Kevin Ryan [1968] Director

The Edinburgh and Leith Distillery Limited
Incorporated: 8 September 2018
Registered Office: Mitchell House, Mitchell Street, Edinburgh, EH6 7BD
Parent: John Crabbie & Company Limited
Officers: Stewart Andrew Hainsworth [1969] Director/Chief Executive Officer; Alan William Robinson [1965] Finance Director

Edinburgh Distillers Limited
Incorporated: 12 April 2018
Registered Office: 17-21 East Mayfield, Edinburgh, EH9 1SE
Major Shareholder: Sandy Herd
Officers: Sandy Herd [1968] Director

The Edinburgh Distillery Company Ltd.
Incorporated: 14 July 2014
Registered Office: 43 Craiglockhart Gardens, Edinburgh, EH14 1LZ
Shareholder: Gregor Alexander Jack Mathieson
Officers: Gregor Alexander Jack Mathieson [1967] Director; Gordon Robert Watt [1965] Director

Edinburgh Gin Limited
Incorporated: 26 September 2013
Registered Office: Russell House, Dunnet Way, East Mains Industrial Estate, Broxburn, W Lothian, EH52 5BU
Parent: Ian MacLeod Distillers Ltd
Officers: Leonard Stuart Russell [1961] Director; Michael James Younger [1960] Director

The Edinburgh Rum Company Limited
Incorporated: 19 January 2017
Registered Office: 22 Garscube Terrace, Edinburgh, EH12 6BQ
Major Shareholder: Bruce Gordon Fraser Casely
Officers: Bruce Casely, Secretary; Bruce Gordon Fraser Casely [1971] Finance Director

Edinburgh Whisky Ltd.
Incorporated: 10 May 2013
Registered Office: 15 Atholl Crescent, Edinburgh, EH3 8HA
Shareholder: Gregor Alexander Jack Mathieson
Officers: Iain Lindsay Hamilton [1955] Director; Gregor Alexander Jack Mathieson [1967] Director; Gordon Robert Watt [1965] Director

Edmunds Cocktails Ltd
Incorporated: 26 November 2018
Registered Office: 92 Barons Road, Bury St Edmunds, Suffolk, IP33 2LY
Major Shareholder: Tom Mayes
Officers: Tom Mayes [1988] Director/Salesman

Edradour Distillery Company Limited
Incorporated: 19 June 2002 *Employees:* 16
Net Worth: £17,537,428 *Total Assets:* £17,985,994
Registered Office: Edradour Distillery, Pitlochry, Perthshire, PH16 5JP
Major Shareholder: Andrew William Symington
Officers: Graham Keith Cox, Secretary; Graham Keith Cox [1947] Director/Solicitor; Andrew William Symington [1963] Director/Chief Executive Officer

Edrington Distillers Limited
Incorporated: 31 January 1927 *Employees:* 562
Net Worth: £111,700,000 *Total Assets:* £165,700,000
Registered Office: 100 Queen Street, Glasgow, G1 3DN
Parent: The Edrington Group Limited
Officers: Martin Alexander Cooke, Secretary; Martin Alexander Cooke [1961] Director/Company Secretary; Ian Barrett Curle [1961] Director; Graham Robert Hutcheon [1963] Director; Paul Andrew Hyde [1972] Director/Chartered Accountant; Scott John McCroskie [1967] Director/Chartered Accountant

The Edrington Group Limited
Incorporated: 25 April 1961 *Employees:* 2,255
Net Worth: £429,500,000 *Total Assets:* £1,904,000,000
Registered Office: 100 Queen Street, Glasgow, G1 3DN
Parent: Kintail Trustees Limited
Officers: Martin Alexander Cooke, Secretary; Alice Mary Cleoniki Avis [1962] Director; Ian Barrett Curle [1961] Director; Stefanie FitzGenerald [1961] Director/Marketing Vice President [German]; Crawford Scott Gillies [1956] Director; Graham Robert Hutcheon [1963] Director/Chemical Engineer; Paul Andrew Hyde [1972] Director/Accountant; Scott John McCroskie [1967] Director/Chartered Accountant; David Hedley Richardson [1951] Director/Chartered Accountant

Eight Vodka Limited
Incorporated: 8 November 2018
Registered Office: 12th Floor, 6 New Street Square, London, EC4A 3BF
Shareholders: Juan David Vintimilla Palacios; Jason Kingsley Drummond
Officers: Jason Kingsley Drummond [1969] Director

El Gin Findrassie Ltd
Incorporated: 20 July 2015 *Employees:* 2
Net Worth: £958 *Total Assets:* £24,125
Registered Office: Findrassie House, Findrassie, Elgin, Moray, IV30 5PS
Shareholder: Leah Catherine Miller
Officers: Leah Catherine Miller [1975] Director/Operations Manager

El Pulpo Loco Ltd
Incorporated: 22 January 2019
Registered Office: 28 Mast Lane, North Shields, Tyne & Wear, NE30 3DE
Shareholders: Vincent Allen; Angus Robertson Wear
Officers: Dr Vincent Allen [1967] Director/Physicist; Angus Robertson Wear [1964] Director/Veterinary Scientist

Electric Spirit Company Ltd.
Incorporated: 29 December 2014 *Employees:* 1
Net Worth: £7,962 *Total Assets:* £23,569
Registered Office: 25 Lauderdale Street, Edinburgh, EH9 1DE
Major Shareholder: James Porteous
Officers: James Porteous [1986] Director

Elephant Gin Ltd
Incorporated: 27 September 2012 *Employees:* 10
Net Worth: £529,549 *Total Assets:* £1,003,937
Registered Office: 22 Mount Ephraim, Tunbridge Wells, Kent, TN4 8AS
Shareholders: Robin Gerlach; Tessa Elisabeth Gerlach
Officers: Robin Gerlach, Secretary; Robin Gerlach [1984] Director/Founder [German]; Tessa Elisabeth Gerlach [1986] Director/Film and TV Financing [German]

Elgin Bonding Company Limited
Incorporated: 23 November 1965
Registered Office: George House, Boroughbriggs Road, Elgin, Moray, IV30 1JY
Parent: Speymalt Whisky Distributors Ltd
Officers: Norman Ross, Secretary; Ewen Cameron Mackintosh [1968] Whisky Supply Director; Stephen Alexander Masson Rankin [1971] UK Sales Director; Neil Edward Urquhart [1975] Logistics & Facilities Director

Ellon Spirit Company Ltd
Incorporated: 12 February 2019
Registered Office: 4 Lomond Crescent, Ellon, Aberdeenshire, AB41 9GE
Major Shareholder: Kieren Sean Murphy
Officers: Kieren Sean Murphy [1993] Director/General Manager

Elstead Village Distillers Limited
Incorporated: 10 August 2017
Registered Office: West House, Milford Road, Elstead, Godalming, Surrey, GU8 6HF
Shareholders: Christine Anne Shubrook; Neil Andrew Redit
Officers: Neil Andrew Redit [1966] Director; Christine Anne Shubrook [1960] Director; Paul Richard Shubrook [1948] Director

The Ely Gin Company Ltd.
Incorporated: 14 November 2011 Employees: 6
Net Worth: £87,099 Total Assets: £136,975
Registered Office: 83 St Johns Road, Ely, Cambs, CB6 3BW
Shareholders: James Michael Clark; Nancy Maria Rita de Cleir
Officers: James Michael Clark [1974] Director/Manufacturer

Ely's Cocktails Ltd
Incorporated: 14 May 2018
Registered Office: Sagittarius, 4th Floor, Golderbrook House, 15-19 Great Titchfield Street, London, W1W 8AZ
Parent: Ely's Cocktails SAS
Officers: Ely Niang-Fall [1987] Director/Officer [French]; Guillaume Sudre [1985] Director/Chief Executive Officer (CEO) [French]

Empire Bar Service Ltd
Incorporated: 6 October 2016 Employees: 2
Net Worth Deficit: £2,340 Total Assets: £7,648
Registered Office: 25 Balham High Road, London, SW12 9AL
Officers: Nick Giorgio [1969] Director/Business Administrator

Empirical Trading Co. Limited
Incorporated: 26 September 2017
Registered Office: 21 Bedford Square, London, WC1B 3HH
Parent: Empirical IVS
Officers: Mark Emil Tholstrup Hermansen [1986] Director/Chief Executive Officer [Danish]

EMS Corp Limited
Incorporated: 10 February 2009
Net Worth: £303,308 Total Assets: £336,169
Registered Office: 5 Talbot Road, London, N6 4QS
Shareholders: Sacred Spirits Holdings Ltd; Ian Nicholas Hart
Officers: Ian Hart, Secretary; Ian Nicholas Hart [1965] Director/Consulting; Hilary Whitney [1962] Director

Engin Yard Beverage Co Ltd
Incorporated: 19 July 2018
Registered Office: Park View, 14 Central Parade, Shildon, Co Durham, DL4 1DL
Major Shareholder: Ruth Edith Stephenson
Officers: Ruth Edith Stephenson, Secretary; Ruth Edith Stephenson [1980] Director

English Whisky Co. Limited
Incorporated: 12 February 1981 Employees: 2
Net Worth: £1,822,410 Total Assets: £2,327,734
Registered Office: Roudham House, East Harling, Norwich, NR16 2RJ
Major Shareholder: Andrew Leethem Nelstrop
Officers: Andrew Leethem Nelstrop, Secretary; Andrew Leethem Nelstrop [1971] Director/Farmer; Barbara Ann Nelstrop [1942] Director; Kathryn Anna Nelstrop [1979] Marketing Director

Eoforwic Distilling Company Limited
Incorporated: 21 December 2016
Net Worth: £724 Total Assets: £724
Registered Office: 6 Lynwood View, Copmanthorpe, York, YO23 3SW
Officers: Richard Stark, Secretary; Richard Stark [1972] Director/Marketing Manager

Equilibrium Food & Drink Ltd
Incorporated: 8 January 2018
Registered Office: 231 London Road, Sheffield, S2 4NF
Shareholders: Anthony James Lowe; Wendy Ann Lowe
Officers: Anthony James Lowe [1963] Director

Escubac Limited
Incorporated: 7 March 2014 Employees: 2
Net Worth: £54,433 Total Assets: £59,933
Registered Office: 84b Tyrwhitt Road, London, SE4 1QB
Shareholders: Daniel Arthur Fisher; Andrew Smith
Officers: Daniel Arthur Fisher [1982] Director/Executive [American]; Andrew MacLeod Smith [1983] Director/Distiller

Esker Spirits Ltd
Incorporated: 16 October 2015 Employees: 3
Net Worth Deficit: £62,552 Total Assets: £19,972
Registered Office: 1 Westhall Workshops, Kincardine O'Neil, Aboyne, Aberdeenshire, AB34 5AD
Shareholders: Steven Duthie; Lynne Joan Duthie
Officers: Lynne Joan Duthie [1972] Director; Steven Duthie [1971] Director; Alan David Fergusson [1970] Director

Espensen Spirit Ltd
Incorporated: 2 June 2015 Employees: 5
Net Worth Deficit: £213,796 Total Assets: £48,818
Registered Office: Penrose House, 67 Hightown Road, Banbury, Oxon, OX16 9BE
Shareholders: Philippa Charlotte Gillies; Sam Kim Asta Espensen
Officers: Sam Kim Asta Espensen [1973] Director; Philippa Charlotte Gillies [1955] Director

Esq Vodka Limited
Incorporated: 21 August 2018
Registered Office: 8 Button Bridge, Kinlet, Bewdley, Worcs, DY12 3DH
Shareholder: Andrew James Burns
Officers: Steven Banyard [1972] Director [South African]; Andrew James Burns [1968] Director

The Ethereal Cut Limited
Incorporated: 21 June 2018
Registered Office: 4 Hop Gardens, Farnham, Surrey, GU10 5DQ
Officers: Lisa Claire Prichard [1980] Director; Mark Prichard [1980] Director

Etoh Studio Limited
Incorporated: 25 April 2017
Net Worth Deficit: £22,077 Total Assets: £29,614
Registered Office: 89 Leigh Road, Eastleigh, Hants, SO50 9DQ
Major Shareholder: Omar Sharif Mohamed Bakhaty
Officers: Omar Sharif Mohamed Bakhaty [1988] Director

Etrusca Brewery & Distillery in St. Andrews Ltd
Incorporated: 31 December 2015
Registered Office: 59 Bonnygate, Cupar, Fife, KY15 4BY
Major Shareholder: Giorgio Cozzolino
Officers: Giorgio Cozzolino [1964] Director [Italian]

WJ Evans a'i Gwmni (Ynys Enlli) Cyf
Incorporated: 30 November 2018
Registered Office: 20 Penlan, Pwllheli, Gwynedd, LL53 5DE
Shareholders: Colin Sion Evans; Mair Elizabeth Evans
Officers: Colin Sion Evans, Secretary; Colin Sion Evans [1975] Director; Mair Elizabeth Evans [1974] Director

H.B. Evelyo Ltd.
Incorporated: 28 November 2017
Registered Office: 2nd Floor, Stratus House, Emperor Way, Exeter Business Park, Exeter, Devon, EX1 3QS
Major Shareholder: Philip Everett-Lyons
Officers: Philip Everett-Lyons [1983] Director

Evolution Brewing Ltd
Incorporated: 28 November 2018
Registered Office: Sixty Six North Quay, Great Yarmouth, Norfolk, NR30 1HE
Shareholders: Pilson Group Limited; Samantha Jane Elliott; Gordon Fisher
Officers: Samantha Jane Elliott [1986] Director; Kenneth John Turner [1949] Director

The Exeter Distillery Ltd
Incorporated: 21 August 2017
Registered Office: 2 John Street, Exeter, EX1 1BL
Major Shareholder: Hamish James Gurmin Lothian
Officers: Hamish James Gurmin Lothian [1968] Director

Exeter Gin Ltd
Incorporated: 26 January 2017
Net Worth Deficit: £15,414 *Total Assets:* £25,560
Registered Office: Redwoods Accountants, 2 Clyst Works, Clyst Road, Exeter, EX3 0DB
Major Shareholder: Karen Yvonne Skerratt
Officers: Karen Yvonne Skerratt [1960] Director; Michael David Alexander Skerratt [1966] Director; Lyndsey Ellen Terrell [1983] Director

Exmoor Distillers Ltd
Incorporated: 11 January 2017 *Employees:* 2
Net Worth Deficit: £6,034 *Total Assets:* £47,192
Registered Office: Millennium House, Brannam Crescent, Roundswell Business Park, Barnstaple, Devon, EX31 3TD
Shareholders: John Patrick Cadney; Yuli Cadney
Officers: John Patrick Cadney [1953] Director; Yuli Cadney [1961] Director [Malaysian]

Exploration Distillation Limited
Incorporated: 10 December 2018
Registered Office: 7 Hill Bottom Close, Whitchurch Hill, Reading, Berks, RG8 7PX
Major Shareholder: Anthony Coupland
Officers: Anthony Coupland [1992] Director/Engineer

F.W Exports Ltd
Incorporated: 6 August 2018
Registered Office: 505 Great Western Road, Glasgow, G12 8HN
Shareholders: William Woodburn; Ross David Frame
Officers: Ross David Frame [1990] Director; William Woodburn [1988] Director

Fablas Limited
Incorporated: 3 November 2014
Registered Office: Craigfryn, Caersws Road, Pontdolgoch, Caersws, Powys, SY17 5JD
Shareholders: Mark Jackson; Gillian Vanessa Davies
Officers: Gillian Vanessa Davies [1958] Director; Mark Jackson [1957] Director

Faiers Distillery Ltd
Incorporated: 3 September 2018
Registered Office: 6 The Street, Raydon, Ipswich, Suffolk, IP7 5LP
Major Shareholder: Rory James Faiers
Officers: Rory James Faiers [1987] Director

Fairfields Liqueurs Ltd
Incorporated: 26 July 2018
Registered Office: 36 Cordale Road, Basingstoke, Hants, RG21 3LX
Major Shareholder: Duncan Paul McLeod
Officers: Duncan Paul McLeod [1974] Director/Salesman

Faith and Sons Limited
Incorporated: 8 October 2013
Net Worth Deficit: £40 *Total Assets:* £20,074
Registered Office: 59 Rixtonleys Drive, Irlam, Manchester, M44 6RN
Shareholder: Maria Joao Ferreira Silva
Officers: Maria Joao Ferreira Silva [1982] Director [Portuguese]; Filipe Miguel Sequeira Rocha Sousa [1978] Director [Portuguese]

Fal River Distillery Limited
Incorporated: 13 December 2017
Registered Office: Trevone Quarry, Trevone, Mabe Burnthouse, Penryn, Cornwall, TR10 9JQ
Major Shareholder: Eleanor Mary Louise Demaus
Officers: Eleanor Mary Louise Demaus [1991] Director

Falkirk Gin Ltd
Incorporated: 16 January 2018
Registered Office: Atrium House, Callendar Business Park, Falkirk, Stirlingshire, FK1 1XR
Major Shareholder: George Danskin Stewart
Officers: George Danskin Stewart [1945] Managing Director

Falkirk Whisky Ltd
Incorporated: 29 November 2018
Registered Office: Atrium House, Callendar Business Park, Falkirk, FK1 1XR
Major Shareholder: George Danskin Stewart
Officers: George Danskin Stewart [1945] Director/Manager

Falmouth Gin Limited
Incorporated: 19 January 2018
Registered Office: 21 Brean Down Road, Plymouth, PL3 5PU
Shareholder: Alexander Charles Bernhardt de Vries
Officers: Alexander Charles Bernhardt de Vries [1985] Director/Surveyor

Family of Hounds Limited
Incorporated: 18 November 2016 *Employees:* 1
Net Worth Deficit: £60,267 *Total Assets:* £41,226
Registered Office: c/o Anthony Cowen, 1st Floor, Stanmore House, 15-19 Church Road, Stanmore, Middlesex, HA7 4AR
Shareholders: Andrea Frigerio; Lina Adeeb
Officers: Andrea Frigerio [1977] Director [Italian]

Fancy A Tipple Limited
Incorporated: 3 May 2016
Net Worth Deficit: £2,458 *Total Assets:* £1,954
Registered Office: 3 Greengate, Cardale Park, Harrogate, N Yorks, HG3 1GY
Shareholders: Sarah Lianne Botham; Judith McCourt; Darren James David Shield
Officers: Sarah Lianne Botham [1979] Director; Judith McCourt [1972] Director; Darren James David Shield [1982] Director

Fanny's Distilling Company Limited
Incorporated: 1 August 2013
Net Worth Deficit: £50,984 *Total Assets:* £223,099
Registered Office: 63 Saltaire Road, Shipley, W Yorks, BD18 3JN
Major Shareholder: Spencer Marcus Lund
Officers: Linda Jane Harley [1964] Director; Spencer Marcus Lund [1965] Director/Publican

Farkin Distillery Limited
Incorporated: 4 May 2016
Registered Office: East Glencraigs Cottage, Glencraigs, West Road, Campbeltown, Argyll, PA28 6NS
Officers: Lesley Ann Barford, Secretary; John Valentine Barford [1953] Director/Teacher

Farman & Son Ltd
Incorporated: 19 April 2018
Registered Office: 396 Wilmslow Road, Manchester, M20 3BN
Major Shareholder: Cleo Farman
Officers: Cleo Farman [1970] Director

Fatman and Friends Ltd.
Incorporated: 23 July 2014
Net Worth Deficit: £42,811 *Total Assets:* £8,100
Registered Office: 65 Sutton Square, Urswick Road, London, E9 6EQ
Shareholders: Mathew John Charles Smallbane; Moira Theresa Houlihan
Officers: Moira Theresa Houlihan [1967] Director [New Zealander]; Mathew Smallbane [1976] Director/Chief Executive Officer [Australian]

Fen Spirits Limited
Incorporated: 8 August 2017
Registered Office: 24 Cannon Street, Wisbech, Cambs, PE13 2QW
Major Shareholder: Michelle Winterbourne
Officers: Michelle Winterbourne [1976] Director

Fenney Street Distillery Limited
Incorporated: 3 January 2018
Registered Office: 10 Fenney Street, Salford, M7 2ZL
Major Shareholder: Paul James Carruthers
Officers: Paul James Carruthers [1989] Director

John Fergus & Co Limited
Incorporated: 25 February 2011 *Employees:* 11
Net Worth: £9,900,439 *Total Assets:* £17,824,424
Registered Office: Inchdairnie Distillery, Whitecraigs Road, Glenrothes, Fife, KY6 2RX
Parent: CES Whisky Limited
Officers: John Alastair Evan Fingland [1957] Director/Chartered Accountant; David Alexander Sloan [1962] Director/Accountant

Ferintosh Whisky Limited
Incorporated: 2 September 2015
Registered Office: Flat 1-2, 21 Redshank Avenue, Renfrew, PA4 8SG
Officers: Majid Majidi, Secretary; Majid Majidi [1961] Director/Self Employed [Iranian]

The Field Distillers Ltd
Incorporated: 11 December 2018
Registered Office: Unit 2c Park House Business Centre, South Street, Elgin, Moray, IV30 1JB
Major Shareholder: Robert Alfred Dalgarno
Officers: Robert Alfred Dalgarno [1964] Director

Fifty-Nine Spirits Company Ltd
Incorporated: 11 December 2018
Registered Office: 59 Marston Street, Oxford, OX4 1JU
Officers: Man Lok Dustin Cheng [1996] Director/Student; Sungmin Cho [1997] Director/Student [South Korean]; Alistair Henry Ming Parker [1997] Director/Student; David Samuel Walter Williams [1997] Director/Student

Finnieston Distillery Company Limited
Incorporated: 23 July 2013
Previous: Dram2o Ltd
Net Worth Deficit: £173,147 *Total Assets:* £205,776
Registered Office: c/o WRI Associates Ltd, Third Floor, Turnberry House, 175 West George Street, Glasgow, G2 2LB
Officers: Neil Paterson, Secretary; James Scott Cameron [1986] Director/Strategist; Scott Fraser Kelly [1955] Director; Paul Stewart MacInnes [1953] Director; David Donald McLauchlan [1985] Director; Neil Paterson [1983] Director/Lawyer

Fire Beard Spirits Limited
Incorporated: 6 September 2017
Registered Office: 1 Carrington Close, Croydon, Surrey, CR0 7LZ
Major Shareholder: Nathan Ian Lloyd Reed
Officers: Nathan Ian Lloyd Reed [1987] Director/Distiller

Five Fathoms Spirit Limited
Incorporated: 14 March 2017 *Employees:* 1
Net Worth: £100 *Total Assets:* £100
Registered Office: 1 Ferriby High Road, North Ferriby, E Yorks, HU14 3LD
Major Shareholder: Emma Davison
Officers: Emma Davison [1975] Director

Fixed Axis Ltd
Incorporated: 22 October 2015 *Employees:* 1
Previous: Blackfire Ltd
Net Worth: £50,030 *Total Assets:* £79,012
Registered Office: 33 Thurloe Street, London, SW7 2LQ
Shareholders: William Jonathan Cory Seth-Smith; Guy Pelly
Officers: Jamie Nicholas Murray Wells [1983] Director; Guy Pelly [1982] Director; William Jonathan Cory Seth-Smith [1985] Director

Flagg Ltd
Incorporated: 25 February 2019
Registered Office: 60 Longford Street, Glasgow, G33 2HH
Officers: Andrew McKechnie [1966] Director

Flavour Premium Brands Limited
Incorporated: 2 November 2018
Registered Office: Bank House, 71 Dale Street, Milnrow, Rochdale, Lancs, OL16 3NJ
Major Shareholder: Paul William Sheerin
Officers: Paul William Sheerin [1968] Director/Manager

Flavour Traders Limited
Incorporated: 6 October 2017
Registered Office: The Copper Room, Trinity Way, Salford, M3 7BG
Major Shareholder: Robert Charles Sumner
Officers: Robert Charles Sumner [1971] Director

Flint & Hardings Limited
Incorporated: 9 August 2016
Net Worth Deficit: £23,636 *Total Assets:* £28,472
Registered Office: Hammond Ford & Co Limited, Unit 6 Church Farm, Church Road, Barrow, Suffolk, IP29 5AX
Shareholders: Paul Charie; Christine Nancy Charie
Officers: Christine Nancy Charie [1960] Director

Fogcutter Limited
Incorporated: 6 August 1997
Registered Office: South Manor, High Road, Chipstead, Surrey, CR5 3SD
Officers: Christopher Frank Hayman [1947] Director

Folklore Distillery Ltd
Incorporated: 29 September 2017
Registered Office: 5 Bank View, Leeds, LS7 2EX
Shareholders: Nolan Oscar Kane; Barry Darnell
Officers: Barry Darnell [1980] Director; Nolan Oscar Kane [1980] Director

Food Development Company Limited
Incorporated: 7 September 2009
Net Worth: £317,936 *Total Assets:* £416,502
Registered Office: 32 Oakley Road, Chinnor, Oxon, OX39 4HB
Officers: Sir Norman Murray Pringle, Secretary; Sir Norman Murray Pringle [1941] Director/Chartered Management Accountant; James Wilson Turnbull [1951] Director/Management Consultant

For The Love of Limited
Incorporated: 4 October 2015
Net Worth Deficit: £15,456 *Total Assets:* £4,041
Registered Office: 86-90 Paul Street, London, EC2A 4NE
Major Shareholder: James David Hughston
Officers: James David Hughston [1982] Director

Forager Drinks Limited
Incorporated: 7 September 2018
Registered Office: Suite 2, Sigma House, Hadley Park East, Telford, Salop, TF1 6QJ
Major Shareholder: Camilla Louise Davis
Officers: Camilla Louise Davis [1968] Director

Fords of Wakefield Ltd
Incorporated: 24 September 2018
Registered Office: 6 Howcroft Court, Wakefield, W Yorks, WF2 6TP
Shareholders: Gary James Ford; Victoria Margaret Ford
Officers: Gary James Ford [1975] Product Development Director; Victoria Margaret Ford [1971] Marketing Director

Forest Distillery Ltd
Incorporated: 16 April 2015
Previous: Forest Gin Ltd
Net Worth: £142,777 *Total Assets:* £179,255
Registered Office: Chambers Farm, Bottom of the Oven, Macclesfield Forest, Macclesfield, Cheshire, SK11 0AR
Shareholder: Karl Bond
Officers: Karl Matthew Bond [1978] Director/Account Manager; Lindsay Alex Bond [1979] Director/Beautician

Forest Spirits Ltd
Incorporated: 6 January 2015
Net Worth Deficit: £57,385 *Total Assets:* £118,825
Registered Office: 37 Durham Road, Edinburgh, EH15 1PE
Shareholders: James Nicol; Barry Darnell
Officers: Barry Darnell [1980] Director; James Nicol [1974] Director

Forgan Distillery Ltd
Incorporated: 4 August 2017
Registered Office: 20-22 Wenlock Road, London, N1 7GU
Major Shareholder: Philip Ronald Forgan Robbins
Officers: Philip Ronald Forgan Robbins [1964] Director/Distiller

Formby Spirits Limited
Incorporated: 26 January 2018
Registered Office: Crown House, 91a King Street, Southport, Merseyside, PR8 1LQ
Shareholders: Elizabeth Mary Eaton; Patricia Winifred Giles
Officers: Elizabeth Mary Eaton [1964] Director

Forsaken Limited
Incorporated: 8 August 2018
Registered Office: Harcourts Cottage, Bantham, Kingsbridge, Devon, TQ7 3AD
Major Shareholder: Nicholas James Gilbert
Officers: Nicholas James Gilbert [1984] Marketing Director

Fort Glen Whisky Company Limited
Incorporated: 7 January 2010
Net Worth Deficit: £57,336 *Total Assets:* £6,720
Registered Office: Summit House, 4-5 Mitchell Street, Edinburgh, EH6 7BD
Shareholder: Peter Bowyer
Officers: Peter Bowyer, Secretary; Peter Bowyer [1954] Director

Forth Bridge Brewery and Distillery Limited
Incorporated: 6 February 2018
Registered Office: 43 Christiemiller Avenue, Edinburgh, EH7 6TB
Shareholders: James Stephen Brady; Carolyn Jayne Brady
Officers: Carolyn Jayne Brady [1964] Director; James Stephen Brady [1963] Director

Founding Drinks Ltd
Incorporated: 31 May 2017 *Employees:* 3
Net Worth: £8,994 *Total Assets:* £47,806
Registered Office: 6 Church Walk, Beachamwell, Swaffham, Norfolk, PE37 8BJ
Shareholders: Matthew Douglas Brown; Stephanie Jayne Brown
Officers: Matthew Douglas Brown [1964] Director; Stephanie Jayne Brown [1968] Director

Four Sisters Distillery Limited
Incorporated: 9 August 2017
Registered Office: 18 Penketh Avenue, Astley, Tyldesley, Manchester, M29 7DS
Officers: Kerry Frances Collins [1963] Director; Kate Elizabeth Haslam [1971] Director; Lucy Catherine McAvoy [1979] Director; Hayley Teresa Robinson [1966] Director

Fourfolk Gin Company Ltd
Incorporated: 23 February 2017 *Employees:* 4
Net Worth: £175 *Total Assets:* £16,103
Registered Office: Belle Isle Road, Haworth, W Yorks, BD22 8QQ
Shareholders: Craig Steven Dyson; Scott Michael Dyson
Officers: Sophie Jade Broadley [1991] Director; Craig Steven Dyson [1990] Director/Artist; Scott Michael Dyson [1987] Director/Sales Manager; Lauren Frances Warke [1992] Director

Fowey River Gin Ltd
Incorporated: 19 July 2017
Registered Office: Colwith Farm Distillery, Crewell Moor, Pelyn Cross, Lostwithiel, Cornwall, PL22 0JG
Shareholders: Steven Dustow; William Cole
Officers: William Graham Cole [1967] Director; Steven Dustow [1982] Director

W.C. Fowler & Sons Limited
Incorporated: 28 February 2018
Registered Office: Mulberry Cottage, Back Lane, Bredon, Tewkesbury, Glos, GL20 7LH
Major Shareholder: James Warren Maycock
Officers: James Warren Maycock [1969] Director

Fox Gins Ltd
Incorporated: 28 August 2018
Registered Office: 258 Crow Lane West, Newton-le-Willows, Merseyside, WA12 9YQ
Shareholders: Aimee Toomey; Oliver Beniston
Officers: Oliver Beniston [1980] Director; Aimee Toomey [1979] Director

Foxdenton Estate Company Limited
Incorporated: 2 September 1935 *Employees:* 6
Net Worth: £730,090 *Total Assets:* £947,171
Registered Office: The Copper Room, Deva Centre, Trinity Way, Manchester, M3 7BG
Major Shareholder: Nicholas James Radclyffe
Officers: Jonathan Selwyn Brownson, Secretary/Chartered Accountant; Jonathan Selwyn Brownson [1962] Director/Chartered Accountant; Nicholas James Radclyffe [1959] Director

Foxhole Spirits Limited
Incorporated: 10 February 2016 *Employees:* 3
Net Worth Deficit: £87,925 *Total Assets:* £20,333
Registered Office: Bolney Wine Estate, Foxhole Lane, Bolney, Haywards Heath, W Sussex, RH17 5NB
Major Shareholder: James Philip Marsden-Smedley
Officers: Graham John Linter, Secretary; Graham John Linter [1964] Director; Samantha Martha Linter [1968] Director; James Philip Marsden-Smedley [1989] Director

Frensham Distillery Limited
Incorporated: 18 May 2018
Registered Office: 3 St Mary's Cottages, The Street, Frensham, Farnham, Surrey, GU10 3EA
Shareholders: Louise Jane Gheorghiu; John Leo Alissi
Officers: John Leo Alissi [1948] Director/Operations Manager; Louise Jane Gheorghiu [1983] Marketing Director

Fruity Tipples Limited
Incorporated: 5 June 2015
Net Worth: £4,311 *Total Assets:* £21,613
Registered Office: Brianfield Farm, Snowgatehead, New Mill, Holmfirth, W Yorks, HD9 7DH
Shareholders: Kevan Baldwin; Veronica Judith Baldwin
Officers: Kevan Baldwin [1964] Director; Veronica Judith Baldwin [1968] Director

G & J Distillers Ltd.
Incorporated: 14 April 2011 *Employees:* 118
Net Worth: £7,474,000 *Total Assets:* £26,892,000
Registered Office: Distribution Point, Melbury Park, Clayton Road, Birchwood, Warrington, Cheshire, WA3 6PH
Parent: Quintessential Brands UK Group Limited
Officers: Michael Clifford, Secretary; Warren Michael Scott [1963] Director/Businessman; Vincenzo Visone [1955] Director/Businessman [Italian]

G & J Greenall Group Limited
Incorporated: 24 June 2013
Registered Office: Distribution Point, Clayton Road, Birchwood, Warrington, Cheshire, WA3 6PH
Shareholders: Warren Michael Scott; Vincenzo Visone
Officers: Michael Clifford, Secretary; Warren Michael Scott [1963] Director/Businessman; Vincenzo Visone [1955] Director/Businessman [Italian]

G & J Limited
Incorporated: 24 April 2013
Registered Office: Distribution Point, Clayton Road, Birchwood, Warrington, Cheshire, WA3 6PH
Shareholders: Warren Michael Scott; Vincenzo Visone
Officers: Michael Clifford, Secretary; Warren Michael Scott [1963] Director/Businessman; Vincenzo Visone [1955] Director/Businessman [Italian]

Gaelic Pure Scotch Whisky Limited
Incorporated: 27 April 2011
Net Worth Deficit: £41,195 *Total Assets:* £9,526
Registered Office: Richmond House, Walkern Road, Stevenage, Herts, SG1 3QP
Major Shareholder: Daniel Gerrit Jan Klaassen
Officers: Daniel Gerrit Jan-Klaassen [1974] Director

Galldachd Na H-Alba Brewing Ltd
Incorporated: 22 September 2017
Registered Office: Sunnybrae, Old Well Road, Moffat, Dumfries & Galloway, DG10 9AP
Major Shareholder: Michael Stuart Tough
Officers: Thomas Joseph Barr, Secretary; Michael Stuart Tough [1965] Managing Director

Galleon Liqueurs UK Ltd
Incorporated: 14 April 2012
Net Worth Deficit: £6,045 *Total Assets:* £1,645
Registered Office: 2 College Street Mews, Northampton, NN1 2QF
Major Shareholder: Michael Phillipson
Officers: Michael Phillipson [1979] Director/Technician

The Garden Shed Drinks Company Limited
Incorporated: 23 April 2013 *Employees:* 1
Previous: RG ON3 Limited
Net Worth: £12,797 *Total Assets:* £28,326
Registered Office: 135 Norse Road, Glasgow, G14 9EH
Shareholders: Maxine Natalie Grant; Ryan Grant
Officers: Ryan Grant, Secretary; Maxine Natalie Grant [1981] Director of Marketing; Ryan Grant [1985] Director/Professional Rugby Player; Ruaridh James Howard Jackson [1988] Director/Professional Rugby Player

Garej Spirits Company Limited
Incorporated: 13 October 2014
Registered Office: Rhyd Y Garreg Ddu, Talog, Carmarthen, SA33 6NN
Shareholder: David Anthony Rees
Officers: David Anthony Rees [1961] Director/Artisan Gin Distiller; David Thomas [1969] Director/Artisan Gin Distiller

Gaslight Distillery Limited
Incorporated: 5 October 2016
Net Worth: £1 *Total Assets:* £1
Registered Office: 134 Henniker Gardens, London, E6 3HS
Major Shareholder: Owen Powell
Officers: Owen Powell [1975] Director/Owner

Gateway Spirit Company Limited
Incorporated: 30 October 2017
Registered Office: 34 Cranleigh Court Road, Yate, Bristol, BS37 5DH
Major Shareholder: Matthew Robert Lewis
Officers: Matthew Robert Lewis [1994] Director/Marketing Spirits

Gaymens Gin Ltd
Incorporated: 3 May 2018
Registered Office: 426 Crow Road, Broomhill, Glasgow, G11 7EA
Officers: Paul Wainwright [1972] Director/Section Co-ordinator

Gedrick Distilling Company Limited
Incorporated: 10 November 2014
Net Worth: £200 *Total Assets:* £200
Registered Office: 53 John Street, Montrose, Angus, DD10 8LZ
Officers: Gerard Evans [1959] Director/Master Distiller

The Gentlemen Distillers Ltd
Incorporated: 23 July 2018
Registered Office: 2 Marine Point Apartments, Marine Approach, Burton Waters, Lincoln, LN1 2LW
Major Shareholder: James Wood
Officers: James Wood [1994] Director

Geordie-Gin Co Ltd
Incorporated: 2 October 2014
Net Worth Deficit: £7,126 *Total Assets:* £17,343
Registered Office: 36 Moor Close, North Shields, Tyne & Wear, NE29 8DB
Shareholders: Stuart Lamb; Geoffrey Robinson Graydon
Officers: Geoffrey Graydon [1952] Director/Property Holdings; Adam Dobson Lamb [1992] Director/Banker; Stuart Lamb [1954] Director/IT Consultant

Geordie-Gin Corporation Ltd
Incorporated: 12 February 2018
Registered Office: 6 Trewitt Road, Whitley Bay, Tyne & Wear, NE26 2QS
Major Shareholder: Stuart Lamb
Officers: Adam Dobson Lamb [1992] Director/Financial Analyst; Stuart Lamb [1954] Director/Distiller

Gest Spirits Limited
Incorporated: 22 January 2019
Registered Office: Apartment 102, 10 Dallington Street, London, EC1V 0DB
Shareholders: Shane Michael Frith; Gary John Collett
Officers: Gary John Collett [1978] Director

The Gibraltar Gin Company Limited
Incorporated: 21 September 2018
Registered Office: Morants Hall, Colchester Road, Great Bromley, Colchester, Essex, CO7 7TN
Major Shareholder: Michael Joseph Volf
Officers: Michael Joseph Volf [1959] Director/Owner Care Group

Gibson Whisky Ltd
Incorporated: 24 January 2012
Net Worth Deficit: £15,134 *Total Assets:* £78,818
Registered Office: 25 Huntly Gardens, Glasgow, G12 9AU
Major Shareholder: Thomas Gibson
Officers: Thomas Gibson [1944] Director/Mechanical Engineer

Gin Bothy Limited
Incorporated: 26 March 2015 *Employees:* 5
Net Worth: £39,905 *Total Assets:* £122,361
Registered Office: Garlowbank Smiddy, Kinnordy, Kirriemuir, Angus, DD8 4LH
Major Shareholder: Kim Margaret Cameron
Officers: Kim Margaret Cameron [1976] Director/Proprietor/Producer of Beverages

The Gin Dobry Gin Company Ltd
Incorporated: 9 February 2018
Registered Office: 1 Harmer Court, Park Road, Southborough, Tunbridge Wells, Kent, TN4 0NZ
Major Shareholder: Daniel Robert Dudgeon
Officers: Daniel Robert Dudgeon [1980] Director

Gin Foundry Limited
Incorporated: 21 February 2014 *Employees:* 4
Net Worth: £205 *Total Assets:* £160,727
Registered Office: 13 Princeton Court, 53-55 Felsham Road, London, SW15 1AZ
Shareholders: Olivier Ward; Emile Ward
Officers: Emile Ward [1989] Director; Olivier Ward [1985] Director

The Gin Hub Limited
Incorporated: 28 November 2017
Registered Office: Chivas House, 72 Chancellors Road, London, W6 9RS
Parent: Chivas Brothers Limited
Officers: Stuart MacNab [1964] Director of Tax; Louise Ryan [1973] Managing Director, Marketing [Irish]; Catherine Louise Thompson [1971] Director/General Counsel [Australian]

Gin Jar Drinks Company Ltd
Incorporated: 24 July 2015
Net Worth Deficit: £4,832 *Total Assets:* £27,034
Registered Office: Westlands, Hillside, Axbridge, Somerset, BS26 2AN
Major Shareholder: Chris Jefferies
Officers: Christopher Jefferies [1974] Director/Consultant

Gin Kitchen Limited
Incorporated: 26 April 2016 *Employees:* 5
Net Worth: £1,017 *Total Assets:* £16,198
Registered Office: 2 Club Court, 128 High Street, Dorking, Surrey, RH4 1BD
Shareholders: Kate Danielle Gregory; Helen Muncie
Officers: Kate Danielle Gregory [1973] Director; Dr Helen Muncie [1977] Director

Gin Tales Ltd
Incorporated: 24 February 2015
Net Worth: £2,886 *Total Assets:* £21,148
Registered Office: 9 Arundel Square, London, N7 8AT
Officers: Fiona Louise Flood [1981] Director/Retail

Gin Ting Limited
Incorporated: 4 December 2017
Registered Office: 9 Green Lane, Aldridge, W Midlands, WS9 0LN
Major Shareholder: Kristian Nathan Hindley
Officers: Kristian Nathan Hindley [1980] Director; Louise Hindley [1979] Director

Gin-Ger Gin Limited
Incorporated: 15 February 2018
Registered Office: 2 St Aidan's Row, School Road, Broadway, Worcs, WR12 7AS
Major Shareholder: Paul Merchant
Officers: Paul Merchant [1992] Director

Ginglish Limited
Incorporated: 6 September 2017
Registered Office: 2 Victoria Mead, Thame, Oxon, OX9 3HY
Major Shareholder: George Newport English
Officers: George Newport English [1995] Director

Ginkhana Limited
Incorporated: 7 February 2018
Registered Office: Sunnyside Croft, Blairs, Aberdeen, AB12 5YT
Shareholders: David Lawson; Leeanne Lawson
Officers: Jill Bedawi, Secretary; Jill Bedawi [1969] Director; David Lawson [1973] Director; Leeanne Lawson [1976] Director/Housewife

The Ginking Company Limited
Incorporated: 16 August 2017
Net Worth: £4,289 *Total Assets:* £71,013
Registered Office: Ground Floor Offices, 39 Guildford Road, Lightwater, Surrey, GU18 5SA
Shareholders: Mathieu Elzinga; Michael Florence; John Robert Worontschak
Officers: John Robert Worontschak [1961] Director

Ginmeister Ltd
Incorporated: 31 January 2013 *Employees:* 25
Net Worth: £132,969 *Total Assets:* £766,861
Registered Office: Dovehouse Shott, Smith End Lane, Barley, Royston, Herts, SG8 8LL
Shareholder: Stephen Nicholas Bowyer Marsh
Officers: Stephen Nicholas Bowyer Marsh, Secretary; Richard James Alexander Bridgwood [1965] Director; William Anthony Eustace Holt [1965] Director; Stephen Nicholas Bowyer Marsh [1964] Director/Chartered Accountant; Sean Frederick McCreery [1964] Director/Fund Manager; Giles Jon Ashley Moffatt [1972] Director/Advertising Consultant; Georgina Northern [1975] Director/Chartered Accountant; Martijn Van Buuren [1958] Sales Director [Dutch]

Ginomics Ltd
Incorporated: 30 September 2016
Net Worth: £4,970 *Total Assets:* £5,970
Registered Office: 18 Chalmers Walk, Hillingdon Street, London, SE17 3JJ
Officers: Adam Christopher Mason [1980] Director

Ginsecco Ltd
Incorporated: 12 October 2018
Registered Office: 17 Whitelaw Street, Glasgow, G20 0DG
Shareholders: Jonathan McCall; Craig Gibson
Officers: Craig Gibson [1983] Director/Engineer; Jonathan McCall [1982] Director/Engineer

Ginwimmin Ltd
Incorporated: 12 February 2019
Registered Office: 22 Newton Road, Urmston, Manchester, M41 5AE
Shareholders: Emma Charlotte Hawley; Louise Amanda Kershaw; Fiona Gilmore
Officers: Fiona Gilmore [1971] Director; Emma Charlotte Hawley [1974] Director; Louise Amanda Kershaw [1967] Finance Director

Giorgio's Continental Ltd.
Incorporated: 1 June 1987 *Employees:* 88
Net Worth: £10,100,531 *Total Assets:* £23,144,680
Registered Office: Moorgreen Industrial Park, Dunsil Road, Engine Lane, Newthorpe, Nottingham, NG16 3PX
Officers: Salvatore Devivo [1966] Managing Director

Glasgow Distillery Company Limited
Incorporated: 20 December 2012 *Employees:* 21
Net Worth: £1,044,955 *Total Assets:* £3,287,564
Registered Office: 8 Deanside Road, Glasgow, G52 4XB
Officers: Michael Hayward, Secretary; Rustom Meherdaad Battliwala [1979] Director [Indian]; Michael Hayward [1968] Director; Liam Oliver Hughes [1967] Director; Alan James [1958] Director; Ian McDougall [1972] Director/Certified Chartered Accountant; Eddie Poonawala [1959] Director

Glasgow Gin Company Limited
Incorporated: 20 October 2016
Net Worth: £1 *Total Assets:* £1
Registered Office: 272 Bath Street, Glasgow, G2 4JR
Major Shareholder: Derek Joseph Mair
Officers: Derek Joseph Mair [1961] Director/Businessman

Glasgow Partners Ltd.
Incorporated: 2 February 1998
Net Worth: £2 *Total Assets:* £2
Registered Office: 3 Peel Park Place, East Kilbride, S Lanarks, G74 5LW
Parent: JG Distillers Ltd
Officers: Colin Shields Barclay [1958] Director/Merchant [Canadian]; Gerrard McSherry [1956] Director

Glasgow Whisky Limited
Incorporated: 10 October 2007 *Employees:* 1
Net Worth: £9,823,491 *Total Assets:* £22,168,110
Registered Office: 148 Terregles Avenue, Pollokshields, Glasgow, G41 4RR
Shareholders: Stuart Fullarton Hendry; Graham Russell Taylor
Officers: Stuart Fullarton Hendry, Secretary; Stuart Fullarton Hendry [1965] Director/Chartered Accountant; Graham Russell Taylor [1956] Director/Scotch Whisky Producer; Victoria Jane Taylor [1958] Director/Speech & Language Therapist

Glass Jigsaw Ltd.
Incorporated: 9 May 2011 *Employees:* 1
Previous: Ace Vodka Ltd.
Net Worth Deficit: £28,540 *Total Assets:* £37,955
Registered Office: 2 Hubbard Court, Valley Hill, Loughton, Essex, IG10 3BH
Major Shareholder: James Whittington
Officers: James Whittington [1967] Director/Chief Executive

Glastonbury Distillery Limited
Incorporated: 18 July 2016
Registered Office: The Old Police Station, Newtown, West Pennard, Glastonbury, Somerset, BA6 8NN
Major Shareholder: Stephen Crozier
Officers: Stephen Crozier [1962] Director/Distiller

Glaswegin Distilling Co. Limited
Incorporated: 25 July 2018
Registered Office: Caledonian House, 5 Inchinnan Drive, Inchinnan, Renfrew, PA4 9AF
Major Shareholder: Andrew John McGeoch
Officers: Andrew John McGeoch [1980] Director

Glen Calder Blenders Limited
Incorporated: 16 January 1978
Registered Office: Moffat Distillery, Airdrie, N Lanarks, ML6 8PL
Shareholders: Charoen Sirivadhanabhakdi; Khunying Wanna Sirivadhanabhakdi
Officers: Man Kong Lee [1968] Director/Accountant [Chinese]; Dr Martin John Leonard [1961] Managing Director; Prapakon Thongtheppairot [1971] Director [Thai]

Glen Clyde Ltd.
Incorporated: 1 February 2011
Net Worth: £1 *Total Assets:* £1
Registered Office: 3 Peel Park Place, East Kilbride, S Lanarks, G74 5LW
Parent: Campbell Meyer & Co Ltd
Officers: Colin Shields Barclay [1958] Director/Merchant [Canadian]; Gerrard McSherry [1956] Director

Glen Gordon Whisky Company Limited
Incorporated: 1 August 1986
Registered Office: George House, Boroughbriggs Road, Elgin, Moray, IV30 1JY
Parent: Speymalt Whisky Distributors Ltd
Officers: Norman Ross, Secretary; Ewen Cameron Mackintosh [1968] Whisky Supply Director; Stephen Alexander Masson Rankin [1971] UK Sales Director; Neil Edward Urquhart [1975] Logistics & Facilities Director

Glen Monarch Distillery Limited
Incorporated: 9 June 2017
Registered Office: Flat 1, 180 St Pauls Road, London, N1 2LL
Shareholder: Ashwin Balivada
Officers: Ashwin Balivada [1988] Director [Indian]; Dr Mohan Krishna Balivada [1959] Director/Businessman [Indian]

Glen Moray-Glenlivet Distillery Co. Ltd.
Incorporated: 3 April 2001
Registered Office: Glen Turner Distillery, Starlaw Road, Bathgate, W Lothian, EH47 7BW
Parent: Glen Turner Company Limited
Officers: Jean Pierre Cayard [1942] Director [French]

Glen Scotia Distillery Company Limited
Incorporated: 19 July 2013 *Employees:* 3
Net Worth: £73,773,000 *Total Assets:* £154,226,000
Registered Office: 30 Broadwick Street, London, W1F 8JB
Parent: Loch Lomond Distillery Company Limited
Officers: Colin Matthews [1965] Director; Richard Miles [1966] Director; Nicholas Rose [1957] Director

The Glenallachie Distillers Co Limited
Incorporated: 1 March 2017 *Employees:* 1
Net Worth Deficit: £93,774 *Total Assets:* £476,095
Registered Office: Glenallachie Distillery, Glenallachie, Aberlour, Banffshire, AB38 9LR
Shareholders: William James Walker; Alistair James Graham Stevenson
Officers: Patricia Bridget Savage, Secretary; Patricia Bridget Savage [1959] Commercial Director; Alistair James Graham Stevenson [1958] Director; William James Walker [1945] Managing Director

Glencoe Distilleries Ltd
Incorporated: 14 November 2018
Registered Office: 120 Bothwell Street, Glasgow, G2 7JL
Officers: Munnangisita Ramanajneya Reddy, Secretary; Bhavanam Srinivasa Rao [1968] Director [Indian]; Bhavanam Karan Reddy [1995] Director [Indian]; Munnangi Soma Rushyanth Reddy [2001] Director/Student [Indian]; Munnangisita Ramanajneya Reddy [1966] Director [Indian]

Glendronach Distillery Company Limited
Incorporated: 7 February 1927
Registered Office: 50 Lothian Road, Festival Square, Edinburgh, EH3 9WJ
Parent: The Benriach Distillery Company Limited
Officers: Mary Elizabeth Barrazotto [1960] Director/Senior Vice President General Counsel [American]; Leanne Dean Cunningham [1970] Director/General Manager [American]; Edward Wayne Mayrose [1973] VP, Global Director External Manufacturing [American]; Fiona Colette Michelle West [1968] Director/Marketing

Gleneagles Distillery Limited
Incorporated: 20 December 2018
Registered Office: Briven House, Main Road, Aberuthven, Auchterarder, Perthshire, PH3 1HB
Major Shareholder: Graham Charles Bennett
Officers: Graham Charles Bennett [1958] Director

The Glenglassaugh Distillery Company Limited
Incorporated: 24 October 2006
Net Worth: £2,351,101 *Total Assets:* £2,351,101
Registered Office: 50 Lothian Road, Festival Square, Edinburgh, EH3 9WJ
Parent: The Benriach Distillery Company Limited
Officers: Mary Elizabeth Barrazotto [1960] Director/Senior Vice President General Counsel [American]; Leanne Dean Cunningham [1970] Director/General Manager [American]; Edward Wayne Mayrose [1973] VP, Global Director External Manufacturing [American]; Fiona Colette Michelle West [1968] Director/Marketing

Glenmaster Distillers Limited
Incorporated: 11 September 2017
Registered Office: 101 Rose Street, South Lane, Edinburgh, EH2 3JG
Officers: Gaurav Rajput [1980] Director/Distiller [Indian]

The Glenmorangie Company Limited
Incorporated: 30 December 1948
Net Worth: £10,711,000 *Total Assets:* £10,889,000
Registered Office: The Cube, 45 Leith Street, Edinburgh, EH1 3AT
Shareholders: Diageo PLC; LVMH Moet Hennessy Louis Vuitton SE
Officers: Jean-Marc Rene Boulan [1972] Director [French]; Nauman Saleem Hasan [1969] Director; Thomas Jean Moradpour [1973] Director [French]; Dr Peter Jonathon Nelson [1959] Operations Director; Richard Spencer Yeomans [1979] Director

Glenmorangie Distillery Company Limited, The
Incorporated: 23 May 1936
Registered Office: The Cube, 45 Leith Street, Edinburgh, EH1 3AT
Parent: MacDonald & Muir Limited
Officers: Jean-Marc Rene Boulan [1972] Director [French]; Dr Peter Jonathon Nelson [1959] Director

Glenmorangie Spring Water Company Limited
Incorporated: 7 April 1988
Registered Office: The Cube, 45 Leith Street, Edinburgh, EH1 3AT
Parent: MacDonald & Muir Limited
Officers: Jean-Marc Rene Boulan [1972] Director [French]; Dr Peter Jonathon Nelson [1959] Director

Glenrinnes Distillery Limited
Incorporated: 25 August 2016
Net Worth Deficit: £77,139 *Total Assets:* £3,144,057
Registered Office: Glenrinnes Lodge, Glenrinnes, Keith, Moray, AB55 4BS
Parent: Glenrinnes Farms Limited
Officers: Alexander James Christou [1981] Director; Alasdair James Dougall Locke [1953] Director

The Glens of Antrim Whiskey Company Limited
Incorporated: 18 October 2012
Registered Office: 56 Layde Road, Cushendall, Ballymena, Co Antrim, BT44 0NQ
Major Shareholder: Alastair Paul McLaughlin
Officers: Alastair Paul McLaughlin [1965] Director [Irish]

Glenturret Distillery Limited
Incorporated: 21 January 1981
Registered Office: Glenturret Distillery, Crieff, Perthshire, PH7 4HA
Parent: Highland Distillers Limited
Officers: Martin Alexander Cooke [1961] Director/Company Secretary

Glenturret Limited
Incorporated: 17 December 2018
Registered Office: 100 Queen Street, Glasgow, G1 3DN
Parent: Highland Distillers Limited
Officers: Martin Alexander Cooke [1961] Director/Company Secretary

Matthew Gloag & Son Limited
Incorporated: 14 April 1939
Registered Office: 100 Queen Street, Glasgow, G1 3DN
Parent: Highland Distillers Group Limited
Officers: Martin Alexander Cooke, Secretary; Martin Alexander Cooke [1961] Company Secretary/Director; Suzy Smith [1972] Director

Global Premium Spirits Ltd
Incorporated: 22 October 2009 Employees: 1
Net Worth Deficit: £33,760 Total Assets: £419,674
Registered Office: Suite 12, 2nd Floor, Queens House, 180 Tottenham Court Road, London, W1T 7PD
Shareholders: Elena Pustovoytova; Andrey Sokolov
Officers: Elena Pustovoytova [1980] Director [Russian]; Andrey Sokolov [1968] Director [Russian]

GNR Distillery Limited
Incorporated: 21 June 2018
Registered Office: Manwood Barn, Mersea Road, Abberton, Colchester, Essex, CO5 7NS
Shareholder: Gavin Miklaucich
Officers: Susan Miklaucich, Secretary; Richard Fletcher Frost [1972] Director; Gavin Miklaucich [1966] Director

Godka Ltd
Incorporated: 9 February 2018
Registered Office: 4 Penhill Road, Cardiff, CF11 9PQ
Shareholder: Tom Peddie
Officers: Simon Johns [1988] Director; Tom Peddie [1989] Director/Regional Account Manager

Golden Measure Limited
Incorporated: 18 July 2016 Employees: 1
Net Worth: £100 Total Assets: £47,857
Registered Office: Harden Vale, Ancrum, Jedburgh, Roxburghshire, TD8 6XH
Major Shareholder: Catherine MacInnes
Officers: Catherine MacInnes [1973] Director

Goldings Distillery Ltd
Incorporated: 10 January 2019
Registered Office: Kemp House, 160 City Road, London, EC1V 2NX
Shareholders: David Tait; Janet Tait
Officers: Janet Tait, Secretary; David Tait [1966] Director/Pharmacist; Janet Tait [1966] Director/Administration Officer

Goldman Distillery Ltd
Incorporated: 5 January 2018
Registered Office: 319 St Vincent Street, Glasgow, G2 5RG
Parent: Whyte and MacKay Limited
Officers: Bryan Harold Donaghey [1961] Director

Goldy Gin Limited
Incorporated: 23 December 2016
Registered Office: Flat 2, 23 Mount Street, London, W1K 2RP
Major Shareholder: Justin Daniel O'Shea
Officers: Antonio Michele Conigliaro [1971] Director/Bar Owner; Ramon Mac-Crohon Ron [1975] Director/Entrepreneur [Spanish]; Justin Daniel O'Shea [1979] Director/Entrepreneur [Australian]

The Good Life Gin Company Ltd
Incorporated: 7 December 2017
Registered Office: Anchor House, Burgoine Quay, 8 Lower Teddington Road, Kingston upon Thames, Surrey, KT1 4EU
Major Shareholder: Samuel Rupert Berry
Officers: Samuel Rupert Berry [1989] Director

Good Spirits Ltd
Incorporated: 29 May 2018
Registered Office: 28 Crieff Road, London, SW18 2EA
Shareholders: James Henry Newton Kaye; James Edward Prowse
Officers: James Henry Newton Kaye [1996] Director; James Edward Prowse [1996] Director

Goosnargh Gin Ltd
Incorporated: 22 January 2018
Registered Office: Eccles Moss Farm, Bleasdale Road, Whitechapel, Preston, Lancs, PR3 2ER
Shareholders: Richard Ian Trenchard; Rachel Elizabeth Trenchard
Officers: Rachel Elizabeth Trenchard [1976] Director; Richard Ian Trenchard [1975] Director

Gordon & Company (Distillers) Limited
Incorporated: 17 October 2012 Employees: 6
Net Worth Deficit: £90,740 Total Assets: £224,826
Registered Office: 18 Westerlands Drive, Newton Mearns, Glasgow, G77 6YB
Shareholders: James Gordon; Janet Gordon
Officers: Harvest Gordon [1988] Director; James Gordon [1956] Managing Director; Janet Gordon [1956] Director; Jonathan Gordon [1990] Commercial Director

Gordon & MacPhail Limited
Incorporated: 16 February 2017
Registered Office: George House, Boroughbriggs Road, Elgin, Moray, IV30 1JY
Parent: Speymalt Whisky Distributors Limited
Officers: Norman Ross, Secretary; Ewen Cameron Mackintosh [1968] Director

Gordon Bonding Company Limited
Incorporated: 31 July 1986
Registered Office: George House, Boroughbriggs Road, Elgin, Moray, IV30 1JY
Parent: Speymalt Whisky Distributors Ltd
Officers: Norman Ross, Secretary; Ewen Cameron Mackintosh [1968] Whisky Supply Director; Stephen Alexander Masson Rankin [1971] UK Sales Director; Neil Edward Urquhart [1975] Logistics & Facilities Director

James Gordon Whisky Company Limited
Incorporated: 31 July 1986
Registered Office: George House, Boroughbriggs Road, Elgin, Moray, IV30 1JY
Parent: Speymalt Whisky Distributors Ltd
Officers: Norman Ross, Secretary; Ewen Cameron Mackintosh [1968] Whisky Supply Director; Stephen Alexander Masson Rankin [1971] UK Sales Director; Neil Edward Urquhart [1975] Logistics & Facilities Director

Gorgeous Gin Limited
Incorporated: 13 February 2018
Registered Office: 5 West Road, Newport-on-Tay, Fife, DD6 8HH
Major Shareholder: Gail Marion Sneddon
Officers: Gail Marion Sneddon [1967] Director

Gower Distillery Ltd
Incorporated: 2 February 2018
Registered Office: 8 Axis Court, Mallard Way, Riverside Business Park, Swansea, SA7 0AJ
Shareholders: Daniel Alejandro Tercero; Nicholas Thomas Bryer
Officers: Nicholas Thomas Bryer [1988] Director; Noah Redfern [1977] Director; Daniel Alejandro Tercero [1974] Director

Gordon Graham & Company Limited
Incorporated: 7 January 2003
Registered Office: 8 Milton Road, College Milton North, East Kilbride, S Lanarks, G74 5BU
Parent: Distell International Limited
Officers: Karen Spy, Secretary; Fraser John Thornton [1969] Director

Alistair Graham Limited
Incorporated: 29 April 1936
Registered Office: The Cube, 45 Leith Street, Edinburgh, EH1 3AT
Parent: MacDonald & Muir Limited
Officers: Jean-Marc Rene Boulan [1972] Director [French]; Dr Peter Jonathon Nelson [1959] Director

Grain Artisan Ltd
Incorporated: 19 June 2018
Registered Office: 70 Bank Road, Matlock, Derbys, DE4 3GL
Major Shareholder: Adrian Cole
Officers: Rebecca Kate Morgan [1975] Director/Project Manager

Granite North Spirits Limited
Incorporated: 5 October 2016
Net Worth Deficit: £6,341 *Total Assets:* £10,646
Registered Office: Unit 15 Spires Business Units, Mugiemoss Road, Bucksburn, Aberdeen, AB21 9BG
Major Shareholder: Sandy Matheson
Officers: Sandy Matheson [1987] Director/Engineer; Dr Kirstie Nisbet [1987] Director/Doctor

J. & G. Grant
Incorporated: 30 May 1947
Registered Office: Glenfarclas Distillery, Ballindalloch, Banffshire, AB37 9BD
Shareholder: John Lynburn Scott Grant
Officers: John Lynburn Scott Grant, Secretary; George Stewart Grant [1976] Sales Director; Ishbel Grant [1954] Director; John Lynburn Scott Grant [1951] Director/Distiller

William Grant & Sons Distillers Limited
Incorporated: 1 October 1991 *Employees:* 903
Net Worth: £746,017,984 *Total Assets:* £1,586,162,048
Registered Office: The Glenfiddich Distillery, Dufftown, Keith, Moray, AB55 4DH
Parent: William Grant & Sons Limited
Officers: Douglas John Bagley [1967] Director [Australian]; Ian Collins Bissett [1963] Technical Director; John Ricson Broadbridge [1957] Director; Craig Hamilton Cranmer [1968] Operations Director; Ian Evans [1953] Director; Tracey Diane Foster [1967] UK Manufacturing Director; Patrick Charles Martin Hartless [1969] Supply Chain Director; Ewan John Henderson [1968] Director; Gary Horsfield [1971] Group Packaging and Supply Chain Director; Simon John Hunt [1971] Director [Australian/British]; Colin Thomas Kelly [1962] Global Quality Director; Douglas William Laing [1972] Director/Chartered Accountant; Michael Lamont [1960] Director; Kieran Gerard Phelan [1965] Global Compliance and EHS Director [Irish]; Graham Howard Shoel [1965] Distilleries Engineering Project Director; Judith Anne Sommerville [1970] HR Director; Stuart Henry Watts [1977] Director/Site Leader

William Grant & Sons Distinction Limited
Incorporated: 11 August 2016
Registered Office: Independence House, 84 Lower Mortlake Road, Richmond, Surrey, TW9 2HS
Parent: William Grant & Sons Investments Ltd
Officers: Gregory Justin Bargeton [1973] Director/Lawyer; Ewan John Henderson [1968] Director/Accountant; Paul Henry Rochford [1963] Director

William Grant & Sons Limited
Incorporated: 13 May 1991 *Employees:* 157
Net Worth: £44,784,000 *Total Assets:* £450,376,992
Registered Office: The Glenfiddich Distillery, Dufftown, Keith, Moray, AB55 4DH
Parent: William Grant & Sons Holdings Limited
Officers: Douglas John Bagley [1967] Director [Australian]; John Ricson Broadbridge [1957] Director; Philip Andrew Gladman [1970] Marketing Director; Peter Grant Gordon [1959] Director/Distiller; Rita Marie Greenwood [1968] Director; Ewan John Henderson [1968] Director; Gary Horsfield [1971] Group Packaging and Supply Chain Director; Simon John Hunt [1971] Director [Australian/British]; Michael Lamont [1960] Director; Jonathan Mark Yusen [1970] Director [American]

Graveney Gin Limited
Incorporated: 15 June 2015 *Employees:* 5
Net Worth: £126 *Total Assets:* £32,652
Registered Office: Unit 17 Merton Abbey Mills, Watermill Way, London, SW19 2RD
Major Shareholder: Victoria Christie
Officers: Victoria Elva Christie [1983] Director/Distiller

Great Don Ltd
Incorporated: 8 January 2018
Registered Office: 2nd Floor, Unicorn House, Station Close, Potters Bar, Herts, EN6 1TL
Officers: Emily Ann Aku Fafa Agodzo [1980] Director; Danny McGuinness [1981] Director; Alexander William Durham Wilkinson [1963] Director

Great White Gin Limited
Incorporated: 3 January 2018
Registered Office: 11 Arch View Crescent, Liverpool, L1 7BA
Major Shareholder: Harry Williams
Officers: Harry Williams, Secretary; Harry Williams [1993] Director/Proprietor

The Great Yorkshire Spirit Company Limited
Incorporated: 22 January 2016
Registered Office: W H Prior, Railway Court, Doncaster, S Yorks, DN4 5FB
Shareholders: Philip Craig Lee; Joanne Taylor
Officers: Philip Craig Lee [1970] Director; Joanne Taylor [1979] Director

Green Box Drinks Limited
Incorporated: 13 March 2012
Net Worth: £21,572 *Total Assets:* £178,101
Registered Office: Unit 1A Hazlewood Tower, Golborne Gardens, London, W10 5DT
Major Shareholder: Mark Douglas Hill
Officers: Mark Douglas Hill [1977] Director/Food & Beverage Consultant

Gilbert and John Greenall Limited
Incorporated: 21 September 2011
Registered Office: Distribution Point, Melbury Park, Clayton Road, Birchwood, Warrington, Cheshire, WA3 6PH
Shareholders: Warren Michael Scott; Vincenzo Visone
Officers: Michael Clifford, Secretary; Warren Michael Scott [1963] Director/Businessman; Vincenzo Visone [1955] Director/Businessman [Italian]

Greenwood Spirits Limited
Incorporated: 30 September 2015 *Employees:* 1
Net Worth Deficit: £1,411,896 *Total Assets:* £7,645,300
Registered Office: 49 St James's Street, London, SW1A 1JT
Officers: Barthelemy Timothee Lawrence Edvard Brosseau [1989] Director [French]; Andrew William Rankin [1957] Director; Dan Lawrence Zaum [1965] Director

Grey Dog of Meoble Limited
Incorporated: 4 January 2019
Registered Office: Braeside, Keppoch Farm Road, Arisaig, Highland, PH39 4NH
Shareholders: Rachel Iona Wilkinson; Paula Mary Wilkinson
Officers: Rachel Iona Wilkinson [1982] Director/Marketing Consultant

Greywood Distillery Limited
Incorporated: 25 November 2015
Net Worth: £260 *Total Assets:* £18,753
Registered Office: 57 Falkland Road, Lichfield, Staffs, WS14 0GE
Shareholders: Tomas David Lindsey; Rory Gavin McKerrell
Officers: Tomas David Lindsey [1987] Director; Rory Gavin McKerrell [1986] Director

Griffiths Brothers Distillery Ltd
Incorporated: 10 May 2016
Net Worth Deficit: £29,459 *Total Assets:* £100,445
Registered Office: Amerden Barn, Amerden Lane, Taplow, Maidenhead, Berks, SL6 0EE
Shareholders: Alex Gordon John Griffiths; Andrew Michael James Griffiths
Officers: Andrew Griffiths, Secretary; Alexander Griffiths [1970] Director/IT Manager; Andrew Griffiths [1972] Director/Commercial Manager

Ground Inn Ltd
Incorporated: 21 August 2018
Registered Office: 19a Square Street, Ramsbottom, Bury, Lancs, BL0 9BE
Major Shareholder: Nicholas Michael Greenwood
Officers: Nicholas Michael Greenwood [1988] Director/Manager

Guilty Drinks Limited
Incorporated: 31 January 2005
Registered Office: 69a Greenside Road, London, W12 9JQ
Major Shareholder: Julian Stephen Deghy
Officers: Julian Stephen Deghy [1960] Director/Internet Developer

Guilty Libations Limited
Incorporated: 9 August 2016
Net Worth: £5,944 *Total Assets:* £49,384
Registered Office: 39 Portsmouth Wood Close, Lindfield, Haywards Heath, W Sussex, RH16 2DQ
Major Shareholder: Paul Stanley
Officers: Paul Stanley [1975] Director

Gun Dog Gin Limited
Incorporated: 23 March 2016 *Employees:* 1
Net Worth Deficit: £10,839 *Total Assets:* £75,401
Registered Office: The Orchards, Putley, Ledbury, Herefords, HR8 2QR
Major Shareholder: Charles Gordon Frost
Officers: Susan Margaret Frost [1957] Director

Gyffordes Distillers Ltd
Incorporated: 24 September 2018
Registered Office: Highfield, 115 Cross Oak Road, Berkhamsted, Herts, HP4 3HZ
Major Shareholder: Peter Burroughes Hughes
Officers: Graham Vernon Appleyard [1969] Managing Director; Peter Burroughes Hughes [1969] Managing Director

H & S Distillers Ltd
Incorporated: 1 June 2017
Registered Office: Pipit Wood, Harbour Way, Bosham, Chichester, W Sussex, PO18 8QH
Major Shareholder: Linus Paul Williams-Silva
Officers: Linus Paul Williams-Silva [1993] Director

The Hackney Distillery Limited
Incorporated: 11 January 2018
Registered Office: Acre House, 11-15 William Road, London, NW1 3ER
Major Shareholder: Alistair James Barclay
Officers: Alistair James Barclay [1989] Director

Half Cock Limited
Incorporated: 10 July 2013
Registered Office: 42 Stewart Road, London, E15 2BB
Officers: Toby Brown [1985] Director; Brett Donahay [1978] Director [Australian]; Ryan Mills [1984] Director

A.D.C. Halford & Company Limited
Incorporated: 9 December 1998
Net Worth: £8 *Total Assets:* £8
Registered Office: 4 Millfield Close, Chester-le-Street, Co Durham, DH2 3HZ
Parent: JG Distillers Ltd
Officers: Caroline Purdie, Secretary; Colin Shields Barclay [1958] Director/Merchant [Canadian]

Halton Turner Brewing Company Ltd
Incorporated: 26 March 2018
Registered Office: 11 Whitley Avenue, Amington, Tamworth, Staffs, B77 3QU
Shareholders: Christopher Paul Turner; Giles Halton
Officers: Christopher Paul Turner [1983] Director

The UK Spirits Industry · dellam

Hamilton Rose Gin Ltd
Incorporated: 27 June 2018
Registered Office: 71-75 Shelton Street, Covent Garden, London, WC2H 9JQ
Shareholders: John Brassey; Rosalind Burns
Officers: John Brassey, Secretary; John Brassey [1980] Director/Tax Adviser; Rosalind Burns [1989] Director/Tax Adviser

The Handmade Gin Company Ltd
Incorporated: 17 May 2016
Previous: The Hand Made Gin Company Ltd
Net Worth: £76,065 Total Assets: £132,143
Registered Office: Seymour Chambers, 92 London Road, Liverpool, L3 5NW
Major Shareholder: Peter Golightly
Officers: Peter Golightly, Secretary; Peter Golightly [1964] Director; Eric Simon Healing [1969] Director

Hankey Bannister & Company Limited
Incorporated: 6 January 1976
Registered Office: Moffat Distillery, Airdrie, N Lanarks, ML6 8PL
Shareholders: Charoen Sirivadhanabhakdi; Khunying Wanna Sirivadhanabhakdi
Officers: Man Kong Lee [1968] Director/Accountant [Chinese]; Dr Martin John Leonard [1961] Managing Director; Prapakon Thongtheppairot [1971] Director [Thai]

Harbour Gin Company Ltd
Incorporated: 14 September 2018
Registered Office: 10 Lilac Avenue, Great Sankey, Warrington, Cheshire, WA5 1LL
Major Shareholder: Christopher George Moore
Officers: Christopher George Moore [1977] Director/Distiller

Harlequin Distillery Ltd
Incorporated: 12 November 2018
Registered Office: 4 Macmillan Drive, Eastbourne, E Sussex, BN21 1SX
Major Shareholder: Susan Sharp
Officers: Susan Sharp [1967] Director

Harley House Craft Distillery Ltd
Incorporated: 17 July 2017
Registered Office: 79 Sutton Road, Seaford, E Sussex, BN25 4QH
Major Shareholder: Heidi Louise Cowley
Officers: Heidi Cowley, Secretary

Harley House Distillery Ltd
Incorporated: 18 July 2017
Registered Office: 79 Sutton Road, Seaford, E Sussex, BN25 4QH
Shareholder: Heidi Louise Cowley
Officers: Joseph Robinson, Secretary; Adam David George Cowley [1970] Director; Heidi Louise Cowley [1973] Director/Accountant; Robert Murray [1982] Director

Harrison Distillery Ltd
Incorporated: 3 September 2018
Registered Office: 8 Sycamore Croft, Skelmanthorpe, Huddersfield, W Yorks, HD8 9UX
Shareholder: Simon Michael Harrison
Officers: Simon Michael Harrison [1979] Director/Operations Manager; Laura Ann Walker [1985] Director/Staff Nurse

Harrogate Distillery Ltd
Incorporated: 10 January 2014 Employees: 6
Net Worth: £97,775 Total Assets: £256,057
Registered Office: Harewell House Farm, Dacre Banks, Harrogate, N Yorks, HG3 4HQ
Major Shareholder: Jane Suzanne Whittaker
Officers: Jessica Ashton Beale, Secretary; Jane Suzanne Whittaker [1969] Sales and Marketing Director; Toby Sam Whittaker [1967] Managing Director

Hart Brothers Limited
Incorporated: 26 March 1992
Net Worth Deficit: £2,859
Registered Office: 4 Millfield Close, Chester-le-Street, Co Durham, DH2 3HZ
Parent: JG Distillers Ltd
Officers: Caroline Purdie, Secretary; Colin Shields Barclay [1958] Director/Merchant [Canadian]; Alistair Robert Greig Hart [1944] Director; Gerrard McSherry [1956] Director/Accountant

Ian Hart Distilling Limited
Incorporated: 4 December 2017
Registered Office: 5 Talbot Road, London, N6 4QS
Parent: Sacred Spirits Holdings Ltd
Officers: Ian Nicholas Hart, Secretary; Ian Nicholas Hart [1965] Director; Hilary Susan Jones [1962] Director

Hatters Distillery Limited
Incorporated: 28 September 2018
Registered Office: 28 Moscow Road East, Edgeley, Stockport, Cheshire, SK3 9QL
Major Shareholder: Sacha Charles Joseph Mannion
Officers: Sacha Charles Joseph Mannion [1990] Director/Distiller

Hawkridge Distillers Ltd
Incorporated: 27 April 2018
Registered Office: Hawkridge House, Hawkridge Hill, Frilsham, Thatcham, Berks, RG18 9XA
Major Shareholder: Elena Breeze
Officers: Elena Breeze [1971] Director/Finance

Hawksburn Spirits International Limited
Incorporated: 24 July 1995
Net Worth Deficit: £7,205
Registered Office: St Peters House, 101 Dorset Road, Bexhill on Sea, E Sussex, TN40 2HU
Shareholder: Timothy John Gordon
Officers: Sharon Anne Gordon, Secretary; Timothy John Gordon [1952] Director/Management Consultant

Hawkshead Distillery Ltd
Incorporated: 29 November 2018
Registered Office: Gilmarver Flat, Wordsworth Street, Hawkshead, Cumbria, LA22 0PA
Major Shareholder: Mark Warburton
Officers: Mark Warburton, Secretary; Mark Warburton [1964] Director

Hawkshead Gin and Spirit Co Ltd
Incorporated: 16 March 2018
Registered Office: Gilmarver Flat, Wordsworth Street, Hawkshead, Cumbria, LA22 0PA
Major Shareholder: Mark Warburton
Officers: Mark Warburton [1964] Director

Hawkshead Spirit Co Ltd
Incorporated: 30 January 2019
Registered Office: Gilmarver Flat, Wordsworth Street, Hawkshead, Cumbria, LA22 0PA
Major Shareholder: Mark Warburton
Officers: Mark Warburton [1964] Director

Hayman Distillers Limited
Incorporated: 26 May 1954
Registered Office: 8b Weir Road, London, SW12 0NA
Parent: Hayman Group
Officers: Christopher Frank Hayman [1947] Director; James Hayman [1976] Director; Miranda Sophie Carin Nevin [1974] Director

Hayter Divisions Limited
Incorporated: 15 March 2017
Registered Office: 88 Derwent Road, Highwoods, Colchester, Essex, CO4 9RU
Major Shareholder: Christopher James Hayter
Officers: Christopher James Hayter [1976] Director/Retail Management; Thomas Jonathan Hayter [1994] Director/Teacher

Hazell & Hazell Distillers Ltd
Incorporated: 9 February 2018
Registered Office: The Jaw, Baldernock, Milngavie, E Dunbartonshire, G62 6HD
Shareholder: Simon Mark Hazell
Officers: Helen Alison Hazell [1960] Director; Simon Mark Hazell [1960] Director

Heart of Suffolk Distillery Limited
Incorporated: 13 October 2017 *Employees:* 2
Net Worth Deficit: £4,650 *Total Assets:* £19,929
Registered Office: Bury Lodge, Bury Road, Stowmarket, Suffolk, IP14 1JA
Major Shareholder: Martyn Jon Luke
Officers: Karen Elizabeth Luke [1963] Director; Martyn Jon Luke [1966] Director

The Hebden Bridge Spirit Company Limited
Incorporated: 20 April 2018
Registered Office: Lauren House, 37a Wakefield Road, Tandem, Huddersfield, W Yorks, HD5 0AN
Shareholders: Michael O'Grady; Avril O'Grady
Officers: Avril O'Grady [1963] Director; Dr Michael O'Grady [1959] Director

Hebridean Distillers Limited
Incorporated: 8 April 2016
Registered Office: 22 East Barnton Avenue, Edinburgh, EH4 6AQ
Shareholders: Iain Stuart Smith; Douglas Alexander Smith
Officers: Douglas Alexander Smith [1972] Manager/Director [British/Australian]; Iain Stuart Smith [1975] Director

The Hebridean Liqueur Company Limited
Incorporated: 18 December 1995
Net Worth: £2,149 *Total Assets:* £2,149
Registered Office: 44 Campbell Street, Helensburgh, Argyll & Bute, G84 8XZ
Major Shareholder: Roy Thomas Lewis
Officers: Thomas McFarlane, Secretary; Penelope Frances Lewis [1958] Director/Fundraiser; Roy Thomas Lewis [1957] Director/Salesman

Helford River Distillery Ltd
Incorporated: 5 May 2016
Net Worth: £3 *Total Assets:* £10,003
Registered Office: Bodergy, Budock Vean Lane, Mawnan Smith, Falmouth, Cornwall, TR11 5LH
Shareholders: Mark Kelly; Simon James Finemore; Connell Carlin Dorrian
Officers: Connell Carlin Dorrian [1972] Director/Chiropractor [Irish]; Simon James Finemore [1973] Director/Chiropractor; Mark Kelly [1970] Director [Irish]

Hendre Distillery Ltd
Incorporated: 13 November 2018
Registered Office: Hendre Glyn Farm, Upper Llanover, Abergavenny, Monmouthshire, NP7 9ER
Major Shareholder: Sioned Haf Leyshon
Officers: Sioned Haf Leyshon [1989] Director; Alan John Williams [1953] Director; Victoria Nancy Williams [1961] Director

The Hendrick's Gin Distillery Limited
Incorporated: 30 August 2002
Registered Office: Girvan Distillery, Grangestone Industrial Estate, Girvan, S Ayrshire, KA26 9PT
Parent: William Grant & Sons Management Limited
Officers: Gregory Justin Bargeton [1973] Director/Lawyer; Ewan John Henderson [1968] Director/Accountant

The Henley Gin Company Limited
Incorporated: 27 September 2017
Registered Office: 4th Floor, New Penderel House, 283-288 High Holborn, London, WC1V 7HP
Officers: David Charles Jenkins [1959] Director/Accountant

Henstone Distillery Limited
Incorporated: 8 July 2015
Net Worth Deficit: £17,109 *Total Assets:* £136,999
Registered Office: Stonehouse, Weston, Oswestry, Salop, SY10 9ES
Officers: Alison Mary Parr, Secretary; Alison Mary Parr [1969] Director; Shane Alexander Parr [1972] Director [Australian]; Alexandra Toller [1957] Director; Christopher Ian Toller [1956] Director

Herbert's Distillery & Co Ltd
Incorporated: 1 October 2018
Registered Office: 23 Kirby Road, Basildon, Essex, SS14 1RX
Major Shareholder: Ryan Jon Herbert
Officers: Ryan Jon Herbert [1984] Director/Production Manager

Hereford & Ludlow Cider Brandy Company Limited
Incorporated: 26 February 2013
Registered Office: Wainbridge House, Clee St Margaret, Craven Arms, Salop, SY7 9DT
Major Shareholder: Michael John Hardingham
Officers: Michael John Hardingham [1956] Director/Distiller

HG Family Enterprise Ltd
Incorporated: 1 May 2015
Registered Office: The Tall House, 29a West Street, Marlow, Bucks, SL7 2LS
Officers: Yvonne Mary Hardaker [1953] Director

HI&PE Limited
Incorporated: 17 November 2015
Net Worth Deficit: £1,433 *Total Assets:* £511
Registered Office: 31 Bassett Crescent East, Bassett, Southampton, SO16 7PD
Major Shareholder: Hillar Peters
Officers: Hillar Peters [1969] Director [Estonian]

Hibernian Beverage Group Limited
Incorporated: 19 April 2018
Registered Office: c/o KRA Accountants Ltd, Office 1, Elsie Whiteley Innovation Centre, Hopwood Lane, Halifax, W Yorks, HX1 5ER
Officers: Larry Murin [1957] Director [Irish]; Lorcan Rossi [1969] Director [Irish]; Gregory Sparks [1951] Director [Irish]

Hidden Gem - Urban Artisan Spirit Ltd
Incorporated: 14 March 2017
Registered Office: 103 Chorley Road, Swinton, Manchester, M27 4AA
Major Shareholder: Carmel Heeran
Officers: Carmel Heeran [1972] Director/Alcohol Production and Sales

High Road Rum Company Limited
Incorporated: 26 August 2016
Registered Office: Old School House, Lotts, Islay, Argyll, PA42 7DD
Officers: Ben Inglis [1992] Director

The High Street Trading Company Limited
Incorporated: 9 November 1994 *Employees:* 2
Net Worth: £131,058 *Total Assets:* £236,342
Registered Office: Suites 4 & 5, Main Street, Milngavie, Glasgow, G62 6BJ
Major Shareholder: Roy Thomas Lewis
Officers: Thomas McFarlane, Secretary; Penelope Frances Lewis [1958] Director/Charity Fundraiser; Roy Thomas Lewis [1957] Director/Salesman

High Water Distilling Company Limited
Incorporated: 23 August 2018
Registered Office: Pennycomequick, Smithick Hill, Falmouth, Cornwall, TR11 3AX
Major Shareholder: Jack Peter Williams
Officers: Jack Peter Williams [1987] Director

Highland Boundary Ltd
Incorporated: 26 January 2016
Net Worth Deficit: £6,352 *Total Assets:* £15,599
Registered Office: Kirklandbank, Alyth, Blairgowrie, Perthshire, PH11 8LL
Shareholders: Marian Cooke Bruce; Simon Alexander Montador
Officers: Dr Marian Cooke Bruce [1966] Director/Artist, Farmer, Business Owner; Simon Alexander Montador [1966] Director/Management Consultant

Highland Distillers Group Limited
Incorporated: 7 July 1887
Net Worth: £59,000,000 *Total Assets:* £153,200,000
Registered Office: 100 Queen Street, Glasgow, G1 3DN
Parent: 1887 Company Limited
Officers: Gemma May Robson, Secretary; Aristotelis Baroutsis [1973] Director [Swedish]; Jeremy McDowell Chaplin [1961] Director; Scott John McCroskie [1967] Director/Chartered Accountant; Michael Stephen Saunders [1966] Director/Chartered Accountant

Highland Distillers Limited
Incorporated: 19 June 1995 *Employees:* 202
Net Worth: £96,600,000 *Total Assets:* £374,300,000
Registered Office: 100 Queen Street, Glasgow, G1 3DN
Parent: 1887 Company Limited
Officers: Gemma May Robson, Secretary; Aristotelis Baroutsis [1973] Director [Swedish]; Jeremy McDowell Chaplin [1971] Director; Graham Robert Hutcheon [1963] Director; Scott John McCroskie [1967] Director/Chartered Accountant

Highland Toddy Ltd
Incorporated: 24 September 2013
Registered Office: Seacrest, Barbaraville, Invergordon, Ross-shire, IV18 0NA
Officers: William Ross, Secretary; William MacKay Ross [1933] Director/Retired

Highland Whisky Limited
Incorporated: 22 March 2005
Net Worth Deficit: £19,893 *Total Assets:* £13,548
Registered Office: 1 Royal Bank Place, Buchanan Street, Glasgow, G1 3AA
Shareholders: Christopher Ronald Parker; Alexander William Parker
Officers: Alexander William Parker, Secretary; Alexander William Parker [1973] Director; Heather Patricia Parker [1941] Director; Naomi Parker [1973] Director/Administrator

Highlands Spirit Ltd.
Incorporated: 4 July 2007
Registered Office: 1 Aspen Court, High Street, Crieff, Perthshire, PH7 3HZ
Shareholder: Charles Duncan Brown
Officers: Charles Duncan Brown, Secretary; Charles Duncan Brown [1947] Horticulturist/Director; Robert Grafham [1952] Director

Hin Ltd
Incorporated: 12 December 2018
Registered Office: 1b Carram Way, Lincoln, LN1 1AB
Shareholders: Christopher Puttick; Mathew Kalum Graham
Officers: Mathew Kalum Graham [1985] Director; Christopher Puttick [1993] Director

Hinch Distillery Holdings Limited
Incorporated: 27 February 2018
Registered Office: Killaney Lodge, 19 Carryduff Road, Lisburn, Co Antrim, BT27 6TZ
Parent: CD PTC Limited (as Trustee of The Cross Family Trust)
Officers: Terence Martin Cross [1950] Director; Derek Hardy [1961] Director; Patrick Joseph McGibbon [1971] Director/Accountant; Michael Morris [1961] Sales Director [Irish]

Hinch Distillery Limited
Incorporated: 4 August 2016 *Employees:* 2
Previous: Killaney Estates Limited
Net Worth Deficit: £132,655 *Total Assets:* £1,969,733
Registered Office: Killaney Lodge, 19 Carryduff Road, Lisburn, Co Antrim, BT27 6TZ
Parent: Hinch Distillery Holdings Limited
Officers: Patrick Martin Cross [1975] Director; Terence Martin Cross [1950] Director; Derek Hardy [1961] Director; Patrick Joseph McGibbon [1971] Director/Accountant; Michael Morris [1961] Sales Director [Irish]

Hinch Whiskey Company Limited
Incorporated: 27 February 2018
Registered Office: Killaney Lodge, 19 Carryduff Road, Lisburn, Co Antrim, BT27 6TZ
Parent: Hinch Distillery Limited
Officers: Terence Martin Cross [1950] Director; Derek Hardy [1961] Director; Patrick Joseph McGibbon [1971] Director/Accountant; Michael Morris [1961] Sales Director [Irish]

Hinton's of Bewdley Ltd
Incorporated: 1 February 2017
Net Worth Deficit: £1,582 *Total Assets:* £11,827
Registered Office: 25 Damson Way, Bewdley, Worcs, DY12 1EZ
Major Shareholder: Nicholas James Hinton
Officers: Andrea Clare Hinton, Secretary; Nicholas James Hinton [1969] Technical Director

HMS Spirits Company Limited
Incorporated: 12 December 2016
Net Worth Deficit: £14,808 *Total Assets:* £32,855
Registered Office: 6 Coleville Avenue, Fawley, Southampton, SO45 1DA
Officers: Benjamin Charles Maguire [1983] Director/Sales Manager

Hoggnorton Limited
Incorporated: 29 December 2015
Net Worth Deficit: £22,534 *Total Assets:* £14,050
Registered Office: Belmont Cottage, Holymoorside, Chesterfield, Derbys, S42 7DS
Shareholders: Michael Paul Norton; Adrian Hogg
Officers: Michael Woolgar-Norton, Secretary; Adrian Hogg [1958] Director/Founder; Michael Paul Woolgar-Norton [1971] Director/Founder

Holler Brewery Limited
Incorporated: 21 December 2017
Registered Office: 19-23 Elder Place, Brighton, BN1 4GF
Parent: Ironstone Brewery Ltd
Officers: Steve James Keegan [1982] Director; Davinder Singh Sahota [1975] Director

Holme Gin Limited
Incorporated: 4 December 2017
Registered Office: 1 The Forum, Minerva Business Park, Lynch Wood, Peterborough, Cambs, PE2 6FT
Major Shareholder: Nicholas Collett
Officers: Nicholas Collett [1965] Director

Holy Grail Beverages Limited
Incorporated: 13 April 2018
Registered Office: 30 St Clares Walk, Brigg, S Humbers, DN20 8JS
Shareholders: Rebecca Sturgeon; Frank Bosco
Officers: Rebecca Sturgeon, Secretary; Frank Bosco [1954] Director

The Holyrood Distillery Ltd
Incorporated: 1 April 2016
Registered Office: The Capital Building, 12-13 St Andrew Square, Edinburgh, EH2 2AF
Parent: Newmake Limited
Officers: Robert Francis Carpenter [1964] Director/Lawyer [Canadian]; William Farrar [1958] Director; David Graham Robertson [1968] Director

The Honey Gin Company Limited
Incorporated: 20 July 2017
Registered Office: 9 Glen Rise, Glen Parva, Leicester, LE2 9HA
Officers: Stephen Patrick Anderson [1988] Commercial Director; Geoffrey Dylan Woodward [1988] Creative Director

Honey Spirits Co Ltd
Incorporated: 19 December 2016
Net Worth Deficit: £33,464 *Total Assets:* £27,741
Registered Office: The Barn, Tagg Lane, Monyash, Bakewell, Derbys, DE45 1JP
Major Shareholder: Ineta McKaite
Officers: James Edward Maxwell Mather [1976] Director; Ineta Mickaite [1981] Managing Director [Lithuanian]

The Hooting Owl Distillery Ltd
Incorporated: 5 April 2018
Registered Office: Barmby Moor House, Hull Road, Barmby Moor, York, YO42 4EZ
Major Shareholder: Dominic Oseman M'Benga
Officers: Sarah Jane Cairney [1968] Director; Neil Anthony Hepplewhite [1968] Sales Director; Dominic Oseman M'benga [1965] Director

Horseguards London Dry Gin Limited
Incorporated: 27 July 2017
Registered Office: Suite D, Pinbrook Court, Venny Bridge, Exeter, EX4 8JQ
Shareholders: Paul Brian McCarthy; London IP Exchange Limited
Officers: Gordon Charles Fitzjohn [1954] Director; Paul Brian McCarthy [1963] Director; Simon Rendell [1962] Director

Horsforth Distillery Ltd
Incorporated: 14 May 2018
Registered Office: The Cottage, 40 Bachelor Lane, Horsforth, Leeds, LS18 5NA
Major Shareholder: Johannes Lukas Stanta
Officers: Dr Johannes Lukas Stanta [1978] Director/Chief Executive [Austrian]

Hothams Limited
Incorporated: 18 January 2018
Registered Office: 20-22 Hepworths Arcade, Silver Street, Hull, HU1 1JU
Officers: Emma Kinton, Secretary; Emma Kinton [1975] Director/Teacher; Simon Pownall [1971] Director/Manager

House of Elrick Gin Limited
Incorporated: 15 April 2016
Net Worth Deficit: £106,643 *Total Assets:* £463,376
Registered Office: Elrick House, Newmachar, Aberdeen, AB21 7PY
Major Shareholder: Stuart Ingram
Officers: Stuart Ingram [1977] Director

House of St Giles Ltd
Incorporated: 1 April 2016
Net Worth Deficit: £606 *Total Assets:* £168,900
Registered Office: Mercury House, Shipstones Business Center, North Gate, Nottingham, NG7 7FN
Officers: Peter Robson, Secretary; Peter Robson [1959] Director

Howards of Kent Limited
Incorporated: 7 November 2011
Registered Office: 30 Cromwell Avenue, Bromley, Kent, BR2 9AQ
Major Shareholder: Claire Brinan
Officers: David Brinan, Secretary; Claire Brinan [1961] Director

Hoyle Bottom Spirits Ltd
Incorporated: 27 April 2018
Registered Office: Oswaldtwistle Mills Business Centre, Clifton Mill, Pickup Street, Oswaldtwistle, Lancs, BB5 0EY
Major Shareholder: Jamie McNally
Officers: Jamie McNally [1987] Managing Director; Owen McNally [1984] Director

HS (Distillers) Limited
Incorporated: 7 June 1996 *Employees:* 3
Net Worth: £27,000 *Total Assets:* £27,000
Registered Office: 100 Queen Street, Glasgow, G1 3DN
Shareholders: Highland Distillers Group Limited; SUS Holdings 2 Limited
Officers: Ashleigh Kay Clark, Secretary; Ashleigh Kay Clark [1985] Director/Legal Counsel; Pryce William David Greenow [1970] Director/Sales & Marketing, President International Region; Scott John McCroskie [1967] Director/Chartered Accountant

Hukleys Limited
Incorporated: 15 August 2016
Registered Office: Abbey Fields, 242 London Road, Stretton on Dunsmore, Rugby, Warwicks, CV23 9JA
Officers: Jessica Hughes [1991] Director/Sales

Hunter Douglas Scotch Whisky Limited
Incorporated: 11 March 2015
Net Worth: £100 *Total Assets:* £100
Registered Office: c/o Cloch Solicitors, 94 Hope Street, Glasgow, G2 6PH
Parent: The Shieling Scotch Whisky Co Ltd
Officers: Andrew Ross Crombie [1964] Director/Stonemason

Hurlingham International Limited
Incorporated: 28 January 1993
Registered Office: Avalon House, 72 Lower Mortlake Road, Richmond, Surrey, TW9 2JY
Parent: Distell International Holdings Limited
Officers: Karen Spy, Secretary; Fraser John Thornton [1969] Director

Hurricane Rum Company Limited
Incorporated: 29 January 2018
Registered Office: 1 Stephen Street, London, W1T 1AL
Major Shareholder: Arlo Brady
Officers: Arlo Brady [1977] Director

Hussingtree Blends Limited
Incorporated: 27 October 2017
Registered Office: Tythe Barn, Church Lane, Martin Hussingtree, Worcester, WR3 8TQ
Shareholders: Richard William Meredith; Elaine Joan Meredith; Duncan Thompson Gilroy
Officers: Duncan Thompson Gilroy [1978] Director/Design & Marketing Consultant; Elaine Joan Meredith [1951] Director/Accountant - Retired; Richard William Meredith [1949] Director/Teacher - Retired

Idle Saint Spirits Limited
Incorporated: 19 March 2015
Registered Office: 1 Nepaul Road, London, SW11 2QQ
Shareholder: Julia Ruzicka
Officers: Adam Colin Devonshire, Secretary; Adam Colin Devonshire [1984] Director; Julia Ruzicka [1975] Director/Musician [Australian]; Mr Damien Craig Sayell [1984] Director

The Ilkley Gin Company Ltd
Incorporated: 1 November 2018
Registered Office: 8a Beechwood Centre, Church Street, Woodlesford, Leeds, LS26 8RE
Major Shareholder: Andrew Carthy
Officers: Andrew Carthy [1982] Director/Motor Engineer

Illicit Spirits Ltd
Incorporated: 17 July 2017
Registered Office: Unit 3 Bridge Court, 12 Cook Street, Glasgow, G5 8JN
Officers: Darran Edmond [1987] Director/Owner

In The Welsh Wind Distillery Ltd
Incorporated: 24 January 2018
Registered Office: Plas-Y-Wern, Tresaith, Cardigan, Ceredigion, SA43 2JP
Shareholders: Ellen Catherine Wakelam; Alexander Peter Jungmayr
Officers: Alexander Peter Jungmayr [1981] Director; Ellen Catherine Wakelam [1983] Director

Incharvie Group Limited
Incorporated: 9 April 2018
Registered Office: Lahill, Upper Largo, Leven, Fife, KY8 6JE
Shareholders: William James Garnock; James Anstey Preston Wild
Officers: William James Garnock [1990] Director; James Anstey Preston Wild [1991] Director

Incognito Ltd
Incorporated: 24 August 2017
Registered Office: Finnieston House, 1129 Argyle Street, Finnieston, Glasgow, G51 1JW
Shareholders: Maurice Howard Clark; Graham Kenneth Suttle; Scott John Arnot
Officers: Maurice Clark, Secretary; Scott John Arnot [1980] Director; Maurice Howard Clark [1980] Director; Graham Kenneth Suttle [1979] Director

Independent Spirits Limited
Incorporated: 14 August 2007
Registered Office: 27 Nasmyth Street, London, W6 0HA
Major Shareholder: Fairfax Alexander Charles Hall
Officers: Fairfax Hall, Secretary; Stamford Timothy John Galsworthy [1976] Director; Fairfax Hall [1974] Director

Inshriach Distilling Limited
Incorporated: 24 May 2016
Net Worth: £12,350 *Total Assets:* £48,520
Registered Office: Inshriach House, Inshriach, Aviemore, Highland, PH22 1QP
Major Shareholder: Walter Harry Micklethwait
Officers: Walter Harry Micklethwait [1978] Director/Estate Manager

Inspirited Ltd
Incorporated: 23 January 2019
Registered Office: 27 Glasgow Road, Chapelton, Aberdeenshire, ML10 6RS
Shareholders: Lawrence Nicholson; James Nicholson
Officers: James Nicholson [1963] Director; Lawrence Nicholson [1994] Director

Inver House Distillers Limited
Incorporated: 12 March 1964 *Employees:* 212
Net Worth: £106,847,000 *Total Assets:* £158,866,000
Registered Office: Moffat Distillery, Airdrie, N Lanarks, ML6 8PL
Shareholders: Khunying Wanna Sirivadhanabhakdi; Chareon Sirivadhanabhakdi
Officers: Jorgen Bornhoft [1942] Director [Danish]; Sithichai Chaikriangkrai [1954] Director [Thai]; Michael Hin Fah Chye [1959] Director [Singaporean]; Dr Martin John Leonard [1961] Managing Director; Thapana Sirivadhanabhakdi [1975] Director/Chairman [Thai]; Prapakon Thongtheppairot [1971] Director [Thai]

Inverroche International Limited
Incorporated: 20 May 2016
Net Worth: £100 Total Assets: £100
Registered Office: 27 Old Gloucester Street, London, WC1N 3AX
Major Shareholder: Leonora Scott
Officers: Leonora Scott [1955] Director

Invoke Distillery Ltd
Incorporated: 29 November 2018
Registered Office: East Millwood, Maidstone Road, Wrotham Heath, Sevenoaks, Kent, TN15 7SR
Shareholders: Lee Hall; James Hackney
Officers: James Hackney [1978] Director/Manager; Lee Hall [1980] Director/Teacher

Invoke Distilling Co. Ltd
Incorporated: 23 November 2018
Registered Office: East Millwood, Maidstone Road, Wrotham Heath, Sevenoaks, Kent, TN15 7SR
Shareholders: Lee Hall; James Hackney
Officers: James Hackney [1978] Director/Manager; Lee Hall [1980] Director/Teacher

The Irish Gin Company Ltd
Incorporated: 19 April 2018
Registered Office: 35 Legilly Road, Dungannon, Co Tyrone, BT70 1QG
Major Shareholder: Cathal Peter McVeigh
Officers: Cathal Peter McVeigh [1989] Director

Irish Whiskey Company Limited - The
Incorporated: 23 March 1989
Net Worth Deficit: £995 Total Assets: £5
Registered Office: The Hill, 30 Newcastle Road, Ballynahinch, Co Down, BT24 8NF
Shareholder: Nicholas Howard Ward
Officers: Nicholas Howard Ward, Secretary; Adrian Gawain Moir [1953] Director/Marketing Consultant; Nicholas Howard Ward [1949] Director/Accountant; Eric Wrixon [1947] Director/Marketing Consultant

The Ironbridge Gorge Gin Company Ltd
Incorporated: 17 January 2019
Registered Office: 25 Croppings Park, Lightmoor, Telford, Salop, TF4 3GB
Major Shareholder: Derek Clive Bowen
Officers: Derek Clive Bowen [1963] Director/Salesman

The Islay Boys Limited
Incorporated: 17 December 2012
Net Worth: £16,303 Total Assets: £68,227
Registered Office: The Brewery, Islay House Square, Bridgend, Islay, Argyll, PA44 7NZ
Shareholders: Donald MacKenzie; Jason McGuire MacKay Smith
Officers: Donald MacKenzie [1962] Director/Brand Ambassador; Jason McGuire MacKay Smith [1969] Director

Islay Rum Company Ltd
Incorporated: 3 November 2008
Registered Office: 101 Rose Street, South Lane, Edinburgh, EH2 3JG
Major Shareholder: Gilbert Buchanan Stevenson
Officers: Dr Gilbert Buchanan Stevenson [1977] Director

Islay Spirits (No. 2) Limited
Incorporated: 12 April 2017 Employees: 2
Net Worth Deficit: £4,963 Total Assets: £73,741
Registered Office: 2 Stewart Street, Milngavie, Glasgow, G62 6BW
Shareholders: Harry Brian Crook; Andrew Brian Crook; The Vintage Malt Whisky Company Limited
Officers: Caroline Sanderson James, Secretary; Andrew Brian Crook [1976] Director; Caroline Sanderson James [1968] Director

The Islay Spirits Company Limited
Incorporated: 1 February 2017
Registered Office: 2 Stewart Street, Milngavie, Glasgow, G62 6BW
Shareholders: Caroline Sanderson James; Andrew Brian Crook
Officers: Caroline James, Secretary; Caroline Sanderson James [1968] Director/Solicitor

Isle of Arran Gin Company Limited
Incorporated: 22 December 2016
Net Worth: £100 Total Assets: £100
Registered Office: Bay Stores, Whiting Bay, Isle of Arran, KA27 8PZ
Officers: Stuart Fraser [1971] Director/Shop Owner; George Frank Grassie [1974] Director; Ross Hamilton [1971] Director; George Laird [1971] Director/Healthcare Services Executive

Isle of Barra Distillers Ltd
Incorporated: 9 January 2017 Employees: 3
Net Worth Deficit: £49,763 Total Assets: £1,914
Registered Office: Trinity House, 31 Lynedoch Street Park, Glasgow, G3 6EF
Major Shareholder: Michael Joseph Morrison
Officers: Michael Joseph Morrison [1991] Director

Isle of Bute Gin Company Limited
Incorporated: 26 January 2018
Registered Office: Pavilion 1, Finnieston Business Park, Minerva Way, Glasgow, G3 8AU
Shareholders: Simon Tardivel; Merchant City Brewing Company Limited
Officers: Allan Douglas Rimmer [1982] Director; Simon Tardivel [1986] Director/Distiller; Douglas Gordon George Wheatley [1959] Director

Isle of Harris Distillers Limited
Incorporated: 4 December 2007 Employees: 21
Net Worth: £5,885,679 Total Assets: £9,860,436
Registered Office: Isle of Harris Distillery, Tarbert, Isle of Harris, HS3 3DJ
Officers: Anderson Duke Bakewell [1948] Director; Simon David Erlanger [1959] Director; Hugh Grant [1958] Director; Elsa Vivien Jack [1971] Director/Management Consultant; Sebastien Le Page [1971] Director [French]; Ronald Bannatyne MacEachran [1957] Director/Business Consultant; Dirk Saltzherr [1977] Director [Dutch]

Isle of Iona Gin Limited
Incorporated: 19 February 2019
Registered Office: Cnoc Oran, Isle of Iona, PA76 6SP
Shareholders: Bryan Livingston; Glen MacDonald
Officers: Bryan Livingston [1968] Director; Glen MacDonald [1984] Director

Isle of Lewis Distillers Limited
Incorporated: 11 May 2018
Registered Office: 14 Crowlista, Uig, Stornoway, Isle of Lewis, HS2 9JF
Shareholders: Richard Alun Campbell Davies; Edward Dickon Green
Officers: Richard Alun Campbell Davies [1971] Director

Isle of Mull Gin Distillery Limited
Incorporated: 13 February 2018
Registered Office: Treetops, Gowkhouse Road, Kilmacolm, Renfrewshire, PA13 4DJ
Major Shareholder: Leslie McDonald MacLeod
Officers: Leslie McDonald MacLeod [1961] Director

Isle of Mull Gin Limited
Incorporated: 13 February 2018
Registered Office: Treetops, Gowkhouse Road, Kilmacolm, Renfrewshire, PA13 4DJ
Major Shareholder: Leslie McDonald MacLeod
Officers: Leslie McDonald MacLeod [1961] Director

Isle of Skye Distillers Ltd
Incorporated: 21 March 2016 *Employees:* 2
Net Worth: £6,395 *Total Assets:* £86,353
Registered Office: Hillfoot, Viewfield Road, Portree, Isle of Skye, IV51 9ES
Major Shareholder: Alistair MacCaskill Wilson
Officers: Alistair MacCaskill Wilson [1981] Director

Isle of Wight Distillery Ltd
Incorporated: 14 May 2014 *Employees:* 8
Net Worth: £164,438 *Total Assets:* £367,523
Registered Office: Rosemary Vineyard, Smallbrooke Lane, Ryde, Isle of Wight, PO33 4BE
Shareholders: Vincent Hugh Nolan; Xavier Lee Baker; Conrad Gauntlett
Officers: Xavier Lee Baker [1977] Director/Brewer; Conrad Martin Gauntlett [1953] Director/Farmer; Vincent Hugh Nolan [1962] Director/Chairman

Isledon Gin Ltd
Incorporated: 30 April 2018
Registered Office: 40b Endymion Road, London, N4 1EQ
Shareholders: Stefan Ben Brierley; Daniel Ivan Brierley
Officers: Dr Daniel Ivan Brierley [1981] Director/Scientist; Stefan Ben Brierley [1985] Director/IT Consultant

The Italian Gin Company Limited
Incorporated: 14 February 2018
Registered Office: 2 Farriers Yard, 9a Ockendon Road, Islington, London, N1 3NN
Shareholders: Kristin Margaret Hickey; Jacqueline Simone Ferrier
Officers: Jacqueline Simone Ferrier [1977] Director [Australian]; Kristin Margaret Hickey [1967] Director [New Zealander]

Jackson Distillers Limited
Incorporated: 23 May 2017
Registered Office: Charlesfield Farm, St Boswells, Melrose, Roxburghshire, TD6 0HH
Major Shareholder: Trevor Howard Jackson
Officers: Trevor Howard Jackson [1966] Director

Jackson's Gin Ltd
Incorporated: 12 November 2018
Registered Office: 123 Thirsk Avenue, Sale, Cheshire, M33 4GW
Shareholders: Ashley Martin Jackson; Adina Simone Aikens
Officers: Adina Simone Aikens [1995] Director; Ashley Martin Jackson [1994] Director

Jacob's Gin Limited
Incorporated: 4 September 2018
Registered Office: Fitzgerald & Law LLP, 4th Floor, 283-288 New Penderel House, High Holborn, London, WC1V 7HP
Major Shareholder: David Charles Jenkins
Officers: David Charles Jenkins [1959] Director

The Jacobite Spirit Company Ltd
Incorporated: 28 January 2019
Registered Office: 538 Paisley Road West, Glasgow, G51 1RJ
Officers: Euan Fullerton [1980] Director; Jamie Paul Vincent Smith [1978] Film Director; Anthony Stapleton [1975] Director

Jacqson Limited
Incorporated: 6 September 2016 *Employees:* 1
Net Worth Deficit: £6,447 *Total Assets:* £15,989
Registered Office: 101 Bourn View Road, Huddersfield, W Yorks, HD4 7LA
Major Shareholder: Darryl Dumigan
Officers: Dr Darryl Dumigan [1964] Director

C S James & Sons Limited
Incorporated: 14 September 2005
Registered Office: 2 Stewart Street, Milngavie, Glasgow, G62 6BW
Shareholders: Caroline Crawford Crook; Harry Brian Crook
Officers: Caroline Crawford Crook, Secretary/Director; Harry Brian Crook [1942] Director

Jawbox Spirits Company Ltd
Incorporated: 8 August 2014
Registered Office: 155-157 Donegall Pass, Belfast, BT7 1DT
Officers: Shane Joseph Braniff [1963] Director; Steven Clark Pattison [1979] Director; Richard Henderson Ryan [1977] Director; Gerry White [1958] Director [Irish]

JDB Spirits Ltd
Incorporated: 11 December 2015
Registered Office: 20-22 Wenlock Road, London, N1 7GU
Major Shareholder: Janek Burstein
Officers: Ekaterina Berkova, Secretary; Janek Burstein [1969] Director/Product Development [Swedish]

Jedhart Distillery Limited
Incorporated: 28 August 2013
Net Worth Deficit: £175 *Total Assets:* £80
Registered Office: Mossburn House, Camptown, Jedburgh, Roxburghshire, TD8 6PJ
Parent: Mossburn Distillers Ltd
Officers: John Neil MacLeod Mathieson, Secretary; Francesco Annibali [1966] Director [Italian]; John Neil MacLeod Mathieson [1961] Director/Line Shipper; Dr Alan Gray Rutherford [1942] Director

Jefferson & Bennett Distillers Ltd
Incorporated: 31 December 2018
Registered Office: 18 Tignel Court, Boddington Gardens, London, W3 9AR
Major Shareholder: Svetlana Muhonen
Officers: Svetlana Muhonen [1955] Director [Finnish]

Jervis Trading Limited
Incorporated: 12 July 2017
Registered Office: 6 Station View, Chester, CH2 3DT
Shareholders: Peter Jervis; Laura Jervis
Officers: Laura Jervis [1987] Director; Peter Jervis [1986] Director

Jesmond Distilling Co Ltd
Incorporated: 19 June 2015
Registered Office: 24 Nuns Moor Road, Newcastle upon Tyne, NE4 9AU
Officers: Elfi Mathilda Maria Middelbeek [1985] Director/Analyst [Dutch]

Jewel Isle Global Productions Ltd
Incorporated: 15 March 2012
Net Worth Deficit: £17,152 *Total Assets:* £200
Registered Office: 69 Durban Road, Tottenham, London, N17 8ED
Major Shareholder: Anita Beatrice Witter
Officers: Anita Beatrice Witter [1960] Director

Jim & Tonic Limited
Incorporated: 4 March 2016 *Employees:* 2
Net Worth: £6,499 *Total Assets:* £27,379
Registered Office: Incuba Business Centre, Brewers Hill Road, Dunstable, Beds, LU6 1AA
Major Shareholder: John James Mark
Officers: John James Mark [1979] Director/Property Consultant; Matthew James Warren [1985] Director; Nick Woodward [1987] Director/Property Manager

Jivana Spirits Ltd.
Incorporated: 13 November 2017
Registered Office: Flat 1, Philips House, 8 Ravenswood Road, London, SW12 9PL
Shareholders: Rachitha Seneviratne; Caishenkama Ltd
Officers: Vikram Pathak [1992] Director/Investments; Rachitha Seneviratne [1991] Director/Marketing [Australian]

JKM Spirits Limited
Incorporated: 12 March 2018
Registered Office: 2 Chantry Croft, Leeds, LS15 9DN
Officers: Mark Freeman [1991] Managing Director; Kane Lee [1991] Managing Director; James Douglas Tran [1991] Managing Director

Jo & Matt Ltd
Incorporated: 10 March 2015 *Employees:* 2
Net Worth: £5,226 *Total Assets:* £23,287
Registered Office: 24 Studholme Street, Peckham, London, SE15 1DD
Shareholders: Matthew Joel Broughton; Josephine Hughes
Officers: Matthew Joel Broughton [1972] Director; Josephine Hughes [1979] Director

James Johnstone Distillers Ltd.
Incorporated: 10 March 2015
Registered Office: Regent Court, 70 West Regent Street, Glasgow, G2 2QZ
Officers: Dr Tina Ingwersen-Matthiesen [1973] Director [German]; Christoph Arnold Maab [1960] Finance Director [German]

Jones Gin Ltd
Incorporated: 22 May 2018
Registered Office: 61 Hartford Road, Davenham, Northwich, Cheshire, CW9 8JE
Shareholders: Karen Elizabeth Murray; Neil Ronald Murray
Officers: Karen Elizabeth Murray [1980] Director; Neil Ronald Murray [1973] Managing Director

Jonomade Limited
Incorporated: 4 July 2018
Registered Office: Oxford House, Mount Ephraim Road, Tunbridge Wells, Kent, TN1 1EN
Shareholders: Deborah Easton Blackmore; Matthew Charles Blackmore
Officers: Deborah Easton Blackmore [1965] Director/Chief Executive; Joshua Robert Blackmore [1997] Director/Distiller; Matthew Charles Blackmore [1968] Director/General Manager

Jorvik Distillery Limited
Incorporated: 8 January 2019
Registered Office: Suite 146, 5 High Street, Maidenhead, Berks, SL6 1JN
Major Shareholder: Donald John Stewart
Officers: Donald John Stewart [1963] Director/Solicitor

Jose Reyes Bodega Ltd
Incorporated: 31 March 2016
Net Worth: £831 *Total Assets:* £182,001
Registered Office: Mercury House, Shipstone Business Centre, North Gate, Nottingham, NG7 7FN
Officers: Peter Robson, Secretary; Peter Robson [1959] Director

The Juggling King Rum Company Limited
Incorporated: 11 July 2018
Registered Office: Blackwell House, Guildhall Yard, London, EC2V 5AE
Major Shareholder: Jack Gervaise-Brazier
Officers: Jack Gervaise-Brazier [1985] Director; Dewi John Hitchcock [1963] Director

Juniper Street Gin Company Limited
Incorporated: 10 July 2017
Registered Office: 33 Lisburn Lane, Liverpool, L13 9AE
Officers: Paul Edward Martin [1960] Director/Owner

JustaGinCompany Limited
Incorporated: 7 June 2018
Registered Office: 21 Crowshaw Drive, Rochdale, Lancs, OL12 0SR
Major Shareholder: Steven Mallalieu
Officers: Steven Mallalieu [1985] Director

Justerini & Brooks, Limited
Incorporated: 22 December 1900 *Employees:* 51
Net Worth: £1,399,778,048 *Total Assets:* £1,432,017,024
Registered Office: 61 St James's Street, London, SW1A 1LZ
Parent: Diageo Great Britain Limited
Officers: Gavin Paul Crickmore [1958] Director/Chartered Accountant; James Matthew Crayden Edmunds [1974] Director/Solicitor; Sharon Lynnette Fennessy [1967] Director/Group Treasurer [Irish]; David Heginbottom [1970] Director/Group Treasurer; Aniko Mahler [1976] Director/Head of Statutory Compliance [Hungarian]; Kara Elizabeth Major [1977] Director [American]; Edward Martin Peachey [1973] Commercial Financial Director

JW Distillers Limited
Incorporated: 30 January 2015 *Employees:* 8
Net Worth: £113,995 *Total Assets:* £516,809
Registered Office: Great Yeldham Hall, Church Road, Great Yeldham, Halstead, Essex, CO9 4PT
Major Shareholder: John Anthony Walters
Officers: John Anthony Walters [1967] Director

K1 Beer PLC
Incorporated: 10 July 2012
Net Worth Deficit: £245,872 *Total Assets:* £12,046
Registered Office: Building 3, Chiswick Park, 566 Chiswick High Road, London, W4 5YA
Major Shareholder: Keyvan Foroshani
Officers: Keyvan Foroshani [1963] Director/Chief Executive

Charlie Kaane Enterprises Ltd.
Incorporated: 12 August 2016
Net Worth: £10,933 *Total Assets:* £10,933
Registered Office: 11 Kinloss Gardens, London, N3 3DU
Major Shareholder: Charles Chibueze Odunukwe
Officers: Juliet Uju Odunukwe, Secretary; Chibueze Charles Odunukwe [1990] Managing Director [Nigerian]

Kac70 Limited
Incorporated: 15 August 2018
Registered Office: 17 Carlton House Terrace, London, SW1Y 5AS
Major Shareholder: Craig Malcolm Rochford
Officers: Dr Craig Malcolm Rochford [1970] Director/Engineer

Kafecal Global Company Ltd
Incorporated: 4 January 2018
Registered Office: Nelson House, 2 Hamilton Terrace, Leamington Spa, Warwicks, CY32 4LY
Major Shareholder: Carmelo Signorello
Officers: Alessandra Percolla, Secretary; Carmelo Signorello [1977] Director [Italian]

Kammerling's Investment Holdings Ltd
Incorporated: 9 August 2011
Net Worth: £720,104 *Total Assets:* £721,544
Registered Office: Harwood House, 43 Harwood Road, London, SW6 4QP
Shareholder: Alex David Kammerling
Officers: George Ivor James [1957] Director; Alex David Kammerling [1975] Director; Heinz Peter Kammerling [1948] Director/Business Consultant; Basit Nasim [1978] Director/Equity Trader, Finance; Oliver Max Rivers [1966] Director/Strategy Consultant

Kammerlings Limited
Incorporated: 2 February 2010 *Employees:* 2
Net Worth Deficit: £712,584 *Total Assets:* £43,302
Registered Office: Harwood House, 43 Harwood Road, London, SW6 4QP
Major Shareholder: Alex David Kammerling
Officers: George Ivor James [1957] Director; Alex David Kammerling [1975] Director; Heinz Peter Kammerling [1948] Director/Business Consultant; Basit Nasim [1978] Director/Equity Trader, Finance; Oliver Max Rivers [1966] Director/Strategy Consultant

Kelpie Whisky Limited
Incorporated: 20 January 2017
Registered Office: Oak Cottage, Pedley Lane, Marthall, Knutsford, Cheshire, WA16 7SY
Major Shareholder: Nick Paul Speakman
Officers: Nick Paul Speakman [1969] Director

The Kelpies Whisky Limited
Incorporated: 28 November 2013
Registered Office: Atrium House, Callendar Business Park, Callendar Road, Falkirk, FK1 1XR
Major Shareholder: George Danskin Stewart
Officers: George Danskin Stewart, Secretary; George Danskin Stewart [1945] Director/Electrician

Kelso Gin Company Limited
Incorporated: 8 July 2016
Net Worth: £11,584 *Total Assets:* £17,682
Registered Office: 3 Spylaw Farm Cottages, Kelso, Roxburghshire, TD5 8DY
Shareholders: Andrew MacKenzie Crow; Rob Armstrong
Officers: Oliver John Drake, Secretary; Andrew MacKenzie Crow [1955] Director/Retired Racehorse Trainer

Kendal Brewery Ltd
Incorporated: 19 September 2017
Registered Office: Masons Yard 24, 22 Stramongate, Kendal, Cumbria, LA9 4BN
Shareholders: Jonathan Gillis Ritson; Darren Lincoln
Officers: Darren Lincoln [1968] Director/Joiner

The Kendal Mint Cake Company Limited
Incorporated: 27 June 2012 *Employees:* 3
Net Worth: £53,524 *Total Assets:* £121,148
Registered Office: 15 Lowther Street, Kendal, Cumbria, LA9 4DH
Officers: Michael Andrew Pennington [1956] Director

Kettlesing Gin Limited
Incorporated: 31 October 2016
Registered Office: New Chartford House, Centurion Way, Cleckheaton, W Yorks, BD19 3QB
Major Shareholder: Caron Gail Thompson
Officers: Ian Thompson [1963] Director; Richard Ian Thompson [1993] Director

Kiko Mezcal Ltd
Incorporated: 11 July 2018
Registered Office: Fieldfisher, Riverbank House, 2 Swan Lane, London, EC4R 3TT
Major Shareholder: Glynn James Pegler
Officers: Glynn James Pegler [1983] Director

Kilchoman Distillery Company Ltd.
Incorporated: 12 November 2001 *Employees:* 29
Net Worth: £4,995,726 *Total Assets:* £13,973,451
Registered Office: The Old Surgery, School Road, Tarbert, Argyll, PA29 6UL
Officers: Katherine Alison Wills, Secretary; Niels Ladefoged [1963] Director [Danish]; Dr John Laurence Thorogood [1952] Director/Drilling Global Consultant; Jonathan Michael Turnbull [1951] Director; Simon March Turnbull [1949] Director; Anthony John Vernon Wills [1956] Director

Killowen Distillery Ltd
Incorporated: 3 July 2017
Registered Office: 23 Donaghaguy Road, Warrenpoint, Co Down, BT34 3RZ
Major Shareholder: Brendan Carty
Officers: Brendan Carty [1986] Director/Chartered Architect [Irish]

Kimbland Distillery Ltd
Incorporated: 16 August 2017
Registered Office: 53a Hertford Road, Stevenage, Herts, SG2 8SA
Shareholder: Sebastian James Anthony Aiden Hadfield-Hyde
Officers: Sebastian James Anthony Aiden Hadfield-Hyde [1985] Overseas Director

Kindred Gin Ltd
Incorporated: 23 October 2018
Registered Office: Acre House, 11-15 William Road, London, NW1 3ER
Officers: Jim Chapman [1987] Director; John Phillip Chapman [1987] Director; Samantha Chapman [1977] Director; Ian Haste [1976] Director; Nicola Louise Haste [1980] Director

Kinelarty Limited
Incorporated: 22 October 2018
Registered Office: 55 Drumnaconagher Road, Crossgar, Downpatrick, Co Down, BT30 9JH
Shareholders: Andrew Montgomery; Paula Maxwell
Officers: Paula Maxwell [1978] Commercial Director [Irish]; Andrew Montgomery [1974] Director

The Kingsbarns Company of Distillers Ltd
Incorporated: 5 May 2009 *Employees:* 23
Net Worth Deficit: £2,267,220 *Total Assets:* £6,888,285
Registered Office: 4 Melville Crescent, Edinburgh, EH3 7JA
Parent: Wemyss Distillery Limited
Officers: Isabella Alethea Wemyss, Secretary; Karen Margaret Stewart [1968] Director of Marketing; William John Wemyss [1970] Director

Kingston Distillers Ltd.
Incorporated: 12 December 2013
Net Worth Deficit: £16,741 *Total Assets:* £48,291
Registered Office: 28 Portsmouth Road, Kingston upon Thames, Surrey, KT1 2ND
Major Shareholder: Neil Beckitt
Officers: Neil Beckitt [1966] Director/Engineer

The Kingston upon Hull Liqour Company Limited
Incorporated: 9 January 2017
Registered Office: 51 Chantry Way East, Swanland, North Ferriby, E Yorks, HU14 3QF
Officers: Iain Todd [1969] Director

Kinrara Distillery Limited
Incorporated: 8 February 2017 *Employees:* 2
Net Worth Deficit: £134,770 *Total Assets:* £112,360
Registered Office: Lochindorb Lodge, Lochindorb Estate, Grantown on Spey, Moray, PH26 3PY
Shareholders: Duncan Kirk Fletcher; Kevin Paterson Fletcher
Officers: Duncan Kirk Fletcher [1967] Director; Kevin Paterson Fletcher [1969] Director; Stuart Nicol McMillan [1971] Director; Douglas Wood [1975] Director

Kirklee Scotch Whisky Limited
Incorporated: 20 February 2004 *Employees:* 2
Net Worth: £1,494,371 *Total Assets:* £1,580,819
Registered Office: 14 Mirrlees Drive, Glasgow, G12 0SH
Officers: Alan William Lundie, Secretary/Scotch Whisky Blender & Broker; Alan William Lundie [1951] Director/Scotch Whisky Blender & Broker; Anne Marion Young Lundie [1949] Director/Teacher

Kirkwood Distillery Limited
Incorporated: 15 March 2017
Net Worth Deficit: £14,494 *Total Assets:* £56,672
Registered Office: Wellside, Livesey Road, Ludlow, Salop, SY8 1EZ
Major Shareholder: Scott Harold Kirkwood
Officers: Alison Janet Caffyn, Secretary; Scott Harold Kirkwood [1968] Director

Klerck Distillery Ltd
Incorporated: 24 January 2019
Registered Office: 35 Ballards Lane, London, N3 1XW
Major Shareholder: Paul Alexander Klerck
Officers: Dr Paul Alexander Klerck [1973] Director

The Knockdhu Distillery Company Limited
Incorporated: 9 September 1988
Registered Office: Moffat Distillery, Airdrie, N Lanarks, ML6 8PL
Shareholders: Charoen Sirivadhanabhakdi; Khunying Wanna Sirivadhanabhakdi
Officers: Man Kong Lee [1968] Director/Accountant [Chinese]; Dr Martin John Leonard [1961] Managing Director; Prapakon Thongtheppairot [1971] Director [Thai]

Knockeen Hills Spirits Ltd
Incorporated: 15 October 2012
Net Worth Deficit: £21,109 *Total Assets:* £1,951
Registered Office: Rose Cottage, Templeton, Devon, EX16 8BP
Major Shareholder: Marie Constance Stibbe
Officers: Alan Stibbe [1947] Director

Knowcal Limited
Incorporated: 13 November 2006 *Employees:* 3
Net Worth: £80,466 *Total Assets:* £164,842
Registered Office: Fleming Court, Leigh Road, Eastleigh, Southampton, SO50 9PD
Major Shareholder: Stephen Paul Bowler
Officers: Renata Bowler, Secretary; Stephen Paul Bowler [1971] Director/Business Consultant

KO Gin Limited
Incorporated: 15 May 2018
Registered Office: 73 Cornhill, London, EC3V 3QQ
Major Shareholder: Vladislav Shevelev
Officers: Vladislav Shevelev [1998] Director [Maltese]

Koolvibes Limited
Incorporated: 30 March 2016 *Employees:* 2
Net Worth Deficit: £1,475 *Total Assets:* £18,448
Registered Office: 776-778 International House, Barking Road, London, E13 9PJ
Shareholder: Gillian Gibbs
Officers: Gillian Gibbs, Secretary; Gillian Gibbs-Sawyers [1974] Director/Registered Nurse; Michael Sawyers [1978] Director/Chef

Kozuba & Sons Limited
Incorporated: 25 June 2015
Registered Office: Highlands House, Basingstoke Road, Spencers Wood, Reading, Berks, RG7 1NT
Major Shareholder: Zbigniew Kozuba
Officers: Maciej Kozuba, Secretary; Jakub Kozuba [1982] Director/Manager [Polish]; Maciej Kozuba [1976] Director/Manager [Polish]

Krupnikoz Ltd
Incorporated: 28 February 2019
Registered Office: 18 Baytree Gardens, Plymouth, PL2 2QQ
Major Shareholder: Paul Anthony Kozakiewicz
Officers: Paul Anthony Kozakiewicz [1975] Director

KSSM International Limited
Incorporated: 17 July 2015
Registered Office: 153 Mortimer Street, Herne Bay, Kent, CT6 5HA
Shareholders: Stuart James Pike; Stuart Pearson; Kieran David Wyatt-Nicole
Officers: Michael James Chatfield [1980] Director; Stuart Pearson [1975] Director; Stuart James Pike [1963] Director; Kieran David Wyatt-Nicole [1980] Director

Label 5 First Blending Company Limited
Incorporated: 24 December 2013
Net Worth: £10,000 *Total Assets:* £10,000
Registered Office: Glen Turner Distillery, Starlaw Road, Bathgate, W Lothian, EH47 7BW
Parent: Glen Turner Company Limited
Officers: Jean Pierre Cayard [1942] Director [French]

Hunter Laing & Company Limited
Incorporated: 11 February 2013 *Employees:* 32
Net Worth: £8,184,797 *Total Assets:* £20,675,920
Registered Office: 16 Park Circus, Glasgow, G3 6AX
Parent: Hunter Laing Holdings Limited
Officers: Scott Laing, Secretary; David John Armour [1966] Director; Lorraine Elizabeth Gillen [1977] Director/Production Manager; Andrew William Douglas Laing [1982] Director; Scott Hepburn Laing [1979] Director; Stewart Hunter Laing [1946] Director

Andrew Laing & Company Limited
Incorporated: 11 March 2015
Net Worth: £100 *Total Assets:* £100
Registered Office: c/o Cloch Solicitors, 94 Hope Street, Glasgow, G2 6PH
Parent: The Shieling Scotch Whisky Co Ltd
Officers: Andrew Ross Crombie [1964] Director/Stonemason

Lakeland Moon Limited
Incorporated: 16 May 2011
Previous: Tenton Management Ltd
Net Worth: £8,798 *Total Assets:* £24,758
Registered Office: 15 Lowther Street, Kendal, Cumbria, LA9 4DH
Shareholders: Michael Andrew Pennington; Frederic William Fulton Pennington
Officers: Frederic William Fulton Pennington [1952] Director/Builder; Michael Andrew Pennington [1956] Director/Bar Owner

The Lakes Distillery Company PLC
Incorporated: 12 September 2011 *Employees:* 64
Previous: The Lakes Distillery Company Limited
Net Worth: £5,796,000 *Total Assets:* £10,870,000
Registered Office: 1st Floor Offices, Grandstand Garage, Kenton Road, Gosforth, Newcastle upon Tyne, NE3 4NB
Officers: Andrew John Davison, Secretary; Paul Richard Currie [1964] Director; Timothy Bahram Neville Farazmand [1960] Director; Richard John Hutton [1968] Director; Nigel John Mills [1958] Director; Paul Anthony Neep [1953] Consultant/Director; David Peter Robinson [1984] Director; Dr Alan Gray Rutherford [1942] Director & Consultant

Lambeth Spirits Ltd
Incorporated: 11 June 2014
Registered Office: 21 Rowan Shaw, Tonbridge, Kent, TN10 3QB
Shareholder: Sandra Ann Lambeth
Officers: Candice Elizabeth Lambeth [1987] Director/Solicitor; Sandra Ann Lambeth [1957] Director/Credit Risk Manager

Lamson Wine Company Limited
Incorporated: 6 March 2018
Registered Office: Health & Energy Drinks, Bridge House, 64-72 Mabgate, Leeds, LS9 7DZ
Major Shareholder: Robert (Elias) Wilson
Officers: Robert Wilson [1941] Director (CEO)

Land's End Gin Limited
Incorporated: 15 January 2019
Registered Office: 10 Tremayne Close, Devoran, Truro, Cornwall, TR3 6QE
Shareholders: Roger Wolens; Michael Bearcroft
Officers: Michael Bearcroft [1945] Director; Roger Wolens [1940] Director

Landeavour Distillery Ltd
Incorporated: 6 November 2018
Registered Office: 2 The Woodlands, Linton, Cambridge, CB21 4UF
Shareholders: Luke Henry Hammond; Angharad Wyn Hammond
Officers: Luke Henry Hammond [1986] Director/Manager

Lang Brothers Limited
Incorporated: 25 April 2003
Registered Office: Russell House, Dunnet Way, Broxburn, W Lothian, EH52 5BU
Parent: Ian MacLeod Distillers Ltd
Officers: Michael James Younger, Secretary; Leonard Stuart Russell [1961] Director

Langholm Distillery Limited
Incorporated: 28 November 2013
Registered Office: Burnfoot Farm House, Westerkirk, Langholm, Dumfries & Galloway, DG13 0NG
Shareholders: Christopher John Harrison; Christopher John Harrison
Officers: Leslie John Harrison, Secretary; Christopher John Harrison [1966] Director/Cider Maker

Langs Consulting Ltd.
Incorporated: 21 April 2015 *Employees:* 2
Net Worth: £65,620 *Total Assets:* £84,933
Registered Office: 57-59 High Street, Dunblane, Perthshire, FK15 0EE
Major Shareholder: David Kinniburgh Lang
Officers: David Kinniburgh Lang [1970] Director/Business Executive

Langstane Liquor Company Limited
Incorporated: 16 June 2015 *Employees:* 3
Net Worth Deficit: £13,908 *Total Assets:* £289,319
Registered Office: 5-9 Bon Accord Crescent, Aberdeen, AB11 6DN
Shareholder: Benjamin Iravani
Officers: Benjamin Iravani [1985] Director/Business Executive; Professor Andrew Justin Radcliffe Porter [1961] Director/Biotech Consultant; Josh Graham Rennie [1985] Director/Business Executive

Lanty Slee Liquor Co Ltd
Incorporated: 26 November 2018
Registered Office: Kemp House, 160 City Road, London, EC1V 2NX
Shareholders: Joe Nichols; John Walmsley
Officers: Joe Nichols [1984] Director/Manager; John Walmsley [1979] Director/Manager

The Last Drop Spirit Company Ltd
Incorporated: 19 October 2018
Registered Office: Whitty Farm, Curland, Taunton, Somerset, TA3 5BD
Major Shareholder: John Cooney
Officers: Ann Cooney, Secretary; John Cooney [1957] Director

Lazy Drinks Ltd.
Incorporated: 24 July 2017
Registered Office: 6 Station View, Chester, CH2 3DT
Shareholders: Peter Jervis; Laura Jervis
Officers: Laura Jervis [1987] Director

LDC Scotland Limited
Incorporated: 26 April 2012 *Employees:* 8
Net Worth: £270,007 *Total Assets:* £1,550,313
Registered Office: 29 Portland Road, Kilmarnock, E Ayrshire, KA1 2BY
Officers: Kenneth James Rose [1973] Director [Australian]; Scott McMurray Watson [1972] Director; Brian David Woods [1974] Director

LDN Spirits Limited
Incorporated: 14 September 2017
Registered Office: 88c Amhurst Road, London, E8 1JH
Major Shareholder: Gabriella Thorpe
Officers: Gabriella Thorpe [1983] Director/Owner

Leeds Gin Limited
Incorporated: 14 December 2015
Net Worth Deficit: £597 *Total Assets:* £46,884
Registered Office: 13-17 Paradise Square, Sheffield, S1 2DE
Parent: True North Brew Co Ltd

Legendary Distillers Ltd
Incorporated: 13 July 2017
Registered Office: 9 Baronscourt Drive, Paisley, Renfrewshire, PA1 2TH
Shareholders: Bryan Charles McCall; Mark Thomas Carden
Officers: Mark Thomas Carden [1976] Managing Director; Bryan Charles McCall [1980] Managing Director

Leith Liqueur Company Limited
Incorporated: 24 August 2005
Net Worth Deficit: £74,816 *Total Assets:* £96,268
Registered Office: 6th Floor, Gordon Chambers, 90 Mitchell Street, Glasgow, G1 3NQ
Shareholders: George Allan Swanson; Arafa Rashid
Officers: Fiona Eddy, Secretary; Kevin Benedict Moore [1957] Director; George Allan Swanson [1950] Director

Lianorin Ltd
Incorporated: 23 July 2018
Registered Office: 214a Kettering Road, Northampton, NN1 4BN
Shareholders: Ma. Annie Grezilda Sambito; Natalie Kilcourse
Officers: Ma. Annie Grezilda Sambito [1988] Director [Filipino]

Libaeration Limited
Incorporated: 11 November 2008
Net Worth Deficit: £15,722 *Total Assets:* £12,393
Registered Office: Ash Tree Farm, 25 Mill Lane, Butterwick, Boston, Lincs, PE22 0JE
Shareholders: Tim Staniland; Annette Staniland
Officers: Annette Staniland [1961] Director/Entrepreneur; Tim Staniland [1963] Director/Entrepreneur

Libation Liberation Limited
Incorporated: 9 September 2015 *Employees:* 3
Net Worth Deficit: £20,974 *Total Assets:* £44,670
Registered Office: 55 Daisy Avenue, Bury St Edmunds, Suffolk, IP32 7PG
Shareholders: Paul Edward Rayner; Timothy Ross Blake; Leanne Vinakadina
Officers: Timothy Ross Blake [1980] Director/Bar Manager; Merrill William Evans [1975] Director/Marketing; Paul Edward Rayner [1975] Director/Chartered Accountant

Liberty Orchards Limited
Incorporated: 22 April 2010 *Employees:* 3
Net Worth Deficit: £16,554 *Total Assets:* £169,754
Registered Office: 14 Fairmont Terrace, Sherborne, Dorset, DT9 3JS
Officers: Robert Francis Imlach [1953] Director/Business Owner; Alison Jean Lemmey [1963] Director/Speech Therapist; Peter John Lemmey [1962] Director/Farmer; Victoria Morland [1965] Director/Publishing Manager

The Lickerish Tooth Ltd
Incorporated: 21 November 2014
Net Worth: £14,031 *Total Assets:* £33,307
Registered Office: 34 High Street, Marske-by-the-Sea, Redcar, Cleveland, TS11 7BE
Major Shareholder: Steven Donnelly
Officers: Steven Donnelly [1975] Director/Safety Manager

Light Spirit Company Limited (The)
Incorporated: 15 April 1985
Registered Office: Independence House, 84 Lower Mortlake Road, Richmond, Surrey, TW9 2HS
Parent: William Grant & Sons Management Limited
Officers: Gregory Justin Bargeton [1973] Director/Lawyer; Ewan John Henderson [1968] Director/Accountant

LighthouseVodka Ltd
Incorporated: 10 April 2018
Registered Office: 1 Marmion Terrace, Whitley Bay, Tyne & Wear, NE25 8AS
Shareholders: Stuart Lamb; Stuart Douglas Parker
Officers: Stuart Lamb [1954] Director; Stuart Douglas Parker [1978] Director

Lillington Distillation Limited
Incorporated: 31 December 2018
Registered Office: Hollybush Cottage, Potbridge, Odiham, Hook, Hants, RG29 1JW
Major Shareholder: James Peter Lillington
Officers: James Peter Lillington [1995] Director/Engineer

Lime Street Distillery Limited
Incorporated: 3 April 2017
Registered Office: 23 Archerfield Road, Allerton, Liverpool, L18 7HS
Major Shareholder: Peter Fawcett
Officers: Peter Fawcett [1975] Director/Sales

The Lincoln Distillery Limited
Incorporated: 2 May 2017
Registered Office: 3 Manrico Drive, Lincoln, LN1 1AD
Major Shareholder: Matthew Felgate
Officers: Matthew Felgate [1983] Director/Business Owner; John Reginald Lock [1951] Director

Lincoln Gin Ltd
Incorporated: 7 January 2016
Registered Office: Hearing House, 104 Moor Lane, North Hykeham, Lincoln, LN6 9AB
Major Shareholder: Captain George Michael Tipler
Officers: Captain George Michael Tipler [1951] Director/Retired

Lincoln Imp Drinks Company Limited
Incorporated: 27 April 2017 *Employees:* 2
Net Worth: £2,213 *Total Assets:* £58,326
Registered Office: Rotaset House, Enterprise Road, Mablethorpe, Lincs, LN12 1NB
Shareholders: Alex Charles Hull; Richard Arnold
Officers: Richard Arnold [1974] Director; Alex Charles Hull [1979] Director

Lincolnshire Gin Ltd
Incorporated: 15 August 2017
Registered Office: 15 Barnes Close, Sleaford, Lincs, NG34 8BF
Major Shareholder: Barbara Ann Daughtrey
Officers: Barbara Ann Daughtrey [1953] Director

Linden and Lime Limited
Incorporated: 18 December 2018
Registered Office: Salisbury House, Station Road, Cambridge, CB1 2LA
Parent: L3 Point Limited
Officers: Paul Nigel Robert Bennett [1959] Director; Dr Mukund Unavane [1972] Director

The Lindores Distilling Co. Ltd
Incorporated: 11 February 2013 *Employees:* 22
Net Worth Deficit: £1,030,027 *Total Assets:* £6,874,879
Registered Office: Lindores, Abbey House, Abbey Road, Newburgh, Fife, KY14 6HH
Parent: Spirex Ltd
Officers: Helen Ruth McKenzie Smith, Secretary; Andrew James McKenzie Smith [1963] Director/Farmer; Dmitry Morgunov [1986] Business Development Director

Lindsay's Still Room Ltd
Incorporated: 18 September 2014
Net Worth Deficit: £3,600 *Total Assets:* £7,038
Registered Office: Postern House, Hagg Lane, Turnditch, Belper, Derbys, DE56 2LX
Major Shareholder: Lindsay Burton
Officers: Lindsay Burton [1975] Director

Linlithgow Distillery Limited
Incorporated: 16 March 2017
Net Worth Deficit: £17,027 *Total Assets:* £29,549
Registered Office: 12 Kettil'stoun Grove, Linlithgow, W Lothian, EH49 6PP
Shareholders: Ross Finlay Jamieson; Alyson Playfair Jamieson
Officers: Alyson Playfair Jamieson [1965] Director/Distiller; Ross Finlay Jamieson [1963] Director/Consultant

The Liqueur Manufactory Limited
Incorporated: 25 April 2018
Registered Office: 11 Halesowen Road, Netherton, Dudley, W Midlands, DY2 9QG
Major Shareholder: Joseph William Mann
Officers: Joseph William Mann [1989] Director

Liquid Lounge Drinks Co. Ltd
Incorporated: 6 November 2017
Registered Office: 5 Horsepool Road, Sheviock, Torpoint, Cornwall, PL11 3EP
Major Shareholder: Thomas B L Pennington
Officers: Thomas B L Pennington [1978] Director

Liquid Revolution Ltd
Incorporated: 3 April 2017
Registered Office: 35 Lemon Street, Truro, Cornwall, TR1 2NR
Shareholders: Gary Gary Watts; Thomas Hannon
Officers: Thomas Hannon [1984] Director; Gary Stephen Watts [1973] Director

Liquid Spirit Ltd
Incorporated: 12 July 2018
Registered Office: Ground Floor, 1-7 Station Road, Crawley, W Sussex, RH10 1HT
Shareholders: Oliver Ullrich; Iris Menne-Ullrich
Officers: Iris Menne-Ullrich [1985] Director/Chief Operating Officer [German]

Liquid Vision Enterprise Limited
Incorporated: 3 March 2011 *Employees:* 5
Net Worth: £333,571 *Total Assets:* £1,202,885
Registered Office: 116a High Street, Sevenoaks, Kent, TN13 1UZ
Shareholders: Monika Wodke; Maciej Wodke
Officers: Monika Wodke, Secretary; Maciej Wodke [1973] Director

Little Brown Dog Spirits Ltd
Incorporated: 20 September 2018
Registered Office: West Aquhorthies Farm, Fetternear, Inverurie, Aberdeenshire, AB51 5JY
Shareholders: Christopher David John Reid; Andrew William Smith
Officers: Christopher David John Reid [1983] Director; Dr Andrew William Smith [1984] Director

The Little Gin Shop Limited
Incorporated: 7 December 2015
Registered Office: Quay House, Quay Road, Waterside, Thorne, N Yorks, DN8 4JG
Major Shareholder: Justin Adrian Bullas
Officers: Justin Adrian Bullas [1971] Director/Barrister

The Little Red Berry Company Ltd.
Incorporated: 4 October 2017
Registered Office: Unit 3c & 3d Sycamore Business Park, Dishforth Road, Copt Hewick, Ripon, N Yorks, HG4 5DF
Shareholders: Peter Goadby Griffiths; Claire Louise Norton
Officers: Peter Goadby Griffiths [1965] Director; Claire Louise Norton [1983] Director

Little Rotters Limited
Incorporated: 30 August 2016
Net Worth Deficit: £9,332 *Total Assets:* £4,370
Registered Office: 47 Cambridge Road, Ely, Cambs, CB7 4HJ
Major Shareholder: Emily Trotter
Officers: Emily Charlotte Trotter [1975] Director

The Littlemill Distillery Company Limited
Incorporated: 19 July 2013 *Employees:* 3
Net Worth Deficit: £699,000 *Total Assets:* £110,479,000
Registered Office: 30 Broadwick Street, London, W1F 8JB
Parent: Loch Lomond Holdings 1 Limited
Officers: Colin Matthews [1965] Director; Richard Miles [1966] Director; Nicholas Rose [1957] Director

Liveras Limited
Incorporated: 6 January 2011
Registered Office: The Grove, Hadley Green Road, Barnet, Herts, EN5 5PY
Major Shareholder: Luke John Liveras
Officers: Luke John Liveras [1991] Director

Liverpool Gin Distillery Limited
Incorporated: 2 March 2017
Registered Office: The Sovereign Distillery, Wilson Road, Huyton, Knowsley, Merseyside, L36 6AD
Officers: Stewart Andrew Hainsworth [1969] Director; Timothy Richard Hines [1979] Finance Director; Alan William Robinson [1965] Director; Lee Andrew Tayburn [1974] Production Director

Liverpool Spring Gin Limited
Incorporated: 5 June 2018
Registered Office: 11 Arch View Crescent, Liverpool, L1 7BA
Major Shareholder: Harry Williams
Officers: Harry Williams, Secretary; Harry Williams [1993] Director/Proprietor

Llanfairpwll Distillery Ltd
Incorporated: 11 June 2018
Registered Office: 6 Plas Britannia, Church Road, Llanfairpwllgwyngyll, Anglesey, LL61 6AD
Shareholders: Maria Elaine Jones; Ann Katherine Louise Owen
Officers: Maria Elaine Jones [1968] Director; Robert Clayton Laming [1981] Director

LLDR Alexandria Ltd
Incorporated: 15 July 1998 *Employees:* 3
Net Worth Deficit: £1,450,283 *Total Assets:* £3,200,073
Registered Office: 1 Anthony Road, Largs, N Ayrshire, KA30 8EQ
Officers: Henry John Jagielko, Secretary/Accountant; Alexander Bulloch [1927] Director/Wine Merchant; Carol Anne Bulloch [1956] Director; Henry John Jagielko [1952] Director/Accountant; Linda Ellis Lind [1957] Director; Elspeth Revie [1958] Director

LLDY Alexandria Ltd
Incorporated: 2 September 1992 *Employees:* 3
Net Worth: £90,571 *Total Assets:* £199,195
Registered Office: 1 Anthony Road, Largs, N Ayrshire, KA30 8EQ
Parent: LLDR Alexandria Ltd
Officers: Henry John Jagielko, Secretary/Accountant; Alexander Bulloch [1927] Director; Carol Anne Jagielko [1956] Director/Clerkess; Henry John Jagielko [1952] Director/Accountant

Loaded Spirits Ltd
Incorporated: 30 January 2018
Registered Office: 71-75 Shelton Street, Covent Garden, London, WC2H 9JQ
Officers: Sean Roche [1993] Director; Thomas Scott [1990] Director

Loca Beverages Ltd
Incorporated: 23 August 2013
Net Worth Deficit: £42,088 *Total Assets:* £17,037
Registered Office: 1 Garthwood Close, West Bergholt, Colchester, Essex, CO6 3EA
Major Shareholder: Samuel Joseph Trett
Officers: Samuel Joseph Trett [1988] Director/Self Employed

Loch Earn Brewery Ltd
Incorporated: 27 June 2003
Net Worth Deficit: £11,413 *Total Assets:* £69
Registered Office: 100 Wellington Street, Glasgow, G2 6DH
Major Shareholder: Gerald Robert Michaluk
Officers: Generald Robert Michaluk [1960] Director/Consultant; Veronica Michaluk [1989] Director/Student

Loch Ewe Spirits Limited
Incorporated: 22 March 2017
Registered Office: 2nd Floor, North Saltire Court, 20 Castle Terrace, Edinburgh, EH1 2EN
Shareholders: Karamjit Jaiswal; Roshini Sanah Jaiswal; Ayaan Jaiswal Singh
Officers: Andrew Phillip Dutoy [1954] Director/General Manager; Dhanraj Chatamal Gidwaney [1948] Director/Chartered Accountant [Indian]; Nagina Judge Waters [1952] Director

Loch Leven Distillery Limited
Incorporated: 10 May 2017
Net Worth Deficit: £1,827 *Total Assets:* £1,745
Registered Office: Green Hotel, 2 Muirs, Kinross, KY13 8AS
Shareholders: James David Keith Montgomery; Kenneth Campbell
Officers: Kenneth Campbell, Secretary; Kenneth Campbell [1980] Director; James David Keith Montgomery [1957] Director/Hotelier

Loch Lomond Distillers Limited
Incorporated: 12 September 2013 *Employees:* 217
Net Worth: £30,660,000 *Total Assets:* £217,186,000
Registered Office: 30 Broadwick Street, London, W1F 8JB
Parent: Glen Scotia Distillery Company Limited
Officers: Colin Matthews [1965] Director; Richard Miles [1966] Director; Nicholas Rose [1957] Director

Loch Lomond Distillery Company Limited
Incorporated: 19 July 2013 *Employees:* 3
Net Worth Deficit: £35,812,000 *Total Assets:* £154,226,000
Registered Office: 30 Broadwick Street, London, W1F 8JB
Parent: The Littlemill Distillery Company Limited
Officers: Colin Matthews [1965] Director; Richard Miles [1966] Director; Nicholas Rose [1957] Director

Loch Lomond Liquor Company Ltd
Incorporated: 8 May 2018
Registered Office: 13a Alexander Street, Renton, Dumbarton, W Dunbartonshire, G82 4LT
Major Shareholder: Stuart Haggart
Officers: Stuart Haggart [1979] Director/Engineer; Fiona Macpherson [1983] Director/Dental Nurse

Loch Ness Distilling Company Ltd.
Incorporated: 15 December 2014
Registered Office: Oakdale, Drumnadrochit, Inverness, IV63 6TX
Major Shareholder: Jon Beach
Officers: Jon Beach [1970] Director/Restaurant Manager

Loch Ness Drinks Ltd
Incorporated: 8 March 2017
Net Worth Deficit: £2,913 *Total Assets:* £977
Registered Office: Beinn Bhurie, 3 Hillpark Brae, Munlochy, Ross & Cromarty, IV8 8PL
Officers: John Philip Oag [1970] Managing Director

Loch Ness Spirits Limited
Incorporated: 13 October 2015 *Employees:* 3
Net Worth Deficit: £63,092 *Total Assets:* £81,895
Registered Office: Johnston Carmichael, Clava House, Cradlehall Business Park, Inverness, IV2 5GH
Shareholders: Kevin Robert Cameron-Ross; Lorien Cameron-Ross
Officers: Kevin Robert Cameron-Ross [1963] Director; Dr Lorien Cameron-Ross [1975] Director

Loch Shiel Whisky Limited
Incorporated: 7 August 2015
Registered Office: Mercury House, North Gate, Nottingham, NG7 7FN
Major Shareholder: Peter Robson
Officers: Peter Robson, Secretary; Peter Robson [1959] Director

Lochaber Craft Brewing and Distilling Limited
Incorporated: 27 June 2017
Registered Office: 147 Blas, High Street, Fort William, Highland, PH33 6EA
Major Shareholder: Iain Kenney
Officers: Iain Kenney [1969] Director

Lochglen Whisky Company Ltd.
Incorporated: 20 October 2009
Net Worth Deficit: £310,419 *Total Assets:* £1,300
Registered Office: 138 Nethergate, Dundee, DD1 4ED
Officers: Iain John McHattie, Secretary; David Eric Evans [1960] Director; John Neil McHattie [1950] Director

Lochindaal Distillery Limited
Incorporated: 15 August 2006
Registered Office: The Bruichladdich Distillery, Islay, Argyll, PA49 7UN
Parent: Bruichladdich Distillery Company Limited
Officers: Simon Patrick Coughlin, Secretary; Madame Valerie Marie Anne Chapoulaud-Floquet [1962] Director/Chief Executive Officer [French]; Simon Patrick Coughlin [1961] Director; Douglas Adamson Taylor [1976] Director/Chief Executive Officer

Lochlea Distilling Company Limited
Incorporated: 27 April 2016
Net Worth Deficit: £42,589 *Total Assets:* £4,154,356
Registered Office: Caledonia House, 5 Inchinnan Drive, Inchinnan, Renfrew, PA4 9AF
Major Shareholder: Neil James McGeoch
Officers: Neil James McGeoch [1977] Director

Locksley Distilling Company Limited
Incorporated: 14 March 2013 *Employees:* 2
Net Worth: £88,009 *Total Assets:* £157,771
Registered Office: Unit 20C, 1 Portland Works, Randall Street, Sheffield, S2 4SJ
Shareholders: John Andrew Cherry; Dorothy Park Watson
Officers: John Andrew Cherry [1970] Director/Retail Manager & Business Owner; Dorothy Watson [1950] Director/Retired [American]

Lombard Scotch Whisky Limited
Incorporated: 19 November 1985
Registered Office: 7 Orchard Close, Calne, Wilts, SN11 8HA
Officers: Margaret Elizabeth Lombard-Chibnall [1937] Director/Retired; Richard Anthony Lombard-Chibnall [1964] Sales Director

Lonberg Limited
Incorporated: 11 September 2018
Registered Office: 23 Upton Close, London, NW2 1UP
Shareholders: Amer Aziz; Julian Naik
Officers: Amer Aziz [1973] Director; Julian Naik [1978] Director [South African]

Lonburg 449 Limited
Incorporated: 12 July 2017
Registered Office: Flat 6, 121 Lower Richmond Road, London, SW15 1EX
Major Shareholder: Tim Flett
Officers: Tim Flett, Secretary; Tim Flett [1979] Director

Londinio Liqueurs Ltd.
Incorporated: 9 February 2018
Net Worth: £1,795 *Total Assets:* £1,795
Registered Office: Basement Flat, 198 Munster Road, London, SW6 6AU
Major Shareholder: Jake Coventry
Officers: Jake Coventry [1991] Director

London Alcohol Company Ltd
Incorporated: 23 April 2010 *Employees:* 1
Net Worth: £70,641 *Total Assets:* £1,591,884
Registered Office: 3rd Floor, 207 Regent Street, London, W1B 3HH
Officers: Zakar Oganian [1985] Director

London Botanical Drinks Limited
Incorporated: 16 March 2018
Registered Office: 39-45 Bermondsey Street, London, SE1 3XF
Shareholders: Paul Mathew; Bloodandsand Limited
Officers: Daniel Paul Hatton [1982] Ventures Director; Paul Mathew [1976] Director/Drinks Consultant

London Brewery Limited
Incorporated: 2 July 2018
Registered Office: 55 Oakdale, London, N14 5RG
Major Shareholder: Ilyas Demirci
Officers: Ilyas Demirci [1990] Director

London Craft Distillers Ltd
Incorporated: 26 March 2015
Registered Office: 18 Romney Road, Willesborough, Ashford, Kent, TN24 0RW
Major Shareholder: Daniel Peter Todd
Officers: Daniel Todd [1984] Director/Retail Manager

London Distillery - Battersea Ltd
Incorporated: 18 October 2016
Registered Office: 58 Druid Street, London, SE1 2EZ
Parent: The London Distillery Company Ltd
Officers: Simon Bessant [1970] Director; Killian O'Sullivan [1978] Director [Irish]

The London Distillery Company Ltd
Incorporated: 24 June 2011 *Employees:* 5
Net Worth: £79,648 *Total Assets:* £490,926
Registered Office: 58 Druid Street, London, SE1 2EZ
Officers: Nicholas James Anthony Vye Taylor, Secretary; Simon Jonathan Bessant [1970] Director; Robert McClatchey [1965] Director; Killian O'Sullivan [1978] Director; Simon Derek Seaton [1968] Director

The London Dry Gin Company Limited
Incorporated: 9 June 2014
Registered Office: Distribution Point, Melbury Park, Clayton Road, Birchwood, Warrington, Cheshire, WA3 6PH
Shareholders: Warren Michael Scott; Vincenzo Visone
Officers: Michael Clifford, Secretary; Warren Michael Scott [1963] Director/Businessman; Vincenzo Visone [1955] Director/Businessman [Italian]

London Fortifiers Limited
Incorporated: 28 March 2018
Registered Office: 18 Stoke Newington High Street, London, N16 7PL
Major Shareholder: Michael James Rogers
Officers: Michael James Rogers [1980] Director

London Heaven Spirits Company UK Ltd
Incorporated: 26 February 2013
Net Worth: £1 *Total Assets:* £1
Registered Office: Suite 122, Bradford Court Business Centre, 123-131 Bradford Street, Birmingham, B12 0NS
Officers: Surjit Kaur [1952] Director [Indian]

The London Rum Company Holdings Limited
Incorporated: 22 August 2018
Registered Office: 33 Albion Street, Hyde Park, London, W2 2AX
Shareholders: Karl Peter Hennessy; Ravi Kumar Das
Officers: Charlotte Augusta Das [1987] Director/Teacher; Dr Ravi Kumar Das [1986] Director/Neuropharmacology Stuff; Karl Peter Hennessy [1963] Director/Insurancey Stuff

London Rum Limited
Incorporated: 31 August 2017
Registered Office: 92 Greenbank Drive, Sunderland, Tyne & Wear, SR4 0JX
Major Shareholder: Stephen Anthony Brace
Officers: Stephen Anthony Brace [1991] Director/Business Development

London Society of Mixologists
Incorporated: 12 May 2016
Registered Office: Shepherd and Wedderburn LLP, Condor House, 10 St Paul's Churchyard, London, EC4M 8AL
Parent: Whyte and MacKay Limited
Officers: Bryan Harold Donaghey [1961] Director

London Spice Company Limited
Incorporated: 24 October 2016
Net Worth Deficit: £7,268 *Total Assets:* £1,404
Registered Office: 2 Woodhall Avenue, Pinner, Harrow, Middlesex, HA5 3DX
Shareholder: Sandeep Raithatha
Officers: Sandeep Raithatha [1973] Director; Sheetal Raithatha [1975] Director

London Spiced Dry Limited
Incorporated: 9 October 2017
Net Worth: £100 *Total Assets:* £100
Registered Office: 85 Eaststand Apartments, Highbury Stadium Square, London, N5 1FF
Shareholders: Steven Stellakis Kyprianou; Georgi Dinkov Radev
Officers: Steven Stellakis Kyprianou [1974] Director; Georgi Dinkov Radev [1981] Director; Samuel Benzie Robson [1986] Director [Australian]

London Vodka Ltd
Incorporated: 19 August 2014
Registered Office: Suite 149, The Tower, 1 St George Wharf, London, SW8 2DA
Parent: London Alcohol Company Ltd.
Officers: Zakar Oganian, Secretary; Zakar Oganian [1985] Director

Lone Wolf Spirits Limited
Incorporated: 6 May 2016 *Employees:* 4
Net Worth: £713,000 *Total Assets:* £1,141,000
Registered Office: Brewdog, Balmacassie Drive, Balmacassie Commercial Park, Ellon, Aberdeenshire, AB41 8BX
Parent: Brewdog PLC
Officers: Alan Martin Dickie [1982] Director; Neil Allan Simpson [1971] Finance Director; James Bruce Watt [1982] Director

Long Gin Ltd
Incorporated: 22 August 2017
Registered Office: 23 Grant Drive, Corby, Northants, NN18 8SX
Officers: Sandro Rasgado [1981] Director [Portuguese]

Long Walk Spirits Limited
Incorporated: 1 June 2018
Registered Office: 130 Old Street, London, EC1V 9BD
Officers: Steve Ballantyne [1980] Director; Mark Taylor [1980] Director

Longtooth Gin Limited
Incorporated: 15 February 2018
Registered Office: Eldo House, Kempson Way, Bury St Edmunds, Suffolk, IP32 7AR
Major Shareholder: Kevin Arnold
Officers: Kevin Arnold [1965] Director; Peter Filler [1959] Director

Lost Roots Limited
Incorporated: 26 January 2017
Registered Office: 3rd Floor, 86-90 Paul Street, London, EC2A 4NE
Shareholders: Jack Calderwood; Alexander Maximilian Carlton Heal
Officers: Jack Calderwood [1992] Director/Consultant; Alexander Maximilian Carlton Heal [1992] Director/Analyst

Lough Neagh Distillers - 1837 Ltd
Incorporated: 26 November 2018
Registered Office: Inverlodge, 51 Bannfoot Road, Derrytrasna, Co Armagh, BT66 6PH
Major Shareholder: Vernon Fox
Officers: Vernon Fox [1973] Director [Irish]

The Lowestoft Distillery Company Limited
Incorporated: 11 July 2017 *Employees:* 1
Net Worth Deficit: £6,672 *Total Assets:* £1,945
Registered Office: Lothing House, Quay View Business Park, Lowestoft, Suffolk, NR32 2HD
Major Shareholder: Grant Robert Bartlett
Officers: Grant Robert Bartlett, Secretary; Grant Robert Bartlett [1964] Director

W. P. Lowrie & Company Limited
Incorporated: 30 January 2017
Registered Office: Ruthven Villa, Montrose Road, Auchterarder, Perth & Kinross, PH3 1BZ
Major Shareholder: Robert Daniel Fergus Hartley
Officers: Robert Daniel Fergus Hartley [1965] Director

Lucent Drinks Ltd
Incorporated: 25 January 2018
Registered Office: 71-75 Shelton Street, Covent Garden, London, WC2H 9JQ
Shareholders: Steven Roy Adams; Martyn Christopher Withers
Officers: Martyn Withers, Secretary; Steven Roy Adams [1973] Director/Founder; Martyn Christopher Withers [1970] Director/Chief Executive Officer

Ludlow Apple Brandy Distillery Limited
Incorporated: 22 February 2012
Registered Office: Wainbridge House, Clee St Margaret, Craven Arms, Salop, SY7 9DT
Major Shareholder: Michael John Hardingham
Officers: Michael John Hardingham [1956] Director/Distiller

Ludlow Distillery Limited
Incorporated: 17 December 2008
Net Worth Deficit: £3,238 *Total Assets:* £62,902
Registered Office: Wainbridge House, Clee St Margaret, Craven Arms, Salop, SY7 9DT
Shareholders: Barbara Eileen Hardingham; Michael John Hardingham
Officers: Michael John Hardingham, Secretary; Barbara Eileen Hardingham [1939] Director; Michael John Hardingham [1956] Director

Ludlow Vineyard Limited
Incorporated: 17 November 2003
Registered Office: Wainbridge House, Clee St Margaret, Craven Arms, Salop, SY7 9DT
Shareholders: Barbara Eileen Hardingham; Barbara Eileen Hardingham; Michael John Hardingham
Officers: Michael John Hardingham, Secretary/Administrator; Barbara Eileen Hardingham [1939] Director/Administrator; Michael John Hardingham [1956] Director/Administrator

Ludlow Whisky Limited
Incorporated: 3 June 2013
Registered Office: Wainbridge House, Clee St Margaret, Craven Arms, Salop, SY7 9DT
Major Shareholder: Michael John Hardingham
Officers: Michael John Hardingham [1956] Director/Distiller

Lujo Distilling Company Limited
Incorporated: 9 March 2018
Registered Office: 88 Bawtry Road, Bessacarr, Doncaster, S Yorks, DN4 7BQ
Shareholders: Andrea Michelle Adlam; Alison Louise Coates
Officers: Andrea Michelle Adlam [1970] Director; Jason Paul Adlam [1971] Director; Alison Louise Coates [1967] Director; Gary Coates [1970] Director

Lumber Distillers Limited
Incorporated: 6 March 2018
Registered Office: The Newbury, 137 Bartholomew Street, Newbury, Berks, RG14 5HB
Major Shareholder: Peter Lumber
Officers: Peter Lumber [1968] Director

Wm. Lundie & Company
Incorporated: 7 August 1974
Net Worth: £3,550,900 *Total Assets:* £3,754,690
Registered Office: Rechlerich, Ballindalloch, Moray, AB37 9BD
Officers: Douglas Malcolm Burd Belford, Secretary; Douglas Malcolm Burd Belford [1973] Director/Chartered Accountant; John Lynburn Scott Grant [1951] Director

Lundin Distilling Company Limited
Incorporated: 12 June 2015
Net Worth Deficit: £36,835 *Total Assets:* £40,462
Registered Office: 1 West Fergus Place, Kirkcaldy, Fife, KY1 1UR
Major Shareholder: Iain George Brown
Officers: Iain George Brown [1976] Director/Solicitor/Finance

Luxbev Limited
Incorporated: 4 October 2017
Registered Office: 71-75 Shelton Street, Covent Garden, London, WC2H 9JQ
Major Shareholder: Hernando Ramirez
Officers: Hernando Ramirez, Secretary; Hernando Ramirez [1969] Director [French]

Luxco Drinks Limited
Incorporated: 12 March 2018
Registered Office: 1 Park Row, Leeds, LS1 5AB
Officers: David Bratcher [1967] Director [American]; Donn Lux [1960] Director [American]

Luxury Spirit Co Limited
Incorporated: 29 March 2017
Registered Office: 3rd Floor, 16 Gordon Street, Glasgow, G1 3PT
Major Shareholder: Ernesto Mainardi
Officers: Ernesto Mainardi [1943] Director/Distiller [Italian]

Luxury Trading Company Limited
Incorporated: 7 January 2013
Registered Office: 3 Hardman Street, Manchester, M3 3HF
Major Shareholder: John Edgar
Officers: John Edgar [1970] Director

LWD Holdings Limited
Incorporated: 4 June 2018
Registered Office: Apartment 8, 41 Notting Hill, Belfast, BT9 5NS
Major Shareholder: Raymond McLaughlin
Officers: Raymond McLaughlin [1980] Director [Irish]

Lymm Gin Limited
Incorporated: 10 July 2017
Registered Office: 57 School Drive, Lymm, Cheshire, WA13 9UR
Shareholders: David Owen Hughes; Lisa Hughes
Officers: David Owen Hughes [1977] Director; Lisa Hughes [1980] Director

Lytham Distillers Limited
Incorporated: 5 April 2016
Registered Office: 18 Derby Road, Lytham St Annes, Lancs, FY8 4BZ
Shareholders: Michael Graham Wolstencroft; Patrick Alexander Jolin
Officers: Patrick Alexander Jolin [1965] Director; Michael Graeme Wolstencroft [1965] Director

Lytham Distillery Company Ltd
Incorporated: 13 August 2018
Registered Office: 19 Park Road, Lytham St Annes, Lancs, FY8 1PW
Shareholders: Simon Alexander Smith; Jonathan Harrison; Jake Andrew Crimmin
Officers: Jake Andrew Crimmin [1976] Director; Jonathan Harrison [1982] Director; Simon Alexander Smith [1972] Director

Lytham Gin Company Ltd
Incorporated: 14 March 2018
Registered Office: 19 Park Road, Lytham St Annes, Lancs, FY8 1PW
Shareholders: Simon Alexander Smith; Jonathan Harrison; Jake Andrew Crimmin
Officers: Jake Andrew Crimmin [1976] Director/Bar Owner; Jonathan Harrison [1982] Director/Designer; Simon Alexander Smith [1972] Director/Consultant

The Macallan Distillers Limited
Incorporated: 25 April 1946
Net Worth: £584,899,968 *Total Assets:* £702,000,000
Registered Office: The Macallan Distillery, Craigellachie, Banffshire, AB38 9RX
Parent: HS (Distillers) Limited
Officers: Ashleigh Kay Clark, Secretary; Alan William Frizzell [1964] Director/Chartered Accountant; Pryce William David Greenow [1970] Director/Sales & Marketing, President International Region; Kunimasa Himeno [1957] Director/Senior General Manager, Group Strategy Planning [Japanese]; Scott John McCroskie [1967] Director/Chartered Accountant; John Alexander McLaren [1951] Director/Merchant Banker

J. MacArthur Jr. & Co. Limited
Incorporated: 12 December 1972
Registered Office: Moffat Distillery, Airdrie, N Lanarks, ML6 8PL
Shareholders: Charoen Sirivadhanabhakdi; Khunying Wanna Sirivadhanabhakdi
Officers: Man Kong Lee [1968] Director/Accountant [Chinese]; Dr Martin John Leonard [1961] Managing Director; Prapakon Thongtheppairot [1971] Director [Thai]

MacDonald & Muir Limited
Incorporated: 3 April 1936 *Employees:* 207
Net Worth: £209,982,000 *Total Assets:* £273,318,016
Registered Office: The Cube, 45 Leith Street, Edinburgh, EH1 3AT
Parent: The Glenmorangie Company Limited
Officers: Jean-Marc Rene Boulan [1972] Director [French]; Nauman Saleem Hasan [1969] Director; Thomas Jean Moradpour [1973] Director [French]; Dr Peter Jonathon Nelson [1959] Operations Director; Richard Spencer Yeomans [1979] Director

MacDonald Martin Distilleries Limited
Incorporated: 13 December 1995
Registered Office: The Cube, 45 Leith Street, Edinburgh, EH1 3AT
Parent: The Glenmorangie Company Limited
Officers: Jean-Marc Rene Boulan [1972] Director [French]; Dr Peter Jonathon Nelson [1959] Director

MacDuff & Company Limited
Incorporated: 4 December 1991
Net Worth Deficit: £157,060
Registered Office: 6 Newton Place, Glasgow, G3 7PR
Officers: David Alexander Sloan, Secretary; Per Steen Molin Heinze [1946] Director [Danish]; Thomas Just Karberg [1964] Director [Danish]; David Alexander Sloan [1962] Director/Accountant; Andrew Torrance [1979] Director

MacDuff (Scotch Whisky) Limited
Incorporated: 16 July 1991
Registered Office: 6 Newton Place, Glasgow, G3 7PR
Officers: David Alexander Sloan, Secretary; Per Steen Molin Heinze [1946] Director [Danish]; Thomas Just Karberg [1964] Director [Danish]; David Alexander Sloan [1962] Director/Accountant; Andrew Torrance [1979] Director

MacDuff International (Scotch Whisky) Limited
Incorporated: 16 July 1991 *Employees:* 9
Net Worth: £10,292,918 *Total Assets:* £16,000,089
Registered Office: 6 Newton Place, Glasgow, G3 7PR
Officers: David Alexander Sloan, Secretary; Per Steen Molin Heinze [1946] Director [Danish]; Thomas Just Karberg [1964] Director [Danish]; David Alexander Sloan [1962] Director/Accountant; Andrew Torrance [1979] Director

Mackintosh Gin Limited
Incorporated: 26 March 2018
Registered Office: c/o Ashton McGill Ltd, The Flour Mill, Exchange Street, Dundee, DD1 3DE
Shareholders: James Alexander McIntosh; Deborah Ann Bowie
Officers: Deborah Ann Bowie [1974] Director; James Alexander McIntosh [1975] Director

Ian MacLeod and Company Limited
Incorporated: 24 May 1966
Registered Office: Russell House, Dunnet Way, Broxburn, W Lothian, EH52 5BU
Parent: Ian MacLeod Distillers
Officers: Michael James Younger, Secretary; Angela Mary Russell [1965] P.R. Director; David William Hodder Russell [1940] Director/Whisky Broker; Edith Stuart Russell [1932] Director/Housewife; Leonard Stuart Russell [1961] Marketing Director; Peter James Sidney Russell [1927] Director/Whisky Broker

Ian MacLeod Distillers Limited
Incorporated: 26 November 1957 *Employees:* 153
Net Worth: £62,203,000 *Total Assets:* £145,944,992
Registered Office: Russell House, Dunnet Way, Broxburn, W Lothian, EH52 5BU
Shareholders: Leonard Stuart Russell; Leonard Stuart Russell and Others as Trustees of The Leonard Stuart Russell 2003 Family Trust
Officers: Michael James Younger, Secretary; Gordon John Doctor [1959] Director/Whisky Blender; Richard William Farrar [1958] Director; Laura Agnes Anne Rankine [1979] HR Director; Angela Mary Russell [1965] P.R. Director; David William Hodder Russell [1940] Director/Whisky Broker; Edith Stuart Russell [1932] Director/Housewife; Leonard Stuart Russell [1961] Managing Director; Peter James Sidney Russell [1927] Director/Whisky Broker; Ian Alexander Shackleton [1965] Sales Director; Michael James Younger [1960] Finance Director

Macmillan Scotch Whisky Company Limited
Incorporated: 7 September 2005
Net Worth: £2 *Total Assets:* £2
Registered Office: Bank Chambers, 31 The Square, Cumnock, E Ayrshire, KA18 1AT
Officers: Dato Pang Lay Terry Joseph Lee [1935] Director [Singaporean]

MacNab Distilleries Limited
Incorporated: 1 September 1933
Net Worth: £2,601,000 *Total Assets:* £4,738,000
Registered Office: Chivas House, 72 Chancellors Road, London, W6 9RS
Parent: Allied Domecq Spirits & Wine Limited
Officers: Stuart MacNab [1964] Director/Accountant; Vincent Turpin [1978] Director/Chief Financial Officer [French]

Douglas MacNiven & Company Limited
Incorporated: 2 December 1935
Registered Office: The Cube, 45 Leith Street, Edinburgh, EH1 3AT
Parent: James Martin & Company Limited
Officers: Jean-Marc Rene Boulan [1972] Director [French]; Dr Peter Jonathon Nelson [1959] Director

Madame Jennifer Distillery Limited
Incorporated: 27 March 2017
Net Worth Deficit: £6,527 *Total Assets:* £4,392
Registered Office: 3 Goldstone Street, Hove, E Sussex, BN3 3RJ
Shareholders: Inger Christine Smith; Ian Curtis
Officers: Ian Curtis [1974] Director; Inger Christine Smith [1973] Director

Madrise Ltd
Incorporated: 23 July 2018
Registered Office: 214a Kettering Road, Northampton, NN1 4BN
Shareholders: Herminia Ablaza; Patrick James Terry
Officers: Herminia Ablaza [1968] Director [Filipino]

The Maeden Group Ltd
Incorporated: 22 August 2017
Registered Office: 31 Grafton Gardens, Pennington, Lymington, Hants, SO41 8AS
Officers: Matthew England [1984] Director/Hotel Manager

Mahiki Trading Limited
Incorporated: 30 January 2019
Registered Office: Regina House, 124 Finchley Road, London, NW3 5JS
Parent: Mahiki Brands Holding Limited
Officers: Piers Benedict Adam [1964] Director; Andreas Werner Herb [1970] Director [German]

Maiden Batch Ltd
Incorporated: 30 August 2018
Registered Office: Gallone & Co, 14 Newton Place, Glasgow, G3 7PY
Officers: David MacInnes Ferguson [1981] Director; Andrew Hamilton [1986] Director; Stuart William Hogg [1992] Director; Alastair Kellock [1981] Director; Billy Milligan [1980] Director

The Maidstone Distillery Ltd
Incorporated: 3 August 2018
Registered Office: 52 Roseacre Lane, Bearsted, Maidstone, Kent, ME14 4JG
Major Shareholder: Darren Charles Graves
Officers: Darren Charles Graves [1976] Director; Samantha Louise Graves [1984] Director

Malt of the Earth Whisky Company Ltd.
Incorporated: 21 June 2013
Net Worth: £771 *Total Assets:* £7,675
Registered Office: 4 McGregor Avenue, Balloch, W Dunbartonshire, G83 8DG
Major Shareholder: Thomas Christian Mills
Officers: Thomas Christian Mills [1983] Director/Whisky Blender/Dealer

The Malt Whisky Investment Company Limited
Incorporated: 7 December 2012
Registered Office: 145 St Vincent Street, Glasgow, G2 5JF
Shareholders: Andrew John Greig Hart; Donald Stuart Greig Hart
Officers: Laurette Margaret Keenan Hart, Secretary; Andrew John Greig Hart [1977] Sales Director; Donald Stuart Greig Hart [1946] Director

Manchester Liquor Co. Limited
Incorporated: 12 April 2017
Registered Office: 27 Provis Road, Manchester, M21 9EN
Major Shareholder: Dominic James Clancy
Officers: Dominic James Clancy [1988] Director/Self Employed

Manchester Still Ltd.
Incorporated: 9 May 2016 *Employees:* 3
Net Worth Deficit: £16,059 *Total Assets:* £21,477
Registered Office: Flat 37, 7 Collier Street, Manchester, M3 4NA
Officers: Dr. Michael Peter Down, Secretary; Prof Craig Edward Banks [1979] Director/Dean of Research - MMU; Dr Michael Peter Down [1989] Director/Research Associate; Samuel James Rowley-Neale [1989] Director/PhD Research Associate

Mannequin Ltd.
Incorporated: 16 July 2010
Registered Office: High View House, Heath Lane, Ewshot, Farnham, Surrey, GU10 5AL
Major Shareholder: Colin William Roy
Officers: Colin William Roy [1970] Director

Marblehead Brand Development Limited
Incorporated: 21 September 2011
Previous: Greenalls Brewery Limited
Registered Office: Distribution Point, Melbury Park, Clayton Road, Birchwood, Warrington, Cheshire, WA3 6PH
Shareholders: Warren Michael Scott; Vincenzo Visone
Officers: Michael Clifford, Secretary; Warren Michael Scott [1963] Director/Businessman; Vincenzo Visone [1955] Director/Businessman [Italian]

Margate Distillery Ltd
Incorporated: 23 January 2018
Registered Office: 35 High Street, Margate, Kent, CT9 1DX
Shareholders: Rhys Huelin; Jason Freedman
Officers: Rhys Huelin, Secretary; Rhys Huelin [1981] Director

Marron (Lincoln) Ltd
Incorporated: 9 May 2011
Net Worth Deficit: £56,811 *Total Assets:* £23,794
Registered Office: 9 Broadbeck, Waddingham, Lincoln, DN21 4TH
Shareholders: Ronald Edgar; Margaret Edgar
Officers: Margaret Edgar [1951] Director/Retired; Ronald Edgar [1949] Director/Sales Person

James Martin & Company, Limited
Incorporated: 23 September 1912
Registered Office: The Cube, 45 Leith Street, Edinburgh, EH1 3AT
Parent: The Glenmorangie Company Limited
Officers: Jean-Marc Rene Boulan [1972] Director [French]; Dr Peter Jonathon Nelson [1959] Director

Martin-Wells Distillery Ltd.
Incorporated: 5 February 2016 *Employees:* 1
Net Worth: £3,116 *Total Assets:* £37,135
Registered Office: 4 Wolstonbury Walk, Shoreham-by-Sea, W Sussex, BN43 5GU
Major Shareholder: Thomas Antony Martin-Wells
Officers: Dr Thomas Antony Martin-Wells [1984] Director

The Masham Distillery Company Limited
Incorporated: 30 April 2018
Registered Office: Suite 146, 5 High Street, Maidenhead, Berks, SL6 1JN
Major Shareholder: Donald John Stewart
Officers: Donald John Stewart [1963] Director

Mason & Summers Limited
Incorporated: 22 October 1947
Registered Office: One Fleet Place, London, EC4M 7WS
Shareholders: Charoen Sirivadhanabhakdi; Khunying Wanna Sirivadhanabhakdi
Officers: Man Kong Lee [1968] Director/Accountant [Chinese]; Dr Martin John Leonard [1961] Managing Director; Prapakon Thongtheppairot [1971] Director [Thai]

Masons Yorkshire Gin Ltd
Incorporated: 22 November 2012 *Employees:* 26
Net Worth: £441,644 *Total Assets:* £990,712
Registered Office: Masons Distillery, 74 Bedale Road, Aiskew, Bedale, N Yorks, DL8 1DD
Shareholders: Karl Warren Mason; Catherine Mason
Officers: Karl Mason, Secretary; Catherine Mason [1967] Director; Karl Warren Mason [1967] Director

Master of Malt Limited
Incorporated: 12 March 2018
Registered Office: Unit 1 Ton Business Park, 2-8 Morley Road, Tunbridge Wells, Kent, TN9 1RA
Parent: Atom Supplies Limited
Officers: Joel John Kelly [1980] Director/Solicitor

Masters of Malt Limited
Incorporated: 12 March 2018
Registered Office: Unit 1 Ton Business Park, 2-8 Morley Road, Tunbridge Wells, Kent, TN2 3EF
Parent: Atom Supplies Limited
Officers: Joel John Kelly [1980] Director/Solicitor

Mastropasqua & Brothers Ltd.
Incorporated: 6 May 2016
Registered Office: c/o Sabino Antonio Mastrapasqua, 26 Baberton Mains Brae, Edinburgh, EH14 3HH
Major Shareholder: Sabino Antonio Mastrapasqua
Officers: Sabino Antonio Mastrapasqua [1973] Director [Italian]

Matisse Spirits Company Limited
Incorporated: 20 May 2004 *Employees:* 2
Net Worth: £800,675 *Total Assets:* £1,067,537
Registered Office: 6 Logie Mill, Edinburgh, EH7 4HG
Parent: Holy Grail
Officers: John Crilly, Secretary/Finance Manager; Chang SEN-Ho [1959] Business Director [Taiwanese]

Matugga Beverages Limited
Incorporated: 1 April 2015
Net Worth Deficit: £43,786 *Total Assets:* £28,172
Registered Office: 71-75 Shelton Street, Covent Garden, London, WC2H 9JQ
Shareholders: Jacine Louise Rutasikwa; Donald Paul Rutasikwa
Officers: Janet Agatha Cooper, Secretary; Donald Paul Rutasikwa [1977] Director; Jacine Louise Rutasikwa [1978] Director

Matugga Distillers Limited
Incorporated: 27 April 2018
Registered Office: 1a Young Square, Brucefield Industrial Estate, Livingston, W Lothian, EH54 9BX
Officers: Donald Paul Rutasikwa [1977] Director/Engineer & Distiller; Jacine Louise Rutasikwa [1978] Director/Marketing Professional

Mavarac UK Limited
Incorporated: 22 February 2019
Registered Office: 1 Knightsbridge Green, London, SW1X 7NE
Major Shareholder: Alexander Johnson
Officers: Ross Adam Archer [1986] Director [Irish]; Alexander Johnson [1987] Director

Maverick Brands Limited
Incorporated: 13 March 2018
Registered Office: Unit 1 Ton Business Park, 2-8 Morley Road, Tonbridge, Kent, TN9 1RA
Parent: Atom Supplies Limited
Officers: Joel John Kelly [1980] Director/Solicitor

Maverick Drinks Limited
Incorporated: 12 March 2018
Registered Office: Unit 1 Ton Business Park, 2-8 Morley Road, Tonbridge, Kent, TN9 1RA
Parent: Atom Supplies Limited
Officers: Joel John Kelly [1980] Director/Solicitor

Maverick Spirits Limited
Incorporated: 13 March 2018
Registered Office: Unit 1 Ton Business Park, 2-8 Morley Road, Tonbridge, Kent, TN9 1RA
Parent: Atom Supplies Limited
Officers: Joel John Kelly [1980] Director/Solicitor

Maxchater Ltd
Incorporated: 21 September 2015 *Employees:* 2
Net Worth Deficit: £10,555 *Total Assets:* £22,563
Registered Office: Sunnyside, Corseley Road, Groombridge, Tunbridge Wells, Kent, TN3 9RP
Major Shareholder: Max Chater
Officers: Max Chater [1987] Director

Wm Maxwell (Scotch Whisky) Limited
Incorporated: 27 July 1990
Registered Office: Russell House, Dunnett Way, Broxburn, W Lothian, EH52 5BU
Parent: Ian MacLeod Distillers
Officers: Michael James Younger, Secretary; David William Hodder Russell [1940] Director/Whisky Broker; Leonard Stuart Russell [1961] Managing Director; Peter James Sidney Russell [1927] Director/Whisky Broker

Mayfield Distilling Company Ltd
Incorporated: 6 February 2017
Registered Office: Woodlands, Mayfield Grange, Little Trodgers Lane, Mayfield, E Sussex, TN20 6BF
Parent: A.H. Rackham Ltd
Officers: James Arthur Rackham [1953] Director/Chairman

McCaigs Distillery Ltd
Incorporated: 2 February 2015
Net Worth Deficit: £238,880 *Total Assets:* £18,520
Registered Office: 93 George Street, Edinburgh, EH2 3ES
Officers: David Eric Robertson [1978] Business Development Director

McCallums Liqueurs Ltd
Incorporated: 22 February 2018
Registered Office: Bank End Fisheries, Bank End Road, Finningley, Doncaster, S Yorks, DN9 3NT
Major Shareholder: Andrew David McCallum
Officers: Andrew David McCallum [1967] Director/Horticulturist

Alastair McIntosh Management Services Limited
Incorporated: 6 October 1995
Net Worth: £115,567 *Total Assets:* £239,897
Registered Office: Dilston, Hill Road, Gullane, E Lothian, EH31 2BE
Shareholder: Alastair McIntosh
Officers: Alastair Stiles McIntosh, Secretary; Alastair Stiles McIntosh [1940] Director; Carol Patricia McIntosh [1944] Director; Charles Rome McIntosh [1965] Director

McKerr Farming Ltd
Incorporated: 18 September 2018
Registered Office: Forth Mains Farm, Climpy, Forth, S Lanarks, ML11 8EN
Shareholders: Jennifer McKerr; Stephen McKerr
Officers: Jennifer McKerr [1983] Director/Farmer; Stephen McKerr [1979] Director/Fencer

McLean's Gin Ltd
Incorporated: 11 January 2018
Registered Office: Burnbank Farm, Strathaven, S Lanarks, ML10 6QF
Major Shareholder: Colin McLean
Officers: Colin McLean [1989] Director/Head Ginologist

McMillan MacRaild Ltd
Incorporated: 15 June 2015
Previous: The Corrymuckloch Distillery Company Ltd
Net Worth Deficit: £5,734 *Total Assets:* £262
Registered Office: 1 Broomlee Mains Court, West Linton, Peebles-shire, EH46 7BP
Shareholders: Angus William McRaild; Jonathan William Allan McMillan
Officers: Jonathan William Allan McMillan, Secretary; Angus William MacRaild [1985] Director/Auctioneer; Jonathan William Allan McMillan [1987] Director/Sales Manager

Meadowside Blending Company Limited
Incorporated: 1 May 1985 *Employees:* 2
Net Worth: £1,511,521 *Total Assets:* £2,432,321
Registered Office: 145 St Vincent Street, Glasgow, G2 5JF
Shareholders: Andrew John Greig Hart; Donald Stuart Greig Hart; Laurette Margaret Keenan Hart
Officers: Laurette Margaret Keenan Hart, Secretary/Landlady; Andrew John Greig Hart [1977] Sales Director; Donald Stuart Greig Hart [1946] Director/Exporter

The Mersey Gin Company Limited
Incorporated: 24 December 2018
Registered Office: 49 Sycamore Crescent, Macclesfield, Cheshire, SK11 8LW
Major Shareholder: Gary Stuart Crosbie
Officers: Gary Stuart Crosbie [1964] Director

Mews Gin Company Limited
Incorporated: 12 November 2014 *Employees:* 3
Net Worth Deficit: £24,921 *Total Assets:* £10,505
Registered Office: Little Ridings, Norrels Drive, East Horsley, Surrey, KT24 5DL
Shareholders: Daniel Robert Alan Mew; Jill Barbara Duval Mew; Richard Martin Mew
Officers: Daniel Robert Alan Mew [1989] Director; Jill Barbara Duval Mew [1960] Director; Richard Martin Mew [1956] Director

Mezcal Reina Limited
Incorporated: 7 November 2016
Registered Office: 65 Oakwood Court, London, W14 8JF
Shareholder: Monica Torroella
Officers: Susana Franyutti [1977] Director/PR and Marketing; Monica Torroella [1978] Director/Designer [British/Mexican]

Mezky Ltd
Incorporated: 20 June 2018
Registered Office: Mezky Ltd, Park House, 10 Park Street, Bristol, BS1 5HX
Shareholders: Antony James Williams; Robert Huw Ellis
Officers: Robert Huw Ellis [1980] Director/Musician; Antony James Williams [1982] Director/Musician

Mill House Distillery Limited
Incorporated: 16 March 2018
Registered Office: Yorkshire Accountancy Limited, County House, Dunswell Road, Cottingham, E Yorks, HU16 4JT
Major Shareholder: John Mark Cook
Officers: John Mark Cook [1974] Director

Millom Distillery Limited
Incorporated: 13 June 2018
Registered Office: 3 Market Square, Millom, Cumbria, LA18 4HZ
Officers: Jacqueline Gandy, Secretary; William Guy Lovell [1969] Director; Sean Anthony Shuttleworth [1989] Managing Director

Joseph Mills (Denaturants) Limited
Incorporated: 3 October 1975 *Employees:* 3
Net Worth: £877,575 *Total Assets:* £2,964,848
Registered Office: 3rd Floor, 5 Temple Street, Liverpool, L2 5RH
Shareholder: Christopher Mason Mills
Officers: Christopher Mason Mills [1962] Director/Industrial Chemist

Mint Drinks Company Limited
Incorporated: 19 May 2016
Registered Office: c/o Christian Douglass Accountants Ltd, Cooper Way, Parkhouse, Carlisle, CA3 0JG
Officers: Matthew David Hughes [1969] Director

J. & A. Mitchell and Company, Limited
Incorporated: 10 August 1897 *Employees:* 78
Net Worth: £18,906,872 *Total Assets:* £20,268,120
Registered Office: Springbank Distillery, Well Close, Campbeltown, Argyll, PA28 6ET
Officers: Stuart Alexander Campbell, Secretary; Stuart Alexander Campbell [1961] Director/Company Secretary; Neil Clapperton [1958] Director; Ian Edward [1935] Director/Retired; Patrick Bernard Lefebvre [1965] Director

Mitchell's Glengyle Limited
Incorporated: 25 September 2000
Net Worth: £1,637,041 *Total Assets:* £2,377,487
Registered Office: Springbank Distillery, Well Close, Campbeltown, Argyll, PA28 6ET
Parent: J & A Mitchell and Co Ltd
Officers: Stuart Alexander Campbell, Secretary; Neil Clapperton [1958] Director

MK Drinks Company Limited
Incorporated: 25 October 2018
Registered Office: c/o Bluecube House, Unit 3 Blackhill Drive, Wolverton Mill, Milton Keynes, Bucks, MK12 5TS
Officers: James Gear, Secretary; Paul Metcalfe [1987] Director; Alice Faye Warren [1991] Director

Modern Botanicals Limited
Incorporated: 7 February 2019
Registered Office: 71-75 Shelton Street, London, WC2H 9JQ
Major Shareholder: Nikita Stepanov
Officers: Nikita Stepanov, Secretary; Nikita Stepanov [1996] Director [Russian]

Moffat & Towers Limited
Incorporated: 12 October 1995
Registered Office: Moffat Distillery, Airdrie, N Lanarks, ML6 8PL
Shareholders: Khunying Wanna Sirivadhanabhakdi; Chareon Sirivadhanabhakdi
Officers: Dr Martin John Leonard [1961] Managing Director; Prapakon Thongtheppairot [1971] Director [Thai]

Molotov Brand Limited
Incorporated: 5 February 2018
Registered Office: 43 Park Place, Leeds, LS1 2RY
Officers: Vanessa Heidi Javed [1972] Director; Dayle Ivan Roane [1970] Managing Director

Montoscar Enterprises Limited
Incorporated: 16 February 2015 *Employees:* 2
Net Worth Deficit: £6,076 *Total Assets:* £21,274
Registered Office: Hillcrest, Hinton Parva, Swindon, Wilts, SN4 0DH
Major Shareholder: Harry William Meakin
Officers: Cyril Camus [1971] Director [French]; William Ashley King [1965] Director; Harry William Meakin [1980] Director/Marketing & Sales; Andre Eon Russell [1964] Director [South African]

Montrose Scotch Whisky Ltd.
Incorporated: 30 April 1973
Net Worth: £4,938 *Total Assets:* £4,938
Registered Office: 4 Millfield Close, Chester-le-Street, Co Durham, DH2 3HZ
Parent: JG Distillers Ltd
Officers: Gerrard McSherry, Secretary/Director; Colin Shields Barclay [1958] Director/Merchant [Canadian]

Moody Rum Ltd
Incorporated: 10 July 2018
Registered Office: Companies House, Default Address, Cardiff, CF14 8LH
Major Shareholder: Mike Moody
Officers: Mike Moody [1989] Director

Moores of Warwick Limited
Incorporated: 6 October 2017
Registered Office: Arkham, 9 Emscote Road, Warwick, CV34 4PH
Major Shareholder: Martin Keith Moore
Officers: Lorraine Moore [1967] Director/Manager; Martin Keith Moore [1960] Director/Accountant

Moorland Distillery Limited
Incorporated: 7 April 2016
Net Worth Deficit: £24,280 *Total Assets:* £39,428
Registered Office: Unit 22 Callywith Gate Industrial Estate, Launceston Road, Bodmin, Cornwall, PL31 2RQ
Major Shareholder: Brian Paul Farmer
Officers: Brian Paul Farmer [1958] Director

Moorland Spirit Company Limited
Incorporated: 30 April 2014 *Employees:* 7
Net Worth: £203,770 *Total Assets:* £245,883
Registered Office: 32 Portland Terrace, Newcastle upon Tyne, NE2 1QP
Shareholder: Walter John Buchanan Riddell
Officers: Christopher Lawrance Garden [1982] Director/Distiller; Cairbry Robert Meredith Hill [1975] Director; Sir Walter John Buchanan Riddell [1974] Director/Consultancy; Howard Southern [1960] Director; Valentine Thomas Warner [1972] Director/Cook, Writer, Broadcaster

Mooshine Ltd
Incorporated: 8 November 2018
Registered Office: Buckenhill Manor, Buckenhill, Bromyard, Herefords, HR7 4PG
Major Shareholder: Desmond Damian Andrews
Officers: Desmond Damian Andrews [1961] Director/Stonemason

Morangie Mineral Water Company Limited
Incorporated: 7 April 1988
Registered Office: The Cube, 45 Leith Street, Edinburgh, EH1 3AT
Parent: MacDonald & Muir Limited
Officers: Jean-Marc Rene Boulan [1972] Director [French]; Dr Peter Jonathon Nelson [1959] Director

Morangie Springs Limited
Incorporated: 7 April 1988
Registered Office: The Cube, 45 Leith Street, Edinburgh, EH1 3AT
Parent: MacDonald & Muir Limited
Officers: Jean-Marc Rene Boulan [1972] Director [French]; Dr Peter Jonathon Nelson [1959] Director

Morant Bay Distillery Co Limited
Incorporated: 22 September 2014 *Employees:* 2
Net Worth Deficit: £2,671 *Total Assets:* £21,740
Registered Office: 58 Croydon Road, Caterham, Surrey, CR3 6QB
Officers: Andrew McEniry, Secretary; Nicki Louise Townsend [1975] Director/Team Manager; Peter Townsend [1965] Director

Stanley Morrison & Co. Ltd
Incorporated: 18 October 2011 *Employees:* 2
Net Worth: £223,192 *Total Assets:* £243,950
Registered Office: 32 Main Road, Kirkoswald, Maybole, S Ayrshire, KA19 8HY
Shareholders: Stanley Walker Morrison; Stanley Andrew Morrison
Officers: Nicholas John White, Secretary; Stanley Walker Morrison [1941] Director; Stanley Andrew Morrison [1977] Director

Morrison Bowmore Distillers Limited
Incorporated: 27 July 1989 *Employees:* 180
Net Worth: £138,266,000 *Total Assets:* £176,492,992
Registered Office: Springburn Bond, Carlisle Street, Glasgow, G21 1EQ
Officers: Madame Del Pino Bermudez de La Puente Sanchez-Aguilera [1974] Director/Associate General Counsel [Spanish]; Jose Padilla Munoz [1959] Senior Director International Supply Chain Finance [Spanish]; Michael John Ord [1965] Director of Scotch & Irish Whiskies

Morrison Glasgow Distillers Limited
Incorporated: 19 June 2012 *Employees:* 18
Previous: The Glasgow Distilling Company Limited
Net Worth: £7,481,808 *Total Assets:* £9,972,933
Registered Office: 100 Stobcross Road, Glasgow, G3 8QQ
Officers: Michael David Acks [1967] Director [American]; Scott Grier [1941] Director; Kenneth Andrew McAllister [1971] Director/Chartered Accountant; Katrina Croft Morrison [1959] Director/Marketing & Tourism Consultant; Stanley Andrew Morrison [1977] Director; Stanley Walker Morrison [1941] Director; Douglas Charles Ross [1962] Director

Mossburn Distillers Limited
Incorporated: 9 August 2013 *Employees:* 2
Net Worth Deficit: £1,661,253 *Total Assets:* £5,841,532
Registered Office: Mossburn House, Camptown, Jedburgh, Roxburghshire, TD8 6PJ
Officers: John Neil MacLeod Mathieson, Secretary; Etienne Jean Marie Guyot D'Asnieres de Salins [1966] Managing Director [French]; John Neil MacLeod Mathieson [1961] Director/Line Shipper; Frederik Dag Arfst Paulsen [1950] Director [Swedish]; Eric Charles Turner [1959] Director

Mourne Dew Limited
Incorporated: 27 February 2017
Net Worth: £47,603 *Total Assets:* £59,749
Registered Office: 13 Kilbroney Road, Rostrevor, Co Down, BT34 3BH
Major Shareholder: Donal Farrell
Officers: Donal Joseph Farrell [1961] Director/Barrister [Irish]; Noel Brendan Mills [1951] Director/Retired [Irish]

The UK Spirits Industry

Mourne Mountains Whiskey Co. Ltd.
Incorporated: 25 September 2017
Registered Office: 7 Rathfriland Road, Hilltown, Newry, Co Down, BT34 5TA
Major Shareholder: David Lowry
Officers: David Lowry [1973] Director/Pharmacist [Irish]

Mousehole Brewery Limited
Incorporated: 19 March 2018
Registered Office: Jamies Wheal Whidden, Carbis Bay, St Ives, Cornwall, TR26 2QX
Major Shareholder: Joanne Michell
Officers: Joanne Michell [1974] Director/Home Keeper

Mr & Mrs Gin Ltd
Incorporated: 10 January 2017
Registered Office: Suite 3.49, Canterbury Court, 1-3 Brixton Road, London, SW9 6DE
Major Shareholder: Nicola Gurung
Officers: Nicola Gurung, Secretary; Nicola Gurung [1980] Director

Mr Bonds Tonic Limited
Incorporated: 10 June 2016
Registered Office: Hill Farm Studios, Wainlode Lane, Norton, Gloucester, GL2 9LN
Major Shareholder: Nicholas James Hine
Officers: Richard James Fredrick Hine, Secretary; Nicholas James Hine [1970] Managing Director

Mr Kegz Ltd
Incorporated: 5 September 2018
Registered Office: 22 Burgh Way, Walsall, W Midlands, WS2 7RG
Major Shareholder: Conor Aston Johns
Officers: Conor Aston Johns [1992] Director/Support Worker

Mudlark Investments Ltd
Incorporated: 20 December 2017
Registered Office: 5 Newcroft Road, Woolton, Liverpool, L25 6EP
Major Shareholder: Dougal Freeman
Officers: Dougal Freeman [1970] Director/Accountant

Charles Muirhead & Son. Limited
Incorporated: 30 September 1936
Registered Office: The Cube, 45 Leith Street, Edinburgh, EH1 3AT
Parent: The Glenmorangie Company Limited
Officers: Jean-Marc Rene Boulan [1972] Director [French]; Dr Peter Jonathon Nelson [1959] Director

Mulberry Distillery Limited
Incorporated: 22 June 2018
Registered Office: Acre House, 11-15 William Road, London, NW1 3ER
Shareholders: Richard Joseph Hargroves; Suman Mitra
Officers: Richard Joseph Hargroves [1968] Director; Suman Mitra [1975] Director/Hotelier and Restaurateur

The Mull Gin Company Ltd
Incorporated: 26 January 2018
Registered Office: Treetops, Gowkhouse Road, Kilmacolm, Renfrewshire, PA13 4DJ
Major Shareholder: Leslie McDonald MacLeod
Officers: Leslie McDonald MacLeod [1961] Director

The Mull Gin Distillery Ltd
Incorporated: 26 January 2018
Registered Office: Treetops, Gowkhouse Road, Kilmacolm, Renfrewshire, PA13 4DJ
Major Shareholder: Leslie McDonald MacLeod
Officers: Leslie McDonald MacLeod [1961] Director

Murphy's Gin Ltd
Incorporated: 1 November 2018
Registered Office: 25 Parker Avenue, Seaforth, Liverpool, L21 1EL
Shareholders: Mark Francis Murphy; Lianne Karen Murphy
Officers: Dr Lianne Karen Murphy [1978] Director/Technical Manager; Dr Mark Francis Murphy [1972] Director/Lecturer

Murphy, Black and Mills Limited
Incorporated: 1 December 2016
Net Worth Deficit: £579 *Total Assets:* £21
Registered Office: 4 Kitchen Street, Liverpool, L1 0AN
Officers: Tom Mills [1983] Director; Paul Murphy [1983] Director

Musicspeller Ltd
Incorporated: 25 June 2018
Registered Office: Suite 1, Fielden House, 41 Rochdale Road, Todmorden, W Yorks, OL14 6LD
Shareholders: Bianca San Jose; Caroline Kendall
Officers: Bianca San Jose [1998] Director [Filipino]

MWBH Bottling Co. Limited
Incorporated: 22 November 1999
Net Worth: £25,602 *Total Assets:* £33,563
Registered Office: 22 Market Place, Kendal, Cumbria, LA9 4TN
Major Shareholder: Paul William Cliburn Smith
Officers: Rebecca Emily Louise Holliday, Secretary; Rebecca Emily Louise Holliday [1979] Director/University Administrator; Barry Reginald Felstead Jones [1945] Director/Licensee; Paul William Cliburn Smith [1949] Director/Solicitor

My Nan's Favourite Ltd
Incorporated: 22 February 2019
Registered Office: Pitch Cottage, Pitch Place, Thursley, Godalming, Surrey, GU8 6QW
Major Shareholder: Christopher Jon Frederick
Officers: Christopher Jon Frederick [1982] Director

Myatt's Fields Limited
Incorporated: 1 February 2017
Net Worth Deficit: £6,107 *Total Assets:* £6,316
Registered Office: 11 Upstall Street, London, SE5 9JE
Officers: Cyrus Jasper Gilbert-Rolfe, Secretary; Cyrus Jasper Gilbert-Rolfe [1966] Director/Partner; Clemency Rachel Lesley Indira Penn [1973] Director/Partner

Myperfectgin Ltd
Incorporated: 31 July 2017
Registered Office: 290 Milton Road East, Edinburgh, EH15 2PQ
Shareholders: Neil Jordan; Matthew Ward
Officers: Neil Lennox Jordan [1972] Director; Matthew Ward [1967] Director

N.Gin Distillery Ltd
Incorporated: 20 August 2018
Registered Office: 8 Stanley Grange Business Village, Ormskirk Road, Knowsley, Prescot, Merseyside, L34 4AR
Shareholders: Samantha Louise Flaherty; Ian John Platt
Officers: Samantha Louise Flaherty [1989] Director/Teacher

NB Distillery Limited
Incorporated: 5 March 2013
Net Worth Deficit: £196,542 *Total Assets:* £103,695
Registered Office: 15 St Andrew Street, North Berwick, E Lothian, EH39 4NU
Shareholders: Vivienne Muir; Stephen Robert Muir
Officers: Vivienne Muir, Secretary; Stephen Robert Muir [1971] Director/Solicitor; Vivienne Muir [1973] Director/Solicitor

Ncn'ean Distillery Limited
Incorporated: 22 March 2013 *Employees:* 6
Previous: Drimnin Distillery Limited
Net Worth: £4,343,493 *Total Assets:* £4,991,578
Registered Office: Ncn'Ean Distillery, Drimnin, by Lochaline, Oban, Argyll & Bute, PA80 5XZ
Shareholders: Annabel Buick Thomas; Julia Lewis; Louise Lewis; Charles Adriaenssen; Jacques de Meuvis
Officers: Annabel Thomas, Secretary; Charles Adriaenssen [1956] Director [Belgian]; Richard John Cole [1954] Director/Banker; Derek Compton Lewis [1946] Director; Benet Dunstan Slay [1961] Managing Director; Annabel Buick Thomas [1983] Director

Neat Distillery Ltd
Incorporated: 17 August 2017
Registered Office: P O Box 199, 3 Hillersdon Avenue, Edgware, Middlesex, HA8 7FG
Shareholders: Adam Woodyatt; Beverley Anita Woodyatt
Officers: Adam Woodyatt [1968] Director/Actor; Beverley Anita Woodyatt [1963] Director/Theatrical Agent/Manager

Neat Spirits Limited
Incorporated: 3 May 2018
Registered Office: 93 London Road, Cheltenham, Glos, GL52 6HL
Parent: Sibling Distillery Limited
Officers: Cicely Star Elliott-Berry [1995] Director; Clarice Bijou Elliott-Berry [1993] Director; Felix Louis Elliott-Berry [1992] Director; Roland Brian Elliott-Berry [1951] Director; Stephanie Judith Elliott-Berry [1965] Director

Nectardigger Ltd
Incorporated: 23 July 2018
Registered Office: Suite 1, Fielden House, 41 Rochdale Road, Todmorden, W Yorks, OL14 6LD
Major Shareholder: Paige Amber Ellis
Officers: Robin Patrick Reyes [1992] Director [Filipino]

H. J. Neill Ltd
Incorporated: 23 December 2015
Net Worth: £270,000 *Total Assets:* £807,000
Registered Office: The Sovereign Distillery, Wilson Road, Huyton, Knowsley, Merseyside, L36 6AD
Shareholders: Judith Margaret Halewood; Ian Alan Douglas
Officers: Stewart Andrew Hainsworth [1969] Director/Chief Executive Officer; Alan William Robinson [1965] Director/Accountant

Nele Drinks Limited
Incorporated: 14 August 2017
Registered Office: 21 Racavan Road, Broughshane, Ballymena, Co Antrim, BT42 4PH
Major Shareholder: Niall Edward Lloyd Esler
Officers: Niall Edward Lloyd Esler [1985] Director/Solicitor

Nene Distillery Limited
Incorporated: 12 October 2017
Registered Office: Keel House, Garth Heads, Newcastle upon Tyne, NE1 2JE
Shareholders: Scott Biggs; Inveniam Corporate Finance Limited; Tier One Capital Investments Limited
Officers: Scott Biggs [1987] Director

Neptune SA Ltd
Incorporated: 12 March 2018
Registered Office: Mays Grove Cottage, Mays Lane, Dedham, Colchester, Essex, CO7 6EW
Officers: Antanas Sadauskas [1965] Director [Lithuanian]

Nero Drinks Company Limited
Incorporated: 12 March 2018
Registered Office: 15 Cumbernauld Road, Stepps, Glasgow, G33 6LE
Officers: Nicola Margaret Morrissey [1975] Director

Nestwonder Ltd
Incorporated: 23 July 2018
Registered Office: Suite 6, First Floor, Wordsworth Mill, Wordsworth Street, Bolton, Lancs, BL1 3ND
Major Shareholder: Paul Westhead
Officers: Josephine Maglanque [1974] Director [Filipino]

New Adventure (Norfolk) Limited
Incorporated: 16 December 2014
Net Worth: £33,117 *Total Assets:* £102,022
Registered Office: 21 Blakeney Close, Norwich, NR4 7QP
Major Shareholder: Major Jonathan Mark Redding
Officers: Jonathan Mark Redding [1960] Director/Retired; Muriel Alison Redding [1958] Director

New Comber Distillery Ltd
Incorporated: 5 May 2017
Registered Office: Sinclair House, 89-100 Royal Avenue, Belfast, BT1 1FE
Major Shareholder: Julia McLaughlin
Officers: Julia McLaughlin [1976] Director

New Dawn Traders Ltd
Incorporated: 10 July 2013
Net Worth Deficit: £3,809 *Total Assets:* £28,844
Registered Office: c/o Linden Accountants Ltd, 21 Sevier Street, Bristol, BS2 9LB
Shareholder: Alexandra Joan Geldenhuys
Officers: Alexandra Joan Geldenhuys [1982] Director/Creative

The New Forest Distillery Ltd
Incorporated: 15 November 2016
Registered Office: 2 Water End Barns, Water End, Eversholt, Beds, MK17 9EA
Shareholders: Valerie Wood; Stephen Ross Wood
Officers: Valerie Wood, Secretary; Stephen Ross Wood [1949] Director

New Forest Spirits Ltd
Incorporated: 12 October 2017
Registered Office: 1a Kingsbury's Lane, Ringwood, Hants, BH24 1EL
Shareholders: Kay Maxine Williams; Mark Steven Williams
Officers: Kay Maxine Williams [1964] Director; Mark Steven Williams [1963] Director

New Found Spirit Scotland Limited
Incorporated: 6 February 2018
Registered Office: Unit 5 Block 1, Duckburn Industrial Estate, Dunblane, Stirling, FK15 0EW
Major Shareholder: Richard Thurlow-Begg
Officers: Richard Thurlow-Begg [1985] Director

New Galloway Inspired Ltd
Incorporated: 31 May 2017
Registered Office: The Smithy, High Street, New Galloway, Dumfries & Galloway, DG7 3RN
Officers: David John Briggs [1951] Director/Chef; Marion Riddell Briggs [1952] Director; Margaret Mary McSorley Walker [1963] Director/Development Manager; Andrew Walker [1967] Director/Chartered Accountant

The New Union Brewing Company Limited
Incorporated: 31 January 2019
Registered Office: 159 Stricklandgate, Kendal, Cumbria, LA9 4RF
Officers: Martin James Boyd [1968] Director/Architectural Technician; Philip Lawrence John Walker [1986] Director/Publican

The New Welsh Whiskey Company Limited
Incorporated: 8 December 1999
Registered Office: Penderyn Distillery, Pontpren, Penderyn, Rhondda Cynon Taf, CF44 0SX
Officers: Huw Thomas, Secretary; Edwina Josette Clark [1951] Director/Stocktaker; Nicholas John Clark [1947] Director/Engineer; Professor Brian Morgan [1947] Director/University Lecturer

Newbury Gin Limited
Incorporated: 25 August 2016
Registered Office: The Vicarage, Cold Ash Hill, Cold Ash, Thatcham, Berks, RG18 9PT
Officers: Steve Leadley [1958] Director; Ann Stancombe [1961] Director

Newcastle Distilling Ltd
Incorporated: 30 November 2016
Registered Office: 6 Peony Place, Newcastle upon Tyne, NE6 1LU
Officers: Michael Bell, Secretary; Leo Bell [1979] Director/Brewer; Michael Bell [1952] Director/Brewer; David Ronald Kell [1946] Director/Retired

Newcastle Gin Co. Limited
Incorporated: 16 June 2015 *Employees:* 4
Net Worth: £4,067 *Total Assets:* £55,660
Registered Office: Bealim House, 17-25 Gallowgate, Newcastle upon Tyne, NE1 4SG
Officers: Harry Vaulkhard [1985] Director; Oliver Tom Vaulkhard [1971] Director

The Newcastle Whisky Distillery Company Limited
Incorporated: 10 October 2016
Registered Office: 5 Market Yard Mews, 194-204 Bermondsey Street, London, SE1 3TQ
Major Shareholder: Gary John Thornton
Officers: Gary John Thornton [1967] Director

Newton Drinks Limited
Incorporated: 28 January 2016 *Employees:* 5
Net Worth Deficit: £76,992 *Total Assets:* £69,497
Registered Office: 50 The Terrace, Torquay, Devon, TQ1 1DD
Shareholders: Jane Cannon; Robin George Cannon
Officers: Jane Canon, Secretary; Jane Canon [1958] Director; Robin George Canon [1953] Director

Nibbs Spirits Limited
Incorporated: 13 April 2018
Registered Office: Hawthorn Cottage, Runfold St George, Badshot Lea, Farnham, Surrey, GU10 1PL
Officers: Richard Michael Sharman, Secretary; Nicola Ann Sharman [1964] Director; Richard Michael Sharman [1961] Director

Nicol Anderson & Company Limited
Incorporated: 30 March 1927
Registered Office: The Cube, 45 Leith Street, Edinburgh, EH1 3AT
Parent: The Glenmorangie Company Limited
Officers: Jean-Marc Rene Boulan [1972] Director [French]; Dr Peter Jonathon Nelson [1959] Director

Nightrep Limited
Incorporated: 8 December 2016
Net Worth Deficit: £2,715 *Total Assets:* £1,197
Registered Office: 28 Innerleithen Way, Perth, PH1 1RN
Major Shareholder: Iain James McDonald
Officers: Iain James McDonald [1966] Director/Consultant

NineTailsDistillery Ltd
Incorporated: 28 August 2018
Registered Office: Iso:Fitness, Church Street, Pontardawe, Swansea, SA8 4JB
Major Shareholder: Cerith James Thomas
Officers: Cerith James Thomas [1991] Director/Businessman

Ninth Wave Gin Company Limited
Incorporated: 19 April 2018
Registered Office: Killaney Lodge, 19 Carryduff Road, Lisburn, Co Antrim, BT27 6TZ
Parent: Hinch Distillery Limited
Officers: Terence Martin Cross [1950] Director; Derek Hardy [1961] Director; Patrick Joseph McGibbon [1971] Director/Accountant; Michael Morris [1961] Sales Director [Irish]

Nip from The Hip Limited
Incorporated: 23 February 2011
Net Worth: £28,876 *Total Assets:* £40,667
Registered Office: Unit 23 Integrame, Bircholt Road, Maidstone, Kent, ME15 9YY
Major Shareholder: Alison Joy Smith
Officers: Alison Smith, Secretary; Alison Joy Smith [1976] Managing Director; Joy Emily Wilding [1953] Production Director

Nitrogin Ltd.
Incorporated: 17 October 2017
Registered Office: Hurlditch Court, Lamerton, Tavistock, Devon, PL19 8QA
Major Shareholder: Brian George Muir
Officers: Brian George Muir [1970] Director/Web Designer

The Nodding Donkey Distillery Company Limited
Incorporated: 3 August 2016
Net Worth Deficit: £56,596 *Total Assets:* £167,352
Registered Office: 14 Laburnum Grove, Chichester, W Sussex, PO19 7DL
Shareholders: James Cameron Jarrold; Nichola Jane Jarrold
Officers: James Cameron Jarrold [1967] Director; Nichola Jane Jarrold [1962] Director

Norcabis Ltd
Incorporated: 24 July 2018
Registered Office: Ground Floor Office, 108 Fore Street, Hertford, SG14 1AB
Major Shareholder: Simon Boswell
Officers: Dominga Madrid [1964] Director [Filipino]

Norfolk Distillery Ltd
Incorporated: 13 March 2015
Registered Office: Drayton Old Lodge, 146 Drayton High Road, Norwich, NR8 6AN
Shareholders: Patrick James Saunders; Sarah Elizabeth Saunders
Officers: Patrick James Saunders [1965] Director/Trails Officer; Sarah Elizabeth Saunders [1968] Director/Teacher

Norfolk Gin Limited
Incorporated: 14 June 2018
Registered Office: 21 Blakeney Close, Norwich, NR4 7QP
Major Shareholder: Major Jonathan Mark Redding
Officers: Jonathan Mark Redding [1960] Director

The Norfolk Rum Company Ltd
Incorporated: 7 January 2019
Registered Office: 20-22 Wenlock Road, London, N1 7GU
Major Shareholder: Susan Richman
Officers: Susan Richman [1972] Director

Norfolk Whisky Co. Limited
Incorporated: 12 December 2005
Registered Office: Roudham House, East Harling, Norwich, NR16 2RJ
Major Shareholder: Andrew Nelstrop
Officers: Andrew Leethem Nelstrop, Secretary; Andrew Leethem Nelstrop [1971] Director/Builder

The North British Distillery Company Limited
Incorporated: 24 October 1885 *Employees:* 179
Net Worth: £49,910,000 *Total Assets:* £64,013,000
Registered Office: Wheatfield Road, Edinburgh, EH11 2PX
Parent: Lothian Distillers Limited
Officers: Fraser William MacDonald, Secretary; Ian Barrett Curle [1961] Director; David Andrew Cutter [1968] Director [Australian]; Graham Robert Hutcheon [1963] Director/Distiller; Alan John Stewart Kilpatrick [1965] Director; Alan Kilpatrick [1980] Director; Pamela Elizabeth Scott [1969] Director

North Tyne Ventures Ltd
Incorporated: 12 April 2018
Registered Office: Lloyds House, Bellingham, Northumberland, NE48 2AZ
Major Shareholder: Richard John Cooper
Officers: Richard John Cooper [1986] Director

North Uist Distillery Ltd
Incorporated: 15 March 2017
Net Worth: £100 *Total Assets:* £47,572
Registered Office: Bayview, Baymore, Grimsay, North Uist, HS6 5HX
Major Shareholder: Jonathan Ingledew
Officers: Jonathan Ingledew [1984] Director

Northern Fried Drinks Limited
Incorporated: 10 July 2018
Registered Office: The House, Schoolhouse Lane, Marley Hill, Gateshead, Tyne & Wear, NE16 5AN
Major Shareholder: Thomas James Featherstone
Officers: Thomas James Featherstone [1983] Director

Northern Spirits Partnership Ltd
Incorporated: 20 June 2016
Net Worth Deficit: £18,327 *Total Assets:* £6,904
Registered Office: Unit 4 Woodrow Business Centre, Woodrow Way, Irlam, Manchester, M44 6NN
Officers: Anthony Paul Mitten [1981] Director; Carl David Mitten [1981] Director; Samuel Ian Mitten [1954] Director; Stephen James Mitten [1980] Director

The Northlew Distillery Ltd
Incorporated: 16 July 2018
Registered Office: Hillside Forge, Northlew, Okehampton, Devon, EX20 3NR
Shareholders: Timothy Lloyd Williams; Daniel Charles Anscomb
Officers: Daniel Charles Anscomb [1985] Director; Timothy Lloyd Williams [1968] Director

The Northumberland Distillery Company Limited
Incorporated: 3 April 2014
Registered Office: 5 Market Yard Mews, 194-204 Bermondsey Street, London, SE1 3TQ
Major Shareholder: Paul Richard Currie
Officers: Paul Richard Currie [1964] Director

The Northumberland Gin Company Limited
Incorporated: 19 April 2017
Net Worth: £20,674 *Total Assets:* £20,822
Registered Office: 36 Leafield Close, Birtley, Chester-le-Street, Co Durham, DH3 1RX
Officers: Jane Monehen [1970] Director/School Secretary; Peter Monehen [1960] Director/IT Consultant; Deborah Renwick [1970] Director/NHS Manager; Ian Douglas Renwick [1965] Director/Chief Executive

Northumberland Spirit Company Ltd
Incorporated: 26 June 2016
Net Worth: £22,617 *Total Assets:* £48,823
Registered Office: Blacksmiths Hall, Rock, Alnwick, Northumberland, NE66 3SB
Shareholder: Neil Jeremy Osborne
Officers: Neil Jeremy Osborne [1965] Director

Northumberland Whisky Ltd
Incorporated: 13 August 2018
Registered Office: 14 Romans Court, Nottingham, NG6 0HF
Shareholders: Richard Bryan Hall; Colin Bland
Officers: Colin Bland [1951] Director/Retired; Richard Bryan Hall [1950] Director/Charity Worker

O'Hara's Spiced Rum Limited
Incorporated: 23 January 2012
Net Worth Deficit: £52,559 *Total Assets:* £25,740
Registered Office: 11 Wych Fold, Hyde, Cheshire, SK14 5ED
Major Shareholder: Andrew Timothy O'Hara
Officers: Andy Ohara [1972] Director/Publican

Ogilvy Spirits Limited
Incorporated: 24 July 2013 *Employees:* 2
Net Worth Deficit: £98,778 *Total Assets:* £161,757
Registered Office: Westby, 64 West High Street, Forfar, Angus, DD8 1BJ
Major Shareholder: Graeme Young Jarron
Officers: Caroline Bruce-Jarron [1983] Director; Graeme Young Jarron [1980] Director/Farming

Oktogin Ltd
Incorporated: 30 January 2017
Registered Office: 50 Widney Road, Knowle, Solihull, W Midlands, B93 9DY
Shareholders: Scott Buchanan Martin; Helen Jane Martin
Officers: Scott Buchanan Martin [1985] Managing Director

Old Brenin Distillery Ltd
Incorporated: 26 June 2018
Registered Office: Unit 30 Pontygwindy Industrial Estate, Caerphilly, Gwent, CF83 3HU
Major Shareholder: Carl Antony Simmonds
Officers: Carl Antony Simmonds [1968] Managing Director

The Old Bushmills Distillery Company Limited
Incorporated: 3 April 1930 *Employees:* 110
Net Worth: £160,582,000 *Total Assets:* £176,020,992
Registered Office: 2 Distillery Road, Bushmills, Co Antrim, BT57 8XH
Parent: JC Overseas Ltd
Officers: Angel Ignacio Abarrategui Diez [1955] Director [Spanish]; Pedro Pablo Barragan [1978] Director/General Counsel [Mexican]; Colum Egan [1969] Director/Distiller [Irish]; David Peter Gosnell [1957] Director

The Old Chapel Brendon Limited
Incorporated: 7 May 2010
Net Worth: £70,676 *Total Assets:* £103,407
Registered Office: The Old Chapel, Brendon, Lynton, Devon, EX35 6PT
Shareholders: Julie Sharron Heap; Umesh Kumar Patel
Officers: Umesh Patel, Secretary; Julie Sharron Heap [1968] Accounts Director; Umesh Kumar Patel [1969] Director

The Old Curiosity Distillery Ltd
Incorporated: 14 May 2014 *Employees:* 3
Previous: The Natural Wine Company (UK) Limited
Net Worth: £84,204 *Total Assets:* £194,936
Registered Office: Room 3, Suite 23, Templeton House, 62 Templeton Street, Glasgow, G40 1DA
Shareholders: Hamish Martin; Liberty Grace Dearden Martin
Officers: Colin Alexander Forgie [1971] Operations Director; Richard Edward Glover [1960] Director/Sales and Marketing Manager; Hamish Martin [1958] Director; Liberty Grace Dearden Martin [1978] Director

Old Smiths Distillery Ltd
Incorporated: 12 February 2018
Registered Office: 5 Ryder Court, Oakley Hay Industrial Estate, Corby, Northants, NN18 9NX
Major Shareholder: James Donald Checkley
Officers: James Donald Checkley [1974] Director

Old Tom Gin Company in St Andrews Ltd
Incorporated: 3 May 2017
Registered Office: 59 Bonnygate, Cupar, Fife, KY15 4BY
Parent: Divino Incanto Wine & Spirits Group UK Ltd
Officers: Giorgio Cozzolino [1964] Director [Italian]

One Point Eight Bar Limited
Incorporated: 15 June 2015 *Employees:* 2
Net Worth Deficit: £38,162 *Total Assets:* £15,214
Registered Office: Grand Union House, 20 Kentish Town Road, London, NW1 9NX
Shareholders: Laetitia Estella Emmeline Lawrence; Hayden John Gale
Officers: Hayden John Gale [1983] Director/Brewer & Operator; Laetitia Estella Emmeline Lawrence [1987] Director/Manager & Operator

One Swan Ltd
Incorporated: 23 February 2018
Registered Office: 29 Josephine Avenue, Limavady, Co Londonderry, BT49 9BA
Major Shareholder: Conor McKay
Officers: Lauren Hutton, Secretary; Conor McKay [1997] Director/Consultancy [Irish]

Orbis Whiskey Limited
Incorporated: 25 June 2012
Registered Office: 31 Squirrels Heath Avenue, Romford, Essex, RM2 6AD
Officers: Kevin Charles Casey [1950] Director; Andrew Ford [1961] Director/Business Development; Abraham Michael Christian Loubser [1932] Director/Businessman [Dutch]

Originalsip Ltd
Incorporated: 27 April 2017
Net Worth: £4,158 *Total Assets:* £17,260
Registered Office: 10 Rutland Gardens, London, N4 1JP
Shareholder: Antonio Pescatori
Officers: Antonio Pescatori [1990] Director/Rectifier [Italian]

Orkney Distilling Limited
Incorporated: 1 February 2016 *Employees:* 2
Net Worth Deficit: £8,165 *Total Assets:* £592,350
Registered Office: Springfields, Berstane Road, St Ola, Kirkwall, Orkney, KW15 1SZ
Shareholders: Stephen Charles Ritchie Kemp; Alyson Stevenson Kemp
Officers: Alyson Stevenson Kemp, Secretary; Alyson Stevenson Kemp [1988] Director; Stephen Charles Ritchie Kemp [1981] Director

Orkney Mead Ltd
Incorporated: 27 March 2018
Registered Office: Highbury, East Road, Kirkwall, Orkney, KW15 1HZ
Shareholders: Donald Sinclair Macpherson Robertson; Michelle Gayne Robertson
Officers: Donald Sinclair Macpherson Robertson [1967] Director; Michelle Gayne Robertson [1970] Director/Manager

Orkney Spirits Limited
Incorporated: 1 November 2017
Registered Office: Orkney Gin Company, Burray, Orkney, KW17 2SS
Major Shareholder: Andrea Watt
Officers: Andrea Watt [1974] Director/Spirit Producer; Gary David Watt [1971] Director/Ships Master

The Orogin Distilling Co. Limited
Incorporated: 22 October 2015 *Employees:* 3
Net Worth Deficit: £198,067 *Total Assets:* £232,358
Registered Office: 10 Elsee Road, Rugby, Warwicks, CV21 3BA
Shareholders: Raymond Valentine Clynick; Jacqueline Margaret Clynick; Raymond Henry Thomas Clynick
Officers: Jacqueline Margaret Clynick [1950] Director; Raymond Henry Thomas Clynick [1990] Director; Raymond Valentine Clynick [1959] Director

Otter Distillery Limited
Incorporated: 26 April 2018
Registered Office: Middle Barn, Mathayes, Luppit, Honiton, Devon, EX14 4SA
Shareholders: David Francis Anderson McCaig; Mary-Ann McCaig
Officers: David Francis Anderson McCaig [1946] Director; Mary-Ann McCaig [1941] Director

Our/London Vodka Limited
Incorporated: 16 April 2014 *Employees:* 5
Net Worth Deficit: £856,003 *Total Assets:* £998,494
Registered Office: Arches 435 and 436, Spurstowe Road, London, E8 1LS
Officers: David Mizrahi [1978] Director/Engineer [American/Czech]

Oxford Distillers Limited
Incorporated: 27 November 2018
Registered Office: 9 Claypit Lane, East Challow, Wantage, Oxon, OX12 9WF
Shareholders: David Lloyd Wilson; Nicola Louise Wilson
Officers: Dr David Lloyd Wilson [1983] Director; Nicola Louise Wilson [1986] Director

Oxford Distillery Limited
Incorporated: 11 April 2012
Registered Office: 32 Station Road, Histon, Cambridge, CB24 9LQ
Major Shareholder: William John Lowe
Officers: William John Lowe [1979] Director

The Oxford Gin Company Limited
Incorporated: 5 September 2017
Registered Office: The Old Tannery, Hensington Road, Woodstock, Oxon, OX20 1JL
Shareholder: Robert Malcolm Ryder
Officers: Robert Malcolm Ryder [1952] Director

The Oxfordshire Gin Company Ltd
Incorporated: 2 October 2017
Registered Office: Manor Farm, Main Street, Hethe, Bicester, Oxon, OX27 8ES
Major Shareholder: Molly Mansfield
Officers: Molly Mansfield [1991] Director

Pant y Foel Gin Ltd
Incorporated: 29 October 2018
Registered Office: Pant Y Foel, Saron, Denbigh, LL16 4TL
Major Shareholder: Lesley Karan Haythorne
Officers: Lesley Karan Haythorne [1965] Director/Dietitian

Papillon Dartmoor Distillery Limited
Incorporated: 27 February 2017
Net Worth Deficit: £8,505 *Total Assets:* £4,050
Registered Office: 19 Old Exeter Street, Chudleigh, Newton Abbot, Devon, TQ13 0LD
Officers: Adam Hyne [1969] Director; Claire Hyne [1974] Director

Paradise Cocktails Ltd
Incorporated: 26 November 2018
Registered Office: Apt 25915, Trevissome Park, Truro, Cornwall, TR4 8UN
Officers: Alexander Wright [1999] Director/Transport Administration//Accountancy

Paradise Rum Limited
Incorporated: 16 January 2019
Registered Office: 3 Logan Close, Enfield, Middlesex, EN3 5NL
Shareholder: Nathan Brown
Officers: Nathan Brown [1993] Director; Kianne Ward [1994] Director

Parlay Drinks Ltd
Incorporated: 11 January 2016
Net Worth Deficit: £20,555 *Total Assets:* £5,785
Registered Office: 29 Wensleydale, Wilnecote, Tamworth, Staffs, B77 4PS
Major Shareholder: Craig Smith
Officers: Craig Smith [1983] Director/Entrepreneur

Patient Wolf Limited
Incorporated: 19 June 2017 *Employees:* 2
Net Worth Deficit: £33,363 *Total Assets:* £741,320
Registered Office: 10 Queen Street Place, London, EC4R 1AG
Major Shareholder: Mark James Stephen
Officers: Mark James Stephen [1980] Director [Australian]

Patterson and Clarke Distillery Limited
Incorporated: 17 July 2017
Registered Office: Finsgate, 5-7 Cranwood Street, London, EC1V 9EE
Parent: Clarke Vineyard Limited
Officers: Nicholas Antony Clarke [1961] Director; Neil Desmond Patterson [1980] Director

The Peak District Distilling Company Limited
Incorporated: 24 April 2016
Net Worth: £1,921,380 *Total Assets:* £1,921,380
Registered Office: The Wire Works, Derwent Works, Matlock Road, Ambergate, Derbys, DE56 2HE
Shareholder: Max Vaughan
Officers: Gareth Neil Stuart Dunn [1971] Director/Businessman; Christopher Geldard [1970] Director/Businessman; Robert Frederick Morgan [1968] Director; Sean Dudley Parrott [1965] Director; Maxwell Lucas Vaughan [1969] Finance Director

Peakys Distillery Ltd
Incorporated: 30 June 2017
Registered Office: 12 Whitfield Park, Glossop, Derbys, SK13 8LG
Major Shareholder: Zara Penn
Officers: Zara Penn [1971] Director/Distiller

Peats Beast Limited
Incorporated: 2 February 2012
Net Worth: £43,997 *Total Assets:* £116,214
Registered Office: 3 Clive Street, Hereford, HR1 2SB
Shareholders: Eamonn Fitzgerald Jones; Gerald Erdich; Aidan Stuart Smith
Officers: Eamonn FitzGeneral Jones, Secretary; Generall Erdich [1959] Director/Distillery Manager [German]; Eamonn FitzGeneral Jones [1963] Director/Spirits Consultant

Peedie Sea Distilling Limited
Incorporated: 3 April 2018
Registered Office: Store Ayre Mills, Ayre Road, Kirkwall, Orkney, KW15 1QZ
Major Shareholder: Ronald Thomas Spence
Officers: Ronald Thomas Spence [1963] Director/Distiller

Pell and Co Spirits Limited
Incorporated: 26 July 2016
Registered Office: Bankside, 300 Peachman Way, Broadland Business Park, Norwich, NR7 0LB
Shareholders: Felicity Ann Malt; Ricky Kennan Malt
Officers: Felicity Ann Malt [1986] Director; Ricky Kennan Malt [1985] Director/Publican

The Pembrokeshire Comestibles Company Limited
Incorporated: 11 May 2018
Registered Office: The Old Convent, Llanbadarn Road, Aberystwyth, Ceredigion, SY23 1WX
Major Shareholder: Sabrina Johnson
Officers: Katherine Elizabeth Price, Secretary; Sabrina Johnson [1947] Director

Penningtons Spirits and Liqueurs Ltd
Incorporated: 8 February 2018
Registered Office: 10 Tanners Yard, 39 Highgate, Kendal, Cumbria, LA9 4ED
Parent: The Kendal Mint Cake Company Limited
Officers: Tim Brownhill [1991] Director/Business Development Manager

Penny Lane Gin Ltd
Incorporated: 12 February 2018
Registered Office: 26 Southway, Liverpool, L15 7JA
Officers: Joseph John Thomas [1987] Director

Penrhos Spirits Ltd
Incorporated: 3 October 2017
Registered Office: Penrhos Farm, Lyonshall, Kington, Herefords, HR5 3LH
Major Shareholder: Richard John Williams
Officers: Richard John Williams [1966] Director/Farmer

The Pentland Still Ltd
Incorporated: 15 November 2017
Net Worth Deficit: £37,112 *Total Assets:* £7,722
Registered Office: Unit 35 Imex Business Centre, Bilston Glen Industrial Estate, Dryden Road, Loanhead, Midlothian, EH20 9LZ
Major Shareholder: Alexander Campbell Morrison
Officers: Alexander Campbell Morrison [1989] Director

Penton Park Brewery Limited
Incorporated: 15 April 2014 *Employees:* 2
Previous: Pentafra Limited
Net Worth: £27 *Total Assets:* £153,757
Registered Office: Midland House, 2 Poole Road, Bournemouth, BH2 5QY
Shareholders: Danielle Marie Rolfe; Guy William Rolfe
Officers: Danielle Marie Rolfe [1981] Director/Self Employed; Guy William Rolfe [1981] Director/Self Employed

The Pentone Family Limited
Incorporated: 29 December 2014
Net Worth Deficit: £8,675 *Total Assets:* £2,269
Registered Office: c/o UHY Hacker Young, St James Building, 79 Oxford Street, Manchester, M1 6HT
Major Shareholder: Philip Michael Robinson
Officers: Philip Michael Robinson [1986] Director

Pentric Distillery Ltd
Incorporated: 14 July 2017
Registered Office: The White House, 44 High Street, Sixpenny Handley, Dorset, SP5 5ND
Major Shareholder: Oscar de Hane Segrave
Officers: Oscar de Hane Segrave [1995] Director

Percy's T Limited
Incorporated: 19 September 2005
Registered Office: Sycamore Farm, Fen Drove, Kirton Holme, Boston, Lincs, PE20 1TS
Major Shareholder: Claire Louisa Hall
Officers: Jessica Ruth Hall, Secretary/Air Stewardess; Claire Louisa Hall [1982] Director

Perfidious Albion Limited
Incorporated: 3 August 2018
Registered Office: 71-75 Shelton Street, Covent Garden, London, WC2H 9JQ
Major Shareholder: Piers Roberts
Officers: Piers Roberts [1980] Director/Accountant

The Perth Distillery Company Limited
Incorporated: 13 February 2018
Registered Office: 28 Innerleithen Way, Perth, PH1 1RN
Major Shareholder: Iain James McDonald
Officers: Elaine Brady [1967] Director; Iain James McDonald [1966] Director

Perthshire Whisky Company Limited
Incorporated: 16 October 1998
Registered Office: Edradour Distillery, Pitlochry, Perthshire, PH16 5JP
Major Shareholder: Andrew William Symington
Officers: Graham Keith Cox, Secretary; Graham Keith Cox [1947] Director/Solicitor; Andrew William Symington [1963] Director/Chief Executive Officer

Pesvebi Ltd
Incorporated: 3 August 2012
Net Worth: £912 *Total Assets:* £54,104
Registered Office: Old Vodka, Church Farm, Ardeley, Stevenage, Herts, SG2 7AH
Major Shareholder: Merab Salamashvili
Officers: Merab Salamashvili [1975] Director [Georgian]

Laurence Philippe Wines Limited
Incorporated: 25 March 1981 *Employees:* 10
Net Worth: £287,400 *Total Assets:* £590,043
Registered Office: 1 Brewery Fields, Great Baddow, Chelmsford, Essex, CM2 7LE
Major Shareholder: Alan William Mark Lawrence
Officers: Alison Bangs, Secretary; Alan William Mark Lawrence [1946] Director

Pickering's Gin Limited
Incorporated: 7 November 2018
Registered Office: Summerhall Distillery, 1 Summerhall, Edinburgh, EH9 1PL
Parent: Summerhall Distillery Limited
Officers: Matthew David Malcolm Gammell [1975] Director; Marcus George Pickering [1974] Director

Pigeon Fisher Gin Co Limited
Incorporated: 15 January 2016
Registered Office: Unit B1, The Devonshire Buildings, Works Road, Chesterfield, Derbys, S43 2PE
Major Shareholder: Adrian Cole
Officers: Adrian Cole [1976] Director/Brewer

Pilgrim Spirit Ltd
Incorporated: 9 October 2017
Registered Office: 3 Percy Street, Alnwick, Northumberland, NE66 1AE
Major Shareholder: Andrew John Petherick
Officers: Andrew John Petherick [1977] Director

Pin Fold Distillery Ltd
Incorporated: 26 February 2019
Registered Office: Old Bell Farm, School Lane, Pilling, Lancs, PR3 6HB
Major Shareholder: Jeremy Ward
Officers: Jeremy Ward [1963] Director/Distiller

The Pink Gin Company Ltd
Incorporated: 9 December 2016
Registered Office: Arisaig Gartocharn, Alexandria, W Dunbartonshire, G83 8ND
Major Shareholder: Sharon Newall
Officers: Sharon Newall [1961] Director

Pipeline Drinks Ltd
Incorporated: 10 July 2018
Registered Office: Kemp House, 160 City Road, London, EC1V 2NX
Officers: John James Mark [1979] Director/Entrepreneur

Pixel Spirits Limited
Incorporated: 14 March 2016 *Employees:* 2
Net Worth Deficit: £17,806 *Total Assets:* £20,714
Registered Office: Loch Leven Hotel, North Ballachulish, Onich, Fort William, Inverness-shire, PH33 6SA
Officers: Craig Innes [1983] Director/Hotelier; Noru Innes [1978] Director/Hotelier [Finnish]

Pocketful of Stones Distillers Limited
Incorporated: 22 February 2016
Net Worth Deficit: £35,558 *Total Assets:* £81,306
Registered Office: Suite D, The Business Centre, Faringdon Avenue, Romford, Essex, RM3 8EN
Shareholders: Shaun Mark Bebington; Paul Motley
Officers: Shaun Mark Bebington [1979] Director [South African]; Paul Charles Motley [1964] Director

Pococello Ltd
Incorporated: 4 July 2014
Net Worth: £38,089 *Total Assets:* £125,443
Registered Office: 4th Floor, 3 Kingly Street, London, W1B 5PD
Shareholders: Thom Luscombe Eliott; James Elliot; James Matthew Chase
Officers: James Matthew Chase [1990] Director; Rupert John Clevely [1957] Director; James Luscome Elliot [1986] Director/Restaurateur; Thom Luscombe Elliot [1983] Director/Restaurateur; Warren Maynard Johnson [1976] Director/PR; Eduardo Piro [1973] Director/Designer [Italian]

Poetic License Distillery Ltd
Incorporated: 12 October 2016
Registered Office: Cottage rear of Roker Hotel, Roker Terrace, Sunderland, Tyne & Wear, SR6 9ND
Major Shareholder: Mark Hird
Officers: Steven Andrew Akers [1981] Director/Certified Chartered Accountant; Nicola Jane Foster Hird [1972] Director; Jonathan Graham [1974] Operations Director; Mark Hird [1973] Director; Luke Smith [1993] Director/Distiller

Polaris Spirits Limited
Incorporated: 10 July 2018
Registered Office: Suite 146, 5 High Street, Maidenhead, Berks, SL6 1JN
Major Shareholder: Donald John Stewart
Officers: Donald John Stewart [1963] Director

Polestar Spirits Limited
Incorporated: 10 July 2018
Registered Office: Suite 146, 5 High Street, Maidenhead, Berks, SL6 1JN
Major Shareholder: Donald John Stewart
Officers: Donald John Stewart [1963] Director

Polo Gin Limited
Incorporated: 18 April 2016
Net Worth: £4,382 *Total Assets:* £20,141
Registered Office: Hill Farm, Wainlodes Lane, Bishops Norton, Gloucester, GL2 9LN
Major Shareholder: Nicholas James Hine
Officers: Rosabella January Hine, Secretary; Nicholas James Hine [1970] Director/Self Employed; Richard James Frederick Valentine Hine [1993] Director; Richenda Gana-Lisa Hine [1970] Director

Port Charlotte Limited
Incorporated: 16 September 1969
Net Worth: £100 *Total Assets:* £100
Registered Office: The Bruichladdich Distillery, Islay, Argyll, PA49 7UN
Parent: Bruichladdich Distillery Company Limited
Officers: Simon Patrick Coughlin, Secretary/Director; Madame Valerie Marie Anne Chapoulaud-Floquet [1962] Director/Chief Executive Officer [French]; Simon Patrick Coughlin [1961] Director; Douglas Adamson Taylor [1976] Director/Chief Executive Officer

Portavadie Distillery Limited
Incorporated: 25 July 2007 *Employees:* 1
Net Worth: £71,709 *Total Assets:* £1,110,483
Registered Office: Craig Lodge, Ostel Bay, Tighnabruaich, Argyll & Bute, PA21 2AH
Major Shareholder: Sarah Stow
Officers: George James Riddell, Secretary; Alexander Bulloch [1927] Director; Sarah Stow [1963] Director

Porthilly Spirit Distillery Limited
Incorporated: 15 January 2019
Registered Office: Acre House, 11-15 William Road, London, NW1 3ER
Parent: West Eleven Limited
Officers: William John Herrmann [1978] Director

The Portsmouth Distillery Company Limited
Incorporated: 4 July 2018
Registered Office: Coastguard Casemate, Fort Cumberland, Fort Cumberland Road, Southsea, Hants, PO4 9LD
Parent: The Rum Club Ltd
Officers: Giles Thomas Collighan [1968] Director/Consultant; Vincent Robert Amos Noyce [1968] Director/Distiller

The Portsmouth Gin Company Limited
Incorporated: 11 April 2018
Registered Office: 77 North Wallington, Fareham, Hants, PO16 8TJ
Major Shareholder: Jake Jefferson Ryan Naylor
Officers: Jake Jefferson Ryan Naylor [1989] Director

Potion Universe Ltd
Incorporated: 23 December 2016
Registered Office: Ground Floor, 2 Woodberry Grove, London, N12 0DR
Shareholders: Tom Ivan Omara-Okello; Michael Hunnygen-Henry
Officers: Michael Hunnygen-Henry [1989] Director/Revenues Officer; Tom Ivan Omara-Okello [1987] Director/Warehouse Operative

Precision Spirits Ltd
Incorporated: 15 January 2019
Registered Office: 126 Greenbank Road, Edinburgh, EH10 5RN
Shareholders: Guy Thomas Wardrop; Luke William Cochrane
Officers: Luke William Cochrane [1996] Director/Student; Guy Thomas Wardrop [1996] Director/Student

Premier Bonding Company Limited
Incorporated: 1 February 2013
Registered Office: 16 Park Circus, Glasgow, G3 6AX
Parent: Hunter Laing & Company Limited
Officers: Stewart Hunter Laing [1946] Director/Manager

Prentice Spirits Ltd
Incorporated: 24 September 2018
Registered Office: 28 Crabtree Leys, Offenham, Evesham, Worcs, WR11 8SE
Major Shareholder: Neil Prentice
Officers: Neil Prentice [1978] Director/Manager

Princetown Distillers Ltd
Incorporated: 13 March 2015 *Employees:* 1
Net Worth: £706,072 *Total Assets:* £758,686
Registered Office: Old Magistrates Court, East Street, Ilminster, Somerset, TA19 0AJ
Major Shareholder: Rowan Maule
Officers: Richard Donald Jameson [1956] Director; Robert Alexander Leask [1965] Director/Chemical Engineer; Rowan Maule [1957] Director/Engineer

Privacy Domains Limited
Incorporated: 26 May 2015
Registered Office: Clyde Offices, 48 West George Street, Glasgow, G2 1BP
Officers: Blake Nordstrom, Secretary; Blake Nordstrom [1960] Director [Swedish]

Pronto Cocktails Limited
Incorporated: 6 March 2017
Registered Office: Unit K2, Rose Industrial Estate, Marlow Bottom, Marlow, Bucks, SL7 3ND
Officers: Professor Kevin Morley [1950] Director; Dominic Roche [1986] Director; Anthony Spackman [1985] Director

Pryzm Cocktails Limited
Incorporated: 23 April 2018
Registered Office: 10 Mynors Crescent, Wythall, Bromsgrove, Worcs, B47 5JG
Major Shareholder: Tye Smith
Officers: Tye Smith, Secretary; Tye Smith [1996] Director

Psychopomp Ltd
Incorporated: 4 April 2014
Net Worth: £134,853 *Total Assets:* £187,351
Registered Office: 44 St Andrews Road, Montpelier, Bristol, BS6 5EH
Shareholders: Daniel Lee Walker; Liam Scott Hirt
Officers: Dr Liam Scott Hirt [1978] Director; Daniel Lee Walker [1982] Director

Puddlebrook Distillery Limited
Incorporated: 19 December 2017
Registered Office: Serenity House, Springfields, Drybrook, Glos, GL17 9BW
Major Shareholder: Sharon Louise Elliott
Officers: Sharon Louise Elliott [1965] Director

The Pulteney Distillery Company Limited
Incorporated: 6 March 1995
Registered Office: Moffat Distillery, Airdrie, N Lanarks, ML6 8PL
Shareholders: Charoen Sirivadhanabhakdi; Khunying Wanna Sirivadhanabhakdi
Officers: Man Kong Lee [1968] Director/Accountant [Chinese]; Dr Martin John Leonard [1961] Managing Director; Prapakon Thongtheppairot [1971] Director [Thai]

Purdy Distillers Limited
Incorporated: 25 July 2018
Registered Office: 16 Avoca Lawn, Warrenpoint, Newry, Co Armagh, BT34 3RJ
Shareholders: Aileen Lorraine Purdy; Kevin Matthew Purdy
Officers: Aileen Lorraine Purdy [1992] Managing Director; Andrew Neil Purdy [1994] Creative Director; John Raymond Purdy [1991] Director; Kevin Matthew Purdy [1997] Director

Pure Cornish Limited
Incorporated: 10 October 2016
Registered Office: 11 Westbridge Road, Trewoon, St Austell, Cornwall, PL25 5TE
Major Shareholder: Stephen William Jarman
Officers: Stephen William Jarman, Secretary; Stephen William Jarman [1953] Director

Pure Distilled Spirit Company Limited
Incorporated: 27 February 2017
Net Worth: £518 *Total Assets:* £20,225
Registered Office: 5 Bankside, Hanborough Business Park, Long Hanborough, Oxon, OX29 8LJ
Shareholders: Edward William Betts; Michael Ian Norman Palij
Officers: Edward William Betts [1966] Director/Chemist; Michael Ian Norman Palij [1966] Director/Master of Wine

Pure Spirit in Wales Limited
Incorporated: 7 September 2017
Registered Office: Llanover House, Llanover Road, Pontypridd, Rhondda Cynon Taf, CF37 4DY
Shareholders: Lee Charles Burton; Christian Sion Phillips
Officers: Lee Charles Burton [1971] Director; Christian Sion Phillips [1971] Director

Pure Sussex Distillery Ltd
Incorporated: 18 July 2017
Registered Office: 79 Sutton Road, Seaford, E Sussex, BN25 4QH
Shareholder: Heidi Cowley
Officers: Heidi Louise Cowley, Secretary; Adam David George Cowley [1970] Director; Heidi Louise Cowley [1973] Director/Accountant

Pure Wild Spirits Ltd
Incorporated: 27 November 2015 *Employees:* 2
Net Worth: £224,195 *Total Assets:* £276,864
Registered Office: c/o Alexander & Co, 17 St Anns Square, Manchester, M2 7PW
Major Shareholder: David Jonathan Wallwork
Officers: Christopher Mark Penny [1968] Director; David Jonathan Wallwork [1968] Director

Q & S Distilling Co Ltd
Incorporated: 12 December 2017
Registered Office: Orchard Lodge, Orchard Hill, Bideford, Devon, EX39 2QY
Shareholders: Simon Roy Lacey; Quinton Davies
Officers: Quinton Davies [1972] Director/Consultant; Simon Roy Lacey [1968] Director

Queen Cleo Rum Ltd
Incorporated: 7 December 2017
Registered Office: 7 Plover Close, Stratford upon Avon, Warwicks, CV37 9EN
Shareholders: Emma Kara Bishop; Nicola Jane Tavener
Officers: Emma Kara Bishop [1987] Director; Nicola Jane Tavener [1987] Director

R & B Distillers Limited
Incorporated: 29 July 2014 *Employees:* 6
Net Worth Deficit: £70,187 *Total Assets:* £8,173,131
Registered Office: 23 Manor Place, Edinburgh, EH3 7DX
Parent: Salvators Investments Limited
Officers: Alasdair MacDonald Day [1965] Director; William Dobbie [1959] Director

R & R Distillery Ireland Ltd
Incorporated: 1 October 2018
Registered Office: 33 Church Road, Holywood, Co Down, BT18 9BU
Major Shareholder: Robin Herron
Officers: Robin Herron [1967] Director

R & T Stills Limited
Incorporated: 15 August 2018
Registered Office: Diablo's on the Quay, Coracle Way, Carmarthen, SA31 3JP
Shareholders: Paul Richard Magness; Alexander Michael Luck
Officers: Alexander Michael Luck [1981] Director; Paul Richard Magness [1975] Director

R2 Distillers Ltd
Incorporated: 3 May 2012
Previous: Sustainable Structures Ltd
Net Worth Deficit: £32,743 *Total Assets:* £60,152
Registered Office: Whitby Court, Abbey Road, Shepley, Huddersfield, W Yorks, HD8 8EL
Shareholders: Raymond Paul Woolhead; Rachel Margaret Woolhead
Officers: Rachel Margaret Woolhead, Secretary; Rachel Margaret Woolhead [1971] Director; Raymond Paul Woolhead [1966] Director

Rabakkan Ltd
Incorporated: 20 August 2018
Registered Office: 14 Bianca Street, Bootle, Merseyside, L20 7DT
Major Shareholder: Julie Anne Sumner
Officers: Julie Anne Sumner [1987] Director/Consultant

Rademon Estate Distillery Limited
Incorporated: 18 April 2012 *Employees:* 9
Net Worth: £166,081 *Total Assets:* £2,342,651
Registered Office: The Distillery, Rademon Estate, Ballynahinch Road, Crossgar, Downpatrick, Co Down, BT30 9HS
Shareholder: Fiona Boyd-Armstrong
Officers: David Boyd-Armstrong [1980] Director; Fiona Boyd-Armstrong [1981] Director

Raer Scotch Whisky Ltd
Incorporated: 5 April 2012
Previous: Philipshill Retirement Village Ltd
Net Worth Deficit: £241,696 *Total Assets:* £1,141,138
Registered Office: Cognitor Accountancy Limited, Forbes House, Harris Business Park, Hanbury Road, Stoke Prior, Bromsgrove, Worcs, B60 4BD
Major Shareholder: James Kean
Officers: Jacob Kean [1996] Director; James Harkins Kean [1960] Director

Rainbow Chaser Limited
Incorporated: 13 March 2007
Net Worth: £39,152 *Total Assets:* £55,869
Registered Office: Compay Ltd, Marlows, Station Road, Northiam, Rye, E Sussex, TN31 6QA
Major Shareholder: Juian Haswell
Officers: Julian Guy Haswell [1958] Director of Sales

Ramsbottom Gin Company Limited
Incorporated: 18 July 2017
Registered Office: 11 Harrison Street, Ramsbottom, Bury, Lancs, BL0 0AH
Officers: Elizabeth Kate Hayhoe [1991] Director; Alexander Ciaran Quayle [1991] Director

The Ramsbury Brewing and Distilling Company Limited
Incorporated: 4 March 2013 *Employees:* 7
Net Worth Deficit: £1,902,932 *Total Assets:* £3,085,206
Registered Office: The Estate Office, Priory Farm, Axford, Marlborough, Wilts, SN8 2HA
Major Shareholder: Carl Stefan Erling Persson
Officers: Alistair Edward Stuart Ewing, Secretary; Carl Stefan Erling Persson [1947] Director [Swedish]

Rare Bird Distillery Limited
Incorporated: 15 February 2016
Net Worth Deficit: £29,711 *Total Assets:* £53,406
Registered Office: Elmwood House, York Road, Kirk Hammerton, York, YO26 8DH
Major Shareholder: Matthew James Robertson Stewart
Officers: Matthew James Robertson Stewart [1968] Director/Distiller

Rathlee Distilling Company Ltd.
Incorporated: 29 October 2001
Net Worth Deficit: £29,616 *Total Assets:* £15,337
Registered Office: 23 Cott Road, Lostwithiel, Cornwall, PL22 0EU
Shareholders: Stuart Graham Leather; Paola Leather
Officers: Paola Andrea Leather, Secretary; Paola Andrea Leather [1975] Company Secretary/Director; Stuart Graham Leather [1977] Director

Raven Spirits Limited
Incorporated: 15 November 2017
Registered Office: 2 Old Skene Road, Kingswells, Aberdeen, AB15 8QA
Shareholders: Callum Downie Sim; Alison Jane Sim
Officers: Alison Jane Sim [1967] Director/Lawyer; Callum Downie Sim [1962] Director/Lawyer; Peter Robert Sim [1964] Director

The Raw Distiller Ltd
Incorporated: 21 August 2017
Registered Office: 4 Fintry Gardens, Bearsden, Glasgow, G61 4RJ
Major Shareholder: Andrew Gold Neilson
Officers: Andrew Gold Neilson [1964] Director/Process Consultant

Raw Distilling Ltd
Incorporated: 28 March 2017
Registered Office: 46 Kiln Garth, Rothley, Leicester, LE7 7LZ
Shareholders: David Hemstock; Michelle Tuddenham
Officers: David John Andrew Hemstock [1977] Director; Michelle Tuddenham [1978] Director

The Really Brilliant Company Limited
Incorporated: 1 April 2014
Net Worth Deficit: £13,321 *Total Assets:* £46,406
Registered Office: Summersday, Spinney Lane, Itchenor, Chichester, W Sussex, PO20 7DJ
Shareholders: Graham Woolston; Gail Lesley Gina Woolston
Officers: Gail Lesley Gina Woolston [1956] Director/Property Developer; Graham Woolston [1953] Director/Business Consultant

Rebel Distillers Ltd
Incorporated: 8 May 2015 *Employees:* 1
Net Worth: £1,992 *Total Assets:* £16,610
Registered Office: 1 Parkshot, Richmond, Surrey, TW9 2RD
Major Shareholder: Matthew McGivern
Officers: Matthew McGivern, Secretary; Matthew McGivern [1983] Director [Irish]

Rebel Rabbet Ltd
Incorporated: 27 May 2015
Net Worth Deficit: £15,861   *Total Assets:* £1,198
Registered Office: 1 Parkshot, Richmond, Surrey, TW9 2RD
Shareholders: Dylan Michael Bell; Matthew McGivern
Officers: Matthew McGivern, Secretary; Matthew McGivern [1983] Director [Irish]; Dylan Michael Bell [1988] Director/Musician

Red Distillery Limited
Incorporated: 17 January 2019
Registered Office: Furnace Place Farm Yard, Killinghurst Lane, Haslemere, Surrey, GU27 2EH
Major Shareholder: Neil Desmond Patterson
Officers: Neil Desmond Patterson [1980] Managing Director

Red Door Gin Company Ltd
Incorporated: 6 April 2018
Registered Office: George House, Boroughbriggs Road, Elgin, Moray, IV30 1JY
Parent: Speymalt Whisky Distributors Limited
Officers: Norman Ross, Secretary; Ewen Cameron Mackintosh [1968] Director

Red Squirrel Brands Ltd
Incorporated: 2 April 2014
Net Worth Deficit: £58,708   *Total Assets:* £4,294
Registered Office: 12 The Inches, Dalgety Bay, Dunfermline, Fife, KY11 9YG
Major Shareholder: Robert Bruce Borthwick
Officers: Robert Bruce Borthwick [1950] Director/Brand Seeding Consultant

Redcastle Spirits Limited
Incorporated: 20 March 2018
Registered Office: Drummygar Mains, Carmyllie, Arbroath, Angus, DD11 2RA
Shareholders: John Alexander Anderson; Fiona Margaret Walsh
Officers: John Alexander Anderson [1959] Director/Farmer; Fiona Margaret Walsh [1977] Director

Redrosesforme Limited
Incorporated: 26 January 2016
Net Worth Deficit: £4,791   *Total Assets:* £4,973
Registered Office: The Sovereign Distillery, Wilson Road, Huyton Business Park, Knowsley, Merseyside, L36 6AD
Parent: Halewood International Limited
Officers: Mark Benjamin Addis [1980] Director; Stewart Andrew Hainsworth [1969] Director/Chief Executive Officer; Alan William Robinson [1965] Finance Director

Renaissance Drinks Ltd
Incorporated: 24 September 2014   *Employees:* 2
Net Worth Deficit: £50,682   *Total Assets:* £1,190
Registered Office: Flat 21, Wyatt House, Frampton Street, London, NW8 8ND
Major Shareholder: Andy Stanforth
Officers: Vadim Alexis Jean [1963] Director; Andy Stanforth [1971] Director

Renaissance Vodka Limited
Incorporated: 8 November 2017
Registered Office: c/o Stewart Gilmour & Co, 3rd Floor, St George's Buildings, 5 St Vincent Place, Glasgow, G1 2DH
Parent: Renaissance Drinks Limited
Officers: Andrew Colin Scott Stanforth, Secretary; Vadim Alexis Jean [1963] Director; Andrew Colin Scott Stanforth [1971] Director

Renegade Spirits Grenada Limited
Incorporated: 5 February 2016   *Employees:* 33
Net Worth: £1,155,632   *Total Assets:* £1,347,563
Registered Office: 2 Babmaes Street, London, SW1Y 6HD
Officers: John Peter Anthony Adams [1958] Director/Chartered Accountant; David Gammie [1985] Director; Jean-Marie Laborde [1948] Director [French]; Graham Robert Starling Lark [1959] Director; Sir John Auld MacTaggart [1951] Managing Director; Mark Bartholomew Reynier [1961] Director; James Anthony Skehan [1951] Director [Irish]

Revelry Brewing & Distilling Ltd
Incorporated: 4 September 2018
Registered Office: Coldred Place, Church Road, Coldred, Dover, Kent, CT15 5AQ
Officers: Christian Maurice Peck [1973] Director/General Manager; Melanie Helen Peck [1981] Director/Receptionist; Benjamin Toms [1975] Director/Photographer; Cassandra Jane Toms [1977] Director/Human Resources

Revelry Spirits Ltd
Incorporated: 6 November 2018
Registered Office: 5 Danby Wynd, Yarm, Cleveland, TS15 9SF
Shareholders: Liam John Price; Katrina Wendy Rosser
Officers: Liam John Price [1973] Director

Revolution Rum Ltd
Incorporated: 11 August 2017
Registered Office: 46 High Street, Esher, Surrey, KT10 9QY
Major Shareholder: Elizabeth Casely
Officers: Elizabeth Casely, Secretary; Elizabeth Casely [1975] Director

Rhucello Limited
Incorporated: 27 October 2015
Net Worth: £13,369   *Total Assets:* £42,096
Registered Office: 69 Cumbrian Way, Wakefield, W Yorks, WF2 8JS
Major Shareholder: David James Burnley
Officers: David James Burnley [1978] Director/Accountant

Rhum Liquor Limited
Incorporated: 15 August 2017
Registered Office: 8 Acer Crescent, Paisley, Renfrewshire, PA2 9LR
Officers: Keith Hamilton Campbell, Secretary; Keith Hamilton Campbell [1979] Director/Account Manager

The Ribble Valley Gin Company Ltd.
Incorporated: 2 February 2018
Registered Office: 19 Little Lane, Longridge, Preston, Lancs, PR3 3NS
Shareholders: Justine Danielle Harrison; Lucas Moyes
Officers: Justine Danielle Harrison [1987] Sales Director; Lucas Moyes [1986] Manufacturing Director

Maurice Richard Ltd
Incorporated: 5 November 2018
Registered Office: First Floor, 85 Great Portland Street, London, W1W 7LT
Shareholders: Alain Maurice Illi; Moreno Gasser; Sandro Richard Gianini
Officers: Moreno Gasser [1987] Director [Swiss]; Sandro Richard Gianini [1987] Director [Swiss]; Alain Maurice Illi [1986] Director [Swiss]

Richie & Nikki Ltd
Incorporated: 26 October 2016
Net Worth Deficit: £11,440 *Total Assets:* £11,048
Registered Office: 102 Great Western Street, Moss Side, Manchester, M14 4RA
Shareholders: Harold Richard McKenzie; Nickeysha Alecia McKenzie
Officers: Harold Richard McKenzie [1974] Director/Barber; Nickeysha Alecia McKenzie [1978] Director/Beautician

William Riddell & Sons Limited
Incorporated: 16 January 2007
Net Worth Deficit: £292,991 *Total Assets:* £1,132,326
Registered Office: 10 Lynedoch Crescent, Glasgow, G3 6EQ
Major Shareholder: Guido Marini
Officers: Rudolf Jozef Koopmans [1956] Director [Belgian]

Riktig Limited
Incorporated: 20 February 2019
Registered Office: 26 Shrewsbury Avenue, London, SW14 8JZ
Major Shareholder: Sebastian Nikolaus Margolis
Officers: Sebastian Nikolaus Margolis [1991] Director/Project Manager [Swedish]

The River Test Distillery Limited
Incorporated: 18 December 2017
Registered Office: Riverbarn Cottage, Longparish, Andover, Hants, SP11 6PJ
Officers: Sarah Kate Nelson, Secretary; Jonathan Bernard Nelson [1968] Director/Distiller; Sarah Kate Nelson [1970] Director/Company Secretary

Riverside Spirits Ltd
Incorporated: 1 November 2011 *Employees:* 4
Previous: Christine's Preserves Ltd
Net Worth: £34,762 *Total Assets:* £127,183
Registered Office: 12 Greys Court, Kingsland Grange, Warrington, Cheshire, WA1 4SH
Shareholders: Hugh Munro; Charlotte Smith
Officers: Hugh Munro [1969] Director/Food Manufacturing; Charlotte Smith [1988] Director/Food Manufacturing

Rivington Distillery Ltd
Incorporated: 4 January 2018
Registered Office: 5 New Road, Anderton, Chorley, Lancs, PR6 9EY
Major Shareholder: Henry Linn
Officers: Henry Linn [1994] Director

Rock Hill Cider Company Limited
Incorporated: 4 July 2018
Registered Office: 53 Amwell Street, London, EC1R 1UR
Shareholders: Charlotte Louise Clifton Robinson; Dickon Hugh Wheelwright Robinson
Officers: Charlotte Louise Clifton Robinson [1947] Director/Bookseller/Cider Maker; Dickon Hugh Wheelwright Robinson [1945] Director/Regeneration Consultant/Cider Maker

Rockwood & Hines Limited
Incorporated: 20 December 2006
Net Worth Deficit: £16,324 *Total Assets:* £116,539
Registered Office: Martlet House, E1 Yeoman Gate, Yeoman Way, Worthing, W Sussex, BN13 3QZ
Major Shareholder: Henri Jean Rene Berthe
Officers: Stuart Ralph Poppleton [1940] Director/Business Consultant

Ron de Mestizo Ltd
Incorporated: 1 April 2016
Net Worth Deficit: £1,006 *Total Assets:* £80,000
Registered Office: Mercury House, Shipstones Business Center, North Gate, Nottingham, NG7 7FN
Officers: Peter Robson, Secretary; Peter Robson [1959] Director

Rosebank Distillery Camelon Limited
Incorporated: 27 November 2012
Registered Office: Atrium House, Callendar Business Park, Callendar Road, Falkirk, Stirlingshire, FK1 1XR
Major Shareholder: George Danskin Stewart
Officers: George Danskin Stewart [1945] Director/Engineer

Rosebank Whisky Limited
Incorporated: 27 November 2007
Registered Office: Atrium House, Callendar Business Park, Falkirk, FK1 1XR
Shareholder: Alan Campbell Stewart
Officers: Fiona Anne Campbell Stewart, Secretary/Land Director; Alan Campbell Stewart [1970] Director/Electrician; Fiona Anne Campbell Stewart [1973] Planning Director

Rosemullion Distillery Ltd
Incorporated: 31 August 2017
Registered Office: 25 Lemon Street, Truro, Cornwall, TR1 2LS
Officers: Andrew James Bradbury [1965] Director/Scientist; Elizabeth Bradbury [1974] Director/Technologist

Round Wood Distillery Ltd
Incorporated: 22 September 2016 *Employees:* 2
Net Worth Deficit: £32,521 *Total Assets:* £79,588
Registered Office: The Elephant House, Little Raveley, Huntingdon, Cambs, PE28 2NF
Major Shareholder: Emily Robertson
Officers: Emily Robertson [1991] Director/Software Developer; Patrick Rupert Waters [1991] Director/Assistant Estate Manager

Row & Company Limited
Incorporated: 13 February 1934
Net Worth: £14,988,040 *Total Assets:* £16,136,183
Registered Office: 100 Queen Street, Glasgow, G1 3DN
Shareholder: Edrington Distillers Limited
Officers: Gemma May Robson, Secretary; Yves Audo [1962] Director [French]; Jeremy McDowell Chaplin [1971] Finance Director; Massimo Antonio Fabris [1970] Commercial Director [Italian]; Frederic Gourgeon [1970] Director [French]

Royal Wootton Bassett Gin Company Ltd
Incorporated: 17 January 2017
Net Worth Deficit: £76 *Total Assets:* £23,556
Registered Office: 27 Vale View, Royal Wootton Bassett, Wilts, SN4 7BY
Major Shareholder: Andrew Malcolm Ferguson Carr
Officers: Andrew Malcolm Ferguson Carr [1965] Sales Director

Royton Gin Ltd
Incorporated: 22 August 2018
Registered Office: Flat 7, Denbydale Way, Royton, Oldham, Lancs, OL2 5TJ
Major Shareholder: Timothy Bowker
Officers: Timothy Bowker [1954] Director/Retired

RSM Solutions (NE) Limited
Incorporated: 29 September 2008 *Employees:* 20
Net Worth: £208,877 *Total Assets:* £1,128,360
Registered Office: 11 Sowerby Way, Durham Lane Industrial Park, Eaglescliffe, Stockton on Tees, Cleveland, TS16 0RB
Major Shareholder: Richard James Marsden
Officers: Richard James Marsden [1974] Director

The Rum Club Ltd
Incorporated: 1 September 2015
Net Worth Deficit: £17,948 *Total Assets:* £8,515
Registered Office: 25 Malvern Road, Southsea, Hants, PO5 2LZ
Shareholders: Giles Thomas Collighan; Vincent Robert Amos Noyce
Officers: Giles Thomas Collighan [1968] Director/Management Consultant; Vincent Robert Amos Noyce [1968] Director/Port Operations Manager; Richard Alexander Oatley [1974] Director/Sales and Marketing

Rum To You Ltd
Incorporated: 15 November 2018
Registered Office: 23 Coney Lane, Keighley, W Yorks, BD21 5JE
Shareholders: John Patrick Mitchell; Helen Willoughby; Luke Willoughby
Officers: Helen Willoughby [1984] Director/Company Secretary

Rumbustian Limited
Incorporated: 9 November 2017
Registered Office: 7 West Street, Hastings, E Sussex, TN34 3AN
Shareholder: Jamie Francis Keenan
Officers: Jamie Francis Keenan [1976] Director; Susan Karen Keenan [1973] Director

Ruskin Spirit Co Ltd
Incorporated: 11 February 2019
Registered Office: Gilmarver Flat, Wordsworth Street, Hawkshead, Cumbria, LA22 0PA
Major Shareholder: Mark Warburton
Officers: Mark Warburton, Secretary; Mark Warburton [1964] Director

Peter J Russell & Company Ltd.
Incorporated: 16 July 2003
Registered Office: Russell House, Dunnet Way, Broxburn, W Lothian, EH52 5BU
Parent: Ian MacLeod Distillers Limited
Officers: Michael James Younger, Secretary; Leonard Stuart Russell [1961] Marketing Director; Lucinda Russell [1966] Director/Race Horse Trainer

Russell Distillers Limited
Incorporated: 29 April 2013 *Employees:* 11
Net Worth Deficit: £449,963 *Total Assets:* £872,949
Registered Office: 50 Melville Street, Edinburgh, EH3 7HF
Shareholders: Stephen Russell; Robert Matthew Russell
Officers: Robert Geoffrey Russell, Secretary; Robert Matthew Russell [1973] Director; Robert Geoffrey Russell [1946] Director; Stephen Geoffrey Russell [1977] Director

Russian Doll Vodka Limited
Incorporated: 12 November 2018
Registered Office: Flat 1, Carlow House, Miller Street, London, NW1 7DN
Major Shareholder: Jordan Ashley Bookman
Officers: Jordan Ashley Bookman [1979] Director

The Rutland Distillery Company Ltd
Incorporated: 8 March 2018
Registered Office: 27 Cedar Street, Braunston in Rutland, Oakham, Rutland, LE15 8QS
Shareholders: Simon Phillips; Joanne Eryl Palmer-Phillips
Officers: Dr Joanne Eryl Palmer-Phillips [1973] Director/Chief Operating Officer; Simon Phillips [1969] Director/Chairman

RWB Drinks Ltd
Incorporated: 28 March 2018
Registered Office: 185 Nursery Road, London, E9 6PB
Major Shareholder: Ross William Butler
Officers: Ross William Butler [1988] Director/Founder

Ryhall Distillery Limited
Incorporated: 22 August 2017
Registered Office: The Lawns, First Drift, Wothorpe, Stamford, Lincs, PE9 3JL
Major Shareholder: Nigel Palfreeman
Officers: Nigel Palfreeman [1962] Managing Director

Sacred Spirits Holdings Ltd
Incorporated: 14 September 2017
Registered Office: 5 Talbot Road, London, N6 4QS
Shareholders: Hilary Susan Jones; Ian Nicholas Hart
Officers: Ian Hart, Secretary; Ian Nicholas Hart [1965] Director; Hilary Susan Jones [1962] Director

Saddleworth Distillery Ltd
Incorporated: 21 January 2016
Previous: RDNS Corporate Consulting Ltd
Net Worth Deficit: £600 *Total Assets:* £240
Registered Office: Hole House Farm, Huddersfield Road, Mossley, Ashton under Lyne, Lancs, OL5 9BT
Shareholders: Alexander David Strachan Smalley; Robert David Neil Smalley
Officers: Robert David Neil Smalley, Secretary; Alexander David Strachan Smalley [1991] Director; Robert David Neil Smalley [1956] Director/Retired

The Saffron Gin Company Limited
Incorporated: 6 August 2014
Registered Office: 9-10 The Crescent, Wisbech, Cambs, PE13 1EH
Major Shareholder: Steven John Charles Foster
Officers: Steven John Charles Foster [1974] Director

The Saffron Spirit Company Limited
Incorporated: 6 August 2014
Registered Office: 9-10 The Crescent, Wisbech, Cambs, PE13 1EH
Major Shareholder: Steven John Charles Foster
Officers: Steven John Charles Foster [1974] Director

Saffron Spirits Limited
Incorporated: 7 August 2014
Registered Office: 9-10 The Crescent, Wisbech, Cambs, PE13 1EH
Major Shareholder: Steven John Charles Foster
Officers: Steven John Charles Foster [1974] Director

Sailor Jerry Limited
Incorporated: 16 April 2002
Registered Office: Independence House, 84 Lower Mortlake Road, Richmond, Surrey, TW9 2HS
Parent: William Grant & Sons Management Limited
Officers: Gregory Justin Bargeton [1973] Director/Lawyer; Ewan John Henderson [1968] Director/Accountant

Saint Patricks Ltd
Incorporated: 15 February 2018
Registered Office: 20-22 Wenlock Road, London, N1 7GU
Major Shareholder: Patrick Hayden
Officers: Patrick Hayden [1987] Director/Founder

Salcombe Cider Company Ltd
Incorporated: 5 December 2016
Registered Office: Holwell Farm, South Huish, Kingsbridge, Devon, TQ7 3EQ
Major Shareholder: Duncan Walker Burnett
Officers: Duncan Walker Burnett [1986] Director/Cider Maker

Salcombe Distilling Company Ltd
Incorporated: 21 July 2014 *Employees:* 18
Net Worth: £681,248 *Total Assets:* £816,737
Registered Office: The Boathouse, 28 Island Street, Salcombe, Devon, TQ8 8DP
Shareholders: Howard Lawrence Davies; Charles Angus Hamilton Lugsdin
Officers: Charlotte Ellen Davies [1977] Finance Director; Howard Lawrence Davies [1977] Director; Charles Angus Hamilton Lugsdin [1976] Director; Nick Simon Marshall [1976] Director

Salcombe Moonshine Ltd
Incorporated: 17 February 2017
Registered Office: c/o Haysom Silverton, Chancery House, 199 Silbury Boulevard, Milton Keynes, Bucks, MK9 1JL
Shareholders: Grant Patey; Peter Stephen Rogers
Officers: Grant Patey [1965] Director; Peter Stephen Rogers [1967] Director

Sangobeg Ltd
Incorporated: 9 March 2006
Net Worth Deficit: £2,520 *Total Assets:* £80,739
Registered Office: Torridon House, 56 Torridon Road, Broughty Ferry, Dundee, DD5 3HB
Shareholder: David Donald Corbett Morrison
Officers: Shonagh Elizabeth Morrison, Secretary; John Gibson [1954] Director/Property Developer; David Donald Corbett Morrison [1944] Director; James Ross Morrison [1966] Director/Property Developer

Sartorial Spirits Limited
Incorporated: 21 September 2015
Net Worth Deficit: £36,962 *Total Assets:* £18,538
Registered Office: The Lilacs, Meadow Farm Lane, Horsham St Faith, Norwich, NR10 3BY
Major Shareholder: Matthew Andrew Seaton Clifford
Officers: Matthew Andrew Seaton Clifford [1972] Director

SB Gin Limited
Incorporated: 24 July 2018
Registered Office: 114 Busby Road, Glasgow, G76 8BG
Major Shareholder: Jaswant Bhart
Officers: Jaswant Bhart [1977] Director/Retailer

Otten Schmidt Ltd.
Incorporated: 22 January 2018
Registered Office: 3 Grange Yard, London, SE1 3AE
Shareholder: Henry James Woodward Parr
Officers: Samuel Henry Bompas [1983] Director; Henry James Woodward Parr [1982] Director

Scotch Malt Distillers Ltd
Incorporated: 21 January 2019
Registered Office: Burnbank, Stirling Street, Blackford, Auchterarder, Perth & Kinross, PH4 1QA
Shareholders: Debra Word; Anthony Reeman-Clark; Zak Shenfield
Officers: Anthony Reeman-Clark, Secretary; Anthony Reeman-Clark [1955] Director; Zak Shenfield [1993] Director/Distiller

The Scotch Malt Whisky Society Limited
Incorporated: 6 May 1983 *Employees:* 72
Net Worth: £783,000 *Total Assets:* £19,495,000
Registered Office: The Vaults, 87 Giles Street, Leith, Edinburgh, EH6 6BZ
Parent: The Artisanal Spirits Company Limited
Officers: William Alexander Bremner, Secretary; Neil Peter James Aitken [1971] Commercial Director; William Alexander Bremner [1973] Finance Director; Jan Willem Damen [1971] Operations Director UK [Dutch]; Kai Ivalo [1965] Director; David John Ridley [1969] Director [Australian]; Paul Henry Skipworth [1968] Non-Executive Director Chairman

Scots' Cheer Limited
Incorporated: 16 July 1998
Net Worth: £5,558 *Total Assets:* £76,971
Registered Office: The Carthouse, Crauchie, East Linton, E Lothian, EH40 3EB
Shareholder: Robin James Ford
Officers: Robin James Ford, Secretary/Director; Derry Gaye Campbell [1954] Director; Robin James Ford [1954] Director

Scottish Independent Distillers Company Limited
Incorporated: 16 January 1928
Registered Office: Russell House, Dunnet Way, East Mains Industrial Estate, Broxburn, W Lothian, EH52 5BU
Parent: Ian MacLeod Distillers Ltd
Officers: Michael James Younger, Secretary; Edith Stuart Russell [1932] Director; Leonard Stuart Russell [1961] Director

Scouse Girls Gin Ltd
Incorporated: 9 January 2018
Registered Office: 173 College Road, Liverpool, L23 3AT
Shareholder: Keith Joseph Gledhill
Officers: Keith Joseph Gledhill [1948] Director; Maureen Francise Gledhill [1954] Director

Scout and Sage Spirits Limited
Incorporated: 22 January 2016
Net Worth Deficit: £2,219 *Total Assets:* £3,513
Registered Office: Fairfields, Semington, Trowbridge, Wilts, BA14 6JD
Major Shareholder: Holly Elizabeth Winifred Bower
Officers: Holly Elizabeth Winifred Bower [1975] Director

Scream Retail Limited
Incorporated: 1 December 1995 *Employees:* 4
Net Worth: £18,677 *Total Assets:* £226,147
Registered Office: Sylvan House, Castle Walk, Wadhurst, E Sussex, TN5 6DB
Shareholders: Brian Michael Wates; Jon Lilly
Officers: Deborah Jane Wates, Secretary; Jon Lilly [1965] Director/Salesman; Brian Michael Wates [1968] Director/Representative

The UK Spirits Industry

Seada Distillery Limited
Incorporated: 19 November 2018
Registered Office: 8 Oakfield Road, Shifnal, Salop, TF11 8HT
Shareholders: Paul Fraser Clayton; Alexander Henry Perry
Officers: Paul Fraser Clayton [1989] Managing Director; Alexander Henry Perry [1987] Director/Chief Executive

Seadwealths Ltd
Incorporated: 20 August 2018
Registered Office: 109 Calgarth Road, Huyton, Knowsley, Merseyside, L36 3UE
Major Shareholder: Rebecca Pollock
Officers: Rebecca Pollock [2000] Director/Sales Assistant

Seaway Royale Limited
Incorporated: 22 May 2018
Registered Office: 37 Shiphay Lane, Torquay, Devon, TQ2 7DU
Major Shareholder: Julian Patrick Niles
Officers: Julian Patrick Niles [1962] Director

Second Son Distillery Limited
Incorporated: 11 October 2016
Net Worth: £2,626 *Total Assets:* £2,626
Registered Office: The Tigers Head, Pytchleys Hollow, Norley, Frodsham, Cheshire, WA6 8NT
Officers: John Robert Whitlow [1988] Director/Business Owner; Anna May IV Williams [1997] Director/Photographer

Seduction Rum Punch UK Ltd
Incorporated: 31 July 2015
Net Worth: £1 *Total Assets:* £1
Registered Office: 154 Fore Street, London, N18 2XA
Major Shareholder: Richard Lenford Allen
Officers: Richard Lenford Allen [1964] Director

Sendivogius Limited
Incorporated: 8 June 2018
Registered Office: 9 Christopher Street, London, EC2A 2BS
Major Shareholder: Piotr Jan Jedrzejewski
Officers: Piotr Jan Jedrzejewski [1983] Managing Director [Polish]

Seven Deadly Sins Ltd
Incorporated: 27 October 2015
Net Worth Deficit: £18,266 *Total Assets:* £1
Registered Office: Unit 3F, 2 Cattedown Road, Plymouth, PL4 0EG
Officers: Kelly Marie Giles [1981] Director/Entrepreneur; Spencer Richard James Ulrich Glazsher [1966] Director/Solicitor

Shakespeare Distillery Limited
Incorporated: 26 June 2015 *Employees:* 1
Net Worth: £8,799 *Total Assets:* £71,215
Registered Office: 13 The Courtyard, Timothys Bridge Road, Stratford upon Avon, Warwicks, CV37 9NP
Major Shareholder: Simon Picken
Officers: Peter David Monks [1971] Director; Simon Picken [1981] Director

Shannon & Thomas Limited
Incorporated: 24 April 2018
Registered Office: The Old Farmhouse, Bollowal Farm, St Just, Penzance, Cornwall, TR19 7NP
Shareholders: Jack Shannon; Archelaus Joseph Harvey Thomas
Officers: Jack Shannon [1986] Director; Archelaus Joseph Harvey Thomas [1985] Director

Shanty Spirit Ltd
Incorporated: 3 May 2017
Registered Office: 34 Station Road, Parkstone, Poole, Dorset, BH14 8UD
Major Shareholder: Hugh Anthony Lambert
Officers: Hugh Anthony Lambert [1971] Director

Shed 1 Distillery Ulverston. Limited
Incorporated: 28 May 2016
Net Worth: £9 *Total Assets:* £25,806
Registered Office: Shed 1, 70 Sunderland Terrace, Ulverston, Cumbria, LA12 7JY
Major Shareholder: Andrew John Arnold-Bennett
Officers: Andrew John Arnold-Bennett [1966] Director

Sheffield Distillery Limited
Incorporated: 8 March 2017
Registered Office: The Commercial Inn, 107-109 Station Road, Chapeltown, Sheffield, S35 2XF
Shareholders: Gary Sheriff; Paul Rothwell Menzies
Officers: Paul Rothwell Menzies [1957] Director/Publican; Gary Sheriff [1954] Director/Brewer

The Shetland Distillery Company Limited
Incorporated: 1 August 2013 *Employees:* 5
Net Worth: £38,920 *Total Assets:* £241,674
Registered Office: Saxa Vord, Haroldswick, Unst, Shetland, ZE2 9EF
Officers: Stuart Nickerson [1956] Director; Wilma Nickerson [1959] Director; Deborah Louise Strang [1965] Director; Frank Allen Strang [1958] Director

The Shetland Whisky Company Limited
Incorporated: 13 December 2018
Registered Office: 56 Druids Park, Murthly, Perth, PH1 4EJ
Shareholders: Wilma Nickerson; Stuart Nickerson
Officers: Stuart Nickerson [1956] Director; Wilma Nickerson [1959] Director

The Shieling Scotch Whisky Co Ltd
Incorporated: 11 March 2015
Net Worth: £100 *Total Assets:* £100
Registered Office: c/o Cloch Solicitors, Standard Buildings, 94 Hope Street, Glasgow, G2 6PH
Major Shareholder: Andrew Ross Crombie
Officers: Andrew Ross Crombie [1964] Director/Stonemason

Shire Gin Limited
Incorporated: 10 January 2018
Net Worth: £1 *Total Assets:* £1
Registered Office: 5 Canal Way, Ellesmere, Salop, SY12 0FE
Major Shareholder: Gareth Lee Glynn
Officers: Gareth Lee Glynn [1981] Director

Shorts Boy Distillery Ltd
Incorporated: 17 July 2018
Registered Office: 205 Ranelagh Gardens, London, SW6 3SG
Shareholders: Ben Gaisford Clyde-Smith; Harry Caldecott Coulthard
Officers: Ben Gaisford Clyde-Smith [1992] Director; Harry Caldecott Coulthard [1991] Director

Shotgun Limited
Incorporated: 29 March 2018
Registered Office: Russell Flooring Co, 11 Water Lane, Halifax, W Yorks, HX3 9HG
Officers: Jason Richard Sutcliffe, Secretary; Jason Richard Sutcliffe [1971] Director

The Shropshire Distillery Limited
Incorporated: 10 January 2018
Net Worth: £1 *Total Assets:* £1
Registered Office: 5 Canal Way, Ellesmere, Salop, SY12 0FE
Major Shareholder: Gareth Lee Glynn
Officers: Gareth Lee Glynn [1981] Director

The Shropshire Gin Company Limited
Incorporated: 20 October 2015 *Employees:* 1
Net Worth: £482 *Total Assets:* £45,883
Registered Office: Severn Suite 11, Business Development Centre, Stafford Park 4, Telford, Salop, TF3 3BA
Major Shareholder: Jeffrey Joshua Lawrence
Officers: Vicki Lawrence, Secretary; Jeffrey Joshua Lawrence [1967] Director

Shropshire Hills Distillery Limited
Incorporated: 5 June 2018
Registered Office: 1a Cathedral Close, Hereford, HR1 2NG
Major Shareholder: Shaun Leslie Ward
Officers: Shaun Leslie Ward [1978] Director/Executive Manager

Sibling Distillery Limited
Incorporated: 5 November 2013 *Employees:* 9
Net Worth: £51,808 *Total Assets:* £115,581
Registered Office: 93 London Road, Cheltenham, Glos, GL52 6HL
Officers: Cicely Star Elliott-Berry [1995] Director/Administrator; Clarice Bijou Elliott-Berry [1993] Director/Administrator; Felix Louis Elliott-Berry [1992] Director/Administrator; Roland Brian Elliott-Berry [1951] Director/Brewer; Stephanie Judith Elliott-Berry [1965] Director/Administrator

Silent Pool Distillers Limited
Incorporated: 19 June 2014
Registered Office: Silent Pool Distillery, Shere Road, Albury, Guildford, Surrey, GU5 9BW
Parent: The Surrey Hills Distilling Company
Officers: Ian Douglas McCulloch [1959] Director

Silhill Brewery Limited
Incorporated: 14 April 2010
Net Worth: £11,993 *Total Assets:* £25,329
Registered Office: 3 Bramshall Drive, Dorridge, Solihull, W Midlands, B93 8TG
Major Shareholder: Mark Seymour Gregory
Officers: Mark Seymour Gregory [1967] Director

Silver Circle Distillery Limited
Incorporated: 28 November 2018
Registered Office: Unit 15 Brickfield Lane, Chandler's Ford, Eastleigh, Hants, SO53 4DR
Shareholders: Joe Howden; Nina Howden
Officers: Joe Howden [1979] Director; Nina Howden [1981] Director [Swedish]

Silverback Distillers Ltd
Incorporated: 14 March 2017
Net Worth: £12,140 *Total Assets:* £54,043
Registered Office: Fairfield House, 104 Whitby Road, Ellesmere Port, Cheshire, CH65 0AB
Major Shareholder: Christine Vivienne Ditchfield
Officers: Stephen James Ditchfield, Secretary; Christine Vivienne Ditchfield [1959] Director/Self Employed; Stephen James Ditchfield [1957] Director/Engineer

The Silvertown Brewery and Distillery Company Limited
Incorporated: 26 May 2017
Registered Office: H6 Sloane Avenue Mansions, Sloane Avenue, London, SW3 3JW
Major Shareholder: Bruce Kenneth McRobie
Officers: Bruce Kenneth McRobie [1962] Director/Chartered Surveyor

Simple Sips International Limited
Incorporated: 13 February 2017
Registered Office: 84 Octavia Close, Mitcham, Surrey, CR4 4BZ
Major Shareholder: Jeffers Kamande Kamau
Officers: Jeffers Kamande Kamau [1982] Director/Computer Internet Security [Ugandan]

The Sin of Gin Ltd
Incorporated: 31 October 2014
Net Worth Deficit: £14,662 *Total Assets:* £2,799
Registered Office: 18 Elmdon Road, Selly Park, Birmingham, B29 7LF
Major Shareholder: Kathryn Patricia Dean
Officers: Kathryn Patricia Dean [1963] Director

Single Estate Spirits Ltd
Incorporated: 22 December 2016
Net Worth Deficit: £12,210 *Total Assets:* £18,700
Registered Office: 26 Thorngrove Crescent, Aberdeen, AB15 7FH
Shareholders: Matthew David Dakers; Jack Arthur Rackham
Officers: Matthew David Dakers [1982] Director; Adrian Joseph Gomes [1979] Director; Jack Arthur Rackham [1987] Director; Andrew Peter Robin Samways [1980] Director

Sip Antics Limited
Incorporated: 5 April 2018
Registered Office: 1F2, 65 Cumberland Street, Edinburgh, EH3 6RD
Major Shareholder: Gary Patrick Bradley
Officers: Gary Patrick Bradley [1982] Director

The Sipping Shed Limited
Incorporated: 19 March 2014 *Employees:* 2
Net Worth Deficit: £5,073 *Total Assets:* £42,485
Registered Office: West Hill House, Allerton Hill, Chapel Allerton, Leeds, LS7 3QB
Officers: Daniel Hipshon [1976] Director; Richard Robinson [1957] Director

Sipsmith Limited
Incorporated: 18 September 2007 *Employees:* 43
Net Worth: £2,725,000 *Total Assets:* £10,079,000
Registered Office: c/o Pitmans LLP, 107 Cheapside, London, EC2V 6DN
Parent: Suntory UK Holdings Limited
Officers: Stamford Timothy John Galsworthy [1976] Director; Pryce William David Greenow [1970] Senior Vice President, Managing Director Europe,; Fairfax Hall [1974] Director; Drew Hester [1979] Director [American]; Leanne Fay Marran [1978] Director [Polish]

Skinny Russian Vodka Ltd
Incorporated: 3 June 2014
Net Worth: £100 *Total Assets:* £100
Registered Office: 14 Hornbeam Crescent, Harrogate, N Yorks, HG2 8QA
Major Shareholder: Paul Grimshaw
Officers: Paul Grimshaw [1966] Director

Skinnybrands Ltd
Incorporated: 2 September 2015 *Employees:* 3
Net Worth: £1,375,318 *Total Assets:* £1,702,059
Registered Office: Ashton Old Baths, Stamford Street West, Ashton under Lyne, Lancs, OL6 7FW
Shareholders: Thomas Neale Bell; Gary Nicholas Conway
Officers: Mihai Albu [1962] Director [Romanian]; Thomas Neale Bell [1989] Director/Alcohol Manufacturer; Gary Nicholas Conway [1971] Director [Irish]

Sky Pirate Ltd
Incorporated: 26 September 2018
Registered Office: 71-75 Shelton Street, London, WC2H 9JQ
Major Shareholder: Michael Bentley
Officers: Michael Bentley [1964] Director

The Skye Vodka Company Ltd
Incorporated: 6 June 2018
Registered Office: 28 Rathad An Fheoir, Portree, Isle of Skye, IV51 9TR
Shareholders: Raymond Macpherson Lamont; Nicola Lamont
Officers: Nicola Lamont [1982] Director/Self Employed; Raymond Macpherson Lamont [1980] Director/Self Employed

Skylark Distillery Ltd
Incorporated: 12 November 2018
Registered Office: 1 Glanville Road, Tavistock, Devon, PL19 0EA
Major Shareholder: Alexander William Palmer-Samborne
Officers: Alexander William Palmer-Samborne [1978] Director

Slains Castle Spirit Company Ltd
Incorporated: 16 August 2018
Registered Office: Mains of Fedderate, Maud, Peterhead, Aberdeenshire, AB42 4QF
Shareholders: Nikki Jane Elrick; Colin William Elrick
Officers: Colin William Elrick [1969] Director; Nikki Jane Elrick [1973] Director

Slamseys Drinks Limited
Incorporated: 16 February 2012
Net Worth: £62,887 *Total Assets:* £101,425
Registered Office: 169 New London Road, Chelmsford, Essex, CM2 0AE
Major Shareholder: Beth Johanna Paterson
Officers: Beth Johanna Paterson [1987] Director; Matthew John Paterson [1981] Director/Agronomist

Sleepy Hollow Spirits Ltd
Incorporated: 14 January 2019
Registered Office: Sleepy Hollow, Belmangate, Guisborough, Cleveland, TS14 7BD
Major Shareholder: Peter James Kay
Officers: Peter James Kay [1975] Director

Sloeberry Spirits Ltd.
Incorporated: 8 February 2012 *Employees:* 1
Net Worth: £7,384 *Total Assets:* £67,466
Registered Office: Northfield Farm, Whissendine Lane, Cold Overton, Oakham, Rutland, LE15 7QF
Major Shareholder: Andrew Hoyle
Officers: Andrew Hoyle [1966] Director/Liqueur Manufacturer

Sloosh Limited
Incorporated: 23 May 2017
Registered Office: 32 Lytton Avenue, London, EN3 6EN
Major Shareholder: Nathaniel Grant
Officers: Nathaniel Grant [1989] Director

Smart Brewing and Distilling Solutions Limited
Incorporated: 1 December 2017
Registered Office: Bourne House, Queen Street, Gomshall, Guildford, Surrey, GU5 9LY
Shareholders: Christopher Andrew Smart; Katherine Smart
Officers: Dr Christopher Andrew Smart [1968] Director

The Smithies Gin Company Ltd
Incorporated: 17 April 2018
Registered Office: Millfield House, Forfar Road, Arbroath, Angus, DD11 3RA
Shareholders: Patricia Elizabeth Smith; Beth Smith; Jill Smith
Officers: Patricia Elizabeth Smith [1958] Director

Snowdonia Distillery Ltd
Incorporated: 7 September 2015 *Employees:* 2
Net Worth: £12,593 *Total Assets:* £72,976
Registered Office: 14 Walshaw Avenue, Colwyn Bay, Conwy, LL29 7YA
Major Shareholder: Christopher Alexander Marshall
Officers: Christopher Marshall, Secretary; Christopher Marshall [1984] Director

Snowdonia Spirit Company Limited
Incorporated: 23 June 2017
Registered Office: 9 Grandfield Avenue, Radcliffe on Trent, Notts, NG12 1AL
Shareholders: Michael Trevena; Iain Sinclair Boyd
Officers: Iain Sinclair Boyd [1963] Director; Michael Trevena [1967] Director

Soak Engineering Ltd
Incorporated: 20 August 2018
Registered Office: Flat D, 247 Fordwych Road, London, NW2 3LY
Major Shareholder: Hermanus Philippus Potgieter
Officers: Hermanus Philippus Potgieter [1987] Director/Civil Engineer [South African]

Soapbox Spirits Ltd
Incorporated: 24 March 2015 *Employees:* 2
Net Worth: £59,413 *Total Assets:* £93,507
Registered Office: 10 Bridge Street, Christchurch, Dorset, BH23 1EF
Shareholders: Lukasz Damian Dwornik; Martin James Jennings
Officers: Lukasz Damian Dwornik [1981] Director [Polish]; Martin James Jennings [1965] Director

The Soho Shebeen Company Limited
Incorporated: 8 May 2014
Registered Office: Distribution Point, Melbury Park, Clayton Road, Birchwood, Warrington, Cheshire, WA3 6PH
Shareholders: Warren Michael Scott; Vincenzo Visone
Officers: Michael Clifford, Secretary; Warren Michael Scott [1963] Director/Businessman; Vincenzo Visone [1955] Director/Businessman [Italian]

The Solent Spirits Company Limited
Incorporated: 29 January 2019
Registered Office: 32 Larkspur Drive, Marchwood, Southampton, SO40 4JX
Shareholders: Robert Joseph Connor; Tammy Marie Connor
Officers: Robert Joseph Connor [1978] Director/Operations Manager; Tammy Marie Connor [1972] Director/Teacher

Solway Spirits Ltd
Incorporated: 4 May 2018
Registered Office: 1 Railway Cottage, Cummertrees, Annan, Dumfries & Galloway, DG12 5QG
Major Shareholder: Andrew Emmerson
Officers: Kathryn Edith Rimmer, Secretary; Andrew Emmerson [1968] Director/Brewer and Distiller

The Somerset Cider Brandy Company Limited
Incorporated: 17 March 1989
Net Worth: £887,360 *Total Assets:* £1,439,011
Registered Office: Pass Vale Farm, Burrow Hill, Kingsbury Episcopi, Martock, Somerset, TA12 6BU
Major Shareholder: Julian Harold Temperley
Officers: Thomas Brian Williams, Secretary; Mark Ernest Hix [1962] Director; William Ion Leyshon [1957] Director/Thatcher; Timothy Dean Stoddart [1983] Director/Cider Maker; Diana Elizabeth Temperley [1948] Director/Housewife; Julian Harold Vazeille Temperley [1945] Director/Farmer; Mary Clementine Temperley [1978] Commercial Director; Matilda Esmeralda Diana Temperley [1981] Director/Public Health Scientist

Somerset Craft Distillery Ltd
Incorporated: 9 October 2018
Registered Office: Barton Lower Farm, Gosling Street, Barton St David, Somerset, TA11 6GS
Shareholders: Barry Davies; Mandy Davies
Officers: Barry Davies [1956] Director; Mandy Davies [1959] Director

Somerset Craft Spirit Company Ltd
Incorporated: 9 October 2018
Registered Office: Barton Lower Farm, Gosling Street, Barton St David, Somerset, TA11 6GS
Shareholders: Barry Davies; Mandy Davies
Officers: Barry Davies [1956] Director; Mandy Davies [1959] Director

Somerset Distillery Ltd
Incorporated: 21 June 2018
Registered Office: Lea Rig, Hillcommon, Taunton, Somerset, TA4 1DU
Shareholder: Thomas William Marney
Officers: Thomas William Marney [1992] Director

Somerset Drinks Ltd
Incorporated: 9 December 2015
Registered Office: 1 Brue Avenue, Bruton, Somerset, BA10 0HZ
Officers: Rosanna Blampied [1989] Director/Personal Assistant; John Foster Yeoman [1961] Director/Farmer; Emma Margaret Miller [1979] Director/Accountant

SOS Gin Ltd
Incorporated: 22 September 2017
Registered Office: 102 Clerk Street, Loanhead, Midlothian, EH20 9RB
Major Shareholder: Mark Munnoch-Wahlberg
Officers: Mark James Munnoch-Wahlberg [1968] Director/Owner

The Soul of The Spirit Limited
Incorporated: 16 March 2018
Registered Office: 21 Culverlands Close, Stanmore, Middlesex, HA7 3AG
Major Shareholder: Koen de Jans
Officers: Koen de Jans [1976] Director [Belgian]

Soul Vodka Ltd
Incorporated: 15 February 2018
Registered Office: 27 Purcells Avenue, Edgware, Middlesex, HA8 8DP
Officers: Gurdarshan Singh Bedi [1955] Director/Beverages & Restaurant

Soulmate Gin Ltd
Incorporated: 5 July 2018
Registered Office: 4 Sandy Hall Lane, Barrowford, Nelson, Lancs, BB9 6QH
Shareholders: Antony Mark Leach; Victoria Joanne Ryan
Officers: Antony Mark Leach [1979] Director; Victoria Joanne Ryan [1980] Director/Teacher

South Causey Distillery Ltd
Incorporated: 2 December 2016
Registered Office: 1 Jesmond Business Court, 217 Jesmond Road, Newcastle upon Tyne, NE2 1LA
Major Shareholder: Susan Jane Moiser
Officers: Susan Jane Moiser [1963] Director

The South Devon Liqueur Company Limited
Incorporated: 9 January 2019
Registered Office: 2 Tower House, Hoddesdon, Herts, EN11 8UR
Major Shareholder: Katie Victoria Musgrave
Officers: Dr Katie Victoria Musgrave [1984] Director

South Loch Ltd
Incorporated: 19 December 2018
Registered Office: 34 Atholl Crescent Lane, Edinburgh, EH3 8ET
Shareholders: Richard Charles Sutherland; James Edward Sutherland
Officers: Alister John Sutherland [1951] Director; James Edward Sutherland [1982] Director; Richard Charles Sutherland [1985] Director; Susan Sutherland [1951] Director

The South London Urban Gin Company Limited
Incorporated: 13 September 2018
Registered Office: 1 & 2 Studley Court Mews, Studley Court, Guildford Road, Chobham, Surrey, GU24 8EB
Major Shareholder: Gareth James Mozley
Officers: Gareth James Mozley [1969] Director

South Side Spirit Limited
Incorporated: 30 May 2014
Registered Office: 20 Braid Mount, Edinburgh, EH10 6JJ
Major Shareholder: John Everett
Officers: Ewen Gillespie, Secretary; John Everett [1964] Director; Ewen Gillespie [1960] Director

Southampton Distillery Ltd
Incorporated: 18 January 2019
Registered Office: Rosemary Vineyard, Ryde, Isle of Wight, PO33 1PX
Shareholders: Gary Foyle; Conrad Gaunlett
Officers: Gary Foyle [1959] Director/Engineer

The Southey Brewing Company Limited
Incorporated: 15 August 2016
Net Worth Deficit: £8,345 *Total Assets:* £30,692
Registered Office: East Lodge, Bedlars Green, Great Hallingbury, Bishop's Stortford, Herts, CM22 7TL
Shareholder: Propstock Community Pubs Limited
Officers: Samuel Jonathan Barber [1986] Director/Brewer; Darren MacRae [1989] Director/Bars Manager

Southwestern Distillery Limited
Incorporated: 27 September 2012 *Employees:* 14
Net Worth: £639,002 *Total Assets:* £954,224
Registered Office: Unit 11 Higher Trevibban Farm, St Ervan, Wadebridge, Cornwall, PL27 7SH
Major Shareholder: Tarquin David Leadbetter
Officers: Tarquin Leadbetter [1987] Managing Director

Sovereign Spirits Ltd.
Incorporated: 18 January 2018
Registered Office: Newstead House, Pelham Road, Nottingham, NG5 1AP
Parent: Clipstone Park Farms Ltd.
Officers: Guy Shaw-Browne [1958] Director/Farmer; Luke Shaw-Browne [1990] Director

Speakeasy Spirits UK Ltd
Incorporated: 4 August 2016
Registered Office: 3 Countess Way, Euxton, Chorley, Lancs, PR7 6PT
Major Shareholder: Michael Ian Fairless
Officers: Amanda Fairless [1970] Director/Health & Safety Advisor; Michael Ian Fairless [1968] Director/Business Development Manager

Spencerfield Spirit Company Limited
Incorporated: 27 April 2005
Registered Office: Russell House, Dunnet Way, Broxburn, W Lothian, EH52 5BU
Parent: Ian MacLeod Distillers
Officers: Leonard Stuart Russell [1961] Director; Michael James Younger [1960] Director

Speyburn-Glenlivet Distillery Co. Limited
Incorporated: 4 November 1991
Registered Office: Moffat Distillery, Airdrie, N Lanarks, ML6 8PL
Shareholders: Chareon Sirivadhanabhakdi; Khunying Wanna Sirivadhanabhakdi
Officers: Man Kong Lee [1968] Director/Accountant [Chinese]; Dr Martin John Leonard [1961] Managing Director; Prapakon Thongtheppairot [1971] Director [Thai]

Speymalt Whisky Distributors Limited
Incorporated: 11 April 1962 *Employees:* 154
Net Worth: £38,177,164 *Total Assets:* £43,225,660
Registered Office: George House, Boroughbriggs Road, Elgin, Moray, IV30 1JY
Officers: Norman Ross, Secretary; James Andrew Bishop [1959] Director; Ian Michael Chapman [1974] Marketing Director; David Thomas King [1964] Sales Director; Ewen Cameron Mackintosh [1968] Director; Stephen Alexander Masson Rankin [1971] Director; Norman Ross [1974] Director/Chartered Accountant; Neil Edward Urquhart [1975] Director; Stuart David Urquhart [1981] Operations Director; Gillian Anne McGregor Watson [1964] Director

Speyside Distillers Company Limited
Incorporated: 2 September 1999 *Employees:* 14
Net Worth: £3,719,146 *Total Assets:* £12,144,597
Registered Office: 197 Bath Street, Glasgow, G2 4HU
Parent: Hoe International Ltd
Officers: Yung Sheng Chang [1953] Director [Taiwanese]; Yu Hung Ho [1964] Director [Taiwanese]; John McDonough [1956] Director

The Speyside Vodka Company Ltd
Incorporated: 4 March 2016
Registered Office: 5 Dunkinty, Elgin, Moray, IV30 8RA
Major Shareholder: Leon Richard Chessor
Officers: Leon Richard Chessor [1985] Director/Inspection

Spice Island Gin Company Ltd
Incorporated: 15 May 2018
Registered Office: 36 Broad Street, Portsmouth, PO1 2JE
Officers: Jane Lowe [1962] Director/Manager; Mark Lowe [1963] Director/Manager

Spirit of Captain Cook Limited
Incorporated: 15 November 2017
Registered Office: Unit 9 Station Road, Stokesley, Middlesbrough, Cleveland, TS9 7AE
Officers: Gwendolyn Toovey [1949] Director/Retired

The Spirit of Coalpit - Ysbryd y Pwll Glo Ltd
Incorporated: 3 December 2018
Registered Office: Plas Newydd, 1a Maesllwyn, Bonllwyn, Ammanford, Carmarthenshire, SA18 2EG
Shareholders: Stephen Walker; Erika Walker
Officers: Erika Walker [1964] Director; Stephen Walker [1958] Director

Spirit of Glasgow Ltd
Incorporated: 3 May 2016 *Employees:* 1
Net Worth Deficit: £6,754 *Total Assets:* £1,036
Registered Office: 272 Bath Street, Glasgow, G2 4JR
Major Shareholder: Christopher Joseph Ross Bradley
Officers: Christopher Joseph Ross Bradley [1988] Director/Vehicle Technician

Spirit of Harrogate Limited
Incorporated: 29 August 2014 *Employees:* 20
Net Worth Deficit: £547,077 *Total Assets:* £751,580
Registered Office: 4 Sceptre House, Hornbeam Square North, Harrogate, N Yorks, HG2 8PB
Parent: ICB Brands Holdings Limited
Officers: Marcus William Black, Secretary; Marcus William Black [1969] Director/Accountant; Michael John Carthy [1956] Director/Chemist

Spirit of Leeds Ltd
Incorporated: 17 December 2018
Registered Office: 8 Ivegate, Yeadon, Leeds, LS19 7RE
Major Shareholder: Gregory Lydon
Officers: Gregory Lydon [1961] Director

Spirit of Leith Ltd
Incorporated: 24 July 2017
Registered Office: 4/2 Huntingdon Place, Edinburgh, EH7 4AT
Shareholders: Linda Kelly; Andrew Kelly
Officers: Andrew Kelly [1959] Director; Linda Kelly [1959] Director

Spirit of Malt House Limited
Incorporated: 6 February 2018
Registered Office: Malthouse Farmhouse, High Street, Lenham, Maidstone, Kent, ME17 2QG
Shareholders: Laurence Digby Porter; Hannah Victoria Goodwin
Officers: Hannah Victoria Goodwin [1965] Director; Laurence Digby Porter [1955] Director

Spirit of Manchester Distillery Limited
Incorporated: 3 July 2017 *Employees:* 2
Net Worth: £24,509 *Total Assets:* £50,140
Registered Office: 125 Buckingham Road, Manchester, M21 0RG
Shareholders: Sebastian Richard John Heeley; Jennie Louise Wiggins
Officers: Sebastian Richard John Heeley [1986] Director/Owner; Jennie Louise Wiggins [1983] Director/Owner

Spirit of The Lakes Limited
Incorporated: 13 November 2008
Net Worth Deficit: £4,882 Total Assets: £74,064
Registered Office: Barf Cottage, Thornthwaite, Keswick, Cumbria, CA12 5SQ
Shareholders: Vincent James Wilkins; John Davidson
Officers: Vincent James Peter Wilkins, Secretary; Dr Michael Gordon Barker [1968] Director; Vincent James Wilkins [1964] Managing Director

Spirit of The Shires Limited
Incorporated: 29 October 2014
Registered Office: 11 The Glade, Stafford, ST17 4JW
Major Shareholder: William Denis Armstrong
Officers: William Denis Armstrong [1956] Director/Taxi Driver; Karen Dawn Peterkin [1960] Director/Financial Manager

Spirit of Unicorn Ltd
Incorporated: 12 May 2018
Registered Office: 30 Cumberland Mills Square, London, E14 3BH
Shareholders: Filip Tesanovic; Yuriy Lugovyy
Officers: Yuriy Lugovyy [1979] Director/Barber; Filip Tesanovic [1986] Director/Bar Manager [Bosnia/Herzegovina]

Spirit of Yorkshire Limited
Incorporated: 16 August 2012 Employees: 12
Net Worth Deficit: £245,882 Total Assets: £1,866,032
Registered Office: Hunmanby Grange, Wold Newton, Driffield, E Yorks, YO25 3HS
Shareholders: Thomas Leslie Mellor; Gillian Mary Mellor
Officers: Gillian Mary Mellor [1960] Director; Thomas Leslie Mellor [1959] Director; David John Greenwood Thompson [1963] Director; Rebecca Suzanne Thompson [1963] Director

Spirit Stories Ltd
Incorporated: 27 January 2016
Registered Office: 9c Arundel Square, London, N7 8AT
Officers: Fiona Louise Flood [1981] Brand Director

Spiritmen Limited
Incorporated: 4 February 2014 Employees: 61
Net Worth: £1,428,369 Total Assets: £1,956,913
Registered Office: Silent Pool Distillery, Shere Road, Albury, Guildford, Surrey, GU5 9BW
Shareholders: James Clifford John Shelbourne; Ian Douglas McCulloch
Officers: Steven Robert Kavanagh [1974] Director/Consultant [Irish]; John Charles Keeling [1962] Director; Ian Douglas McCulloch [1959] Director; James Clifford John Shelbourne [1964] Director

Spirits and Bubbles Limited
Incorporated: 12 August 2015
Net Worth: £532 Total Assets: £14,706
Registered Office: Kemp House, 152-160 City Road, London, EC1V 2NX
Major Shareholder: Nadeem Aziz
Officers: Nadeem Amer Aziz [1973] Director

Spirits Development & Management Company (SDMC) Limited
Incorporated: 16 December 2013
Net Worth: £631,395 Total Assets: £3,439,762
Registered Office: Citypoint, 65 Haymarket Terrace, Edinburgh, EH12 5HD
Major Shareholder: Michel Picard
Officers: Michel Bernard Picard [1942] Director [French]

The Spirits of Bronte Drinks Co. Ltd
Incorporated: 10 June 2016 Employees: 1
Net Worth: £2,631 Total Assets: £13,924
Registered Office: 7 Moorcroft Avenue, Oakworth, Keighley, W Yorks, BD22 7NE
Major Shareholder: Samantha Jane Long
Officers: Samantha Long, Secretary; Samantha Jane Long [1974] Director

Spnet Ltd.
Incorporated: 27 September 2013
Registered Office: Flat 10, Rockford House, 34-38 Heathcoat Street, Nottingham, NG1 3AA
Officers: Jorge Lorenzana, Secretary; Javier Castaneda [1986] Director/Politician [Spanish]; Miguel Castaneda [1983] Director/Consulting [Spanish]

Square Street Distillery Ltd
Incorporated: 27 June 2008
Previous: Bespoke Ale Limited
Net Worth: £3,171 Total Assets: £12,258
Registered Office: The Old Brewery, Back Square Street, Ramsbottom, Bury, Lancs, BL0 9FZ
Major Shareholder: Peter Booth
Officers: Peter Booth [1963] Director/Consultant

St Andrews Botanics Limited
Incorporated: 10 September 2018
Registered Office: 28 Graemeslea View, Aberuthven, Auchterarder, Perth & Kinross, PH3 1FG
Major Shareholder: Shona Robertson Geddes
Officers: Shona Robertson Geddes [1980] Director/Owner

St Andrews Brewers Limited
Incorporated: 23 January 2012 Employees: 49
Net Worth Deficit: £3,316,901 Total Assets: £2,329,965
Registered Office: Eden Mill, Main Street, Guardbridge, St Andrews, Fife, KY16 0US
Major Shareholder: Anthony Kelly
Officers: Anthony Gerard Kelly, Secretary; Anthony Gerard Kelly [1991] Company Secretary/Director; Anthony Kelly [1963] Director [Irish]; Paul Miller [1961] Director

St Davids Gin Limited
Incorporated: 15 January 2019
Registered Office: Flat 13-14, Cross Square, St Davids, Haverfordwest, Pembrokeshire, SA62 6SE
Major Shareholder: Neil Walsh
Officers: Neil Walsh [1975] Director; Ruth Louise Walsh [1982] Director and Company Secretary

St Faiths Distillery Limited
Incorporated: 1 March 2016
Registered Office: The Lilacs, Meadow Farm Lane, Horsham St Faith, Norwich, NR10 3BY
Major Shareholder: Matthew Andrew Seaton Clifford
Officers: Matthew Andrew Seaton Clifford [1972] Director

St. James Distillery Limited
Incorporated: 16 July 2003
Net Worth Deficit: £453,039
Registered Office: 31 Squirrels Heath Avenue, Romford, Essex, RM2 6AD
Shareholders: Kevin Charles Casey; Abraham Michael Loubser; Andrew Ford
Officers: Sally Louise Greenwood, Secretary; Kevin Charles Casey [1950] Director; Andrew Ford [1961] Director/Business Development; Abraham Michael Christian Loubser [1932] Director/Businessman [Dutch]

St.Andrews Gin Company Ltd
Incorporated: 11 November 2015
Registered Office: Unit 9 Bassaguard Estate, Wallace Street, St Andrews, Fife, KY16 8AL
Officers: Patrick Philip Mackey, Secretary; Timothy George Edward Butler [1972] Director; Patrick Philip Mackey [1974] Director

St.Andrews Whisky Company Ltd
Incorporated: 11 November 2015
Registered Office: Unit 9 Bassaguard Estate, Wallace Street, St Andrews, Fife, KY16 8AL
Officers: Patrick Philip Mackey, Secretary; Timothy George Edward Butler [1972] Director; Patrick Philip Mackey [1974] Director

Staffordshire Distillery Ltd
Incorporated: 5 July 2018
Registered Office: 36 Park Road, Alrewas, Burton on Trent, Staffs, DE13 7AG
Major Shareholder: Rachel Evans
Officers: Rachel Evans [1978] Director/Consultant

The Staffordshire Gin Company Ltd
Incorporated: 13 April 2018
Registered Office: 197 High Street, Silverdale, Newcastle, Staffs, ST5 6JZ
Shareholders: Jason Richard Davies; Claire Margaret Gibbs
Officers: Claire Margaret Gibbs, Secretary; Jason Richard Davies [1969] Director/Lecturer

Stargazey Spirits Ltd
Incorporated: 6 February 2019
Registered Office: Dolphins, Trenale, Tintagel, Cornwall, PL34 0HP
Shareholders: Avian Sandercock; Stephen David James Wharton; Craig Russell Penn
Officers: Craig Russell Penn [1970] Director; Avian Sandercock [1968] Director; Stephen David James Wharton [1970] Director

Starling & Wasp Ltd
Incorporated: 21 November 2016
Registered Office: 41 Cowan Wynd, Uddingston, Glasgow, G71 6TP
Major Shareholder: Pauline Jean Rooney
Officers: Pauline Jean Rooney [1966] Director/VP

The Start-Up Drinks Lab Limited
Incorporated: 13 June 2017
Net Worth: £121,474 *Total Assets:* £206,699
Registered Office: Unit 4 Building D, Kelburn Business Park, Port Glasgow, Inverclyde, PA14 6BL
Shareholders: Craig Robert Strachan; Hannah Magdaline Fisher
Officers: John Ross Brodie [1964] Director; Hannah Magdaline Fisher [1983] Marketing Director; Craig Robert Strachan [1988] Finance Director

Steampunk Ltd
Incorporated: 27 May 2014 *Employees:* 2
Net Worth: £6,072 *Total Assets:* £32,139
Registered Office: 12 Ivy Lane, Low Fell, Gateshead, Tyne & Wear, NE9 6QD
Shareholder: Charles Gibbs
Officers: Charlie Gibbs, Secretary; Charlie William Gibbs [1960] Director; Julie Dawn Gibbs [1961] Director

Steel City Craft Spirits Boutique Ltd
Incorporated: 17 April 2018
Registered Office: Apartment 314, Q4 Apartments, 185 Upper Allen Street, Sheffield, S3 7GT
Major Shareholder: John Joseph Patrick Conway
Officers: John Joseph Patrick Conway, Secretary; John Joseph Patrick Conway [1984] Director

Steel River Drinks Ltd
Incorporated: 15 May 2017
Registered Office: East Durham Business Centre, Station Town, Wingate, Cleveland, TS28 5HD
Officers: Jason Byers [1972] Director/Entrepreneur

The Still House Ltd
Incorporated: 8 January 2013
Registered Office: Distribution Point, Melbury Park, Clayton Road, Birchwood, Warrington, Cheshire, WA3 6PH
Shareholders: Warren Michael Scott; Vincenzo Visone
Officers: Michael Clifford, Secretary; Warren Michael Scott [1963] Director/Businessman; Visone Vincenzo [1955] Director/Businessman [Italian]

Still on the Hill Limited
Incorporated: 1 October 2015
Net Worth: £1,088,873 *Total Assets:* £1,490,932
Registered Office: 8 King Edward Street, Oxford, OX1 4HL
Officers: Tagore Ramoutar, Secretary; Neil Graeme Brown [1959] Director/Chartered Accountant; Cory John Mason [1981] Director/Master Distiller [American]; Marcin Adam Miller [1964] Director; Thomas Paul Nicolson [1966] Director; Jeremy Winslow Parsons [1962] Director; Tagore Ramoutar [1966] Managing Director

Still Shining Distillers Ltd
Incorporated: 6 July 2016
Registered Office: Backhill of Davah, St James Place, Inverurie, Aberdeenshire, AB51 5JN
Major Shareholder: Gregor McAulay Thomson
Officers: Hayley Catherine Thomson, Secretary; Gregor McAulay Thomson [1990] Managing Director

Still Wild Limited
Incorporated: 10 August 2018
Registered Office: Cresselly, Kilgetty, Saundersfoot, Pembrokeshire, SA68 0SP
Major Shareholder: James Alexander Hensleigh Harrison-Allen
Officers: James Alexander Hensleigh Harrison-Allen [1988] Director/Manager

Stirling Distillery Company Ltd
Incorporated: 5 April 2018
Registered Office: 12 Alexander Drive, Bridge of Allan, Stirling, FK9 4QB
Shareholders: Cameron McCann; June McCann
Officers: Brian Robert Henderson [1967] Director; Cameron McCann [1967] Director; June McCann [1970] Director

Stirling Gin Ltd.
Incorporated: 25 August 2015
Net Worth Deficit: £77,380 *Total Assets:* £17,831
Registered Office: 12 Alexander Drive, Bridge of Allan, Stirling, FK9 4QB
Shareholders: June McCann; Cameron McCann
Officers: Brian Robert Henderson [1967] Finance Director; Cameron McCann [1967] Director; June McCann [1970] Director

Stockholm Distillers and Vintners Limited
Incorporated: 26 July 2016
Registered Office: 133a Kingston Road, London, SW19 1LT
Major Shareholder: Mukesh Jain
Officers: Mukesh Jain, Secretary; Mukesh Jain [1969] Director [Indian]

Stockport Gin Ltd
Incorporated: 5 November 2018
Registered Office: 17 Orchard Road, Compstall, Stockport, Cheshire, SK6 5JS
Shareholders: Cheryl Anne Sharrocks; Paul John Sharrocks
Officers: Cheryl Anne Sharrocks [1980] Director/Hairdresser; Paul John Sharrocks [1984] Director/Architect

Stokers Spirits Ltd
Incorporated: 23 February 2016
Net Worth Deficit: £1,223
Registered Office: Fiddington House Farm, Fiddington, Tewkesbury, Glos, GL20 7BJ
Shareholder: Ross Hemming
Officers: Ross James Hemming, Secretary; Ross James Hemmings [1976] Managing Director

Stolowa Ltd
Incorporated: 12 July 2017
Registered Office: 20-22 Wenlock Road, London, N1 7GU
Major Shareholder: Dariusz Plazewski
Officers: Dariusz Plazewski [1977] Director [Polish]

Stonedean Limited
Incorporated: 7 January 2009
Net Worth: £22,004 *Total Assets:* £22,004
Registered Office: 23 Manor Place, Edinburgh, EH3 7DX
Parent: R & B Distillers Limited
Officers: Alasdair MacDonald Day, Secretary; Alasdair MacDonald Day [1965] Director

Stonehenge Distillery Limited
Incorporated: 19 February 2018
Registered Office: Windover House, St Ann Street, Salisbury, Wilts, SP1 2DR
Officers: Francis Whiting [1970] Director

Story Brands Limited
Incorporated: 29 June 2011 *Employees:* 2
Net Worth: £115,207 *Total Assets:* £154,527
Registered Office: Lifford Hall, Lifford Lane, Kings Norton, Birmingham, B30 3JN
Major Shareholder: Julian Wilfrid Sollom
Officers: Julian Wilfrid Sollom [1964] Director

Strathearn Distillery Ltd.
Incorporated: 18 January 2013 *Employees:* 3
Net Worth: £188,979 *Total Assets:* £538,754
Registered Office: 57-59 High Street, Dunblane, Perthshire, FK15 0EE
Parent: The Whisky Garden Ltd.
Officers: Amanda Reeman-Clark, Secretary; Thomas David Burke [1952] Director; Thomas James Burke [1978] Director; Anthony Reeman-Clark [1955] Director/Business Executive; Zak Shenfield [1993] Director

Strathleven Distillers Company Limited
Incorporated: 13 April 2006 *Employees:* 3
Net Worth Deficit: £4,749 *Total Assets:* £483,106
Registered Office: 21 Forbes Place, Paisley, Renfrewshire, PA1 1UT
Major Shareholder: Roderick George Christie
Officers: Roderick George Christie [1952] Director/Distiller; Pricilla Joyce Craig [1958] Director

Strathnairn Whisky Limited
Incorporated: 27 February 1964
Registered Office: WJM LLP, The Green House, Beechwood Park North, Inverness, IV2 3BL
Parent: Speymalt Whisky Distributors Ltd
Officers: Norman Ross, Secretary; Ewen Cameron Mackintosh [1968] Whisky Supply Director; Stephen Alexander Masson Rankin [1971] UK Sales Director; Neil Edward Urquhart [1975] Logistics & Facilities Director

Strawhill Estate Distillery Ltd
Incorporated: 1 May 2015 *Employees:* 3
Net Worth Deficit: £24,060 *Total Assets:* £10,321
Registered Office: Quaker Buildings, High Street, Lurgan, Craigavon, Co Armagh, BT66 8BB
Shareholders: Gregory Berry; Norman Mark Pearson
Officers: Adam Berry [1995] Director/Student; Norman Mark Pearson [1974] Director

Strawhill Estate Spirits Company Ltd
Incorporated: 4 October 2017
Registered Office: McCleary & Company Ltd, Quaker Buildings, High Street, Lurgan, Craigavon, Co Armagh, BT66 8BB
Shareholders: Norman Mark Pearson; Gregory Berry
Officers: Adam Berry [1995] Director/Student; Norman Mark Pearson [1974] Director

Strawhill Ltd
Incorporated: 17 October 2012
Previous: Pecan Brewing Ltd
Registered Office: Strawhill, 2 Hall Road, Donaghcloney, Co Down, BT66 7LJ
Officers: Sharon Margaret Berry [1965] Director/Retired Teacher; William Gregory Hamilton Berry [1966] Director/Barrister

The Strontium Gin Company Ltd
Incorporated: 17 January 2019
Registered Office: 206 Regents Park Road, Southampton, SO15 8NY
Major Shareholder: Warwick Ian Newson
Officers: Warwick Ian Newson [1960] Director

The Suffolk Distillery Limited
Incorporated: 4 January 2016 *Employees:* 2
Net Worth: £3,560 *Total Assets:* £42,172
Registered Office: 38 Long Pastures, Glemsford, Sudbury, Suffolk, CO10 7SS
Shareholders: Gary Wilkinson; Melanie Mary Wilkinson
Officers: Gary Wilkinson [1962] Director; Melanie Mary Wilkinson [1962] Director

Suffolk Smugglers Limited
Incorporated: 19 February 2018
Registered Office: Swanley House, Farnham Road, Snape, Saxmundham, Suffolk, IP17 1QW
Officers: Philip Alexander Guy Jervis Kay [1990] Director

Summerhall Distillery Limited
Incorporated: 25 September 2013 *Employees:* 14
Net Worth: £758,269 *Total Assets:* £1,460,160
Registered Office: Summerhall Distillery, 1 Summerhall, Edinburgh, EH9 1PL
Shareholders: Matthew David Malcolm Gammell; Marcus George Pickering
Officers: Matthew David Malcolm Gammell [1975] Director; David Owen Mullen [1968] Executive Creative Director; Marcus George Pickering [1974] Director

Sunderland Gin Limited
Incorporated: 31 August 2017
Registered Office: 92 Greenbank Drive, Sunderland, Tyne & Wear, SR4 0JX
Major Shareholder: Stephen Anthony Brace
Officers: Stephen Anthony Brace [1991] Director/Business Development Executive

Sunfire Spirits Ltd
Incorporated: 21 May 2018
Registered Office: Brookfields, Station Road, Great Fransham, Dereham, Norfolk, NR19 2JB
Officers: Suzanne Elizabeth Bauly, Secretary; Suzanne Elizabeth Bauly [1993] Director/Interior Designer; Ashley Richard John Thurston [1962] Director/Businessman; Daniel Gary Thurston [1991] Director/Receptionist; Sandra Jean Thurston [1964] Director/Teacher

Supermarine Vodka Distillers Limited
Incorporated: 29 March 2017
Net Worth: £100 *Total Assets:* £100
Registered Office: Meadow View, Meadow Lane, Ormskirk, Lancs, L40 2QA
Shareholders: Spitfire Heritage Distillers Limited; Spitfire Heritage Distillers Limited
Officers: Ian Hewitt [1965] Director

Surendran & Bownes Ltd.
Incorporated: 17 August 2017
Registered Office: Flat 54, Reynolds House, Approach Road, London, E2 9JR
Officers: Cameron Bownes [1993] Director; Liam John Lewis [1989] Director

The Surrey Copper Distillery Limited
Incorporated: 23 June 2017
Registered Office: Bourne House, Queen Street, Gomshall, Guildford, Surrey, GU5 9LY
Major Shareholder: Christopher Andrew Smart
Officers: Dr Christopher Andrew Smart [1968] Director

The Surrey Hills Distilling Company Ltd
Incorporated: 2 April 2013
Net Worth Deficit: £65,403 *Total Assets:* £35,124
Registered Office: Silent Pool Distillery, Shere Road, Albury, Guildford, Surrey, GU5 9BW
Parent: Spiritmen Limited
Officers: Ian Douglas McCulloch [1959] Director

Surrey Hills EBT Limited
Incorporated: 2 July 2014
Registered Office: Silent Pool Distillery, Shere Road, Albury, Guildford, Surrey, GU5 9BW
Parent: Spiritmen Limited
Officers: Ian Douglas McCulloch [1959] Director; Mark Douglas Warner [1957] Director

The Surrey Hills Whisky Company Limited
Incorporated: 10 October 2018
Registered Office: The Old Rectory, Church Street, Weybridge, Surrey, KT13 8DE
Shareholders: Steven Robert Kavanagh; Ian Douglas McCulloch; James Clifford John Shelbourne
Officers: Steven Robert Kavanagh [1974] Director [Irish]; John Keeling [1962] Director; Ian Douglas McCulloch [1959] Director; James Clifford John Shelbourne [1964] Director

SV Distilleries Limited
Incorporated: 19 November 2018
Registered Office: Marsh Close, Gowdall Lane, Snaith, Goole, N Yorks, DN14 0AA
Parent: SV Properties Limited
Officers: Richard Hugh Langdon [1946] Director/Retired

Swallow London Ltd
Incorporated: 10 February 2016
Registered Office: 10 London Mews, London, W2 1HY
Shareholders: Jean-Sebastien Dupuy; Gaye Meryl Rainier-Kirkwood
Officers: Jean-Sebastien Dupuy [1974] Director/Drinks Manufacturer/Distributor [French]; Gay Meryl Rainier-Kirkwood [1959] Director/Drinks Manufacturer/Distributor

Sweet Afton Scotch Whisky Limited
Incorporated: 17 July 2017
Registered Office: Clyde Offices, 48 West George Street, Glasgow, G2 1BP
Officers: Otf Doheny [1961] Director

Sweetdram Limited
Incorporated: 10 March 2014 *Employees:* 4
Net Worth Deficit: £473,386 *Total Assets:* £246,384
Registered Office: 84b Tyrwhitt Road, London, SE4 1QB
Parent: Escubac Limited
Officers: Daniel Arthur Fisher [1982] Director/Executive [American]; Andrew MacLeod Smith [1983] Director/Distiller

Sweetwater Distillery Limited
Incorporated: 23 October 2017
Registered Office: Parkleaze Distillery, Ewen, Cirencester, Glos, GL7 6PZ
Shareholders: Emma Samantha Clare Beardshaw; Harry Tucker
Officers: Emma Samantha Clare Beardshaw [1973] Director; Harry Tucker [1984] Director

Swift Half Collective Ltd
Incorporated: 2 May 2017
Registered Office: Hamlet Cottage, St Michaels Church Road, Liverpool, L17 7BD
Shareholder: Conor Foley
Officers: Conor Foley [1985] Managing Director [Irish]; Peter Michael John Hunter [1987] Marketing & Sales Director; Danny McCay [1985] Artistic Director [Irish]

Sword of Spirit Distillery Limited
Incorporated: 4 March 2013
Net Worth Deficit: £6,043 *Total Assets:* £1,397
Registered Office: 8 Ivegate, Yeadon, Leeds, LS19 7RE
Major Shareholder: Gregory Lydon
Officers: Greg Lydon [1961] Director/Distiller

Syndicate 58/6 Limited
Incorporated: 4 July 2012
Net Worth: £1,000 *Total Assets:* £1,000
Registered Office: Dilston, Hill Road, Gullane, E Lothian, EH31 2BE
Officers: Alastair Stiles McIntosh [1940] Director; Charles Rome McIntosh [1965] Director

Tap End Brands Ltd
Incorporated: 12 October 2015
Registered Office: 17 Gleads Croft, Halesowen, W Midlands, B62 0QA
Officers: Kirsty Ann Hughes [1982] Director/Regional Account Manager; Claire Louise Sumner [1980] Director/Key Account Manager

Taplin & Mageean Ltd
Incorporated: 24 August 2018
Registered Office: Croft House, West Burton, Leyburn, N Yorks, DL8 4JW
Shareholders: Chris Edward Taplin; Barry Joseph Mageean
Officers: Barry Joseph Mageean [1995] Director/Distiller; Chris Edward Taplin [1967] Managing Director

Tappers Artisan Spirits Ltd.
Incorporated: 4 April 2016 *Employees:* 1
Net Worth Deficit: £12,549 *Total Assets:* £18,525
Registered Office: 223 Greenbank Road, Wirral, Merseyside, CH48 6DL
Major Shareholder: Stephen Tapril
Officers: Susan Tapril, Secretary; Dr Stephen Tapril [1981] Director/IT Manager

Tarbraxus Distillers Ltd
Incorporated: 4 April 2017
Net Worth Deficit: £10,202 *Total Assets:* £24,301
Registered Office: Dykehead, Tarbrax, West Calder, W Lothian, EH55 8LW
Shareholders: Tabatha Justine, Kerry McCree-Cox; Tarbraxus Consultancy Limited
Officers: Philip Henry Cox [1962] Director; Tabatha Justine McCree-Cox [1970] Director

Tarlogie Springs Limited
Incorporated: 7 April 1988
Registered Office: The Cube, 45 Leith Street, Edinburgh, EH1 3AT
Parent: MacDonald & Muir Limited
Officers: Jean-Marc Rene Boulan [1972] Director [French]; Dr Peter Jonathon Nelson [1959] Director

Tarsier Spirit Ltd
Incorporated: 11 April 2017 *Employees:* 2
Net Worth Deficit: £7,818 *Total Assets:* £17,515
Registered Office: 11 Riverton Road, Manchester, M20 5QH
Shareholders: Sherwin Acebuche; Timothy Jonathan Driver
Officers: Sherwin Acebuche [1977] Director/Head of Sales [British/Filipino]; Timothy Jonathan Driver [1983] Director

Tasty Beverages Limited
Incorporated: 20 March 2017
Net Worth Deficit: £9,387 *Total Assets:* £29,530
Registered Office: 7a Shaftesbury Road, London, N19 4QW
Major Shareholder: Alex David Kammerling
Officers: Alex David Kammerling [1975] Director

Taunton Distiller's Ltd
Incorporated: 4 August 2016
Previous: The Last Drop Gin Company Ltd
Registered Office: 40 St James Buildings, St James Street, Taunton, Somerset, TA1 1JR
Officers: Richard Derek Brice [1955] Director; Michael Anthony Collard [1960] Director; John Terence Cooney [1957] Director; Benjamin Michael Hollin [1993] Director

Taunton Gin Limited
Incorporated: 8 January 2019
Registered Office: 10 Meadow Street, Avonmouth, Bristol, BS11 9AR
Major Shareholder: Stephen Ronald Downey
Officers: Stephen Ronald Downey [1959] Director

Tay Spirits Ltd.
Incorporated: 11 November 2016
Net Worth Deficit: £43,984 *Total Assets:* £80,124
Registered Office: Tayport Distillery, Unit 2 Shanwell Court Industrial Estate, Shanwell Road, Tayport, Fife, DD6 9DX
Officers: Kecia McDougall [1965] Director/Nurse Practitioner [American]

TBD Tipples Ltd
Incorporated: 28 December 2018
Registered Office: 34 Nelson Close, Harleston, Norfolk, IP20 9HL
Major Shareholder: Daniel William Curtis
Officers: Daniel William Curtis [1976] Director

TCBP Holdings Limited
Incorporated: 21 February 2018
Registered Office: 12-15 Donegall Square West, Belfast, BT1 6JH
Major Shareholder: Raymond McLaughlin
Officers: Raymond McLaughlin [1980] Director [Irish]

Tea Rocks Ltd
Incorporated: 14 June 2017
Registered Office: 18 Westerham Road, Keston, Kent, BR2 6HU
Major Shareholder: Victoria Hewlett
Officers: Victoria Hewlett [1973] Director

Tea Venture Limited
Incorporated: 22 January 2016
Net Worth: £110,392 *Total Assets:* £197,442
Registered Office: Alderman Fenwick's House, 98-100 Pilgrim Street, Newcastle upon Tyne, NE1 6SQ
Shareholders: Lukas Passia; Vincent Efferoth
Officers: Alan John Balfour [1957] Director; Vincent Efferoth [1991] Director [German]; Lukas Passia [1990] Director [German]

The Teasmith Spirit Company Limited
Incorporated: 7 July 2016
Net Worth Deficit: £12,963 *Total Assets:* £25,574
Registered Office: 4 New Craig Court, Udny, Ellon, Aberdeenshire, AB41 6QD
Shareholders: Emma Smalley; Nicholas Geoffrey Smalley
Officers: Nicholas Geoffrey Smalley [1983] Director

Telser & Pauli Ltd
Incorporated: 28 March 2017
Registered Office: Carpenter Court, 1 Maple Road, Bramhall, Stockport, Cheshire, SK7 2DH
Shareholders: Marcel Telser; Arno Pauli
Officers: Marcel Telser [1971] Director [Liechtensteiner]

Tempus Gin Limited
Incorporated: 31 January 2017
Registered Office: 422 51 Pinfold Street, Birmingham, B2 4AY
Major Shareholder: Alex Siekierski
Officers: Alex Siekierski [1976] Director

Ten Bears Spirits Limited
Incorporated: 12 May 2011 *Employees:* 2
Net Worth Deficit: £104,357 *Total Assets:* £7,471
Registered Office: Elmwood House, Black Bourton, Oxon, OX18 2PL
Shareholders: Rupert Hart; Edward Stewart-Wood
Officers: Rupert Anthony Clive Hart [1981] Director; Edward John Henry Stewart-Wood [1982] Director

Terrepure Spirits UK Ltd.
Incorporated: 21 June 2012
Net Worth Deficit: £831,008 *Total Assets:* £757
Registered Office: c/o BCS, Windsor House, Station Court, Station Road, Great Shelford, Cambridge, CB22 5NE
Officers: Earl D. Hewlette [1946] Director/Business Executive [American]

Tewkesbury Distillery Ltd
Incorporated: 22 August 2017
Registered Office: No 1 Twyning Cottages, Twyning Green, Twyning, Tewkesbury, Glos, GL20 6DF
Shareholders: Mariane Hodgkinson; Christopher Thomas Hodgkinson
Officers: Mariane Hodgkinson [1982] Director/Owner [German]

Thames Distillers Limited
Incorporated: 6 December 1996 *Employees:* 17
Net Worth Deficit: £896,208 *Total Assets:* £1,204,068
Registered Office: A E Chapman and Son Ltd, Timbermill Way, Gauden Road, London, SW4 6LY
Shareholder: A E Chapman & Son Ltd
Officers: Wellwood George Charles Maxwell, Secretary; Anthony Edward Chapman [1938] Director/Company Chairman; Christopher Frank Hayman [1947] Director; Ian Victor Lockwood [1942] Director; Wellwood George Charles Maxwell [1952] Director/Distiller

J.G. Thomson & Co. Limited
Incorporated: 21 April 2017
Registered Office: The Vaults, 87 Giles Street, Edinburgh, EH6 6BZ
Parent: The Artisanal Spirits Company Limited
Officers: William Alexander Bremner [1973] Director; Kai Ivalo [1965] Director; David John Ridley [1969] Director [Australian]

The Three Graces Distillery Ltd
Incorporated: 17 August 2018
Registered Office: 43 Villiers Street, Leamington Spa, Warwicks, CV32 5YA
Major Shareholder: Thomas Gaston
Officers: Thomas Gaston [1993] Director

The Three Stills Company Limited
Incorporated: 13 March 2013 *Employees:* 6
Net Worth: £696,926 *Total Assets:* £9,540,301
Registered Office: The Borders Distillery, Commercial Road, Hawick, Roxburghshire, TD9 7AQ
Officers: Janine Watson, Secretary; Michael Frank Beamish [1957] Director; Timothy Ado Carton [1959] Director/International Drinks Industry Executive [Irish]; Pierre Dharcourt [1958] Director [French]; Laurence John Fordyce [1962] Director/Project Consultant; John Ronald Kerr Glen [1959] Director; Malcolm Ian Offord [1964] Director; Anthony Brian Roberts [1965] International Commercial Director

Three Wrens Gin Limited
Incorporated: 6 February 2019
Registered Office: The Old Coach House, Cholmondeley Castle Gardens, Cholmondeley, Cheshire, SY14 8AH
Major Shareholder: Nicholas Wadeson
Officers: Nick Wadeson [1979] Director

Tickle Drinks Limited
Incorporated: 13 February 2018
Registered Office: Unit B1, Kembrey Street, Elgin Industrial Estate, Swindon, Wilts, SN2 8UY
Shareholders: Adam Marc Woodley; Tamara Southworth
Officers: Tamara Southworth [1990] Director/Product Developer; Adam Marc Woodley [1990] Director

The Tiny Tipple Company Limited
Incorporated: 30 November 2017 *Employees:* 2
Net Worth: £663 *Total Assets:* £42,939
Registered Office: Lothing House, Quay View Business Park, Lowestoft, Suffolk, NR32 2HD
Shareholders: Karen Rees; Amanda Elisabeth Williams
Officers: Karen Rees, Secretary; Karen Rees [1973] Director; Amanda Elisabeth Williams [1972] Director

Tipo Loco Drinks Co. Limited
Incorporated: 26 January 2018
Registered Office: Bishop's Court, 29 Albyn Place, Aberdeen, AB10 1YL
Major Shareholder: Michael Alexander Ballantyne
Officers: Karina Lianne Jayne Ballantyne [1985] Director; Michael Alexander Ballantyne [1983] Director

Tippling Tonic Limited
Incorporated: 6 August 2018
Registered Office: Acre House, 11-15 William Road, London, NW1 3ER
Shareholders: Richard Joseph Hargroves; Suman Mitra
Officers: Richard Joseph Hargroves [1968] Director; Suman Mitra [1975] Director/Hotelier and Restaurateur

Tipsy Fruit Gins Limited
Incorporated: 18 March 2004
Net Worth: £16,513 *Total Assets:* £84,087
Registered Office: Tipsage Farm, Newnham Bridge, Tenbury Wells, Worcs, WR15 8NU
Shareholders: Michelle Jane Kruger; Douw Gerband Kruger
Officers: Colin Timothy Hingston, Secretary; Colin Timothy Hingston [1949] Director/Compounder; Douw Gerband Kruger [1970] Director/Harvest Manager; Michelle Jane Kruger [1972] Director/Compounder

Tipsy Wight Ltd
Incorporated: 8 February 2013
Net Worth Deficit: £47,641 *Total Assets:* £48,064
Registered Office: Medham Farm, Medham Farm Lane, Cowes, Isle of Wight, PO31 8PH
Shareholder: Michael Peter Green
Officers: Michael Peter Green [1959] Director/Farmer; Ruth Green [1968] Director/Manufacturer

Titanic Distillers Limited
Incorporated: 17 August 2018
Registered Office: 43 Waring Street, Belfast, BT1 2DY
Officers: Richard Stephen Irwin [1973] Director; Stephen Brian Symington [1980] Director

Titanic Gin Ltd
Incorporated: 9 February 2018
Registered Office: 8 Station Road, Holywood, Co Down, BT18 0BP
Shareholder: Peter Martin Lavery
Officers: Peter Martin Lavery [1961] Director [Irish]

Titanic Vodka Ltd
Incorporated: 9 February 2018
Registered Office: 8 Station Road, Holywood, Co Down, BT18 0BP
Shareholder: Peter Martin Lavery
Officers: Peter Martin Lavery [1961] Director [Irish]

Tivoli's Gin Limited
Incorporated: 29 February 2016
Registered Office: The Chancel, Ruardean Woodside, Ruardean, Glos, GL17 9YL
Major Shareholder: Sarah Gordon-Jones
Officers: Sarah Gordon-Jones [1974] Director

Todka Limited
Incorporated: 5 October 2005 *Employees:* 3
Net Worth Deficit: £884 *Total Assets:* £77,324
Registered Office: Bryndon House, 5-7 Berry Road, Newquay, Cornwall, TR7 1AD
Major Shareholder: Frederick Hart
Officers: Nino Alexander Colombo, Secretary; Nino Alexander Colombo [1968] Director/Drink Manufacturer; Frederick Hart [1955] Director/Self Employed; Carole Lesley Phillips [1964] Director/Self Employed

Tolsta Europe Ltd
Incorporated: 4 May 2018
Registered Office: 17 Racecourse Business Park, 69 Bothwell Road, Hamilton, S Lanarks, ML3 0DW
Officers: John McAulay [1951] Director

Tomatin Distillery Company Limited,(The)
Incorporated: 1 November 1985 *Employees:* 56
Net Worth: £30,677,420 *Total Assets:* £43,479,584
Registered Office: Tomatin, Inverness-shire, IV13 7YT
Parent: Takara Holdings Inc.
Officers: Catherine Anne Davis, Secretary; Robert William Anderson [1953] Director/Executive; Stephen Bremner [1976] Director/Executive; Satoshi Higashino [1962] Director/Executive [Japanese]; Hiroyuki Ito [1965] Director [Japanese]; Kazuyoshi Ito [1961] Director/Chief General Manager [Japanese]; Mutsumi Kimura [1963] Director/Executive [Japanese]; Minori Mori [1962] Director/Executive [Japanese]; Masumi Uetsuji [1963] Director/Executive [Japanese]; Toshiya Yamaoka [1971] Director/Executive [Japanese]

Topsham Gin Ltd
Incorporated: 22 October 2018
Registered Office: The Old Stables, Countess Wear Road, Exeter, Devon, EX2 6LR
Major Shareholder: Joanna Partridge Eveleigh
Officers: Joanna Partridge Eveleigh [1972] Director/Distiller

Torabhaig Distillery Limited
Incorporated: 28 August 2013 *Employees:* 8
Net Worth: £843,998 *Total Assets:* £2,183,058
Registered Office: Mossburn House, Camptown, Jedburgh, Roxburghshire, TD8 6PJ
Parent: Mossburn Distillers Ltd
Officers: John Neil MacLeod Mathieson, Secretary; Francesco Annibali [1966] Director [Italian]; John Neil MacLeod Mathieson [1961] Director/Line Shipper; Lady Lucilla Charlotte James Noble [1959] Director; Dr Alan Gray Rutherford [1942] Director

Tors Vodka Limited
Incorporated: 11 May 2015
Net Worth Deficit: £7,128 *Total Assets:* £17,640
Registered Office: Pretoria Vaults, 2nd Floor, 22 North Street, Okehampton, Devon, EX20 1AR
Shareholders: Edward James Stanley Baily; Jonathan William Bright
Officers: Edward James Stanley Baily [1983] Director/Vodka Production; Jonathan William Bright [1982] Director/Vodka Production

Touch Lucky Limited
Incorporated: 5 March 2018
Registered Office: 2 Gidlow Avenue, Wigan, Lancs, WN6 7PF
Major Shareholder: John Rotherham
Officers: John Rotherham [1959] Director

Toulvaddie Distillery Limited
Incorporated: 30 November 2015
Net Worth Deficit: £21,290 *Total Assets:* £3,765
Registered Office: 21 Cromartie Gardens, Tain, Ross-shire, IV19 1BY
Major Shareholder: Heather Nelson
Officers: Heather Nelson [1979] Director/Manager

Towiemore Distillery and Warehousing Limited
Incorporated: 26 April 2017
Registered Office: Parkmore Distillery, Managers House, Dufftown, Keith, Moray, AB55 4DL
Major Shareholder: Edward Odim
Officers: Edward Odim [1958] Director

Tready's Ltd
Incorporated: 9 October 2018
Registered Office: Kemp House, 160 City Road, London, EC1V 2NX
Shareholder: Sean Treadwell
Officers: Deborah Treadwell, Secretary; Sean Treadwell [1966] Director/Engineer

Treganna Gin Ltd
Incorporated: 19 October 2018
Registered Office: 26 Birchfield Crescent, Canton, Cardiff, CF5 1AE
Major Shareholder: Mark Robert Flanagan
Officers: Mark Robert Flanagan [1983] Director/Entrepreneur

Tres Amigos Limited
Incorporated: 19 December 2017
Registered Office: Flat 65, 216 Kennington Road, London, SE11 6HR
Shareholder: Edward Salmon
Officers: Rafael Cortazzo de Lima [1985] Director/Manager [Brazilian]; Ajay Dhokia [1984] Director/Manager; Edward Salmon [1987] Director/Manager

Tres Bombarderos Gin Limited
Incorporated: 3 January 2018
Registered Office: 59 Bonnygate, Cupar, Fife, KY15 4BY
Major Shareholder: Giorgio Cozzolino Cozzolino
Officers: Giorgio Cozzolino Cozzolino [1964] Director [Italian]

Trevethan Distillery Ltd
Incorporated: 21 November 2013
Net Worth Deficit: £39,989 *Total Assets:* £96,234
Registered Office: Unit 20a Prideaux Close, Tamar View Industrial Estate, Saltash, Cornwall, PL12 6LD
Major Shareholder: Robert John Cuffe
Officers: Jane Kathryn Cuffe [1959] Director/Administrator; Robert John Cuffe [1960] Director/Project Manager

The UK Spirits Industry   dellam

Tricort Limited
Incorporated: 14 November 1988
Net Worth Deficit: £871 *Total Assets:* £1,778
Registered Office: South Manor, High Road, Chipstead, Surrey, CR5 3SD
Major Shareholder: Christopher Frank Hayman
Officers: Christopher Frank Hayman [1947] Director

Trossachs Distillery Limited
Incorporated: 28 July 2015 *Employees:* 8
Net Worth: £202,625 *Total Assets:* £560,727
Registered Office: 44 Robertson Way, Callander, Perthshire, FK17 8JF
Shareholders: Dale McQueen; Veronica McQueen
Officers: Veronica McQueen, Secretary; Dale McQueen [1957] Managing Director

True North Brew Co Limited
Incorporated: 9 July 2002 *Employees:* 305
Previous: Forum Cafe Bars Limited
Net Worth: £2,182,204 *Total Assets:* £5,119,779
Registered Office: 13-17 Paradise Square, Sheffield, S1 2DE
Major Shareholder: Kane Steven Yeardley
Officers: Sean Francis Kelly, Finance Director; Sean Francis Kelly [1982] Finance Director; Alex David Liddle [1976] Operations Director; Kane Steven Yeardley [1961] Director

Tubeoptics. Ltd
Incorporated: 31 January 2019
Registered Office: 2nd Floor, College House, 17 King Edwards Road, Ruislip, Middlesex, HA4 7AE
Major Shareholder: Sasha Nekic
Officers: Sasha Nekic [1967] Director

Tudor Court Distillers Limited
Incorporated: 22 February 2018
Registered Office: Tudor Court, Saleway, Droitwich, Worcs, WR9 7JY
Shareholder: Peter Anthony Jewell
Officers: Peter Anthony Jewell [1949] Director

Tuerto Tequila Ltd
Incorporated: 16 July 2018
Registered Office: Flat 2, 134 Valley Drive, Harrogate, N Yorks, HG2 0JS
Shareholders: Matthew Leonard Edgar; Nathan Prail
Officers: Matthew Leonard Edgar [1984] Director; Nathan Prail [1991] Director

Tullibardine Limited
Incorporated: 15 August 2000 *Employees:* 30
Net Worth: £15,427,899 *Total Assets:* £42,996,404
Registered Office: Citypoint, 65 Haymarket Terrace, Edinburgh, EH12 5HD
Major Shareholder: Michel Bernard Picard
Officers: Gabriel Jacques Picard [1970] Director [French]; Michel Bernard Picard [1942] Director [French]

Turncoat Distillery Limited
Incorporated: 9 December 2017
Registered Office: c/o Jon Davies Accountants Ltd, Business First Business Centre, 23 Goodlass Road, Liverpool, L24 9HJ
Major Shareholder: Terence Francis Langton
Officers: Terence Francis Langton [1976] Director

Tweed Valley Distilling Company Ltd
Incorporated: 10 April 2018
Registered Office: 6 Caley Cottages, Caledonian Road, Peebles, EH45 9DW
Major Shareholder: Ben Glasgow
Officers: Ben Glasgow [1980] Director

Twenty Oaks, Ltd
Incorporated: 7 August 2017
Registered Office: Eversheds House, 70 Great Bridgewater Street, Manchester, M1 5ES
Major Shareholder: Sarit Perry
Officers: Sarit Perry [1978] Director [American]

Twisted Gin Ltd
Incorporated: 20 December 2018
Registered Office: The Customs House, 9 Westbay, Bridport, Dorset, DT6 4EN
Major Shareholder: Stephen Blakesley
Officers: Stephen Blakesley [1951] Director/Retired

Twisted Melon Scotland Limited
Incorporated: 3 May 2018
Registered Office: Skippers Rest, Denside, Gardenstown, Banff, Aberdeenshire, AB45 3ZS
Officers: John Cochrane [1974] Director/Lone Working Specialist; Scott James McIntyre [1974] Director/Manager

Twisted Roots Distillery Ltd
Incorporated: 11 August 2016
Registered Office: Twisted Roots, Stone Pit Wood, Easton Road, Bridlington, E Yorks, YO16 4XF
Officers: Piers Moat, Secretary; Piers Moat [1984] Director/Joiner

Twisting Spirits Ltd
Incorporated: 19 January 2016 *Employees:* 2
Net Worth Deficit: £24,173 *Total Assets:* £45,546
Registered Office: High House, Church Lane, Norton, Gloucester, GL2 9LS
Shareholders: Mary Ann Bateman; Richard Paul Bateman
Officers: Mary Ann Bateman, Secretary; Mary Ann Bateman [1978] Director; Richard Paul Bateman [1973] Director

Two Drifters Distillery Ltd
Incorporated: 11 May 2018
Registered Office: Courtfield, Old Ebford Lane, Ebford, Exeter, EX3 0QB
Officers: Gemma Clare Wakeham [1982] Director/Social Media Manager; Dr Russell Jon Wakeham [1983] Director/Scientist

Two Fathoms Distillery Ltd.
Incorporated: 17 November 2017
Registered Office: Hollytree House, Croquet Gardens, Wivenhoe, Colchester, Essex, CO7 9PQ
Officers: Godwin Girth Baron [1962] Director/Distillery Founder

U'Luvka Ltd
Incorporated: 9 January 2013 *Employees:* 3
Net Worth Deficit: £1,319,013 *Total Assets:* £1,679,686
Registered Office: 3a Berghem Mews, Blythe Road, London, W14 0HN
Shareholder: Sunil Laxman Singh Ramsinghani
Officers: Sudhir Vrajlal Dewji [1957] Director/Consultant; Jitendra Gandhi [1952] Director/Business Executive [Canadian]; Maheshchandra Khemka [1954] Director/Accountant [Indian]; Puthiyapurayil Mohandas [1944] Director/Business Executive [Indian]; Ramesh Kumar Rochiram Narang [1949] Director/Commercial Manager [Indian]; Rajesh Laxman Singh Ramsinghani [1960] Director/Business Executive [Indian]; Sunil Laxman Singh Ramsinghani [1964] Executive Director [Indian]

UK Distillers Limited
Incorporated: 21 February 2017
Registered Office: Towngate House, 2-8 Parkstone Road, Poole, Dorset, BH15 2PW
Officers: Paul Comiskey [1974] Director; Andrew Goord [1959] Director; Stephen Harry Stokes [1959] Director; Matthew Mansell Walker [1972] Director; Gary Owen Weldon [1970] Director

UK Dorset Ltd
Incorporated: 5 May 2017
Registered Office: 71-75 Shelton Street, Covent Garden, London, WC2H 9JQ
Major Shareholder: Saidabror Gulyamov
Officers: Shamagdiev Abdurasul [1987] Director [Uzbek]

UK McLouis Liquor Company Limited
Incorporated: 5 February 2018
Registered Office: Kemp House, 152-160 City Road, London, EC1V 2NX
Major Shareholder: Clariephine Almoguerra Angeles
Officers: Clariephine Almoguerra Angeles [1981] Director [Filipino]

Ulster Distilleries Limited
Incorporated: 29 January 2002
Net Worth Deficit: £26,568 *Total Assets:* £337,801
Registered Office: 3 Lough Shore Road, Portaferry, Newtownards, Co Down, BT22 1PD
Shareholder: John Young
Officers: Laura Young, Secretary; Dr John Young [1964] Director/Solicitor

Ulverston Gin Limited
Incorporated: 18 August 2017
Registered Office: 50 Soutergate, Ulverston, Cumbria, LA12 7ES
Major Shareholder: John McKeown
Officers: John McKeown [1967] Director/Distiller

Uncle Nearest Ltd.
Incorporated: 15 February 2018
Registered Office: Suite 106, 268 Belsize Road, London, NW6 4BT
Parent: Uncle Nearest, Inc.
Officers: Dominique Nichole Johnson [1984] Director/Business Executive [American]; Fawn Weaver [1976] Director/Owner/CEO [American]

Unconventional Distillery Co. Ltd
Incorporated: 20 November 2018
Registered Office: 8 Whisby Way, Lincoln, LN6 3LQ
Major Shareholder: Samuel James Owen
Officers: Samuel James Owen [1988] Managing Director

Undaunted Limited
Incorporated: 22 January 2018
Registered Office: 6 Atholl Crescent, Perth, PH1 5JN
Major Shareholder: David John Philip England
Officers: David John Philip England [1970] Director; Pia Margareta England [1976] Director [Swedish]

The Underground Brewing Company Ltd
Incorporated: 22 January 2016
Registered Office: 4 Chartfield House, Castle Street, Taunton, Somerset, TA1 4AS
Major Shareholder: Jeremy Robert Ham
Officers: Jeremy Robert Ham [1967] Director

Union Distillers Ltd
Incorporated: 23 February 2012 *Employees:* 10
Net Worth: £95,535 *Total Assets:* £378,551
Registered Office: E7 Welland Business Park, Valley Way, Market Harborough, Leics, LE16 7PS
Shareholders: Mark Maurice Gamble; Lynda Taylor
Officers: Lynda Taylor, Secretary; Mark Maurice Gamble [1952] Director; Lynda Taylor [1966] Director

Unit Thirteen Limited
Incorporated: 14 September 2017
Registered Office: Unit 12 The Talina Centre, Bagleys Lane, London, SW6 2BW
Shareholders: Charles Monkton Lockhart Smith; Simon John Weston
Officers: Charles Monkton Lockhart Smith, Secretary; Charles Monkton Lockhart Smith [1965] Director; Simon John Weston [1976] Director

United Distillers UK Limited
Incorporated: 18 December 1991
Previous: United Distillers UK PLC
Registered Office: Edinburgh Park, 5 Lochside Way, Edinburgh, EH12 9DT
Parent: Diageo Scotland Limited
Officers: James Matthew Crayden Edmunds, Secretary; James Matthew Crayden Edmunds [1974] Director/Solicitor; Gabor Kovacs [1980] Director [Hungarian]; Kara Elizabeth Major [1977] Director [American]

Universal Robo Innovations Limited
Incorporated: 24 May 2018
Registered Office: 71-75 Shelton Street, London, WC2H 9JQ
Officers: Ankit Mehta [1981] Director [Indian]

Unthank Distillery Limited
Incorporated: 20 July 2018
Registered Office: 14 Essex Street, Norwich, NR2 2BL
Major Shareholder: Adam Peter Knights
Officers: Adam Peter Knights [1972] Director

Urban Vodka Limited
Incorporated: 7 August 2018
Registered Office: Glebe Farm, Lutterworth Road, Blaby, Leicester, LE8 4DP
Officers: Graham Peter Veitch [1968] Director

Ursus Americanus Limited
Incorporated: 19 September 2017
Registered Office: 2 Victoria Grove, Bridport, Dorset, DT6 3AA
Major Shareholder: Christopher Thayer
Officers: Lloyd Brown [1988] Director/Bar Consultant

V K Brands Limited
Incorporated: 24 February 2006
Registered Office: 5th Floor, Casa, Lockoford Lane, Chesterfield, Derbys, S41 7JB
Officers: Shaun Bacon, Secretary/Accountant; Shaun Bacon [1965] Director/Accountant; Steven James Garcia Perez [1956] Director; Mark Peter James [1971] Director

V7 Enterprises Ltd
Incorporated: 1 June 2010
Net Worth: £8,465 *Total Assets:* £13,309
Registered Office: 8 Clarendon House, Clayton Street West, Newcastle upon Tyne, NE1 5EE
Major Shareholder: Michelle Dawn McKenzie
Officers: Michelle Dawn McKenzie [1972] Director/Administrator

Valt Vodka Company Limited
Incorporated: 8 August 2013
Registered Office: 21 Forbes Place, Paisley, Renfrewshire, PA1 1UT
Shareholder: Roderick George Christie
Officers: Roderick Christie, Secretary; Roderick George Christie [1952] Director/Distiller

Vape Pure Ltd
Incorporated: 12 November 2018
Registered Office: 97 Fairfax Road, London, N8 0NJ
Major Shareholder: Colin Paul July
Officers: Colin Paul July [1964] Director/Civil Servant

Verdant Spirits Ltd.
Incorporated: 30 September 2014 *Employees:* 2
Net Worth Deficit: £112,257 *Total Assets:* £160,755
Registered Office: Old Kirkton House, Coupar Angus Road, Newtyle, Blairgowrie, Perthshire, PH12 8TP
Major Shareholder: Andrew Campbell MacKenzie
Officers: Andrew Campbell MacKenzie [1953] Director

Verset Vodka Holdings Limited
Incorporated: 3 January 2018
Registered Office: 117 Culpepper Close, London, N18 2DT
Major Shareholder: Aldo Chiappetta
Officers: Aldo Chiappetta [1980] Director; Simon Willis [1983] Director

Vijobar Ltd
Incorporated: 1 May 2018
Registered Office: 12 Times Court, Retreat Road, Richmond, Surrey, TW9 1AF
Shareholders: Victor Barbara Lanson; Jonathan Eric Dashfield Pusey; Barbara Joyce Spurrier
Officers: Victor Barbara Lanson [1966] Director/Wine & Spirit Consultant [French]; Jonathan Eric Dashfield Pusey [1958] Director; Barbara Joyce Spurrier [1955] Director

The Village Spirit Collective Ltd
Incorporated: 16 July 2018
Registered Office: Blackberry House, New Road, Wormley, Surrey, GU8 5SU
Major Shareholder: Ian Taylor Cox
Officers: Ian Taylor Cox [1967] Director

Vonlevers Limited
Incorporated: 13 June 2018
Registered Office: 60 Court Hill, South Croydon, Surrey, CR2 9NA
Officers: Andrew Evers [1972] Director/Financial Services Manager; Lorna Levin [1975] Director/Project Manager [South African]

VS Distillers Limited
Incorporated: 26 May 2016 *Employees:* 1
Net Worth: £1,264 *Total Assets:* £128,277
Registered Office: Lamb Holm, Orkney, KW17 2SF
Shareholders: Collin Van Schayk; Emile Leonardus Josephus Maria Van Schayk
Officers: Collin Van Schayk [1989] Director [Dutch]; Emile Leonardus Josephus Maria Van Schayk [1958] Director [Dutch]

W & S Distillery Limited
Incorporated: 11 April 2011
Net Worth Deficit: £185,567 *Total Assets:* £791,180
Registered Office: 1st Floor, Sackville House, 143-149 Fenchurch Street, London, EC3M 6BL
Shareholders: Ivor Omson; Oleksandr Nevzorov
Officers: Philip Edward Colgan [1951] Director/Manager

Wallhouse Distillery Limited
Incorporated: 28 January 2019
Registered Office: Wallhouse Farm, Torphichen, Bathgate, W Lothian, EH48 4NQ
Major Shareholder: Lorna Anne Ritchie
Officers: Lorna Anne Ritchie [1976] Director/Distiller

Wally Wonka Ltd
Incorporated: 7 August 2018
Registered Office: Mains of Drummond Farm, Crieff, Perthshire, PH7 4JA
Shareholders: Russell Wallace; Leanne Wallace
Officers: Leanne Wallace [1982] Director/Owner; Russell Wallace [1981] Director/Distiller

Warner's Distillery Limited
Incorporated: 17 May 2012 *Employees:* 21
Previous: Warner Edwards Distillery Limited
Net Worth: £1,693,071 *Total Assets:* £4,156,981
Registered Office: The Distillery, Falls Farm, Harrington, Northampton, NN6 9NU
Shareholders: Christina Keogh; Tom Warner
Officers: Christina Keogh [1983] Director [Irish]; Tom Warner [1978] Director

The Warwickshire Gin Company Limited
Incorporated: 5 October 2018
Registered Office: 1 George Street, Wolverhampton, W Midlands, WV2 4DG
Major Shareholder: David Peter Blick
Officers: David Peter Blick [1973] Director; Helena Harpham [1975] Director

Warwickshire Spirits Limited
Incorporated: 11 January 2018
Registered Office: 19 Griffin Lane, Shirley, Solihull, Warwicks, B90 1TS
Major Shareholder: Richard Townsend
Officers: Richard Townsend [1984] Director

Waters of Deugh Limited
Incorporated: 6 February 2018
Registered Office: 17b King Street, Castle Douglas, Dumfries & Galloway, DG7 1AA
Officers: Belinda Jane Hilton [1969] Director/Designer; Darren Thomas Hilton [1968] Director/IT Consultant; Attica Wheeler [1976] Director/Midwife; Martyn Gary Wheeler [1959] Director/Accountant

Wave'n Ltd
Incorporated: 29 January 2019
Registered Office: 17a Beechfield Road, London, SE6 4NG
Major Shareholder: Nathan Francis
Officers: Nathan Francis [1983] Director/Mixologist

Waveney Valley Spirits Limited
Incorporated: 21 July 2014
Net Worth Deficit: £4,772 *Total Assets:* £9,730
Registered Office: The Barn, South Farm, Tunbeck Road, Alburgh, Harleston, Norfolk, IP20 0BS
Major Shareholder: Janet May Peachey
Officers: Janet May Peachey [1964] Director/Drink Manufacturer

Wayfinder Distillery Limited
Incorporated: 25 April 2018
Registered Office: 5 Technology Park, Colindeep Lane, Colindale, London, NW9 6BX
Shareholders: Laurie Othen; Samantha Othen
Officers: Laurie Othen [1980] Director; Samantha Othen [1981] Director

Weatheralls Distillery Limited
Incorporated: 19 October 2017
Registered Office: 4 Welland Court, Brockeridge Park, Twyning, Tewkesbury, Glos, GL20 6FD
Major Shareholder: Nicholas Mark Weatherall
Officers: Nicholas Mark Weatherall [1974] Director

Wee Beastie Ltd.
Incorporated: 28 December 1994
Registered Office: Moffat Distillery, Airdrie, N Lanarks, ML6 8PL
Shareholders: Charoen Sirivadhanabhakdi; Khunying Wanna Sirivadhanabhakdi
Officers: Roger Hall [1967] Director/Chief Financial Officer; Dr Martin John Leonard [1961] Managing Director; Nial James MacKinlay [1962] UK Sales Director; Prapakon Thongtheppairot [1971] Director [Thai]

Wee Hemp Spirits Ltd
Incorporated: 19 December 2018
Registered Office: 3 Eday Road, Aberdeen, AB15 6JH
Shareholder: Calum James Napier
Officers: Calum James Napier [1984] Director; Rebecca Grace Napier [1983] Director

Wells Gin Limited
Incorporated: 29 March 2018
Registered Office: Russell Flooring Co, 11 Water Lane, Halifax, W Yorks, HX3 9HG
Officers: Jason Richard Sutcliffe, Secretary; Jason Richard Sutcliffe [1971] Director

The Welsh Whisky Company Limited
Incorporated: 24 August 1998 *Employees:* 56
Net Worth: £5,397,234 *Total Assets:* £12,221,553
Registered Office: Penderyn Distillery, Penderyn, Rhondda Cynon Taf, CF44 0SX
Major Shareholder: Nigel Vernon Short
Officers: Huw Thomas, Secretary; Neil Harper Burchell [1958] Director; Stephen Robert Davies [1964] Director; Roy Noble [1942] Director; Martin Stuart Reed [1960] Finance Director; Nigel Vernon Short [1962] Director; Huw Thomas [1967] Director/Chartered Accountant; Glenn Gifford Tutssel [1951] Director; Sian Whitelock [1971] Director

Wemyss Distillery Limited
Incorporated: 26 November 2012
Net Worth Deficit: £30,000 *Total Assets:* £8,179,615
Registered Office: 4 Melville Crescent, Edinburgh, EH3 7JA
Shareholder: William John Wemyss
Officers: William John Wemyss [1970] Director

Wessex Distillery Limited
Incorporated: 4 September 2017
Registered Office: 4th Floor, Imperial House, 8 Kean Street, London, WC2B 4AS
Shareholders: Halewood International Limited; Jonathan James Clark
Officers: Jonathan James Clark [1956] Director; Stewart Andrew Hainsworth [1969] Director

West Highland Distillers Limited
Incorporated: 21 February 2019
Registered Office: Dean Bank Lodge, 10 Dean Bank Lane, Edinburgh, EH3 5BS
Major Shareholder: Seamus Earraghaidheal O'Baoighill
Officers: Seamus Earraghaidheal O'Baoighill [1997] Director

West Midlands Distillery Limited
Incorporated: 1 February 2019
Registered Office: 24 Bryan Budd Close, Rowley Regis, W Midlands, B65 9BB
Officers: Jordan Lunn [1985] Director

West Spirits MCR Ltd
Incorporated: 18 October 2018
Registered Office: 4 The Birchin, Joiner Street, Manchester, M4 1PH
Officers: Samuel Paul Crick [1996] Director/Barman

Westmorland Spirits Limited
Incorporated: 7 January 2010 *Employees:* 1
Net Worth: £117,818 *Total Assets:* £144,894
Registered Office: 73 Cornhill, London, EC3V 3QQ
Shareholder: Matthew Thomas Diarmuid Gilpin
Officers: Gary James Boom [1958] Managing Director [Dutch]; Hugo John Codrington [1964] Director/LLP Partner; Richard James Kirkham Ellis [1985] Director/Spirits Buyer; Matthew Thomas Diarmuid Gilpin [1969] Director; Cato Henning Stonex [1963] Director/Fund Manager; Kristina Lisa Valius-Gilpin [1968] Director [Lithuanian]

Weymouth and Portland Distillery Company Ltd
Incorporated: 23 May 2018
Registered Office: 31 St Johns Road, Wallingford, Oxon, OX10 9AW
Major Shareholder: Victoria Christiana Hamilton
Officers: Victoria Christiana Hamilton [1982] Marketing Director

Whisky and Cognac.Uk Limited
Incorporated: 15 June 2015
Net Worth Deficit: £20,653 *Total Assets:* £3,866
Registered Office: 4 Woodside Place, Glasgow, G3 7QF
Major Shareholder: Heinz Borchardt
Officers: Heinz Borchardt [1948] Director [German]

The Whisky Cellar Limited
Incorporated: 3 November 2016
Net Worth: £23,406 *Total Assets:* £43,998
Registered Office: 93 George Street, Edinburgh, EH2 3ES
Shareholder: Keith Bonnington
Officers: Keith Bonnington [1976] Director

The UK Spirits Industry

The Whisky Club Ltd
Incorporated: 5 August 2015
Net Worth: £1 *Total Assets:* £1
Registered Office: c/o Cloch Solicitors, 94 Hope Street, Glasgow, G2 6PH
Major Shareholder: Philip Adamson Hannay
Officers: Philip Adamson Hannay [1978] Director/Lawyer/Entrepreneur

Whisky Galore Limited
Incorporated: 15 January 2001
Registered Office: 28 Albyn Place, Aberdeen, AB10 1YL
Major Shareholder: Euan Coutts Shand
Officers: Euan Coutts Shand [1956] Director

The Whisky Works Ltd
Incorporated: 29 December 2017
Registered Office: 319 St Vincent Street, Glasgow, G2 5RG
Parent: Whyte and MacKay Limited
Officers: Bryan Harold Donaghey [1961] Director

Whiskymen Limited
Incorporated: 7 April 2018
Registered Office: Silent Pool Distillery, Shere Road, Albury, Guildford, Surrey, GU5 9BW
Parent: Spiritmen Limited
Officers: Steven Robert Kavanagh [1974] Director [Irish]; John Keeling [1962] Director; Ian Douglas McCulloch [1959] Director; James Clifford John Shelbourne [1964] Director

Whitby Distillery Limited
Incorporated: 29 September 2017
Registered Office: Flat 2, 1/2 Gray Street, Whitby, N Yorks, YO21 1EP
Shareholder: Luke William Pentith
Officers: Luke William Pentith [1988] Director/Engineer; Jessica Lucy Slater [1990] Director/PMO Manager

Whitby Gin Limited
Incorporated: 19 December 2016
Net Worth: £1 *Total Assets:* £1
Registered Office: Tudor Lodge, Coronation Avenue, Hinderwell, Saltburn-by-the-Sea, N Yorks, TS13 5HA
Major Shareholder: James Newton
Officers: James Newton [1993] Director/Student

The White House Distillery Limited
Incorporated: 17 August 2018
Registered Office: 14 Westgate, Otley, W Yorks, LS21 3AX
Major Shareholder: Nicholas Andrew Milton Jocelyn
Officers: Nicholas Andrew Milton Jocelyn [1967] Director

White House Gin Limited
Incorporated: 22 August 2018
Registered Office: 14 Westgate, Otley, W Yorks, LS21 3AX
Officers: Nicholas Andrew Milton Jocelyn [1967] Director

White Peak Distillery Limited
Incorporated: 1 April 2016
Net Worth Deficit: £179,370 *Total Assets:* £1,547,363
Registered Office: The Wire Works, Derwent Works, Matlock Road, Ambergate, Derbys, DE56 2HE
Parent: The Peak District Distilling Company Limited
Officers: Maxwell Lucas Vaughan [1969] Finance Director

White Smoke Distillery Ltd
Incorporated: 8 November 2017
Registered Office: Ilex, Ufford Place, Ufford, Woodbridge, Suffolk, IP13 6DR
Major Shareholder: Ben Bewley-Pope
Officers: Ben Bewley-Pope [1983] Director/Businessman

Whitetail Spirits Limited
Incorporated: 5 September 2016
Net Worth Deficit: £4,439 *Total Assets:* £42,150
Registered Office: Tiroran House, Tiroran, Isle of Mull, PA69 6ES
Officers: Katherine Louise MacKay [1962] Director/Hotelier; Laurence MacKay [1957] Director/Hotelier; Jamie Munro [1989] Director/Hotelier

Whitley Neill Limited
Incorporated: 6 May 2004 *Employees:* 1
Net Worth Deficit: £434,893 *Total Assets:* £11,612
Registered Office: The Gables, High Street, Chieveley, Newbury, Berks, RG20 8TE
Major Shareholder: John James Whitley Neill
Officers: Nicola Ann Neill, Secretary; John James Whitley Neill [1972] Director/Spirits Wholesaler

The Whitstable Distillery Ltd
Incorporated: 31 January 2019
Registered Office: The Old Neptune, Marine Terrace, Whitstable, Kent, CT5 1EJ
Shareholder: Justine Laura Setterfield
Officers: Michelle Claire Booth [1974] Director/Cafe Owner; Justine Laura Setterfield [1974] Director/Licensed Bar Staff; Darren Wilton [1970] Director/Licensed Victualler

Whittaker's Distillery Limited
Incorporated: 13 June 2018
Registered Office: Harewell House Farm, Harewell Lane, Dacre Banks, Harrogate, N Yorks, HG3 4HQ
Shareholders: Toby Sam Whittaker; Jane Suzanne Whittaker
Officers: Toby Sam Whittaker [1967] Director

Whyte and MacKay Limited
Incorporated: 20 January 1927 *Employees:* 432
Net Worth: £493,480,992 *Total Assets:* £619,561,024
Registered Office: 4th Floor, St Vincent Plaza, 319 St Vincent Street, Glasgow, G2 5RG
Parent: Whyte and MacKay Group Limited
Officers: Winston Sy Co [1958] Director [Filipino]; Juan Cortes [1973] Director/Economist [Spanish]; Jorge Domecq [1970] Managing Director [Spanish]; Bryan Harold Donaghey [1961] Director; Dr Andrew Chong Buan Lim Tan [1949] Director/Chairman [Filipino]

Wicked Wolf Limited
Incorporated: 30 April 2013
Registered Office: The Old Chapel, Brendon, Devon, EX35 6PT
Shareholder: Umesh Kumar Patel
Officers: Umesh Kumar Patel [1969] Director

Wight Spirits Ltd
Incorporated: 10 March 2015 *Employees:* 3
Net Worth: £35,942 *Total Assets:* £72,237
Registered Office: Rosemary Vineyard, Smallbrook Lane, Ryde, Isle of Wight, PO33 4BE
Major Shareholder: Elspeth Mary Gauntlett
Officers: Elspeth Mary Gauntlett [1966] Director/Self Employed

Wild and Spirited Limited
Incorporated: 10 February 2016
Registered Office: 10 Camerton Hill, Camerton, Bath, BA2 0PT
Major Shareholder: Graeme Stuart Mellis
Officers: Graeme Stuart Mellis [1961] Director

Wild Atlantic Distillery Ltd
Incorporated: 8 February 2019
Registered Office: 20 Trienamongan Road, Castlederg, Co Tyrone, BT81 7XF
Shareholders: Brian Robert Ash; James Nash
Officers: Brian Robert Ash [1972] Director/Engineer

Wild Foragin Ltd
Incorporated: 22 October 2018
Registered Office: Knapp Cottage, Bredwardine, Hereford, HR3 6BZ
Shareholders: Natalie Louise Evans; Jonathan Richard Evans
Officers: Jonathan Richard Evans [1979] Director; Natalie Louise Evans [1981] Director

Wild Thyme Spirits Limited
Incorporated: 17 August 2016 *Employees:* 2
Net Worth Deficit: £53,999 *Total Assets:* £70,226
Registered Office: Tigh Na Uruisg, Upper Kilchattan, Isle of Colonsay, Argyll & Bute, PA61 7YR
Major Shareholder: Eileen Jackson Geekie
Officers: Eileen Jackson Geekie, Secretary; Eileen Jackson Geekie [1962] Director

Willimott House Limited
Incorporated: 17 October 2011
Net Worth Deficit: £76,547 *Total Assets:* £29,010
Registered Office: First Floor, Unit 7 Waterside, Hamm Moor Lane, Addlestone, Surrey, KT15 2SN
Major Shareholder: Benjamin Koffi Vigno Agboli
Officers: Benjamin Koffi Vigno Agboli [1969] Director; Pamela Maud Phyllis Agboli [1979] Director

The Willow Tree Distilling Company Limited
Incorporated: 1 June 2016 *Employees:* 1
Net Worth Deficit: £11,945 *Total Assets:* £11,562
Registered Office: 11 Newport Drive, Alcester, Warwicks, B49 5BL
Major Shareholder: Mary Anne Vincent
Officers: Mary Anne Vincent, Secretary; Mary Anne Vincent [1966] Director/Distiller [Irish]

Wilmington Spirits Limited
Incorporated: 28 March 2018
Registered Office: The Lodge, The Green, Wilmington, E Sussex, BN26 5SP
Major Shareholder: Greg Meyer
Officers: Dr Greg Meyer [1958] Director [American]

Wilson & Morgan Limited
Incorporated: 24 June 2002
Registered Office: 19 Rutland Square, Edinburgh, EH1 2BB
Major Shareholder: Fabio Rossi
Officers: Fabio Rossi [1961] Managing Director [Italian]; Ernesto Serraglia [1958] Director/Chartered Accountant [Italian]

Wilson's Henley Gin Company Limited
Incorporated: 27 September 2017
Registered Office: 4th Floor, New Penderel House, 283-288 High Holborn, London, WC1V 7HP
Officers: David Charles Jenkins [1959] Director/Accountant

The Wimbledon Distillery Company Limited
Incorporated: 30 September 2014
Registered Office: Unit 8 Prince Georges Road, London, SW19 2PT
Major Shareholder: Mark Charles Gordon
Officers: Mark Charles Gordon [1968] Director/Entrepreneur

Winchester Distillery Limited
Incorporated: 2 March 2017
Registered Office: Fleming Court, Leigh Road, Eastleigh, Southampton, SO50 9PD
Major Shareholder: Stephen Paul Bowler
Officers: Stephen Paul Bowler [1971] Director/Entrepreneur

D & M Winchester Ltd.
Incorporated: 29 March 2004 *Employees:* 5
Net Worth: £1,456,924 *Total Assets:* £2,509,464
Registered Office: Coleburn House, Longmorn, Elgin, Moray, IV30 8SN
Shareholders: Dale Winchester; Mark Winchester
Officers: Dale Winchester, Secretary/Director; Dale Winchester [1960] Director; Mark Winchester [1966] Director

Windfall Wood Group Limited
Incorporated: 27 October 2009
Net Worth Deficit: £50,781 *Total Assets:* £10,361
Registered Office: Low Barn, Gwehelog, Usk, Monmouthshire, NP15 1HY
Officers: Sarah Thompson [1976] Director

WL Distillery Ltd
Incorporated: 24 January 2019
Registered Office: 27 Station Estate North, Murton, Seaham, Co Durham, SR7 9SJ
Major Shareholder: Scott Michael Wilson-Laing
Officers: Scott Michael Wilson-Laing [1986] Managing Director

Wolftown Distillery Limited
Incorporated: 5 October 2018
Registered Office: 50 Soutergate, Ulverston, Cumbria, LA12 7ES
Major Shareholder: John McKeown
Officers: John McKeown [1967] Director/Cameraman

Wood and Company Limited
Incorporated: 19 August 2002
Registered Office: Independence House, 84 Lower Mortlake Road, Richmond, Surrey, TW9 2HS
Parent: William Grant & Sons Management Limited
Officers: Gregory Justin Bargeton [1973] Director/Lawyer; Ewan John Henderson [1968] Director/Accountant

Wood Brothers Distilling Company Limited
Incorporated: 13 April 2017 *Employees:* 1
Net Worth Deficit: £15,218 *Total Assets:* £23,525
Registered Office: Elmwood House, Burford Road, Black Bourton, Oxford, OX18 2PL
Major Shareholder: Edward John Henry Stewart-Wood
Officers: Edward John Henry Stewart-Wood [1982] Director/Owner/Distiller

Woodlab Distillery Limited
Incorporated: 13 November 2017
Registered Office: 14 Lisgobban Road, Benburb, Dungannon, Co Tyrone, BT71 7PT
Major Shareholder: Ulrich Conrad Dyer
Officers: Fiona Mary Dyer [1966] Director; Dr Ulrich Conrad Dyer [1961] Managing Director

Wrekin Spirit Limited
Incorporated: 8 February 2018
Registered Office: Sydney House, Farm Sydney, Kynnersley, Telford, Salop, TF6 6EB
Major Shareholder: Isabel Udale-Moseley
Officers: Isabel Udale-Moseley [1968] Director

Y Cwmni Chwisgi Cymraeg Newydd Cyf
Incorporated: 4 January 2000
Registered Office: Penderyn Distillery, Pontpren, Penderyn, Aberdare, Mid Glamorgan, CF44 0SX
Officers: Huw Thomas, Secretary; Huw Thomas [1967] Director

Yarm Brewing and Distilling Co Ltd
Incorporated: 22 March 2018
Registered Office: 11 Sowerby Way, Durham Lane Industrial Park, Eaglescliffe, Stockton on Tees, Cleveland, TS16 0RB
Major Shareholder: Samantha Marsden
Officers: Samantha Marsden [1972] Director

Yarm Gin Ltd
Incorporated: 29 August 2017
Registered Office: Gin Without Borders Ltd, The Manor House (1707), West End, Sedgefield, Co Durham, TS21 2BW
Major Shareholder: Matthew Philip Wilson
Officers: Matthew Philip Wilson [1986] Director/Owner

The Yarm Spirits Company Ltd
Incorporated: 29 August 2017
Registered Office: Gin Without Borders Ltd, The Manor House (1707), West End, Sedgefield, Co Durham, TS21 2BW
Major Shareholder: Matthew Philip Wilson
Officers: Matthew Philip Wilson [1986] Director/Owner

YDC Ltd
Incorporated: 5 June 2015
Net Worth: £35,306 *Total Assets:* £38,467
Registered Office: Unit 11 The Vivars Industrial Centre, Vivars Way, Canal Road, Selby, N Yorks, YO8 8BE
Officers: Craig Law [1987] Director/Consultant

York Distillery Limited
Incorporated: 8 January 2019
Registered Office: Suite 146, 5 High Street, Maidenhead, Berks, SL6 1JN
Major Shareholder: Donald John Stewart
Officers: Donald John Stewart [1963] Director/Solicitor

York Gin Company Limited
Incorporated: 26 February 2016
Net Worth Deficit: £21,768 *Total Assets:* £37,024
Registered Office: 105 Bishopthorpe Road, York, YO23 1NY
Shareholders: Jonathan Farrow; Peter Bryan McNichol
Officers: Harry Cooke [1983] Director; Paul Anthony Crossman [1968] Director; Emma Jo Godivala [1971] Director; Peter Bryan McNichol [1972] Director

Yorkshine Spirit Limited
Incorporated: 14 November 2017
Registered Office: 22 Common Lane, Leeds, LS25 5BU
Officers: Campbell Carruth [1972] Director/Chartered Surveyor; Joe Dunning [1976] Director/Radiographer

The Yorkshire Distillery Company Limited
Incorporated: 24 July 2013
Registered Office: Highley Hall, Clifton, Brighouse, W Yorks, HD6 4HS
Major Shareholder: Jonathan Stanley Kershaw
Officers: Jonathan Stanley Kershaw [1963] Director/Drink Manufacturer

Yorkshire Gin Limited
Incorporated: 5 December 2018
Registered Office: 10-12 Commercial Street, Shipley, W Yorks, BD18 3SR
Major Shareholder: Joseph Philip Blencowe
Officers: Joseph Philip Blencowe [1967] Director

The Yorkshire Rum Company Limited
Incorporated: 12 January 2017
Registered Office: 2 Cherry Way, Nafferton, E Yorks, YO25 4PA
Shareholders: Jonathan Peter Morgan; Sian Morgan
Officers: Sian Morgan, Secretary; Jonathan Peter Morgan [1964] Director/Software Developer; Sian Morgan [1964] Director/Dispenser

The Yorkshire Whisky Company Limited
Incorporated: 23 July 2013
Registered Office: Highley Hall, Clifton, Brighouse, W Yorks, HD6 4HS
Major Shareholder: Jonathan Stanley Kershaw
Officers: Jonathan Stanley Kershaw [1963] Director/Drink Manufacturer

Your Buddy Mary Limited
Incorporated: 29 March 2016
Net Worth: £69 *Total Assets:* £6,460
Registered Office: 17 Picton Close, Salford, M3 6BE
Major Shareholder: Simon Burgess
Officers: Simon Burgess [1984] Director/Drinks Manufacturer

Zero Gravity Spirits Ltd
Incorporated: 8 October 2018
Registered Office: 70 Bank Road, Matlock, Derbys, DE4 3GL
Major Shareholder: Adrian Cole
Officers: Adrian Cole [1976] Director

Zero-Moo Ltd
Incorporated: 28 January 2019
Registered Office: 7 Amethyst Road, Christchurch, Dorset, BH23 3EA
Major Shareholder: Martin David Nicholls
Officers: Martin David Nicholls [1987] Director

Zymurgorium Ltd
Incorporated: 13 September 2016 *Employees:* 3
Net Worth: £447,149 *Total Assets:* £765,763
Registered Office: Unit B6, Fairhills Road, Irlam, Manchester, M44 6BA
Major Shareholder: Aaron Ross Darke
Officers: Aaron Ross Darke [1991] Distiller/Brewer Managing Director; Callum Thomas Darke [1989] Director/Operations/Accounts Manager

This page is intentionally left blank

Index of Directorships

Abarrategui Diez, Angel Ignacio
The Old Bushmills Distillery Co Ltd

Abdurasul, Shamagdiev
UK Dorset Ltd

Ablaza, Herminia
Madrise Ltd

Acebuche, Sherwin
Tarsier Spirit Ltd

Acks, Michael David
Morrison Glasgow Distillers Ltd

Adam, Piers Benedict
Mahiki Trading Limited

Adams, John Peter Anthony
Renegade Spirits Grenada Ltd

Adams, Steven Roy
Lucent Drinks Ltd

Addis, Mark Benjamin
Redrosesforme Limited

Adlam, Andrea Michelle
Lujo Distilling Co Ltd

Adlam, Jason Paul
Lujo Distilling Co Ltd

Adnams, Jonathan
Adnams PLC

Adriaenssen, Charles
Ncn'ean Distillery Limited

Adu-Gyamfi, Princess Serwah
Botan Grey Ltd

Agboli, Benjamin Koffi Vigno
Willimott House Limited

Agboli, Pamela Maud Phyllis
Willimott House Limited

Agodzo, Emily Ann Aku Fafa
Great Don Ltd

Aikens, Adina Simone
Jackson's Gin Ltd

Aird, Samuel Livingstone
The Bootleg Club Limited

Aitken, Neil Peter James
The Scotch Malt Whisky Society Ltd

Akerlund, Jon Andreas
East London Liquor Co Ltd

Akers, Steven Andrew
Poetic License Distillery Ltd

Albu, Mihai
Skinnybrands Ltd

Alissi, John Leo
Frensham Distillery Limited

Allbut, David Jonathan
Bluu Spirit Limited

Allen, Richard Lenford
Seduction Rum Punch UK Ltd

Allen, Scott Duncan
Distillery Process Ltd

Allen, Vincent, Dr
El Pulpo Loco Ltd

Altman, Antony Carl
Derbyshire Distillery Limited

Alura, Gerson
Dimbandit Ltd

Ambler, Richard Charles Quintin
Broad Street Brands Limited

Anderson, David
Dilly Dilly Limited
Drops of Juniper Limited

Anderson, Hugh
Downton Distillery Limited

Anderson, John Alexander
Redcastle Spirits Limited

Anderson, Robert William
Tomatin Distillery Co Ltd,(The)

Anderson, Stephen Patrick
The Honey Gin Co Ltd

Andrews, Charles
Downton Distillery Limited

Andrews, Desmond Damian
Mooshine Ltd

Angeles, Clariephine Almoguerra
UK McLouis Liquor Co Ltd

Annibali, Francesco
Jedhart Distillery Limited
Torabhaig Distillery Limited

Anscomb, Daniel Charles
The Northlew Distillery Ltd

Appleyard, Graham Vernon
Gyffordes Distillers Ltd

Appleyard, Mark
Brittains Beverages Ltd

Archard, Paul
The Black Cow Vodka Co Ltd

Archer, Ross Adam
Mavarac UK Limited

Armour, David John
Hunter Laing & Co Ltd

Armstrong, William Denis
Spirit of The Shires Limited

Arnold, Alison Mary
Dartmoor Whisky Distillery Ltd

Arnold, Guy Rory
Dartmoor Whisky Distillery Ltd

Arnold, Kevin
Longtooth Gin Limited

Arnold, Richard
Lincoln Imp Drinks Co Ltd

Arnold-Bennett, Andrew John
Shed 1 Distillery Ulverston. Ltd

Arnot, Scott John
Incognito Ltd

Ash, Brian Robert
Wild Atlantic Distillery Ltd

Asher, Tracy Margaret
Carrick Thomson Limited

Asher, Wayne
Carrick Thomson Limited

Assi, Nadim
Beam Suntory UK Limited

Aston, Paul Michael
Deerstalker Whisky Co Ltd

Audo, Yves
Row & Co Ltd

Avis, Alice Mary Cleoniki
The Edrington Group Limited

Aziz, Amer
Lonberg Limited

Aziz, Nadeem Amer
Spirits and Bubbles Limited

Bacon, Shaun
V K Brands Limited

Bagley, Douglas John
William Grant & Sons Distillers Ltd
William Grant & Sons Limited

Baily, Edward James Stanley
Tors Vodka Limited

Baker, Xavier Lee
Isle of Wight Distillery Ltd

Bakewell, Anderson Duke
Isle of Harris Distillers Ltd

Bakhaty, Omar Sharif Mohamed
Etoh Studio Limited

Balaguer, Raimundo
Barcelona Spirit Brands UK Ltd

Baldwin, Kevan
Fruity Tipples Limited

Baldwin, Veronica Judith
Fruity Tipples Limited

Balfour, Alan John
Tea Venture Limited

Balgobin, Rolph, Dr
CL World Brands Limited

Balivada, Ashwin
Glen Monarch Distillery Ltd

Balivada, Mohan Krishna, Dr
Glen Monarch Distillery Ltd

Ball, Stephen James
Burnbrae Distillery Co Ltd

Ballantyne, Karina Lianne Jayne
Tipo Loco Drinks Co. Limited

Ballantyne, Michael Alexander
Tipo Loco Drinks Co. Limited

Ballantyne, Steve
Long Walk Spirits Limited

Bamber, Rich
Brennen & Brown Limited

Banerjee, Abhijit
The East India Company Gin Ltd

Banks, Craig Edward, Prof
Manchester Still Ltd.

Banyard, Steven
Esq Vodka Limited

Baptiste, Michael
Black Label Spirits Ltd

Baravelli, Mark William
Conwy Distillery Limited

Barber, Jason Richard
The Black Cow Vodka Co Ltd

Barber, Samuel Jonathan
The Southey Brewing Co Ltd

Barclay, Alistair James
The Barclay Distillery Limited
The Hackney Distillery Limited

Barclay, Colin Shields
Block, Grey and Block Limited
Burnbrae Distillery Co Ltd
Campbell Meyer & Co Limited
Glasgow Partners Ltd.
Glen Clyde Ltd.
A.D.C. Halford & Co Ltd
Hart Brothers Limited
Montrose Scotch Whisky Ltd.

Barford, John Valentine
Farkin Distillery Limited

Bargeton, Gregory Justin
William Grant & Sons Distinction Ltd
The Hendrick's Gin Distillery Ltd
Light Spirit Co Ltd
Sailor Jerry Limited
Wood and Co Ltd

Barker, Michael Gordon, Dr
Spirit of The Lakes Limited

Barnes, Christine
Dr Scotch Whisky Ltd.

Barnes, Robert Edward
Blue Marble Distillery Ltd

Barnett, Daniel James
City of Aberdeen Distillery Ltd

Baron, Godwin Girth
Two Fathoms Distillery Ltd.

Baroutsis, Aristotelis
Highland Distillers Group Ltd
Highland Distillers Limited

Barp, Eduardo Peroni
Diageo Scotland Limited

Barragan, Pedro Pablo
The Old Bushmills Distillery Co Ltd

Barrazotto, Mary Elizabeth
The Benriach Distillery Co Ltd
Glendronach Distillery Co Ltd
The Glenglassaugh Distillery Co Ltd

Barry, Ian Eric
Brighton Spirits Co Ltd

Bartlett, Grant Robert
The Lowestoft Distillery Co Ltd

Bass, Karen Marie
Beachcomber Gin Ltd

Bateman, Mary Ann
Twisting Spirits Ltd

Bateman, Richard Paul
Twisting Spirits Ltd

Bates, Derek Seth
Duration Brewing Ltd

Batstone, David Richard John
Artificer Spirit Limited

Battliwala, Rustom Meherdaad
Glasgow Distillery Co Ltd

Bauly, Suzanne Elizabeth
Sunfire Spirits Ltd

Baxter, James Alexander
Am Byth Distillery Ltd

Bayles, Richard Michael
Chileanspirit Ltd

Beach, David William John
Beach Craft Spirits Limited

Beach, Jon
Loch Ness Distilling Co Ltd.

Beach, Lara Helene
Beach Craft Spirits Limited

Beadle, Peter
Abbey Distillery Ltd

Beamish, Michael Frank
The Three Stills Co Ltd

Bearcroft, Michael
Land's End Gin Limited

Beardshaw, Emma Samantha Clare
Sweetwater Distillery Limited

Beaumont-Hutchings, Celia Elizabeth, Dr
The Chilgrove Gin Co Ltd

Beaumont-Hutchings, Christopher Edward
The Chilgrove Gin Co Ltd

Bebington, Shaun Mark
Pocketful of Stones Distillers Ltd

Beckitt, Neil
Kingston Distillers Ltd.

Beckwith, Paul
The Cotswold Distilling Co Ltd

Bedawi, Jill
Ginkhana Limited

Bedi, Gurdarshan Singh
Soul Vodka Ltd

Bedingham, Mark Francis
The Artisanal Spirits Co Ltd

Beeden, Ashley James
Croft Distillery Ltd

Beer, Rhian Elen
The Beers Spirit Co Ltd

Beer, Robert Anthony
The Beers Spirit Co Ltd

Beevers, Nicholas David Harry
Eastwater Gin Ltd

Belford, Douglas Malcolm Burd
Wm. Lundie & Company

Bell, Iain Ritchie
Company of Dark Spirits Ltd
Dark Spirits Co Ltd

Bell, Leo
Newcastle Distilling Ltd

Bell, Michael
Newcastle Distilling Ltd

Bell, Thomas Neale
Skinnybrands Ltd

Bellis, David Robert
Cherry Drop Gin Ltd
Cygnet Spirits Limited

Beniston, Oliver
Fox Gins Ltd

Benjamin, Paul Andrew
Benjamin & Blum Limited

Bennett, Graham Charles
Gleneagles Distillery Limited

Bennett, Michael
Doncaster Dry Gin Limited

Bennett, Paul Nigel Robert
Linden and Lime Limited

Bentley, Michael
Sky Pirate Ltd

Bermudez de La Puente Sanchez-Aguilera, Del Pino, Madame
Beam Suntory UK Limited
Morrison Bowmore Distillers Ltd

Berry, Adam
Strawhill Estate Distillery Ltd
Strawhill Estate Spirits Co Ltd

Berry, Robert
Asterley Bros, London Ltd

Berry, Samuel Rupert
The Good Life Gin Co Ltd

Berry, Sharon Margaret
Strawhill Ltd

Berry, William Gregory Hamilton
Strawhill Ltd

Berthet, Michael
Clifden Arms Property Ltd
Clifden Arms Trading Ltd

Bessant, Simon
London Distillery - Battersea Ltd

Bessant, Simon Jonathan
The London Distillery Co Ltd

Betts, Edward William
Pure Distilled Spirit Co Ltd

Bewley-Pope, Ben
White Smoke Distillery Ltd

Bhart, Jaswant
SB Gin Limited

Bhiwandiwala, Zhooben Dossabhay
The East India Company Gin Ltd

Biggs, Scott
Nene Distillery Limited

Birchall, Elaine
Caledonian Bottlers PLC

Birkitt, Joanne Claire
Boho Drinks Brands Ltd
Boho Drinks Ltd

Bishop, Emma Kara
Queen Cleo Rum Ltd

Bishop, James Andrew
Speymalt Whisky Distributors Ltd

Bissett, Ian Collins
William Grant & Sons Distillers Ltd

Black, Christopher
Broken Wings Limited

Black, Marcus William
Spirit of Harrogate Limited

Blackford, Hilary Ann Susan
Hilary Blackford Associates Ltd

Blackford, Paul Anthony
Hilary Blackford Associates Ltd

Blackham, James
Atlantis Gin Ltd

Blackmore, Deborah Easton
Jonomade Limited

Blackmore, Joshua Robert
Jonomade Limited

Blackmore, Matthew Charles
Jonomade Limited

Blake, Timothy Ross
Libation Liberation Limited

Blakesley, Stephen
Twisted Gin Ltd

Blampied, Rosanna
Somerset Drinks Ltd

Blanco, Liza
Banideep Ltd

Bland, Colin
Northumberland Whisky Ltd

Blandford-Newson, Christopher John
Distell International Holdings Ltd

Blatch, David
The Bristol Spirit Collective Ltd

Blencowe, Joseph Philip
Yorkshire Gin Limited

Blick, David Peter
The Warwickshire Gin Co Ltd

Bolt, Albyn Rodney
Dartmoor Distillery Limited

Bompas, Samuel Henry
Otten Schmidt Ltd.

Bond, Karl Matthew
Forest Distillery Ltd

Bond, Lindsay Alex
Forest Distillery Ltd

Bondzio, Joerg Thomas Gustav
Corglass Wild Spirit Ltd

Bonnington, Keith
Colonsay Beverages Ltd.
The Whisky Cellar Limited

Bookman, Jordan Ashley
Russian Doll Vodka Limited

Boom, Gary James
Westmorland Spirits Limited

Booth, Adrian
The Copper Tree Partnership Ltd

Booth, Michelle Claire
The Whitstable Distillery Ltd

Booth, Peter
Square Street Distillery Ltd

Borchardt, Heinz
Whisky and Cognac.Uk Limited

Bornhoft, Jorgen
Inver House Distillers Limited

Borthwick, Robert Bruce
Red Squirrel Brands Ltd

Bosco, Frank
Holy Grail Beverages Limited

Botham, Sarah Lianne
Fancy A Tipple Limited

Bottomley, Alan James
Bottomley Distillers Ltd

Boulan, Jean-Marc Rene
Ardbeg Distillery Limited
Ardbeg Limited
Bonding and Transport Company, Ltd
The Glenmorangie Co Ltd
Glenmorangie Distillery Co Ltd, The
Glenmorangie Spring Water Co Ltd
Alistair Graham Limited
MacDonald & Muir Limited
MacDonald Martin Distilleries Ltd
Douglas MacNiven & Co Ltd
James Martin & Company, Ltd
Morangie Mineral Water Co Ltd
Morangie Springs Limited
Charles Muirhead & Son. Ltd
Nicol Anderson & Co Ltd
Tarlogie Springs Limited

Bowen, Derek Clive
The Ironbridge Gorge Gin Co Ltd

Bower, Holly Elizabeth Winifred
Scout and Sage Spirits Limited

Bowie, Deborah Ann
Mackintosh Gin Limited

Bowker, Timothy
Royton Gin Ltd

Bowler, Stephen Paul
Blend Experts Limited
Knowcal Limited
Winchester Distillery Limited

Bownes, Cameron
Surendran & Bownes Ltd.

Bowyer, Peter
The Cognac Growers' Collective Ltd
Fort Glen Whisky Co Ltd

Boyd, Iain Sinclair
Snowdonia Spirit Co Ltd

Boyd, Martin James
The New Union Brewing Co Ltd

Boyd-Armstrong, David
Rademon Estate Distillery Ltd

Boyd-Armstrong, Fiona
Rademon Estate Distillery Ltd

Brace, Stephen Anthony
London Rum Limited
Sunderland Gin Limited

Bradbury, Andrew James
Rosemullion Distillery Ltd

Bradbury, Elizabeth
Rosemullion Distillery Ltd

Bradley, Christopher Joseph Ross
Spirit of Glasgow Ltd

Bradley, Gary Patrick
Sip Antics Limited

Brady, Arlo
Hurricane Rum Co Ltd

Brady, Carolyn Jayne
Forth Bridge Brewery and Distillery

Brady, Elaine
The Perth Distillery Co Ltd

Brady, James Stephen
Forth Bridge Brewery and Distillery

Braniff, Carolynn
Echlinville Distillery Limited

Braniff, Shane Joseph
Dunville & Co. Limited
Echlinville Distillery Limited
Jawbox Spirits Co Ltd

Brassey, John
Hamilton Rose Gin Ltd

Bratcher, David
Luxco Drinks Limited

Brauer, Matthew Campbell
Beeble Liquor Limited

Breckell, Andrew
Bowland Distillery Ltd

Breeze, Elena
Hawkridge Distillers Ltd

Bremner, Stephen
Tomatin Distillery Co Ltd,(The)

Bremner, William Alexander
The Scotch Malt Whisky Society Ltd
J.G. Thomson & Co. Limited

Brett, John Michael
Dark Matter Distillers Limited

Brice, Richard Derek
Taunton Distiller's Ltd

Bridgwood, Richard James Alexander
Ginmeister Ltd

Brierley, Daniel Ivan, Dr
Isledon Gin Ltd

Brierley, Stefan Ben
Isledon Gin Ltd

Briggs, David John
New Galloway Inspired Ltd

Briggs, Marion Riddell
New Galloway Inspired Ltd

Bright, Jonathan William
Tors Vodka Limited

Brinan, Claire
Howards of Kent Limited

Broadbridge, John Ricson
William Grant & Sons Distillers Ltd
William Grant & Sons Limited

Broadley, Sophie Jade
Fourfolk Gin Co Ltd

Brodie, John Ross
The Start-Up Drinks Lab Ltd

Brooker, George
Duck and Crutch Limited

Brosseau, Barthelemy Timothee Lawrence Edvard
Greenwood Spirits Limited

Broughton, Matthew Joel
Jo & Matt Ltd

Brown, Charles Duncan
Highlands Spirit Ltd.

Brown, Iain George
Lundin Distilling Co Ltd

Brown, Lloyd
Ursus Americanus Limited

Brown, Matthew David
Break Line Brewing & Distilling Ltd

Brown, Matthew Douglas
Founding Drinks Ltd

Brown, Nathan
Paradise Rum Limited

Brown, Neil Graeme
Still on the Hill Limited

Brown, Stephanie Jayne
Founding Drinks Ltd

Brown, Stuart William
Deerness Distillery Ltd

Brown, Toby
Half Cock Limited

Brownhill, Tim
Penningtons Spirits and Liqueurs Ltd

Brownson, Jonathan Selwyn
Foxdenton Estate Co Ltd

Brownstein, Marc
Brockmans Gin Limited

Bruce, Alexander Victor
Adelphi Distillery (1826) Ltd
Adelphi Distillery Limited

Bruce, Marian Cooke, Dr
Highland Boundary Ltd

Bruce-Jarron, Caroline
Ogilvy Spirits Limited

Bryer, Nicholas Thomas
Gower Distillery Ltd

Buist, Gordon William
Chivas Brothers Limited

Bullard, Nicholas Ian
Dark Sky Spirits Ltd

Bullas, Justin Adrian
The Little Gin Shop Limited

Bulloch, Alexander
EB Alexandria Ltd
LLDR Alexandria Ltd
LLDY Alexandria Ltd
Portavadie Distillery Limited

Bulloch, Carol Anne
LLDR Alexandria Ltd

Bungay, Dean Apollo
Duchy Beverages Ltd

Burchell, Neil Harper
The Welsh Whisky Co Ltd

Burden, Archibald Robert
Doctor Bird Rum Ltd

Burgess, Simon
Your Buddy Mary Limited

Burke, John Michael
The Bombay Spirits Co Ltd

Burke, Thomas David
Strathearn Distillery Ltd.

Burke, Thomas James
Strathearn Distillery Ltd.

Burnett, Duncan Walker
Salcombe Cider Co Ltd

Burnley, David James
Rhucello Limited

Burns, Andrew James
Esq Vodka Limited

Burns, Matthew
Broken Wings Limited

Burns, Rosalind
Hamilton Rose Gin Ltd

Burrows, Andrew William
Broad Street Brands Limited

Burstein, Janek
JDB Spirits Ltd

Burton, Lee Charles
Pure Spirit in Wales Limited

Burton, Lindsay
Lindsay's Still Room Ltd

Butler, Ross William
RWB Drinks Ltd

Butler, Timothy George Edward
The Distillers of St.Andrews Ltd
St.Andrews Gin Co Ltd
St.Andrews Whisky Co Ltd

Buttery, Stephanie Amanda
Angels Share (MCR) Limited

Byers, Jason
Steel River Drinks Ltd

Cadbury, Dominic, Sir
The Cotswold Distilling Co Ltd

Caddy, Cosmo Edward
Devon Distillery Limited

Cadney, John Patrick
Exmoor Distillers Ltd

Cadney, Yuli
Exmoor Distillers Ltd

Cairney, Sarah Jane
The Hooting Owl Distillery Ltd

Calderwood, Jack
Lost Roots Limited

Cameron, Daniel Malcolm
Dyfi Distillery Ltd

Cameron, James Scott
Finnieston Distillery Co Ltd

Cameron, Kim Margaret
Bothy Trading Limited
Gin Bothy Limited

Cameron, Peter Douglas
Dyfi Distillery Ltd

Cameron-Ross, Kevin Robert
Loch Ness Spirits Limited

Cameron-Ross, Lorien, Dr
Loch Ness Spirits Limited

Campbell, Alistair Carnegie
Adelphi Distillery (1826) Ltd
Adelphi Distillery Limited

Campbell, Derry Gaye
Scots' Cheer Limited

Campbell, Keith Hamilton
Rhum Liquor Limited

Campbell, Kenneth
Loch Leven Distillery Limited

Campbell, Stuart Alexander
J. & A. Mitchell and Company, Ltd

Camus, Cyril
Montoscar Enterprises Limited

Canon, Jane
Newton Drinks Limited

Canon, Robin George
Newton Drinks Limited

Carberry, Paul James
Buxton Distillery Limited

Carbis, David Ernest
Atlantic Distillery Ltd

Carden, Mark Thomas
Legendary Distillers Ltd

Care, Ritchie Lee
Aztec Spirits Ltd

Carpenter, Robert Francis
The Holyrood Distillery Ltd

Carr Jr, Michael
The Benriach Distillery Co Ltd

Carr, Andrew Malcolm Ferguson
Royal Wootton Bassett Gin Co Ltd

Carroll, Charlotte Trudy
Clock Tower Distilleries Ltd

Carruth, Campbell
Yorkshine Spirit Limited

Carruthers, Kit, Dr
Dormont Distilling Limited

Carruthers, Paul James
Fenney Street Distillery Ltd

Carter, Andrew James
Chase Distillery Limited

Carter, Dominic Michael John
Artisan Brands Limited
The Duke's Distilling Co Ltd

Carter, Kerry
Blackingstone Ltd

Carthy, Andrew
The Ilkley Gin Co Ltd

Carthy, Michael John
Spirit of Harrogate Limited

Carton, Timothy Ado
Borders Distillers Limited
The Borders Distillery Co Ltd
Borders Distilling Limited
The Three Stills Co Ltd

Carty, Brendan
Killowen Distillery Ltd

Casely, Bruce Gordon Fraser
The Edinburgh Rum Co Ltd

Casely, Elizabeth
Revolution Rum Ltd

Casey, Kevin Charles
Orbis Whiskey Limited
St. James Distillery Limited

Castaneda, Javier
Spnet Ltd.

Castaneda, Miguel
Spnet Ltd.

Caton, Kathryn Melanie Kiele
Brighton Spirits Co Ltd

Cayard, Jean Pierre
Glen Moray-Glenlivet Distillery Co Ltd
Label 5 First Blending Co Ltd

Chadwick, Jonathan David
Durham Distillery Limited
Durham Gin Limited

Chaikriangkrai, Sithichai
Blairmhor Distillers Limited
Blairmhor Limited
Inver House Distillers Limited

Chang, Yung Sheng
Speyside Distillers Co Ltd

Chaplin, Jeremy McDowell
Highland Distillers Group Ltd

Chaplin, Jeremy McDowell
Highland Distillers Limited
Row & Co Ltd

Chapman, Anthony Edward
Thames Distillers Limited

Chapman, Ian Michael
Speymalt Whisky Distributors Ltd

Chapman, Jim
Kindred Gin Ltd

Chapman, John Phillip
Kindred Gin Ltd

Chapman, Robin
The East India Company London Dry Gin

Chapman, Samantha
Kindred Gin Ltd

Chapoulaud-Floquet, Valerie Marie Anne, Madame
The Botanist Limited
Lochindaal Distillery Limited
Port Charlotte Limited

Charie, Christine Nancy
Flint & Hardings Limited

Chase, James Matthew
Chase Distillery Limited
Pococello Ltd

Chase, William Leonard
Chase Distillery Limited

Chater, Max
Maxchater Ltd

Chatfield, Michael James
KSSM International Limited

Checkley, James Donald
Old Smiths Distillery Ltd

Cheng, Man Lok Dustin
Fifty-Nine Spirits Co Ltd

Cherry, John Andrew
Locksley Distilling Co Ltd

Chessor, Leon Richard
The Speyside Vodka Co Ltd

Chiappetta, Aldo
Verset Vodka Holdings Limited

Chillery, Scott
East London Liquor Co Ltd

Chinn, Steven Gregory
Chinn-Chinn Ginn Limited

Chisholm, Thomas
Buck and Birch Ltd

Cho, Sungmin
Fifty-Nine Spirits Co Ltd

Chougule, Vikrant Sham
Csatrina Holdings Ltd

Christie, Roderick George
Cask Coin Ltd
Caskcoin Holdings Limited
Strathleven Distillers Co Ltd
Valt Vodka Co Ltd

Christie, Victoria Elva
Graveney Gin Limited

Christou, Alexander James
Glenrinnes Distillery Limited

Chruszczyk, Ewelina
Bimber Distillery Ltd

Church, Teresa Carol
Annandale Distillery Co Ltd

Chye, Michael Hin Fah
Inver House Distillers Limited

Cikurel, Katia, Dr
The Cotswold Distilling Co Ltd

Claessens, Michael Joseph Francis
Willem Barentsz Limited

Clancy, Dominic James
Manchester Liquor Co. Limited

Clapperton, Neil
J. & A. Mitchell and Company, Ltd
Mitchell's Glengyle Limited

Clark Hutchison, Andrew Ronald
Dark Art Gin Limited

Clark, Ashleigh Kay
HS (Distillers) Limited

Clark, Edwina Josette
The New Welsh Whiskey Co Ltd

Clark, James Michael
The Ely Gin Co Ltd.

Clark, Jennifer Anne
Chalgrove Artisan Distillery Ltd

Clark, Jonathan James
Wessex Distillery Limited

Clark, Maurice Howard
Incognito Ltd

Clark, Nicholas John
The New Welsh Whiskey Co Ltd

Clark, Robert Stanley
Chalgrove Artisan Distillery Ltd

Clark, Thomas Bradshaw
American Beverage Marketers Ltd

Clarke, Lowri Thomas
The Crosstown Cocktail Co Ltd

Clarke, Nicholas Antony
Patterson and Clarke Distillery Ltd

Clayton, David James
The Big Hill Distillery Ltd

Clayton, Paul Fraser
Seada Distillery Limited

Clevely, Rupert John
Pococello Ltd

Clifford, Matthew Andrew Seaton
Sartorial Spirits Limited
St Faiths Distillery Limited

Clifford, Ryan Michael
Bombini Ltd

Clyde-Smith, Ben Gaisford
Shorts Boy Distillery Ltd

Clynick, Jacqueline Margaret
The Orogin Distilling Co. Ltd

Clynick, Raymond Henry Thomas
The Orogin Distilling Co. Ltd

Clynick, Raymond Valentine
The Orogin Distilling Co. Ltd

Co, Winston Sy
Whyte and MacKay Limited

Coakley, Matthew James
Atom Distillery Ltd

Coates, Alison Louise
Lujo Distilling Co Ltd

Coates, Gary
Lujo Distilling Co Ltd

Cochrane, John
Twisted Melon Scotland Limited

Cochrane, Luke William
Precision Spirits Ltd

Codrington, Hugo John
Westmorland Spirits Limited

Coe, Ruth
Dartmoor Distillery Limited

Cole, Adrian
Pigeon Fisher Gin Co Limited
Zero Gravity Spirits Ltd

Cole, Richard John
Ncn'ean Distillery Limited

Cole, William Graham
Fowey River Gin Ltd

Colgan, Philip Edward
W & S Distillery Limited

Collard, Alice Jane
Collards Distillery Limited

Collard, Michael Anthony
Taunton Distiller's Ltd

Collard, Penelope Jane
Collards Distillery Limited

Collard, Thomas James
Collards Distillery Limited

Collard, William James Nimrod
Collards Distillery Limited

Collett, Gary John
Gest Spirits Limited

Collett, Nicholas
Holme Gin Limited

Collighan, Giles Thomas
The Portsmouth Distillery Co Ltd
The Rum Club Ltd

Collings, Michael George Spencer
Spencer Collings & Co Limited

Collins, Kerry Frances
Four Sisters Distillery Ltd

Collins, Matthew Simon
Devon Coast Distillery Limited

Colombo, Nino Alexander
Todka Limited

Comiskey, Paul
UK Distillers Limited

Conigliaro, Antonio Michele
Goldy Gin Limited

Connor, Robert Joseph
The Solent Spirits Co Ltd

Connor, Tammy Marie
The Solent Spirits Co Ltd

Conway, Anthony Thomas
Droylsden Craft Limited

Conway, Gary Nicholas
Skinnybrands Ltd

Conway, James Henry Kelshaw
Canebrake Ltd

Conway, John Joseph Patrick
Steel City Craft Spirits Boutique Ltd

Conway, Laura Greig
Club Rum Limited

Conyard, Amy Jane
Bottomley Distillers Ltd

Cook, John Mark
Mill House Distillery Limited

Cooke, Harry
York Gin Co Ltd

Cooke, Martin Alexander
Edrington Distillers Limited
Glenturret Distillery Limited
Glenturret Limited
Matthew Gloag & Son Limited

Cooney, John
The Last Drop Spirit Co Ltd

Cooney, John Terence
Taunton Distiller's Ltd

Cooper, Jason Karl
Checkers Gin Ltd

Cooper, Richard John
North Tyne Ventures Ltd

Cortes, Juan
Whyte and MacKay Limited

Coughlin, Simon Patrick
The Botanist Limited
Lochindaal Distillery Limited
Port Charlotte Limited

Coulter, Emma Margaret
Deshi Liqueur Ltd

Coulter, John Anthony Francis Hugh
Deshi Liqueur Ltd

Coulter, Rosalind Sylvia Ann
Deshi Liqueur Ltd

Coulthard, Harry Caldecott
Shorts Boy Distillery Ltd

Coupland, Anthony
Exploration Distillation Ltd

Courage, Christopher John
Brothers Drinks Co. Limited

Coutures, Jean-Christophe
Chivas Brothers Limited

Couvreur, Marthe Georgette Andree
Michel Couvreur (Scotch Whiskies) Ltd

Coventry, Jake
Londinio Liqueurs Ltd.

Cowan, Andrew Leo
Matthew D'Arcy & Co Ltd

Cowell, Robert
Dockers Spirit Co Ltd

Cowley, Adam David George
Harley House Distillery Ltd
Pure Sussex Distillery Ltd

Cowley, Heidi Louise
Harley House Distillery Ltd
Pure Sussex Distillery Ltd

Cox, Graham Keith
Edradour Distillery Co Ltd
Perthshire Whisky Co Ltd

Cox, Ian Taylor
The Village Spirit Collective Ltd

Cox, Philip Henry
Tarbraxus Distillers Ltd

Cox, Thomas Matthew
Cox & Mall Ltd

Cozzolino, Giorgio
Etrusca Brewery & Distillery in St. Andrews
Old Tom Gin Company in St Andrews Ltd

Cozzolino, Giorgio Cozzolino
Tres Bombarderos Gin Limited

Crabtree, Leo
Beaufort Spirit Ltd

Craig, Doreen
William Craig & Co Ltd

Craig, Pricilla Joyce
Strathleven Distillers Co Ltd

Cranmer, Craig Hamilton
William Grant & Sons Distillers Ltd

Cremin, Steven
The Ecclefechan Whisky Co Ltd

Crick, Samuel Paul
West Spirits MCR Ltd

Crickmore, Gavin Paul
Diageo Great Britain Limited
Diageo Scotland Limited
Justerini & Brooks, Limited

Crimmin, Jake Andrew
Lytham Distillery Co Ltd
Lytham Gin Co Ltd

Crombie, Andrew Ross
Hunter Douglas Scotch Whisky Ltd
Andrew Laing & Co Ltd
The Shieling Scotch Whisky Co Ltd

Crook, Andrew Brian
Islay Spirits (No. 2) Limited

Crook, Harry Brian
C S James & Sons Limited

Crosbie, Gary Stuart
The Mersey Gin Co Ltd

Cross, Patrick Martin
Hinch Distillery Limited

Cross, Terence Martin
Cross Distillery Limited
Hinch Distillery Holdings Ltd
Hinch Distillery Limited
Hinch Whiskey Co Ltd
Ninth Wave Gin Co Ltd

Crossman, Paul Anthony
York Gin Co Ltd

Crow, Andrew MacKenzie
Kelso Gin Co Ltd

Crow, Simon David
Dartmoor Whisky Distillery Ltd

Crozier, Stephen
Glastonbury Distillery Limited

Cubitt, Robert Peter
Checkers Gin Ltd

Cuffe, Jane Kathryn
Trevethan Distillery Ltd

Cuffe, Robert John
Trevethan Distillery Ltd

Cunningham, Douglas Brougham
Armadillo Spirits Limited

Cunningham, Leanne Dean
The Benriach Distillery Co Ltd
Glendronach Distillery Co Ltd
The Glenglassaugh Distillery Co Ltd

Curle, Ian Barrett
Edrington Distillers Limited
The Edrington Group Limited
The North British Distillery Co Ltd

Curley, Carol Jane
Black Cat Drinks Ltd

Curley, Mark Vincent
Black Cat Drinks Ltd

Curley, Vincent John
Black Cat Drinks Ltd

Currie, Paul Richard
The Lakes Distillery Company PLC
The Northumberland Distillery Co Ltd

Curtis, Daniel William
TBD Tipples Ltd

Curtis, Ian
Madame Jennifer Distillery Ltd

Cutter, David Andrew
The North British Distillery Co Ltd

Dakers, Matthew David
Single Estate Spirits Ltd

Dakers-Black, Iain George
Black Arid Kegs Ltd

Dalgarno, Robert Alfred
The Field Distillers Ltd

Dalnas, Anthony George
Black Powder Gin Co Ltd

Dalrymple, Michael Norman
Dalrymples Distillery Ltd

Damen, Jan Willem
The Scotch Malt Whisky Society Ltd

Dammery-Quigley, Alice
The Edale Gin Co Ltd

Dampier, Luke
The Churchill Distillery Ltd

Danvers, Thomas Asher
The 8o8 Drinks Co Ltd

Darke, Aaron Ross
Zymurgorium Ltd

Darke, Callum Thomas
Zymurgorium Ltd

Darnell, Barry
Folklore Distillery Ltd
Forest Spirits Ltd

Das, Charlotte Augusta
The London Rum Company Holdings Ltd

Das, Ravi Kumar, Dr
The London Rum Company Holdings Ltd

Daughtrey, Barbara Ann
A Little Luxury Distillery Ltd
A Little Luxury Ltd
Lincolnshire Gin Ltd

Daughtrey, Laura Elizabeth
A Little Luxury Distillery Ltd
A Little Luxury Ltd

Davidson, Gail
Daisy Distillery Limited

Davidson, Stephen Robert
Daisy Distillery Limited

Davies, Barry
Somerset Craft Distillery Ltd
Somerset Craft Spirit Co Ltd

Davies, Charlotte Ellen
Salcombe Distilling Co Ltd

Davies, Gillian Vanessa
Fablas Limited

Davies, Howard Lawrence
Salcombe Distilling Co Ltd

Davies, Jason Richard
The Staffordshire Gin Co Ltd

Davies, Mandy
Somerset Craft Distillery Ltd
Somerset Craft Spirit Co Ltd

Davies, Quinton
Q & S Distilling Co Ltd

Davies, Richard Alun Campbell
Isle of Lewis Distillers Ltd

Davies, Stephen Robert
The Welsh Whisky Co Ltd

Davis, Camilla Louise
Forager Drinks Limited

Davison, Emma
Five Fathoms Spirit Limited

Dawson, Michael
Blessed Skye Limited

Day, Alasdair MacDonald
R & B Distillers Limited
Stonedean Limited

De Grey Allingham, Peter David
Archangel Distilleries Ltd

De Haan, Benjamin Thomas
Brewhouse Spirits Limited

De Haan, Tamara Jill
Brewhouse Spirits Limited

De Jans, Koen
The Soul of The Spirit Limited

De Lima, Rafael Cortazzo
Tres Amigos Limited

De Souza, Jude Christopher
Archangel Distilleries Ltd

De Vries, Alexander Charles Bernhardt
Falmouth Gin Limited

Dean, Kathryn Patricia
The Sin of Gin Ltd

Deghy, Julian Stephen
Guilty Drinks Limited

Del Mundo, Marilyn
Crystaldrifter Ltd

Demaus, Eleanor Mary Louise
Fal River Distillery Limited

Demirci, Ilyas
London Brewery Limited

Denier, Dennis Troy
Croft Distillery Ltd

Deschamps, Alexandra Marie Elisabeth
Michel Couvreur (Scotch Whiskies) Ltd

Deschamps, Cyril
Michel Couvreur (Scotch Whiskies) Ltd

Devivo, Salvatore
Giorgio's Continental Ltd.

Devonshire, Adam Colin
Idle Saint Spirits Limited

Dewji, Sudhir Vrajlal
U'Luvka Ltd

Dharcourt, Pierre
The Three Stills Co Ltd

Dhokia, Ajay
Tres Amigos Limited

Dickie, Alan Martin
Lone Wolf Spirits Limited

Dimond, Paul Christopher
Branscombe Vale Brewery Ltd

Ditchfield, Christine Vivienne
Silverback Distillers Ltd

Ditchfield, Stephen James
Silverback Distillers Ltd

Dobbie, William
R & B Distillers Limited

Docherty, Stephen Christopher Alexander
Dark Matter Distillers Limited

Doctor, Gordon John
Ian MacLeod Distillers Limited

Doheny, Otf
Sweet Afton Scotch Whisky Ltd

Domecq, Jorge
Whyte and MacKay Limited

Donaghey, Bryan Harold
Goldman Distillery Ltd
London Society of Mixologists
The Whisky Works Ltd
Whyte and MacKay Limited

Donahay, Brett
Half Cock Limited

Donneky, Christopher
Cantails Limited

Donneky, Myles
Cantails Limited

Donnelly, Steven
The Lickerish Tooth Ltd

Dorrian, Connell Carlin
Helford River Distillery Ltd

Dover, Alexander Thomas
Bitter Salvation Ltd

Dover, Alexandra Lynette
Bitter Salvation Ltd

Down, Michael Peter, Dr
Manchester Still Ltd.

Downey, Stephen Ronald
Taunton Gin Limited

Driver, Jonathan Paul Norman
The 8o8 Drinks Co Ltd
Compass Box Delicious Whisky Ltd.

Driver, Timothy Jonathan
Tarsier Spirit Ltd

Drnec, Harry Francis
The 8o8 Drinks Co Ltd

Drummond, Jason Kingsley
Eight Vodka Limited

Duckenfield, James Jeffrey
Duckenfield Ltd

Duckenfield, Jane Caroline
Duckenfield Ltd

Dudgeon, Daniel Robert
The Gin Dobry Gin Co Ltd

Duggan Edwards, Dan John
Dr Junipers Ltd.

Dulieu, Nicola Joy
Adnams PLC

Dumigan, Darryl, Dr
Jacqson Limited

Duncan, Amanda Jane
Ealing Distillery Ltd

Duncan, Simon Francis Anson
Ealing Distillery Ltd

Duncan, Stuart Beange
De Facto Spirits Limited

Dunn, Gareth Neil Stuart
The Peak District Distilling Co Ltd

Dunn, Kevin
Dunnford Craft Distillers Ltd

Dunning, Joe
Yorkshire Spirit Limited

Dupuy, Jean-Sebastien
Swallow London Ltd

Dustow, Steven
Fowey River Gin Ltd

Dustow, Steven Michael
Colwith Farm Distillery Ltd

Duthie, Lynne Joan
Esker Spirits Ltd

Duthie, Steven
Esker Spirits Ltd

Dutoy, Andrew Phillip
Loch Ewe Spirits Limited

Dwornik, Lukasz Damian
Soapbox Spirits Ltd

Dyer, Fiona Mary
Woodlab Distillery Limited

Dyer, Ulrich Conrad, Dr
Woodlab Distillery Limited

Dyson, Craig Steven
Fourfolk Gin Co Ltd

Dyson, Scott Michael
Fourfolk Gin Co Ltd

Eaton, Elizabeth Mary
Formby Spirits Limited

Economou, Anastasios
Brockmans Gin Limited

Edgar, Dean Philip
Black Label Spirits Ltd

Edgar, John
Luxury Trading Co Ltd

Edgar, Margaret
Marron (Lincoln) Ltd

Edgar, Matthew Leonard
Cool Brew Dept Ltd
Tuerto Tequila Ltd

Edgar, Ronald
Marron (Lincoln) Ltd

Edmond, Darran
Illicit Spirits Ltd

Edmunds, James Matthew Crayden
3R Whisky Limited
Carillon U.K. Limited
Diageo Balkans Limited
Diageo Distilling Limited
Diageo Great Britain Limited
Diageo Scotland Limited
Justerini & Brooks,Limited
United Distillers UK Limited

Edward, Ian
J. & A. Mitchell and Company, Ltd

Edwards, Elizabeth Bernadette
The Brixham Gin Co Ltd.

Edwards, Jamie
Druid's Distillery Ltd

Efferoth, Vincent
Tea Venture Limited

Egan, Colum
The Old Bushmills Distillery Co Ltd

Ellefsen, Benedict James Olaf
Atom Supplies Limited

Elliot, James Luscome
Pococello Ltd

Elliot, Thom Luscombe
Pococello Ltd

Elliott, Samantha Jane
Evolution Brewing Ltd

Elliott, Sharon Louise
Puddlebrook Distillery Limited

Elliott, Yvonne
Diageo Scotland Limited

Elliott-Berry, Cicely Star
Neat Spirits Limited
Sibling Distillery Limited

Elliott-Berry, Clarice Bijou
Dowdeswell Distillery Limited
Neat Spirits Limited
Sibling Distillery Limited

Elliott-Berry, Felix Louis
Neat Spirits Limited
Sibling Distillery Limited

Elliott-Berry, Roland Brian
Neat Spirits Limited
Sibling Distillery Limited

Elliott-Berry, Stephanie Judith
Neat Spirits Limited
Sibling Distillery Limited

Ellis, Andrew Robert
The Crosstown Cocktail Co Ltd

Ellis, Richard James Kirkham
Westmorland Spirits Limited

Ellis, Robert Huw
Mezky Ltd

Elmegirab, Adam Abdulrahim
Dr Adam Elmegirabs Bitters Ltd

Elrick, Colin William
Slains Castle Spirit Co Ltd

Elrick, Nikki Jane
Slains Castle Spirit Co Ltd

Emmerson, Andrew
Solway Spirits Ltd

England, David John Philip
Undaunted Limited

England, Matthew
The Maeden Group Ltd

England, Pia Margareta
Undaunted Limited

English, George Newport
Ginglish Limited

Erdich, Generald
Peats Beast Limited

Erlanger, Simon David
Isle of Harris Distillers Ltd

Erskine, Allan Robert
Colonsay Beverages Ltd.

Esler, Niall Edward Lloyd
Nele Drinks Limited

Espensen, Sam Kim Asta
Espensen Spirit Ltd

Evans, Colin Sion
WJ Evans a'i Gwmni (Ynys Enlli) Cyf

Evans, David Eric
Lochglen Whisky Co Ltd.

Evans, Gerard
Gedrick Distilling Co Ltd

Evans, Ian
Distilled Experience Ltd
William Grant & Sons Distillers Ltd

Evans, Jonathan Richard
Wild Foragin Ltd

Evans, Mair Elizabeth
WJ Evans a'i Gwmni (Ynys Enlli) Cyf

Evans, Merrill William
Libation Liberation Limited

Evans, Natalie Louise
Wild Foragin Ltd

Evans, Rachel
Staffordshire Distillery Ltd

Evans, Richard Charles
Alcohols Limited

Eveleigh, Joanna Partridge
Topsham Gin Ltd

Everett, John
South Side Spirit Limited

Everett-Lyons, Philip
H.B. Evelyo Ltd.

Everitt, Neil John
Brockmans Gin Limited

Evers, Andrew
Vonlevers Limited

Ewen, James
Dark Matter Distillers Limited

Fabris, Massimo Antonio
Row & Co Ltd

Faiers, Rory James
Faiers Distillery Ltd

Fair, April Ashley
Braefoot Distillery Ltd

Fairless, Amanda
Speakeasy Spirits UK Ltd

Fairless, Michael Ian
Speakeasy Spirits UK Ltd

Falconer, James Keith Ross
Adelphi Distillery (1826) Ltd
Adelphi Distillery Limited

Farazmand, Timothy Bahram Neville
The Lakes Distillery Company PLC

Farman, Cleo
Farman & Son Ltd

Farmer, Brian Paul
Moorland Distillery Limited

Farrar, Richard William
Ian MacLeod Distillers Limited

Farrar, William
The Holyrood Distillery Ltd

Farrell, Anthony
The Belfast Gin and Spirits School

Farrell, Donal Joseph
Mourne Dew Limited

Fawcett, Peter
Lime Street Distillery Limited

Featherstone, Thomas James
Northern Fried Drinks Limited

Felgate, Matthew
The Lincoln Distillery Limited

Fennessy, Sharon Lynnette
Diageo Great Britain Limited
Diageo Scotland Limited
Justerini & Brooks, Limited

Fenton, Sophia Emma
Cornish Spirit Co Ltd

Ferguson, David MacInnes
Maiden Batch Ltd

Fergusson, Alan David
Esker Spirits Ltd

Ferrier, Jacqueline Simone
The Italian Gin Co Ltd

Ferrier, Jolyon Alexander Donald
Beets Incorporated Ltd

Filler, Peter
Longtooth Gin Limited

Finemore, Simon James
Helford River Distillery Ltd

Fingland, John Alastair Evan
John Fergus & Co Limited

Finn, James Michael
Malcolm Browne Distillery Co Ltd

Fisher, Daniel Arthur
Escubac Limited
Sweetdram Limited

Fisher, Hannah Magdaline
The Start-Up Drinks Lab Ltd

FitzGenerald, Stefanie
The Edrington Group Limited

Fitzjohn, Gordon Charles
Horseguards London Dry Gin Ltd

Flaherty, Samantha Louise
N.Gin Distillery Ltd

Flanagan, Mark Robert
Treganna Gin Ltd

Fleck, Alex
The Belfast Artisan Distillery Ltd

Fletcher, Duncan Kirk
Kinrara Distillery Limited

Fletcher, Kevin Paterson
Kinrara Distillery Limited

Flett, Tim
Lonburg 449 Limited

Flood, Fiona Louise
Gin Tales Ltd
Spirit Stories Ltd

Foley, Conor
Swift Half Collective Ltd

Ford, Andrew
Orbis Whiskey Limited
St. James Distillery Limited

Ford, Gary James
Fords of Wakefield Ltd

Ford, Robin James
Scots' Cheer Limited

Ford, Victoria Margaret
Fords of Wakefield Ltd

Fordyce, Laurence John
Borders Distillers Limited
The Borders Distillery Co Ltd
Borders Distilling Limited
The Three Stills Co Ltd

Forgie, Colin Alexander
The Old Curiosity Distillery Ltd

Foroshani, Keyvan
K1 Beer PLC

Foster Hird, Nicola Jane
Poetic License Distillery Ltd

Foster Yeoman, John
Somerset Drinks Ltd

Foster, Steven John Charles
The Saffron Gin Co Ltd
The Saffron Spirit Co Ltd
Saffron Spirits Limited

Foster, Thomas Matthew
Blackingstone Ltd

Foster, Tracey Diane
William Grant & Sons Distillers Ltd

Fowkes, Robert Andrew
Brockmans Gin Limited

Fox, Vernon
Lough Neagh Distillers - 1837 Ltd

Foyle, Gary
Southampton Distillery Ltd

Frame, Ross David
F.W Exports Ltd

Francis, Nathan
Wave'n Ltd

Francis, Terri Nicole
Atom Supplies Limited

Francis-Baum, Marc
East London Liquor Co Ltd

Frantzen, Jean Arnaud
Michel Couvreur (Scotch Whiskies) Ltd

Franyutti, Susana
Mezcal Reina Limited

Franzen, Patrik Ulf Mattias
East London Liquor Co Ltd

Fraser, Stuart
Isle of Arran Gin Co Ltd

Frederick, Christopher Jon
My Nan's Favourite Ltd

Freeman, Dougal
Mudlark Investments Ltd

Freeman, Mark
JKM Spirits Limited

Freestone, Hollie
Duck and Crutch Limited

Freyne, Aidan Patrick Bernard
Deya Brewing Co Ltd

Freyne, Regine Patricia
Deya Brewing Co Ltd

Freyne, Theodore Robert Sean
Deya Brewing Co Ltd

Frigerio, Andrea
Family of Hounds Limited

Frizzell, Alan William
The Macallan Distillers Ltd

Frost, Richard Fletcher
GNR Distillery Limited

Frost, Susan Margaret
Gun Dog Gin Limited

Fujarczuk, Andrea Susanne Bauder
Docked Distillery International Ltd

Fuller, Mark Benton
Belfast Distillers Ltd

Fullerton, Euan
The Jacobite Spirit Co Ltd

Gahagan, Patrick
Bonny Gin Ltd

Gale, Hayden John
One Point Eight Bar Limited

Galley, Asher Lewis
Commonwealth Gin Ltd

Galsworthy, Stamford Timothy John
Independent Spirits Limited
Sipsmith Limited

Gamble, Mark Maurice
Union Distillers Ltd

Gammell, Matthew David Malcolm
Pickering's Gin Limited
Summerhall Distillery Limited

Gammie, David
Renegade Spirits Grenada Ltd

Gandhi, Jitendra
U'Luvka Ltd

Garcia Perez, Steven James
Corky's Brands Limited
V K Brands Limited

Garden, Christopher Lawrance
Moorland Spirit Co Ltd

Gardiner, Andrew
Boozy Infusion Limited

Gardiner, Anita Michelle
Boozy Infusion Limited

Garnock, William James
Incharvie Group Limited

Gasser, Moreno
Maurice Richard Ltd

Gaston, Thomas
The Three Graces Distillery Ltd

Gauntlett, Conrad Martin
Isle of Wight Distillery Ltd

Gauntlett, Elspeth Mary
Wight Spirits Ltd

Geddes, Shona Robertson
St Andrews Botanics Limited

Geekie, Eileen Jackson
Wild Thyme Spirits Limited

Geldard, Christopher
The Peak District Distilling Co Ltd

Geldenhuys, Alexandra Joan
New Dawn Traders Ltd

Gerlach, Robin
Elephant Gin Ltd

Gerlach, Tessa Elisabeth
Elephant Gin Ltd

Gervaise-Brazier, Jack
The Juggling King Rum Co Ltd

Gheorghiu, Louise Jane
Frensham Distillery Limited

Gianini, Sandro Richard
Maurice Richard Ltd

Gibbs, Charlie William
Steampunk Ltd

Gibbs, Julie Dawn
Steampunk Ltd

Gibbs-Sawyers, Gillian
Koolvibes Limited

Gibson, Craig
Ginsecco Ltd

Gibson, Emyr Wyn
Afallon Mon Cyf

Gibson, John
Sangobeg Ltd

Gibson, Thomas
Gibson Whisky Ltd

Gidwaney, Dhanraj Chatamal
Loch Ewe Spirits Limited

Gilbert, Nicholas James
Forsaken Limited

Gilbert-Rolfe, Cyrus Jasper
Myatt's Fields Limited

Gilchrist, Alan Colin
55 Above Ltd

Giles, Kelly Marie
Seven Deadly Sins Ltd

Gillen, Lorraine Elizabeth
Hunter Laing & Co Ltd

Gillespie, Ewen
South Side Spirit Limited

Gillett, Charlotte
Deer Island Distillery Limited

Gillies, Crawford Scott
The Edrington Group Limited

Gillies, Philippa Charlotte
Espensen Spirit Ltd

Gilmore, Fiona
Ginwimmin Ltd

Gilpin, Matthew Thomas Diarmuid
Westmorland Spirits Limited

Gilroy, Duncan Thompson
Hussingtree Blends Limited

Giorgio, Nick
Empire Bar Service Ltd

Gladman, Philip Andrew
William Grant & Sons Limited

Glaister, Daniel Britt
Coyote Ventures Limited

Glaser, John Reppert
Compass Box Delicious Whisky Ltd.
Compass Box Whisky Supply Ltd

Glasgow, Ben
Tweed Valley Distilling Co Ltd

Glazsher, Spencer Richard James Ulrich
Seven Deadly Sins Ltd

Gledhill, Keith Joseph
Scouse Girls Gin Ltd

Gledhill, Maureen Francise
Scouse Girls Gin Ltd

Glen, Iain David
Brothers Drinks Co. Limited

Glen, John Ronald Kerr
The Three Stills Co Ltd

Gloeckner, Phillipa Nickerson
Damsons in Distress Limited

Glover, Richard Edward
The Old Curiosity Distillery Ltd

Glynn, Gareth Lee
Shire Gin Limited
The Shropshire Distillery Ltd

Gobres, Edilon
Bethera Ltd

Godivala, Emma Jo
York Gin Co Ltd

Golightly, Peter
The Handmade Gin Co Ltd

Gomes, Adrian Joseph
Single Estate Spirits Ltd

Goodwin, Hannah Victoria
Spirit of Malt House Limited

Goord, Andrew
UK Distillers Limited

Gordon, Harvest
Gordon & Company (Distillers) Ltd

Gordon, James
Gordon & Company (Distillers) Ltd

Gordon, Janet
Gordon & Company (Distillers) Ltd

Gordon, Jonathan
Gordon & Company (Distillers) Ltd

Gordon, Mark Charles
The Wimbledon Distillery Co Ltd

Gordon, Peter Grant
William Grant & Sons Limited

Gordon, Timothy John
Hawksburn Spirits International Ltd

Gordon-Jones, Sarah
Tivoli's Gin Limited

Gosnell, David Peter
The Old Bushmills Distillery Co Ltd

Gourgeon, Frederic
Row & Co Ltd

Grafham, Robert
Highlands Spirit Ltd.

Graham, Bryan
The Ecclefechan Whisky Co Ltd

Graham, Jonathan
Poetic License Distillery Ltd

Graham, Mathew Kalum
Hin Ltd

Grant, George Stewart
J. & G. Grant

Grant, Hugh
Isle of Harris Distillers Ltd

Grant, Ishbel
J. & G. Grant

Grant, John Lynburn Scott
Broxburn Bottlers Limited
J. & G. Grant
Wm. Lundie & Company

Grant, Maxine Natalie
The Garden Shed Drinks Co Ltd

Grant, Nathaniel
Sloosh Limited

Grant, Ryan
The Garden Shed Drinks Co Ltd

Grassie, George Frank
Isle of Arran Gin Co Ltd

Graves, Darren Charles
The Maidstone Distillery Ltd

Graves, Samantha Louise
The Maidstone Distillery Ltd

Gray, Andrew Duncan
The Burnsland Distillery Co Ltd

Graydon, Geoffrey
Geordie-Gin Co Ltd

Green, Michael Peter
Tipsy Wight Ltd

Green, Ruth
Tipsy Wight Ltd

Greenow, Pryce William David
Beam Suntory UK Limited
HS (Distillers) Limited
The Macallan Distillers Ltd
Sipsmith Limited

Greenwood, Nicholas Michael
Ground Inn Ltd

Greenwood, Rita Marie
William Grant & Sons Limited

Gregory, Kate Danielle
Gin Kitchen Limited

Gregory, Mark Seymour
Silhill Brewery Limited

Grier, Scott
Morrison Glasgow Distillers Ltd

Griffiths, Alexander
Griffiths Brothers Distillery Ltd

Griffiths, Andrew
Griffiths Brothers Distillery Ltd

Griffiths, Peter Goadby
The Little Red Berry Co Ltd.

Grimshaw, Paul
Skinny Russian Vodka Ltd

Gurung, Nicola
Mr & Mrs Gin Ltd

Guyot D'Asnieres de Salins, Etienne Jean Marie
Mossburn Distillers Limited

Hackney, James
Invoke Distillery Ltd
Invoke Distilling Co. Ltd

Hadfield-Hyde, Sebastian James Anthony Aiden
Kimbland Distillery Ltd

Haggart, Stuart
Loch Lomond Liquor Co Ltd

Hainsworth, Stewart Andrew
Aber Falls Distillery Limited
The Edinburgh and Leith Distillery
Liverpool Gin Distillery Ltd
H. J. Neill Ltd
Redrosesforme Limited
Wessex Distillery Limited

Hall, Bernadette Kylie
Anura Drinks Ltd

Hall, Claire Louisa
Drink It Limited
Percy's T Limited

Hall, Fairfax
Independent Spirits Limited
Sipsmith Limited

Hall, Felicity Eleanor
Bramley and Gage Limited

Hall, Graham Howard
Anura Drinks Ltd

Hall, Lee
Invoke Distillery Ltd
Invoke Distilling Co. Ltd

Hall, Richard Bryan
Northumberland Whisky Ltd

Hall, Roger
Wee Beastie Ltd.

Hall, Timothy Giles
Bramley and Gage Limited

Ham, Jeremy Robert
The Underground Brewing Co Ltd

Hamilton, Andrew
Maiden Batch Ltd

Hamilton, Emma
The Country Garden Drinks Co Ltd

Hamilton, Gordon James
Adelphi Distillery (1826) Ltd
Adelphi Distillery Limited

Hamilton, Iain Lindsay
Edinburgh Whisky Ltd.

Hamilton, Matthew James
The Country Garden Drinks Co Ltd

Hamilton, Ross
Isle of Arran Gin Co Ltd

Hamilton, Victoria Christiana
Weymouth and Portland Distillery Co Ltd

Hammersley, Alan Ronald
78 Dbar Limited

Hammersley, Jack Oliver
78 Dbar Limited

Hammond, Luke Henry
Landeavour Distillery Ltd

Hankey, Carl
Avalon Distillery Co Ltd

Hannay, Philip Adamson
The Whisky Club Ltd

Hannon, Thomas
Liquid Revolution Ltd

Hansen, Thor Hvid
Crossbill Distilling Limited

Hardaker, Yvonne Mary
HG Family Enterprise Ltd

Harding, Richard William
The Cornish Distilling Co Ltd

Hardingham, Barbara Eileen
Ludlow Distillery Limited
Ludlow Vineyard Limited

Hardingham, Michael John
Hereford & Ludlow Cider Brandy Co Ltd
Ludlow Apple Brandy Distillery Ltd
Ludlow Distillery Limited
Ludlow Vineyard Limited
Ludlow Whisky Limited

Hardy, Derek
Hinch Distillery Holdings Ltd
Hinch Distillery Limited
Hinch Whiskey Co Ltd
Ninth Wave Gin Co Ltd

Hargroves, Richard Joseph
Mulberry Distillery Limited
Tippling Tonic Limited

Harley, Linda Jane
Fanny's Distilling Co Ltd

Harper, Jonathan Edward
The Boutique Distillery Ltd

Harpham, Helena
The Warwickshire Gin Co Ltd

Harriman, Benjamin Peter
The Bloomsbury Distillery Ltd

Harris, David John
Broxburn Bottlers Limited

Harris, Michael
Broker's Gin Limited

Harrison, Christopher John
Langholm Distillery Limited

Harrison, Jonathan
Lytham Distillery Co Ltd
Lytham Gin Co Ltd

Harrison, Justine Danielle
The Ribble Valley Gin Co Ltd.

Harrison, Sean Jessop
Coates & Co. (Plymouth) Ltd

Harrison, Simon Michael
Harrison Distillery Ltd

Harrison-Allen, James Alexander Hensleigh
Still Wild Limited

Hart, Alistair Robert Greig
Hart Brothers Limited

Hart, Andrew John Greig
The Malt Whisky Investment Co Ltd
Meadowside Blending Co Ltd

Hart, Donald Stuart Greig
The Malt Whisky Investment Co Ltd
Meadowside Blending Co Ltd

Hart, Frederick
Todka Limited

Hart, Ian Nicholas
EMS Corp Limited
Ian Hart Distilling Limited
Sacred Spirits Holdings Ltd

Hart, Rupert Anthony Clive
Ten Bears Spirits Limited

Hartless, Patrick Charles Martin
William Grant & Sons Distillers Ltd

Hartley, Robert Daniel Fergus
The Craft Scottish Spirits Co Ltd
W. P. Lowrie & Co Ltd

Harvey, Andrew Graham
Bishopsgate Distillery & Wine Co Ltd

Harvey, Simon
4607 Distillery Limited

Hasan, Nauman Saleem
The Glenmorangie Co Ltd
MacDonald & Muir Limited

Haslam, Kate Elizabeth
Four Sisters Distillery Ltd

Haste, Ian
Kindred Gin Ltd

Haste, Nicola Louise
Kindred Gin Ltd

Haswell, Julian Guy
Rainbow Chaser Limited

Hatton, Daniel Paul
London Botanical Drinks Ltd

Havenhand, Amy Jayne
Deco Spirits Limited

Hawley, Emma Charlotte
Ginwimmin Ltd

Hayden, Patrick
Saint Patricks Ltd

Hayhoe, Elizabeth Kate
Ramsbottom Gin Co Ltd

Hayman, Christopher Frank
Fogcutter Limited
Hayman Distillers Limited
Thames Distillers Limited
Tricort Limited

Hayman, James
Hayman Distillers Limited

Haynes, Kerryn Louise
Diageo Great Britain Limited

Haynes, Stephen Paul
The Corrupt Drinks Co Ltd

Hayter, Christopher James
Hayter Divisions Limited

Hayter, Thomas Jonathan
Hayter Divisions Limited

Haythorne, Lesley Karan
Pant y Foel Gin Ltd

Hayward, Benjamin
Antibio UK Ltd

Hayward, Michael
Glasgow Distillery Co Ltd

Hayward, Roger John
Antibio UK Ltd

Hayward, Simon
Amber Valley Gin Ltd

Hazell, Helen Alison
Hazell & Hazell Distillers Ltd

Hazell, Simon Mark
Hazell & Hazell Distillers Ltd

Hazlett, Joanna
Brennen & Brown Limited

Heal, Alexander Maximilian Carlton
Lost Roots Limited

Heald, Michael Guy Hilliard
Adnams PLC

Healing, Eric Simon
The Handmade Gin Co Ltd

Heap, Julie Sharron
The Old Chapel Brendon Limited

Heard, John Reford
The Cornish Distillery Co Ltd

Heeley, Sebastian Richard John
Curious Liquids Limited
Drinks of Manchester Limited
Spirit of Manchester Distillery Ltd

Heeran, Carmel
Hidden Gem - Urban Artisan Spirit Ltd

Heginbottom, David
Diageo Great Britain Limited
Justerini & Brooks, Limited

Heinze, Per Steen Molin
CES Whisky Limited
MacDuff & Co Ltd
MacDuff (Scotch Whisky) Ltd
MacDuff International (Scotch Whisky)

Hemmings, Ross James
Stokers Spirits Ltd

Hemstock, David John Andrew
Raw Distilling Ltd

Henderson, Brian Robert
Stirling Distillery Co Ltd
Stirling Gin Ltd.

Henderson, Ewan John
Drambuie Liqueur Co Ltd.
William Grant & Sons Distillers Ltd
William Grant & Sons Distinction Ltd
William Grant & Sons Limited
The Hendrick's Gin Distillery Ltd
Light Spirit Co Ltd
Sailor Jerry Limited
Wood and Co Ltd

Hendry, Stuart Fullarton
Glasgow Whisky Limited

Hennessy, Karl Peter
The London Rum Company Holdings Ltd

Hepplewhite, Neil Anthony
The Hooting Owl Distillery Ltd

Herb, Andreas Werner
Mahiki Trading Limited

Herbert, Ryan Jon
Herbert's Distillery & Co Ltd

Herd, Sandy
Edinburgh Distillers Limited

Hermansen, Mark Emil Tholstrup
Empirical Trading Co. Limited

Hernon, William
Calder Glen Ltd

Herrmann, William John
Porthilly Spirit Distillery Ltd

Herron, Robin
R & R Distillery Ireland Ltd

Hester, Drew
Sipsmith Limited

Hester, Karen
Adnams PLC

Hewitt, Ian
Supermarine Vodka Distillers Ltd

Hewlett, Victoria
Tea Rocks Ltd

Hewlette, Earl
Terrepure Spirits UK Ltd.

Hickey, Kristin Margaret
The Italian Gin Co Ltd

Hicklin, John Justin Delany
The 8o8 Drinks Co Ltd

Higashino, Satoshi
Tomatin Distillery Co Ltd,(The)

Higgins, Robert William
Eccentric Gin Co Limited

Hill, Cairbry Robert Meredith
Moorland Spirit Co Ltd

Hill, David Kenneth
Aurora Brewing Limited

Hill, Mark Douglas
Green Box Drinks Limited

Hillsman, Richard
Broker's Gin Limited

Hilton, Belinda Jane
Waters of Deugh Limited

Hilton, Darren Thomas
Waters of Deugh Limited

Himeno, Kunimasa
The Macallan Distillers Ltd

Hincks, Alexandra Lesley
Brockmans Gin Limited

Hindley, Kristian Nathan
Gin Ting Limited

Hindley, Louise
Gin Ting Limited

Hine, Lucy Catherine
East Neuk Organic Brewing & Distilling

Hine, Nicholas James
Mr Bonds Tonic Limited
Polo Gin Limited

Hine, Richard James Frederick Valentine
Polo Gin Limited

Hine, Richenda Gana-Lisa
Polo Gin Limited

Hines, Timothy Richard
Liverpool Gin Distillery Ltd

Hingston, Colin Timothy
Tipsy Fruit Gins Limited

Hinkebein, William Andrew
American Beverage Marketers Ltd

Hinton, Nicholas James
Hinton's of Bewdley Ltd

Hipshon, Daniel
The Sipping Shed Limited

Hird, Mark
Poetic License Distillery Ltd

Hirt, Brett
The Bristol Spirit Collective Ltd

Hirt, Liam Scott, Dr
Psychopomp Ltd

Hisamitsu, Tetsuji
Ben Nevis Distillery (Fort William)

Hitchcock, Dewi John
The Juggling King Rum Co Ltd

Hix, Mark Ernest
The Somerset Cider Brandy Co Ltd

Hiza, Daniel Paul
50 Degrees North Limited

Hiza, Ritu Manocha
50 Degrees North Limited

Ho, Yu Hung
Speyside Distillers Co Ltd

Hobbs, Antony Nicholas
Blue Sky Drinking Ltd

Hodgkinson, Mariane
Tewkesbury Distillery Ltd

Hogg, Adrian
Hoggnorton Limited

Hogg, John Malcolm
The Ecclefechan Whisky Co Ltd

Hogg, Stuart William
Maiden Batch Ltd

Holliday, Rebecca Emily Louise
MWBH Bottling Co. Limited

Hollin, Benjamin Michael
Taunton Distiller's Ltd

Holloway, Rupert Vere
Conker Spirit Limited

Holt, William Anthony Eustace
Ginmeister Ltd

Horsburgh, William Fredrick
The Ecclefechan Whisky Co Ltd

Horsfield, Gary
William Grant & Sons Distillers Ltd
William Grant & Sons Limited

Hosang, Kirby Anthony
CL World Brands Limited

Houlihan, Moira Theresa
Fatman and Friends Ltd.

Howard, David
Cabin Pressure Spirits Ltd

Howatson, David
Dallinger Gin Limited

Howden, Joe
Silver Circle Distillery Ltd

Howden, Nina
Silver Circle Distillery Ltd

Hoyle, Andrew
Sloeberry Spirits Ltd.

Hudson, Miranda Lilian
Duration Brewing Ltd

Huelin, Rhys
Margate Distillery Ltd

Hughes, Daniel Charles
The Bristol Rum Co Ltd

Hughes, David Owen
Lymm Gin Limited

Hughes, Jessica
Hukleys Limited

Hughes, Josephine
Jo & Matt Ltd

Hughes, Kirsty Ann
Tap End Brands Ltd

Hughes, Liam Oliver
Glasgow Distillery Co Ltd

Hughes, Lisa
Lymm Gin Limited

Hughes, Matthew David
Mint Drinks Co Ltd

Hughes, Michael
Central Line Holdings Limited

Hughes, Peter Burroughes
Gyffordes Distillers Ltd

Hughes, Simon Grant Jason
Copper Frog Distilling Limited

Hughston, James David
For The Love of Limited

Hull, Alex Charles
Lincoln Imp Drinks Co Ltd

Hull, Jack Adam
Commonwealth Gin Ltd

Hunnygen-Henry, Michael
Potion Universe Ltd

Hunt, John Simon
Broughton Ales Limited

Hunt, Simon John
William Grant & Sons Distillers Ltd
William Grant & Sons Limited

Hunter, Peter Michael John
Swift Half Collective Ltd

Hurl, Vincent
Crosskeys Whiskey Co Ltd

Hutcheon, Graham Robert
Edrington Distillers Limited
The Edrington Group Limited
Highland Distillers Limited
The North British Distillery Co Ltd

Hutton, Richard John
The Lakes Distillery Company PLC

Hyde, Christopher Robert Corsie
The Balno Distillery Limited

Hyde, Fiona
The Balno Distillery Limited

Hyde, Paul Andrew
Edrington Distillers Limited
The Edrington Group Limited

Hyne, Adam
Papillon Dartmoor Distillery Ltd

Hyne, Claire
Papillon Dartmoor Distillery Ltd

Illi, Alain Maurice
Maurice Richard Ltd

Imlach, Robert Francis
Liberty Orchards Limited

Ingledew, Jonathan
North Uist Distillery Ltd

Inglis, Ben
High Road Rum Co Ltd

Ingram, Stuart
House of Elrick Gin Limited

Ingwersen-Matthiesen, Tina, Dr
James Johnstone Distillers Ltd.

Innes, Craig
Pixel Spirits Limited

Innes, Noru
Pixel Spirits Limited

Iravani, Benjamin
Langstane Liquor Co Ltd

Irvine, Gareth James
Copeland Distillery Company (NI) Ltd
Copeland Spirits Ltd

Irwin, Richard Stephen
Titanic Distillers Limited

Ito, Hiroyuki
Tomatin Distillery Co Ltd,(The)

Ito, Kazuyoshi
Tomatin Distillery Co Ltd,(The)

Ivalo, Kai
The Artisanal Spirits Co Ltd
The Scotch Malt Whisky Society Ltd
J.G. Thomson & Co. Limited

Jack, Elsa Vivien
Isle of Harris Distillers Ltd

Jackson, Ashley Martin
Jackson's Gin Ltd

Jackson, Barrie Mason
Cwmni Distyllfa Llanberis Cyf

Jackson, Mark
Fablas Limited

Jackson, Penelope Margaret
The Cognac Growers' Collective Ltd

Jackson, Ruaridh James Howard
The Garden Shed Drinks Co Ltd

Jackson, Trevor Howard
Jackson Distillers Limited

Jagielko, Carol Anne
LLDY Alexandria Ltd

Jagielko, Henry John
EB Alexandria Ltd
LLDR Alexandria Ltd
LLDY Alexandria Ltd

Jain, Mukesh
Stockholm Distillers and Vintners

James, Alan
Glasgow Distillery Co Ltd

James, Caroline Sanderson
Islay Spirits (No. 2) Limited
The Islay Spirits Co Ltd

James, George Ivor
Kammerling's Investment Holdings Ltd
Kammerlings Limited

James, Mark Peter
Corky's Brands Limited
V K Brands Limited

Jameson, Richard Donald
Princetown Distillers Ltd

Jamieson, Alyson Playfair
Linlithgow Distillery Limited

Jamieson, Ross Finlay
Linlithgow Distillery Limited

Jan-Klaassen, Daniel Gerrit
Gaelic Pure Scotch Whisky Ltd

Jarman, Stephen William
Pure Cornish Limited

Jarrold, James Cameron
The Nodding Donkey Distillery Co Ltd

Jarrold, Nichola Jane
The Nodding Donkey Distillery Co Ltd

Jarron, Graeme Young
Ogilvy Spirits Limited

Jaume, Christopher Mark
Cooper King Distillery Ltd

Javed, Vanessa Heidi
Molotov Brand Limited

Jean, Vadim Alexis
Renaissance Drinks Ltd
Renaissance Vodka Limited

Jedrzejewski, Piotr Jan
Sendivogius Limited

Jefferies, Christopher
Gin Jar Drinks Co Ltd

Jenkins, David Charles
The Henley Gin Co Ltd
Jacob's Gin Limited
Wilson's Henley Gin Co Ltd

Jenkins, Jon Robert
&Spirit Limited

Jenner, Harry
Burning Barn Limited

Jenner, Katherine
Burning Barn Limited

Jennings, Martin James
Soapbox Spirits Ltd

Jensen, Christian Erboe
Bermondsey Distillery Limited

Jervis, Laura
Jervis Trading Limited
Lazy Drinks Ltd.

Jervis, Peter
Jervis Trading Limited

Jewell, Peter Anthony
Tudor Court Distillers Limited

Jocelyn, Nicholas Andrew Milton
The White House Distillery Ltd
White House Gin Limited

Johns, Conor Aston
Mr Kegz Ltd

Johns, Simon
Godka Ltd

Johnson, Alexander
Mavarac UK Limited

Johnson, Dominique Nichole
Uncle Nearest Ltd.

Johnson, Sabrina
The Pembrokeshire Comestibles Co Ltd

Johnson, Warren Maynard
Pococello Ltd

Johnston, David Melville Steele
Colonsay Beverages Ltd.

Jolin, Patrick Alexander
Lytham Distillers Limited

Jones, Adrian Lee
Chase Distillery Limited

Jones, Barry Reginald Felstead
MWBH Bottling Co. Limited

Jones, Eamonn FitzGeneraId
Peats Beast Limited

Jones, Hilary Susan
Ian Hart Distilling Limited
Sacred Spirits Holdings Ltd

Jones, Maria Elaine
Llanfairpwll Distillery Ltd

Jones, Owen
Aztec Spirits Ltd

Jones, Samantha Ann
Deco Spirits Limited

Jones, Tobin
The Berkshire Distillery Ltd

Jordan, Neil Lennox
Myperfectgin Ltd

July, Colin Paul
Vape Pure Ltd

Jungmayr, Alexander Peter
In The Welsh Wind Distillery Ltd

Kaberry, Benjamin Andrew
The Big Hill Distillery Ltd

Kain, Edward Bramley
Bramley and Gage Limited

Kain, Michael Colin
Bramley and Gage Limited

Kaiser, Christian James
Barford Imports Limited

Kaiser, Jurgen
Barford Imports Limited

Kaiser, Marcus Jurgen
Barford Imports Limited

Kamau, Jeffers Kamande
Simple Sips International Ltd

Kammerling, Alex David
Kammerling's Investment Holdings Ltd
Kammerlings Limited
Tasty Beverages Limited

Kammerling, Heinz Peter
Kammerling's Investment Holdings Ltd
Kammerlings Limited

Kane, Nolan Oscar
Folklore Distillery Ltd

Karberg, Thomas Just
CES Whisky Limited
MacDuff & Co Ltd
MacDuff (Scotch Whisky) Ltd
MacDuff International (Scotch Whisky)

Kato, Archard Lwihula
Alko Vintages UK Ltd

Kaur, Surjit
London Heaven Spirits Company UK Ltd

Kavanagh, Steven Robert
Spiritmen Limited
The Surrey Hills Whisky Co Ltd
Whiskymen Limited

Kay, Peter James
Sleepy Hollow Spirits Ltd

Kay, Philip Alexander Guy Jervis
Suffolk Smugglers Limited

Kaye, James Henry Newton
Good Spirits Ltd

Kayley, Ali Jane
Coyote Ventures Limited

Kean, Jacob
Raer Scotch Whisky Ltd

Kean, James Harkins
Raer Scotch Whisky Ltd

Keegan, Steve James
Holler Brewery Limited

Keeling, John
The Surrey Hills Whisky Co Ltd
Whiskymen Limited

Keeling, John Charles
Spiritmen Limited

Keenan, Jamie Francis
Rumbustian Limited

Keenan, Susan Karen
Rumbustian Limited

Kell, David Ronald
Newcastle Distilling Ltd

Kellock, Alastair
Maiden Batch Ltd

Kelly, Andrew
Spirit of Leith Ltd

Kelly, Anthony
Blendworks Ltd
Eden Mill Distillers Ltd
St Andrews Brewers Limited

Kelly, Anthony Gerard
Blendworks Ltd
Eden Mill Distillers Ltd
St Andrews Brewers Limited

Kelly, Colin Thomas
William Grant & Sons Distillers Ltd

Kelly, Joel John
Atom Brands Limited
Atom Cask Holdings Limited
Atom Drinks Limited
Atom Group Limited
Atom Scotland Limited
Atom Supplies Limited
Master of Malt Limited
Masters of Malt Limited
Maverick Brands Limited
Maverick Drinks Limited
Maverick Spirits Limited

Kelly, Linda
Spirit of Leith Ltd

Kelly, Mark
Helford River Distillery Ltd

Kelly, Mark Anthony
Brew House Yorkshire Limited

Kelly, Nicholas Stephen
Azure Distilleries Limited

Kelly, Scott Fraser
Finnieston Distillery Co Ltd

Kelly, Sean Francis
True North Brew Co Limited

Kemp, Alyson Stevenson
Orkney Distilling Limited

Kemp, Stephen Charles Ritchie
Orkney Distilling Limited

Kenney, Iain
Lochaber Craft Brewing and Distilling

Keogh, Christina
Warner's Distillery Limited

Kershaw, Jonathan Stanley
The Yorkshire Distillery Co Ltd
The Yorkshire Whisky Co Ltd

Kershaw, Louise Amanda
Ginwimmin Ltd

Khan Tyler-Street, Rubina
Curio Spirits Co Ltd

Khemka, Maheshchandra
U'Luvka Ltd

Killen, Gillian
The Belfast Gin and Spirits School

Killen, Samuel John Ian
The Belfast Gin and Spirits School
The Belfast Whiskey School Ltd

Kilpatrick, Alan
The North British Distillery Co Ltd

Kilpatrick, Alan John Stewart
The North British Distillery Co Ltd

Kimura, Mutsumi
Tomatin Distillery Co Ltd,(The)

King, David Thomas
Speymalt Whisky Distributors Ltd

King, William Ashley
Montoscar Enterprises Limited

Kingsley, Robert
Berwick Brewrey Co Ltd

Kingsley, Sarah Louise
Berwick Brewrey Co Ltd

Kinton, Emma
Hothams Limited

Kirkwood, Scott Harold
Kirkwood Distillery Limited

Kishimoto, Taketoshi
Demball Limited

Klerck, Paul Alexander, Dr
Klerck Distillery Ltd

Knight, William Richard
The Cuba Trading Co Ltd

Knights, Adam Peter
Unthank Distillery Limited

Koopmans, Rudolf Jozef
William Riddell & Sons Limited

Kovacs, Gabor
3R Whisky Limited
Carillon U.K. Limited
Diageo Balkans Limited
Diageo Distilling Limited
United Distillers UK Limited

Kozakiewicz, Paul Anthony
Krupnikoz Ltd

Kozuba, Jakub
Kozuba & Sons Limited

Kozuba, Maciej
Kozuba & Sons Limited

Kruger, Douw Gerband
Tipsy Fruit Gins Limited

Kruger, Michelle Jane
Tipsy Fruit Gins Limited

Kyprianou, Steven Stellakis
London Spiced Dry Limited

Laborde, Jean-Marie
Renegade Spirits Grenada Ltd

Lacey, Simon Roy
Q & S Distilling Co Ltd

Ladefoged, Niels
Kilchoman Distillery Co Ltd.

Laing, Andrew Arthur
Dark Matter Distillers Limited

Laing, Andrew William Douglas
Ardnahoe Distillery Co Ltd
Hunter Laing & Co Ltd

Laing, Douglas William
William Grant & Sons Distillers Ltd

Laing, Frederick Hamilton
Clyde Bottlers Ltd

Laing, Scott Hepburn
Ardnahoe Distillery Co Ltd
Hunter Laing & Co Ltd

Laing, Stewart Hunter
Hunter Laing & Co Ltd
Premier Bonding Co Ltd

Laird, Andrew Robert John
3 Lids Rum Ltd

Laird, George
Isle of Arran Gin Co Ltd

Lamb, Adam Dobson
Geordie-Gin Co Ltd
Geordie-Gin Corporation Ltd

Lamb, Fiona Isobel
Carse of Stirling Distillers Ltd

Lamb, Matthew David Cheyne
Carse of Stirling Distillers Ltd

Lamb, Richard John Watson
Carse of Stirling Distillers Ltd

Lamb, Stuart
Geordie-Gin Co Ltd
Geordie-Gin Corporation Ltd
LighthouseVodka Ltd

Lambert, Hugh Anthony
Shanty Spirit Ltd

Lambert, Jean Marc
Compass Box Delicious Whisky Ltd.
John Dewar and Sons Limited

Lambeth, Candice Elizabeth
Lambeth Spirits Ltd

Lambeth, Sandra Ann
Lambeth Spirits Ltd

Laming, Robert Clayton
The Anglesey Distillery Ltd
Llanfairpwll Distillery Ltd

Lamont, Michael
Drambuie Liqueur Co Ltd.
William Grant & Sons Distillers Ltd
William Grant & Sons Limited

Lamont, Nicola
The Skye Vodka Co Ltd

Lamont, Raymond Macpherson
The Skye Vodka Co Ltd

Lang, David Kinniburgh
Langs Consulting Ltd.

Langdon, Richard Hugh
SV Distilleries Limited

Langton, Terence Francis
Turncoat Distillery Limited

Lanson, Victor Barbara
Vijobar Ltd

Lark, Graham Robert Starling
Renegade Spirits Grenada Ltd

Latham, William Anthony
Cwmni Distyllfa Llanberis Cyf

Lavery, Peter Martin
Belfast Titanic Whiskey Distillery Ltd
Titanic Gin Ltd
Titanic Vodka Ltd

Law, Craig
YDC Ltd

Law, Martin John, Dr
Dr Gin Limited

Lawrence, Alan William Mark
Laurence Philippe Wines Ltd

Lawrence, Jeffrey Joshua
The Shropshire Gin Co Ltd

Lawrence, Laetitia Estella Emmeline
One Point Eight Bar Limited

Lawson, David
Ginkhana Limited

Lawson, Leeanne
Ginkhana Limited

Lawton, John Gregory
Dartmoor Distillery Limited

Le Page, Sebastien
Isle of Harris Distillers Ltd

Leach, Antony Mark
Soulmate Gin Ltd

Leadbetter, Tarquin
Southwestern Distillery Ltd

Leadley, Steve
Newbury Gin Limited

Leask, Robert Alexander
Princetown Distillers Ltd

Leather, Paola Andrea
Rathlee Distilling Co Ltd.

Leather, Stuart Graham
Rathlee Distilling Co Ltd.

Lee, Kane
JKM Spirits Limited

Lee, Man Kong
The Balblair Distillery Co Ltd
R. Carmichael & Sons Limited
James Catto & Co Ltd
Glen Calder Blenders Limited
Hankey Bannister & Co Ltd
The Knockdhu Distillery Co Ltd
J. MacArthur Jr. & Co. Limited
Mason & Summers Limited
The Pulteney Distillery Co Ltd
Speyburn-Glenlivet Distillery Co.

Lee, Pang Lay Terry Joseph, Dato
Macmillan Scotch Whisky Co Ltd

Lee, Philip Craig
The Great Yorkshire Spirit Co Ltd

Lefebvre, Cesar Vincent Remi
Docked Distillery International Ltd

Lefebvre, Patrick Bernard
J. & A. Mitchell and Company, Ltd

Leggat, Caraline Sara
Delicious Drinks Limited

Leggat, Christopher George
Delicious Drinks Limited

Leivers, Ian David
The Belvoir Gin Distillery Ltd

Leivers, Laura Elizabeth
The Belvoir Gin Distillery Ltd

Lejkowski, Marta Magdalena
Benjamin & Blum Limited

Lemmey, Alison Jean
Liberty Orchards Limited

Lemmey, Peter John
Liberty Orchards Limited

Leonard, Martin John, Dr
The Balblair Distillery Co Ltd
Blairmhor Distillers Limited
Blairmhor Limited
R. Carmichael & Sons Limited
James Catto & Co Ltd
Glen Calder Blenders Limited
Hankey Bannister & Co Ltd
Inver House Distillers Limited
The Knockdhu Distillery Co Ltd
J. MacArthur Jr. & Co. Limited
Mason & Summers Limited
Moffat & Towers Limited
The Pulteney Distillery Co Ltd
Speyburn-Glenlivet Distillery Co.
Wee Beastie Ltd.

Leonard, Richard
Anstie Distillers International Ltd

Lettice, Claire
Botanical Alchemy Ltd

Levin, Lorna
Vonlevers Limited

Lewis, Derek Compton
Drimnin Estate Trading Limited
Ncn'ean Distillery Limited

Lewis, Fiona
Clwydian Range Distillery Ltd

Lewis, Liam John
Surendran & Bownes Ltd.

Lewis, Louise
Drimnin Estate Trading Limited

Lewis, Matthew Robert
Gateway Spirit Co Ltd

Lewis, Norman John, Dr
Anno Distillers Limited

Lewis, Penelope Frances
The Hebridean Liqueur Co Ltd
The High Street Trading Co Ltd

Lewis, Roy Thomas
The Hebridean Liqueur Co Ltd
The High Street Trading Co Ltd

Leyshon, Sioned Haf
Hendre Distillery Ltd

Leyshon, William Ion
The Somerset Cider Brandy Co Ltd

Liddle, Alex David
True North Brew Co Limited

Lillington, James Peter
Lillington Distillation Ltd

Lilly, Jon
Scream Retail Limited

Lincoln, Darren
Kendal Brewery Ltd

Lind, Linda Ellis
LLDR Alexandria Ltd

Lindley, Stacey Amanda
AM Distilling Ltd

Lindsey, Tomas David
Greywood Distillery Limited

Ling, Robert Harry
Alcohols Limited

Linn, Henry
Rivington Distillery Ltd

Linter, Graham John
Foxhole Spirits Limited

Linter, Samantha Martha
Foxhole Spirits Limited

Little, Hugh Wilson McIntosh
Dark Matter Distillers Limited

Liveras, Luke John
Liveras Limited

Livingston, Bryan
Isle of Iona Gin Limited

Livingstone, Scott
Chivas Brothers Limited

Lochhead, Iain MacGregor
The Bombay Spirits Co Ltd
John Dewar and Sons Limited

Lock, John Reginald
The Lincoln Distillery Limited

Locke, Alasdair James Dougall
Glenrinnes Distillery Limited

Lockwood, Ian Victor
Thames Distillers Limited

Loftus, Ronald John
Black Powder Gin Co Ltd

Logan, Andrew Kenneith
Atom Supplies Limited

Lombard-Chibnall, Margaret Elizabeth
Lombard Scotch Whisky Limited

Lombard-Chibnall, Richard Anthony
Lombard Scotch Whisky Limited

Long, Mark William
Brindle Distillery Limited

Long, Samantha Jane
The Spirits of Bronte Drinks Co. Ltd

Longden, Aaron
Beaumonde Desserts Limited

Lothian, Hamish James Gurmin
The Exeter Distillery Ltd

Loubser, Abraham Michael Christian
Orbis Whiskey Limited
St. James Distillery Limited

Louden, Adrian Ross
Contract Bottlers Glasgow Ltd

Lovell, William Guy
Millom Distillery Limited

Lowe, Anthony James
Equilibrium Food & Drink Ltd

Lowe, Jane
Spice Island Gin Co Ltd

Lowe, Lucy Nadine
Cambridge Distillery Ltd

Lowe, Mark
Spice Island Gin Co Ltd

Lowe, William John
Cambridge Distillery Ltd
Oxford Distillery Limited

Lowry, David
Mourne Mountains Whiskey Co Ltd

Lowry, Nathan Nicholas
Amber Glen Scotch Whisky Co., Ltd

Lowthian, Ian Stuart
John Dewar and Sons Limited

Luck, Alexander Michael
R & T Stills Limited

Lugovyy, Yuriy
Spirit of Unicorn Ltd

Lugsdin, Charles Angus Hamilton
Salcombe Distilling Co Ltd

Luke, Karen Elizabeth
Heart of Suffolk Distillery Ltd

Luke, Martyn Jon
Heart of Suffolk Distillery Ltd

Lulham, Michael Brian Julian
Burnbrae Distillery Co Ltd

Lumber, Peter
Lumber Distillers Limited

Lund, Spencer Marcus
Fanny's Distilling Co Ltd

Lundie, Alan William
Kirklee Scotch Whisky Limited

Lundie, Anne Marion Young
Kirklee Scotch Whisky Limited

Lunn, Jordan
Dr Eamers Emporium Limited
West Midlands Distillery Ltd

Lunn, Lorna
Dr Eamers Emporium Limited

Luthra, Dhruv
Back Bar Spirits Limited

Lux, Donn
Luxco Drinks Limited

Lydon, Greg
Sword of Spirit Distillery Ltd

Lydon, Gregory
Spirit of Leeds Ltd

Lyle, Timothy Harold Garnett
Broad Street Brands Limited

M'benga, Dominic Oseman
The Hooting Owl Distillery Ltd

Maab, Christoph Arnold
James Johnstone Distillers Ltd.

Mac-Crohon Ron, Ramon
Goldy Gin Limited

MacAlister Hall, Emma
Beinn An Tuirc Distillers Ltd

MacAlister Hall, Kenneth Arthur
Beinn An Tuirc Distillers Ltd

MacAlister Hall, Niall Donald Andrew
Beinn An Tuirc Distillers Ltd

MacAngus, Daniel Manuel
Castleheather Facilities Management Ltd

MacDonald, Elizabeth Jean
Adelphi Distillery (1826) Ltd
Adelphi Distillery Limited

MacDonald, Glen
Isle of Iona Gin Limited

MacDonald, Jamie John
Company of Dark Spirits Ltd
Dark Spirits Co Ltd

MacEachran, Ronald Bannatyne
Isle of Harris Distillers Ltd

MacInnes, Catherine
Golden Measure Limited

MacInnes, Paul Stewart
Finnieston Distillery Co Ltd

MacKay, Ian Anderson
Carse of Stirling Distillers Ltd

MacKay, Katherine Louise
Whitetail Spirits Limited

MacKay, Laurence
Whitetail Spirits Limited

MacKenzie, Amelia Ann
Castleheather Facilities Management Ltd

MacKenzie, Andrew Campbell
Verdant Spirits Ltd.

MacKenzie, Donald
The Islay Boys Limited

MacKinlay, Nial James
Wee Beastie Ltd.

MacLennan, Danny
Clyde Bottlers Ltd

MacLeod, Dawn Louise
Dram in a Can Limited

MacLeod, Iona
Askival Rum Ltd

MacLeod, Leslie McDonald
Isle of Mull Gin Distillery Ltd
Isle of Mull Gin Limited
The Mull Gin Co Ltd
The Mull Gin Distillery Ltd

MacLeod, Skye
Askival Rum Ltd

MacNab, Stuart
Chivas Brothers Pernod Ricard
The Gin Hub Limited
MacNab Distilleries Limited

MacRae, Darren
The Southey Brewing Co Ltd

MacRaild, Angus William
McMillan MacRaild Ltd

MacTaggart, John Auld, Sir
Renegade Spirits Grenada Ltd

Mackey, Patrick Philip
The Distillers of St.Andrews Ltd
St.Andrews Gin Co Ltd
St.Andrews Whisky Co Ltd

Mackie, William
Blinders Pubs & Clubs Ltd

Mackintosh, Ewen Cameron
Avonside Whisky Limited
The Benromach Distillery Co Ltd
Elgin Bonding Co Ltd
Glen Gordon Whisky Co Ltd
Gordon & MacPhail Limited
Gordon Bonding Co Ltd
James Gordon Whisky Co Ltd
Red Door Gin Co Ltd
Speymalt Whisky Distributors Ltd
Strathnairn Whisky Limited

Maclaren of Maclaren, Donald
Amber Glen Scotch Whisky Co., Ltd

Macpherson, Fiona
Loch Lomond Liquor Co Ltd

Madrid, Dominga
Norcabis Ltd

Mafi, Katherine Victoria
The Dirty Drinks Collective Ltd

Mageean, Barry Joseph
Taplin & Mageean Ltd

Maglanque, Josephine
Nestwonder Ltd

Magness, Paul Richard
R & T Stills Limited

Maguire, Benjamin Charles
HMS Spirits Co Ltd

Mahler, Aniko
Justerini & Brooks,Limited

Mainardi, Ernesto
Luxury Spirit Co Limited

Mair, Crispin John
Ditchling Spirits Limited

Mair, Derek Joseph
Glasgow Gin Co Ltd

Majidi, Majid
Ferintosh Whisky Limited

Major, Kara Elizabeth
3R Whisky Limited
Carillon U.K. Limited
Diageo Balkans Limited
Diageo Distilling Limited
Justerini & Brooks,Limited
United Distillers UK Limited

Mall, Ashim
Cox & Mall Ltd

Mallalieu, Steven
JustaGinCo Ltd

Mallows, Andrew Bernard
Bottlers & Distillers (Wales) Ltd

Mallows, Rhys Andrew
Bottlers & Distillers (Wales) Ltd

Malt, Felicity Ann
Pell and Co Spirits Limited

Malt, Ricky Kennan
Pell and Co Spirits Limited

Malvisi, Geoffrey Peter
3D Shapie Limited

Mann, Joseph William
The Liqueur Manufactory Ltd

Mannion, Sacha Charles Joseph
Hatters Distillery Limited

Mansfield, Molly
The Oxfordshire Gin Co Ltd

Manton, Liam
Alderman's Drinks Ltd.

Margolis, Sebastian Nikolaus
Riktig Limited

Marinov, Pavel
Doggy John Distillery Limited

Mark, John James
Jim & Tonic Limited
Pipeline Drinks Ltd

Marney, Thomas William
Somerset Distillery Ltd

Marran, Leanne Fay
Sipsmith Limited

Marsden, Richard James
RSM Solutions (NE) Limited

Marsden, Samantha
Yarm Brewing and Distilling Co Ltd

Marsden-Smedley, James Philip
Foxhole Spirits Limited

Marsh, Paul Anthony
Clock Tower Distilleries Ltd

Marsh, Stephen Nicholas Bowyer
Ginmeister Ltd

Marshall, Christopher
Snowdonia Distillery Ltd

Marshall, Nick Simon
Salcombe Distilling Co Ltd

Marshall, Stephen Joseph
East Neuk Organic Brewing & Distilling

Marston, Benedict John
Chalk & Charcoal Limited

Marston, Kate
Chalk & Charcoal Limited

Marten, Lewis Benedict Sinclair
Duration Brewing Ltd

Martin, Hamish
The Old Curiosity Distillery Ltd

Martin, Liberty Grace Dearden
The Old Curiosity Distillery Ltd

Martin, Paul Edward
Juniper Street Gin Co Ltd

Martin, Scott Buchanan
Oktogin Ltd

Martin, William Richard
Cornish Spiritsmith Ltd

Martin-Wells, Thomas Antony, Dr
Martin-Wells Distillery Ltd.

Mason, Adam Christopher
Ginomics Ltd

Mason, Catherine
Masons Yorkshire Gin Ltd

Mason, Cory John
Still on the Hill Limited

Mason, Karl Warren
Masons Yorkshire Gin Ltd

Massey, Catherine
Butlers Cross Limited

Massey, David Julian
Butlers Cross Limited

Masters, Nicholas James Whishaw
180 East Limited

Masterson, Paul
Deeside Distillers Ltd

Mastrantuono, Alessandro
2H1O Limited

Mastrantuono, Guido Pietro
2H1O Limited

Mastrapasqua, Sabino Antonio
Mastropasqua & Brothers Ltd.

Mather, James Edward Maxwell
Honey Spirits Co Ltd

Matheson, Claire
The Balno Distillery Limited

Matheson, Donald John Marshall
The Balno Distillery Limited

Matheson, Sandy
Granite North Spirits Limited

Mathew, Paul
London Botanical Drinks Ltd

Mathieson, Gregor Alexander Jack
The Edinburgh Distillery Co Ltd.
Edinburgh Whisky Ltd.

Mathieson, John Neil MacLeod
Jedhart Distillery Limited
Mossburn Distillers Limited
Torabhaig Distillery Limited

Matthews, Colin
Glen Scotia Distillery Co Ltd
The Littlemill Distillery Co Ltd
Loch Lomond Distillers Limited
Loch Lomond Distillery Co Ltd

Mattu, Sukhveer Singh
Drinkology Limited

Maule, Rowan
Princetown Distillers Ltd

Maxwell, Paula
Kinelarty Limited

Maxwell, Wellwood George Charles
Thames Distillers Limited

Maycock, James Warren
W.C. Fowler & Sons Limited

Mayes, Tom
Edmunds Cocktails Ltd

Mayfield, David Richard
The Cornish Gin Mine Ltd

Mayrose, Edward Wayne
The Benriach Distillery Co Ltd
Glendronach Distillery Co Ltd
The Glenglassaugh Distillery Co Ltd

McAllister, Kenneth Andrew
Morrison Glasgow Distillers Ltd

McAllister, Sinead Elizabeth
Matthew D'Arcy & Co Ltd

McAulay, John
Tolsta Europe Ltd

McAvoy, Lucy Catherine
Four Sisters Distillery Ltd

McBain, Gordon White
Artificer Spirit Limited

McCaig, David Francis Anderson
Otter Distillery Limited

McCaig, Mary-Ann
Otter Distillery Limited

McCall, Bryan Charles
Legendary Distillers Ltd

McCall, Jonathan
Ginsecco Ltd

McCallum, Andrew David
McCallums Liqueurs Ltd

McCallum, Ashley
AM Distilling Ltd

McCann, Cameron
Stirling Distillery Co Ltd
Stirling Gin Ltd.

McCann, June
Stirling Distillery Co Ltd
Stirling Gin Ltd.

McCarney, Stephen Lawrence
Broughton Ales Limited

McCarthy, Paul Brian
Horseguards London Dry Gin Ltd

McCay, Danny
Swift Half Collective Ltd

McClatchey, Robert
The London Distillery Co Ltd

McClune, Iain
Bright Spirits Limited

McCourt, Judith
Fancy A Tipple Limited

McCree-Cox, Tabatha Justine
Tarbraxus Distillers Ltd

McCreery, Sean Frederick
Ginmeister Ltd

McCroskie, Scott John
Edrington Distillers Limited
The Edrington Group Limited
HS (Distillers) Limited
Highland Distillers Group Ltd
Highland Distillers Limited
The Macallan Distillers Ltd

McCulloch, Ian Douglas
Silent Pool Distillers Limited
Spiritmen Limited
The Surrey Hills Distilling Co Ltd
Surrey Hills EBT Limited
The Surrey Hills Whisky Co Ltd
Whiskymen Limited

McDonald, Iain James
Nightrep Limited
The Perth Distillery Co Ltd

McDonough, John
Speyside Distillers Co Ltd

McDougall, Ian
Glasgow Distillery Co Ltd

McDougall, Kecia
Tay Spirits Ltd.

McGeoch, Andrew John
Glaswegin Distilling Co. Ltd

McGeoch, Neil James
Lochlea Distilling Co Ltd

McGibbon, Patrick Joseph
Hinch Distillery Holdings Ltd
Hinch Distillery Limited
Hinch Whiskey Co Ltd
Ninth Wave Gin Co Ltd

McGirr, Joseph Michael
The Boatyard Distillery Ltd

McGivern, Matthew
Rebel Distillers Ltd
Rebel Rabbet Ltd

McGlone, Sean
Bright Spirits Limited

McGowan, David Andrew
Broughton Ales Limited

McGrane, Enda, Dr
Drumeland Distillery Ltd

McGuinness, Danny
Great Don Ltd

McGuinness, Thomas Stanley
Atom Supplies Limited

McHattie, John
The Dundee Distillery Co Ltd

McHattie, John Neil
Lochglen Whisky Co Ltd.

McIntosh, Alastair Stiles
Alastair McIntosh Management Services
Syndicate 58/6 Limited

McIntosh, Alister Douglas
Chivas Brothers Limited

McIntosh, Carol Patricia
Alastair McIntosh Management Services

McIntosh, Charles Rome
Alastair McIntosh Management Services
Syndicate 58/6 Limited

McIntosh, James Alexander
Mackintosh Gin Limited

McIntyre, Bridget Fiona
Adnams PLC

McIntyre, James Matthew
Cragside Spirit Co Ltd

McIntyre, Scott James
Twisted Melon Scotland Limited

McIvor, David
Be Rude Not To Ltd

McKay, Conor
One Swan Ltd

McKechnie, Andrew
Flagg Ltd

McKenzie Smith, Andrew James
The Lindores Distilling Co. Ltd

McKenzie, Harold Richard
Richie & Nikki Ltd

McKenzie, Michelle Dawn
V7 Enterprises Ltd

McKenzie, Nickeysha Alecia
Richie & Nikki Ltd

McKeown, John
Ulverston Gin Limited
Wolftown Distillery Limited

McKeown, Michael Anthony
Matthew D'Arcy & Co Ltd

McKerr, Jennifer
McKerr Farming Ltd

McKerr, Stephen
McKerr Farming Ltd

McKerrell, Rory Gavin
Greywood Distillery Limited

McLaren, John Alexander
The Macallan Distillers Ltd

McLauchlan, David Donald
Finnieston Distillery Co Ltd

McLaughlin, Alastair Paul
The Glens of Antrim Whiskey Co Ltd

McLaughlin, Julia
New Comber Distillery Ltd

McLaughlin, Raymond
DWD Whiskey Co Ltd
LWD Holdings Limited
TCBP Holdings Limited

McLean, Colin [1982]
Bloodline Spirits Ltd

McLean, Colin [1989]
McLean's Gin Ltd

McLean, Julie
Bloodline Spirits Ltd

McLeod, Duncan Paul
Fairfields Liqueurs Ltd

McMillan, Jonathan William Allan
McMillan MacRaild Ltd

McMillan, Stuart Nicol
Kinrara Distillery Limited

McNally, Jamie
Hoyle Bottom Spirits Ltd

McNally, Owen
Hoyle Bottom Spirits Ltd

McNichol, Peter Bryan
York Gin Co Ltd

McQueen, Dale
Trossachs Distillery Limited

McQuillan, Alan
The Bloomsbury Distillery Ltd

McRobie, Bruce Kenneth
The Silvertown Brewery and Distillery Co

McSherry, Gerrard
Block, Grey and Block Limited
Burnbrae Distillery Co Ltd
Campbell Meyer & Co Limited
Glasgow Partners Ltd.
Glen Clyde Ltd.
Hart Brothers Limited

McSorley Walker, Margaret Mary
New Galloway Inspired Ltd

McVeigh, Cathal Peter
The Irish Gin Co Ltd

Meakin, Harry William
Montoscar Enterprises Limited

Mehta, Ankit
Universal Robo Innovations Ltd

Mehta, Sanjiv Mahendra
The East India Company Gin Ltd

Mellis, Graeme Stuart
Wild and Spirited Limited

Mellor, Gillian Mary
Spirit of Yorkshire Limited

Mellor, Thomas Leslie
Spirit of Yorkshire Limited

Menne-Ullrich, Iris
Liquid Spirit Ltd

Menzies, Paul Rothwell
Sheffield Distillery Limited

Merchant, Paul
Gin-Ger Gin Limited

Meredith, Elaine Joan
Hussingtree Blends Limited

Meredith, Richard William
Hussingtree Blends Limited

Metcalfe, Paul
MK Drinks Co Ltd

Mew, Daniel Robert Alan
Mews Gin Co Ltd

Mew, Jill Barbara Duval
Mews Gin Co Ltd

Mew, Richard Martin
Mews Gin Co Ltd

Meyer, Greg, Dr
Wilmington Spirits Limited

Michael Bell, Dylan
Rebel Rabbet Ltd

Michaluk, Generald Robert
Loch Earn Brewery Ltd

Michaluk, Veronica
Loch Earn Brewery Ltd

Michell, Joanne
Mousehole Brewery Limited

Mickaite, Ineta
Honey Spirits Co Ltd

Micklethwait, Walter Harry
Inshriach Distilling Limited

Middelbeek, Elfi Mathilda Maria
Jesmond Distilling Co Ltd

Midgley, Bruce Christopher
Brentingby Gin Ltd

Miklaucich, Gavin
GNR Distillery Limited

Miles, Richard
Glen Scotia Distillery Co Ltd
The Littlemill Distillery Co Ltd
Loch Lomond Distillers Limited
Loch Lomond Distillery Co Ltd

Millar, Gregory Leslie
Dartmoor Whisky Distillery Ltd

Miller, Douglas Robert
Canebrake Ltd

Miller, Emma Margaret
Somerset Drinks Ltd

Miller, Keith James
Diageo Scotland Limited

Miller, Leah Catherine
El Gin Findrassie Ltd

Miller, Marcin Adam
Still on the Hill Limited

Miller, Paul
Blendworks Ltd
Eden Mill Distillers Ltd
St Andrews Brewers Limited

Miller, Servel, Dr
Caribbean Flaava Limited

Milligan, Billy
Maiden Batch Ltd

Mills, Christopher Mason
Joseph Mills (Denaturants) Ltd

Mills, Nigel John
The Lakes Distillery Company PLC

Mills, Noel Brendan
Mourne Dew Limited

Mills, Philip Stuart
Camden Distillers Limited

Mills, Ryan
Half Cock Limited

Mills, Thomas Christian
Malt of the Earth Whisky Co Ltd.

Mills, Tom
Murphy, Black and Mills Ltd

Milne, Alan David
City of Aberdeen Distillery Ltd

Minionis, Samuel
Amber Glen Scotch Whisky Co., Ltd

Minns, Steven
Abbey Distillery Ltd

Mitra, Suman
Mulberry Distillery Limited
Tippling Tonic Limited

Mitten, Anthony Paul
Northern Spirits Partnership Ltd

Mitten, Carl David
Northern Spirits Partnership Ltd

Mitten, Samuel Ian
Northern Spirits Partnership Ltd

Mitten, Stephen James
Northern Spirits Partnership Ltd

Mizrahi, David
Our/London Vodka Limited

Moat, Piers
Twisted Roots Distillery Ltd

Moffatt, Giles Jon Ashley
Ginmeister Ltd

Mohandas, Puthiyapurayil
U'Luvka Ltd

Moir, Adrian Gawain
Irish Whiskey Co Ltd - The

Moiser, Susan Jane
South Causey Distillery Ltd

Monehen, Jane
The Northumberland Gin Co Ltd

Monehen, Peter
The Northumberland Gin Co Ltd

Monks, Peter David
Shakespeare Distillery Limited

Montador, Simon Alexander
Highland Boundary Ltd

Montgomery, Andrew
Kinelarty Limited

Montgomery, James David Keith
Loch Leven Distillery Limited

Moody, Mike
Moody Rum Ltd

Moore, Christopher George
Harbour Gin Co Ltd

Moore, Kevin Benedict
Leith Liqueur Co Ltd

Moore, Lorraine
Moores of Warwick Limited

Moore, Lucy Catriona, Dr
Bitter Union Limited

Moore, Martin Keith
Moores of Warwick Limited

Moore, Thomas Samuel
Bitter Union Limited

Moradpour, Thomas Jean
The Glenmorangie Co Ltd
MacDonald & Muir Limited

Morgan, Brian, Professor
The New Welsh Whiskey Co Ltd

Morgan, Jonathan Peter
The Yorkshire Rum Co Ltd

Morgan, Rebecca Kate
Grain Artisan Ltd

Morgan, Robert Frederick
The Peak District Distilling Co Ltd

Morgan, Sian
The Yorkshire Rum Co Ltd

Morgunov, Dmitry
The Lindores Distilling Co. Ltd

Mori, Minori
Tomatin Distillery Co Ltd,(The)

Morland, Victoria
Liberty Orchards Limited

Morley, Kevin, Professor
Pronto Cocktails Limited

Morris, Michael
Hinch Distillery Holdings Ltd
Hinch Distillery Limited
Hinch Whiskey Co Ltd
Ninth Wave Gin Co Ltd

Morrison, Alexander Campbell
The Pentland Still Ltd

Morrison, Andrew
Clydeside Distillery Limited

Morrison, David Donald Corbett
Dallas Dhu Ltd
Sangobeg Ltd

Morrison, James Ross
Sangobeg Ltd

Morrison, Jeffrey Scott
Azenja Limited

Morrison, Katrina Croft
Morrison Glasgow Distillers Ltd

Morrison, Michael Joseph
Isle of Barra Distillers Ltd

Morrison, Robert
Brain Brew UK Limited

Morrison, Stanley Andrew
Stanley Morrison & Co. Ltd
Morrison Glasgow Distillers Ltd

Morrison, Stanley Walker
Stanley Morrison & Co. Ltd
Morrison Glasgow Distillers Ltd

Morrissey, Nicola Margaret
Nero Drinks Co Ltd

Motley, Paul Charles
Pocketful of Stones Distillers Ltd

Motojima, Yoshisuke
Ben Nevis Distillery (Fort William)
Demball Limited

Moyes, Lucas
The Ribble Valley Gin Co Ltd.

Mozley, Gareth James
The South London Urban Gin Co Ltd

Muhonen, Svetlana
Jefferson & Bennett Distillers Ltd

Muir, Brian George
Nitrogin Ltd.

Muir, Stephen Robert
NB Distillery Limited

Muir, Vivienne
NB Distillery Limited

Mullen, David Owen
Summerhall Distillery Limited

Mullett, Susan Rosemary
Bath Botanics Limited

Mulligan, David
Ban Poitin Ltd

Muncie, Helen, Dr
Gin Kitchen Limited

Munnoch-Wahlberg, Mark James
SOS Gin Ltd

Munoz, Jose Padilla
Beam Suntory UK Limited
Morrison Bowmore Distillers Ltd

Munro, Hugh
Riverside Spirits Ltd

Munro, Jamie
Whitetail Spirits Limited

Murin, Larry
Hibernian Beverage Group Ltd

Murphy, Kieren Sean
Ellon Spirit Co Ltd

Murphy, Lianne Karen, Dr
Murphy's Gin Ltd

Murphy, Mark Francis, Dr
Murphy's Gin Ltd

Murphy, Paul
Murphy, Black and Mills Ltd

Murray Wells, Jamie Nicholas
Fixed Axis Ltd

Murray, Claire Margaret
Dunnet Bay Distillers Ltd.

Murray, Karen Elizabeth
Jones Gin Ltd

Murray, Martin John
Dunnet Bay Distillers Ltd.

Murray, Neil Ronald
Jones Gin Ltd

Murray, Robert
Harley House Distillery Ltd

Musgrave, Katie Victoria, Dr
The South Devon Liqueur Co Ltd

Myburgh, Ivor West
Anura Drinks Ltd

Myburgh, Renee Monique
Anura Drinks Ltd

Naik, Julian
Lonberg Limited

Napier, Calum James
Wee Hemp Spirits Ltd

Napier, Rebecca Grace
Wee Hemp Spirits Ltd

Narang, Ramesh Kumar Rochiram
U'Luvka Ltd

Nasim, Basit
Kammerling's Investment Holdings Ltd
Kammerlings Limited

Nathan, Steven Jeffrey
Distell International Holdings Ltd

Navale, Samrat Ashok
The East India Company Gin Ltd

Naylor, Jake Jefferson Ryan
The Portsmouth Gin Co Ltd

Neep, Paul Anthony
The Lakes Distillery Company PLC

Neill, John James Whitley
Whitley Neill Limited

Neilson, Abbie Louise, Dr
Cooper King Distillery Ltd

Neilson, Andrew Gold
The Raw Distiller Ltd

Nekic, Sasha
Tubeoptics. Ltd

Nelson, Heather
Toulvaddie Distillery Limited

Nelson, Jonathan Bernard
The River Test Distillery Ltd

Nelson, Peter Jonathon, Dr
Ardbeg Distillery Limited
Ardbeg Limited
Bonding and Transport Company, Ltd
The Glenmorangie Co Ltd
Glenmorangie Distillery Co Ltd, The
Glenmorangie Spring Water Co Ltd
Alistair Graham Limited
MacDonald & Muir Limited
MacDonald Martin Distilleries Ltd
Douglas MacNiven & Co Ltd
James Martin & Company, Ltd
Morangie Mineral Water Co Ltd
Morangie Springs Limited
Charles Muirhead & Son. Ltd
Nicol Anderson & Co Ltd
Tarlogie Springs Limited

Nelson, Sarah Kate
The River Test Distillery Ltd

Nelstrop, Andrew Leethem
English Whisky Co. Limited
Norfolk Whisky Co. Limited

Nelstrop, Barbara Ann
English Whisky Co. Limited

Nelstrop, Kathryn Anna
English Whisky Co. Limited

Neville, Quentin John
Artisan Blending Limited

Nevin, Miranda Sophie Carin
Hayman Distillers Limited

Newall, Sharon
Arisaig Distillers Ltd
The Pink Gin Co Ltd

Newburg, Daniel
Craft Distilling Expo Limited

Newson, Warwick Ian
The Strontium Gin Co Ltd

Newton, James
Whitby Gin Limited

Ngoma, Kenna
Beaumonde Desserts Limited

Niang-Fall, Ely
Ely's Cocktails Ltd

Nicholls, Martin David
Zero-Moo Ltd

Nichols, Joe
Lanty Slee Liquor Co Ltd

Nicholson, James
Inspirited Ltd

Nicholson, Lawrence
Inspirited Ltd

Nickerson, Stuart
The Shetland Distillery Co Ltd
The Shetland Whisky Co Ltd

Nickerson, Wilma
The Shetland Distillery Co Ltd
The Shetland Whisky Co Ltd

Niclasen, Martin
Crossbill Distilling Limited

Nicol, Finlay James Gowl
1725 Limited

Nicol, Harriet Mary Alexandra
1725 Limited

Nicol, James
Forest Spirits Ltd

Nicolson, Thomas Paul
Still on the Hill Limited

Niles, Julian Patrick
Seaway Royale Limited

Nisbet, Christopher William
Colonsay Beverages Ltd.

Nisbet, Kirstie, Dr
Granite North Spirits Limited

Noble, Lucilla Charlotte James, Lady
Torabhaig Distillery Limited

Noble, Roy
The Welsh Whisky Co Ltd

Nolan, Vincent Hugh
Isle of Wight Distillery Ltd

Nolte, Werner
Angola Beverages Holding Co Ltd
Distell International Holdings Ltd
Distell International Limited

Nordstrom, Blake
Privacy Domains Limited

Norgaard, Soren
Cu Dhub Distilling Co Ltd

Northern, Georgina
Ginmeister Ltd

Norton, Claire Louise
The Little Red Berry Co Ltd.

Notley, Philip Andrew
Demon Vodka Limited

Noyce, Vincent Robert Amos
The Portsmouth Distillery Co Ltd
The Rum Club Ltd

O'Baoighill, Seamus Earraghaidheal
West Highland Distillers Ltd

O'Brien, Eamon
British and Colonial Merchants of Jamaica

O'Donnell, Catrina
Cloughmor Consulting Ltd

O'Donnell, Ruairi
Cloughmor Consulting Ltd

O'Grady, Avril
The Hebden Bridge Spirit Co Ltd

O'Grady, Michael, Dr
The Hebden Bridge Spirit Co Ltd

O'Shea, Justin Daniel
Goldy Gin Limited

O'Sullivan, Killian
London Distillery - Battersea Ltd
The London Distillery Co Ltd

Oag, John Philip
Loch Ness Drinks Ltd

Oatley, Richard Alexander
The Rum Club Ltd

Odim, Edward
Coleburn Distillery Limited
Towiemore Distillery and Warehousing

Odunukwe, Chibueze Charles
Charlie Kaane Enterprises Ltd.

Oenga, Elkanah Ondieki
Alko Vintages UK Ltd

Offord, Malcolm Ian
The Three Stills Co Ltd

Oganian, Zakar
London Alcohol Co Ltd
London Vodka Ltd

Ohara, Andy
O'Hara's Spiced Rum Limited

Ollman, Simon Keith
Clwydian Range Distillery Ltd

Omara-Okello, Tom Ivan
Potion Universe Ltd

Omarkongolo, Moses
Black Label Spirits Ltd

Oosthuizen, Nardus
Burn Stewart (U.S. Holdings) Ltd

Ord, Michael John
Morrison Bowmore Distillers Ltd

Ortiz, Hector
Compass Box Delicious Whisky Ltd.

Osborne, Neil Jeremy
Northumberland Spirit Co Ltd

Osmond-Evans, Anthony William David
The Beautiful Distillery Ltd

Othen, Laurie
Wayfinder Distillery Limited

Othen, Samantha
Wayfinder Distillery Limited

Owen, Owen Arwyn
Afallon Mon Cyf

Owen, Owen Gethin
Afallon Mon Cyf

Owen, Samuel James
Unconventional Distillery Co. Ltd

Palfreeman, Nigel
Ryhall Distillery Limited

Palij, Michael Ian Norman
Pure Distilled Spirit Co Ltd

Palmer-Phillips, Joanne Eryl, Dr
The Rutland Distillery Co Ltd

Palmer-Samborne, Alexander William
Skylark Distillery Ltd

Papworth, David Keith
Broad Street Brands Limited

Park, Ian Edward
The Ecclefechan Whisky Co Ltd

Park, Robert Alfred
The Ecclefechan Whisky Co Ltd

Parker, Alexander William
Highland Whisky Limited

Parker, Alistair Henry Ming
Fifty-Nine Spirits Co Ltd

Parker, Heather Patricia
Highland Whisky Limited

Parker, Naomi
Highland Whisky Limited

Parker, Stuart Douglas
LighthouseVodka Ltd

Parr, Alison Mary
Henstone Distillery Limited

Parr, Henry James Woodward
Otten Schmidt Ltd.

Parr, Shane Alexander
Henstone Distillery Limited

Parrott, Sean Dudley
The Peak District Distilling Co Ltd

Parsley, Mark Philip
Bashiba Gin Ltd

Parsons, Jeremy Winslow
Still on the Hill Limited

Passia, Lukas
Tea Venture Limited

Patel, Hina
Diageo Great Britain Limited
Diageo Scotland Limited

Patel, Umesh Kumar
The Old Chapel Brendon Limited
Wicked Wolf Limited

Patel, Vishal Ghanshyam
Csatrina Holdings Ltd

Paterson, Beth Johanna
Slamseys Drinks Limited

Paterson, Matthew John
Slamseys Drinks Limited

Paterson, Neil
Broken Wings Limited
Finnieston Distillery Co Ltd

Patey, Grant
Salcombe Moonshine Ltd

Pathak, Vikram
Jivana Spirits Ltd.

Patterson, Neil Desmond
Patterson and Clarke Distillery Ltd
Red Distillery Limited

Pattison, Steven Clark
Jawbox Spirits Co Ltd

Paulsen, Frederik Dag Arfst
Mossburn Distillers Limited

Payne, Matthew Edward Charles
45 West Distillers Limited

Peachey, Edward Martin
Justerini & Brooks,Limited

Peachey, Janet May
Waveney Valley Spirits Limited

Pearce, Michael Garrick
Anno Distillers Limited

Pearson, Norman Mark
Strawhill Estate Distillery Ltd
Strawhill Estate Spirits Co Ltd

Pearson, Stuart
KSSM International Limited

Pechar, Edward
Broker's Gin Limited

Peck, Christian Maurice
Revelry Brewing & Distilling Ltd

Peck, Melanie Helen
Revelry Brewing & Distilling Ltd

Peddie, Tom
Godka Ltd

Pegler, Glynn James
Kiko Mezcal Ltd

Pelly, Guy
Fixed Axis Ltd

Penn, Clemency Rachel Lesley Indira
Myatt's Fields Limited

Penn, Craig Russell
Stargazey Spirits Ltd

Penn, Zara
Peakys Distillery Ltd

Pennington, Frederic William Fulton
Lakeland Moon Limited

Pennington, Michael Andrew
The Kendal Mint Cake Co Ltd
Lakeland Moon Limited

Pennington, Thomas B L
Liquid Lounge Drinks Co. Ltd

Penny, Christopher Mark
Pure Wild Spirits Ltd

Penrose, Andrew Graham
Devon Coast Distillery Limited

Pentith, Luke William
Whitby Distillery Limited

Perry, Alexander Henry
Seada Distillery Limited

Perry, Sarit
Twenty Oaks, Ltd

Persson, Carl Stefan Erling
The Ramsbury Brewing and Distilling Co

Pescatori, Antonio
Originalsip Ltd

Peterkin, Karen Dawn
Spirit of The Shires Limited

Peters, Hillar
HI&PE Limited

Petherick, Andrew John
Pilgrim Spirit Ltd

Petszaft, Justin Toby
Atom Supplies Limited

Phelan, Kieran Gerard
William Grant & Sons Distillers Ltd

Phillips, Carole Lesley
Todka Limited

Phillips, Christian Sion
Pure Spirit in Wales Limited

Phillips, Matthew James
The Bombay Spirits Co Ltd
John Dewar and Sons Limited

Phillips, Rosanna Charlotte
Eastwater Gin Ltd

Phillips, Simon
The Rutland Distillery Co Ltd

Phillips, William Charles Henry
The Armagnac Co Ltd

Phillipson, Michael
Galleon Liqueurs UK Ltd

Picard, Gabriel Jacques
Tullibardine Limited

Picard, Michel Bernard
Spirits Development & Management Company (SDMC)
Tullibardine Limited

Picken, Simon
Shakespeare Distillery Limited

Pickering, Marcus George
Pickering's Gin Limited
Summerhall Distillery Limited

Pike, Stuart James
KSSM International Limited

Pirie, Brian
AJC Homes Scotland Limited

Piro, Eduardo
Pococello Ltd

Plazewski, Dariusz
Bimber Distillery Ltd
Stolowa Ltd

Podoswa Marrun, Nitzan
Csatrina Holdings Ltd

Pollock, Rebecca
Seadwealths Ltd

Poonawala, Eddie
Glasgow Distillery Co Ltd

Poppleton, Stuart Ralph
Rockwood & Hines Limited

Porteous, James
Electric Spirit Co Ltd.

Porter, Andrew Justin Radcliffe, Professor
Langstane Liquor Co Ltd

Porter, Laurence Digby
Spirit of Malt House Limited

Porter-Smith, Robert Alan
Clifden Arms Property Ltd
Clifden Arms Trading Ltd

Potgieter, Hermanus Philippus
Soak Engineering Ltd

Powell, Owen
Gaslight Distillery Limited

Pownall, Simon
Hothams Limited

Prail, Nathan
Tuerto Tequila Ltd

Prehn, Nikolas Felix
Donnach Whisky Limited

Prentice, John Mark
Copeland Spirits Ltd

Prentice, Neil
Prentice Spirits Ltd

Price, Liam John
Revelry Spirits Ltd

Prichard, Lisa Claire
The Ethereal Cut Limited

Prichard, Mark
The Ethereal Cut Limited

Pringle, Norman Murray, Sir
Food Development Co Ltd

Prior, David Neil
Bladnoch Distillery Limited

Prowse, James Edward
Good Spirits Ltd

Pugh, Stephen Crommelin
Adnams PLC

Pullinger, Paul Stephen
The 808 Drinks Co Ltd

Purdie, Caroline Amy
Campbell Meyer & Co Limited

Purdy, Aileen Lorraine
Purdy Distillers Limited

Purdy, Andrew Neil
Purdy Distillers Limited

Purdy, John Raymond
Purdy Distillers Limited

Purdy, Kevin Matthew
Purdy Distillers Limited

Pusey, Jonathan Eric Dashfield
Vijobar Ltd

Pustovoytova, Elena
Global Premium Spirits Ltd

Puttick, Christopher
Hin Ltd

Pykett, Alex
Clifden Arms Property Ltd
Clifden Arms Trading Ltd

Pykett, Roy Frederick
Clifden Arms Property Ltd
Clifden Arms Trading Ltd

Quayle, Alexander Ciaran
Ramsbottom Gin Co Ltd

Quinn, Geoff
Buxton Distillery Limited

Quinn, Gordon Rodger
Badachro Distillery Ltd

Quinn, Vanessa
Badachro Distillery Ltd

Rackham, Jack Arthur
Single Estate Spirits Ltd

Rackham, James Arthur
Mayfield Distilling Co Ltd

Rackovs, Aleksandrs
Bros Distilling Ltd

Rackovs, Vitalijs
Bros Distilling Ltd

Radclyffe, Nicholas James
Foxdenton Estate Co Ltd

Radev, Georgi Dinkov
London Spiced Dry Limited

Radice, Daniel Brett
Anno Distillers Limited

Radosa, Lukas, Dr
Animal Spirits Ltd

Rae, William David
The 808 Drinks Co Ltd

Rafeeq, Atash Afzal
Caribbean Drinks Ltd

Rainier-Kirkwood, Gay Meryl
Swallow London Ltd

Raithatha, Sandeep
London Spice Co Ltd

Raithatha, Sheetal
London Spice Co Ltd

Rajput, Gaurav
Glenmaster Distillers Limited

Ramirez, Hernando
Luxbev Limited

Ramoutar, Tagore
Still on the Hill Limited

Ramsinghani, Rajesh Laxman Singh
U'Luvka Ltd

Ramsinghani, Sunil Laxman Singh
U'Luvka Ltd

Rankin, Andrew William
Greenwood Spirits Limited

Rankin, Stephen Alexander Masson
Avonside Whisky Limited
The Benromach Distillery Co Ltd
Elgin Bonding Co Ltd
Glen Gordon Whisky Co Ltd
Gordon Bonding Co Ltd
James Gordon Whisky Co Ltd
Speymalt Whisky Distributors Ltd
Strathnairn Whisky Limited

Rankine, Laura Agnes Anne
Ian MacLeod Distillers Limited

Rao, Bhavanam Srinivasa
Glencoe Distilleries Ltd

Raper, John Charles
Brittains Beverages Ltd

Rasgado, Sandro
Long Gin Ltd

Rattray, William John
Dark Matter Distillers Limited

Ray, Jonathan Cleeve
Brighton Spirits Co Ltd

Rayner, Paul Edward
Libation Liberation Limited

Read, Claire Angela
Cupids Bow 35 Limited

Read, Nicholas Charles
Cupids Bow 35 Limited

Read, Thomas, Dr
The Cornish Distilling Co Ltd

Reason, Andrew John, Dr
Anno Distillers Limited

Redding, Jonathan Mark
New Adventure (Norfolk) Ltd
Norfolk Gin Limited

Redding, Muriel Alison
New Adventure (Norfolk) Ltd

Reddy, Bhavanam Karan
Glencoe Distilleries Ltd

Reddy, Munnangi Soma Rushyanth
Glencoe Distilleries Ltd

Reddy, Munnangisita Ramanajneya
Glencoe Distilleries Ltd

Redfern, Noah
Gower Distillery Ltd

Redit, Neil Andrew
Elstead Village Distillers Ltd

Reed, Archie Patrick Finton
Arundo Limited

Reed, Martin Stuart
The Welsh Whisky Co Ltd

Reed, Nathan Ian Lloyd
Fire Beard Spirits Limited

Reed, Nicola Jane
Beeble Liquor Limited

Reeman-Clark, Anthony
Scotch Malt Distillers Ltd
Strathearn Distillery Ltd.

Rees, David Anthony
Garej Spirits Co Ltd

Rees, Karen
The Tiny Tipple Co Ltd

Reid, Christopher David John
Little Brown Dog Spirits Ltd

Reid, William
The Ecclefechan Whisky Co Ltd

Rendell, Simon
Horseguards London Dry Gin Ltd

Rennie, Josh Graham
Langstane Liquor Co Ltd

Renshaw, Claire
CP Infusions Ltd

Renshaw, Paul
CP Infusions Ltd

Renwick, Deborah
The Northumberland Gin Co Ltd

Renwick, Ian Douglas
The Northumberland Gin Co Ltd

Revie, Elspeth
LLDR Alexandria Ltd

Reyes, Robin Patrick
Nectardigger Ltd

Reyes, Toni Rose
Ataxirola Ltd

Reynier, Mark Bartholomew
Renegade Spirits Grenada Ltd

Richards, James Henry
Copper Drinks Limited

Richardson, David Hedley
The Edrington Group Limited

Richman, Susan
The Norfolk Rum Co Ltd

Richmond, Arthur William
Caledonian Bottlers PLC

Riddell, Walter John Buchanan, Sir
Moorland Spirit Co Ltd

Ridley, David John
The Artisanal Spirits Co Ltd
The Scotch Malt Whisky Society Ltd
J.G. Thomson & Co. Limited

Rigby, David James
Central Line Holdings Limited

Riley, Carly
Dr Junipers Ltd.

Rimmer, Allan Douglas
Isle of Bute Gin Co Ltd

Ritchie, Lorna Anne
Wallhouse Distillery Limited

Rivers, Oliver Max
Kammerling's Investment Holdings Ltd
Kammerlings Limited

Roane, Dayle Ivan
Molotov Brand Limited

Robbins, Philip Ronald Forgan
Forgan Distillery Ltd

Roberts, Anthony Brian
Borders Distillers Limited
The Borders Distillery Co Ltd
Borders Distilling Limited
The Three Stills Co Ltd

Roberts, Piers
Perfidious Albion Limited

Robertson, David Eric
McCaigs Distillery Ltd

Robertson, David Graham
The Holyrood Distillery Ltd

Robertson, Donald Sinclair Macpherson
Orkney Mead Ltd

Robertson, Emily
Round Wood Distillery Ltd

Robertson, Michelle Gayne
Orkney Mead Ltd

Robinson, Alan William
Aber Falls Distillery Limited
The Edinburgh and Leith Distillery
Liverpool Gin Distillery Ltd
H. J. Neill Ltd
Redrosesforme Limited

Robinson, Amanda Louise
Artisan Distillery (Staffordshire)

Robinson, Charlotte Louise Clifton
Rock Hill Cider Co Ltd

Robinson, David Peter
The Lakes Distillery Company PLC

Robinson, Dickon Hugh Wheelwright
Rock Hill Cider Co Ltd

Robinson, Hayley Teresa
Four Sisters Distillery Ltd

Robinson, Ian Booth
Alnwick Rum Co Ltd

Robinson, John
Artisan Distillery (Staffordshire)

Robinson, Philip Michael
The Pentone Family Limited

Robinson, Richard
The Sipping Shed Limited

Robson, Peter
House of St Giles Ltd
Jose Reyes Bodega Ltd
Loch Shiel Whisky Limited
Ron de Mestizo Ltd

Robson, Peter Joseph
Devine Distillates Group (Manufacturing)

Robson, Samuel Benzie
London Spiced Dry Limited

Roche, Dominic
Pronto Cocktails Limited

Roche, Sean
Loaded Spirits Ltd

Rochford, Craig Malcolm, Dr
Kac70 Limited

Rochford, Paul Henry
William Grant & Sons Distinction Ltd

Rogers, Christopher
Annandale Distillery Co Ltd

Rogers, Michael James
London Fortifiers Limited

Rogers, Peter Stephen
Salcombe Moonshine Ltd

Rolfe, Danielle Marie
Penton Park Brewery Limited

Rolfe, Guy William
Penton Park Brewery Limited

Rooney, Pauline Jean
Starling & Wasp Ltd

Rose, Kenneth James
LDC Scotland Limited

Rose, Nicholas
Glen Scotia Distillery Co Ltd
The Littlemill Distillery Co Ltd
Loch Lomond Distillers Limited
Loch Lomond Distillery Co Ltd

Rose, Scott
Dutch Courage Spirits Limited

Rose, Wayne
Cheshire Distilleries Limited

Ross, Alexander Walter
Ben Nevis Distillery (Fort William)

Ross, Douglas Charles
Dr Scotch Whisky Ltd.
Morrison Glasgow Distillers Ltd

Ross, Norman
Speymalt Whisky Distributors Ltd

Ross, William MacKay
Highland Toddy Ltd

Rossi, Fabio
Wilson & Morgan Limited

Rossi, Lorcan
Hibernian Beverage Group Ltd

Rotherham, John
Touch Lucky Limited

Rowley-Neale, Samuel James
Manchester Still Ltd.

Roy, Colin William
Mannequin Ltd.

Rudman, Elizabeth
Corner Fifty Three Distilling Ltd

Rudman, Thomas
Corner Fifty Three Distilling Ltd

Russell, Andre Eon
Montoscar Enterprises Limited

Russell, Angela Mary
Ian MacLeod Distillers Limited
Ian MacLeod and Co Ltd

Russell, David William Hodder
Ian MacLeod Distillers Limited
Ian MacLeod and Co Ltd
Wm Maxwell (Scotch Whisky) Ltd

Russell, Edith Stuart
Ian MacLeod Distillers Limited
Ian MacLeod and Co Ltd
Scottish Independent Distillers Co Ltd

Russell, Leonard Stuart
Broxburn Bottlers Limited
Edinburgh Gin Limited
Lang Brothers Limited
Ian MacLeod Distillers Limited
Ian MacLeod and Co Ltd
Wm Maxwell (Scotch Whisky) Ltd
Peter J Russell & Co Ltd.
Scottish Independent Distillers Co Ltd
Spencerfield Spirit Co Ltd

Russell, Lucinda
Peter J Russell & Co Ltd.

Russell, Peter James Sidney
Ian MacLeod Distillers Limited
Ian MacLeod and Co Ltd
Wm Maxwell (Scotch Whisky) Ltd

Russell, Robert Geoffrey
Russell Distillers Limited

Russell, Robert Matthew
Russell Distillers Limited

Russell, Stephen Geoffrey
Russell Distillers Limited

Russell, Walter James
Caskcoin Holdings Limited

Rutasikwa, Donald Paul
Matugga Beverages Limited
Matugga Distillers Limited

Rutasikwa, Jacine Louise
Matugga Beverages Limited
Matugga Distillers Limited

Rutherford, Alan Gray, Dr
Compass Box Delicious Whisky Ltd.
Jedhart Distillery Limited
The Lakes Distillery Company PLC
Torabhaig Distillery Limited

Ruzicka, Julia
Idle Saint Spirits Limited

Ryan, Clare Louise
The Edge Gin Ltd

Ryan, Louise
The Gin Hub Limited

Ryan, Michael Kevin
The Edge Gin Ltd

Ryan, Richard Henderson
Jawbox Spirits Co Ltd

Ryan, Victoria Joanne
Soulmate Gin Ltd

Ryder, Robert Malcolm
The Oxford Gin Co Ltd

Sadauskas, Antanas
Neptune SA Ltd

Sahota, Davinder Singh
Holler Brewery Limited

Salamashvili, Merab
Pesvebi Ltd

Salaya, Rosalyn
Amethystcave Ltd

Salmon, Edward
Tres Amigos Limited

Saltzherr, Dirk
Isle of Harris Distillers Ltd

Sambito, Ma. Annie Grezilda
Lianorin Ltd

Samways, Andrew Peter Robin
Single Estate Spirits Ltd

San Jose, Bianca
Musicspeller Ltd

Sandercock, Avian
Stargazey Spirits Ltd

Sandhu, Avtar Singh
Beerdsman Limited

Sandhu, Balwinder Kaur
Beerdsman Limited

Sandhu, Ragbhir Singh
Beerdsman Limited

Sandhu, Sukhwinder Kaur
Beerdsman Limited

Saunders, Braden Edward
Doghouse Distillery Limited

Saunders, Michael Stephen
Highland Distillers Group Ltd

Saunders, Patrick James
Black Shuck Ltd
Norfolk Distillery Ltd

Saunders, Sarah Elizabeth
Black Shuck Ltd
Norfolk Distillery Ltd

Savage, Patricia Bridget
The Glenallachie Distillers Co Ltd

Sawyers, Michael
Koolvibes Limited

Sayell, Damien Craig, Mr
Idle Saint Spirits Limited

Scothern, Lewis
Distillutions Ltd

Scothern, Paul
Distillutions Ltd

Scott, Leonora
Avinshaw Industries Limited
Inverroche International Ltd

Scott, Michael James
Avinshaw Industries Limited

Scott, Pamela Elizabeth
The North British Distillery Co Ltd

Scott, Sorcha
Askival Rum Ltd

Scott, Thomas
Loaded Spirits Ltd

Scott, Warren Michael
1761 Limited
Thomas Dakin Artisan Distillers Ltd
Thomas Dakin Craft Distillers Ltd
Thomas Dakin Distiller Limited
Thomas Dakin Limited
G & J Distillers Ltd.
G & J Greenall Group Limited
G & J Limited
Gilbert and John Greenall Ltd
The London Dry Gin Co Ltd
Marblehead Brand Development Ltd
The Soho Shebeen Co Ltd
The Still House Ltd

Seaton, Simon Derek
The London Distillery Co Ltd

Seczkowski, Przemyslaw Piotr
Bournemouth Distillers Limited

Seed, Donna
Bowland Distillery Ltd

Segrave, Oscar de Hane
Pentric Distillery Ltd

Sen-Ho, Chang
Matisse Spirits Co Ltd

Seneviratne, Rachitha
Jivana Spirits Ltd.

Serraglia, Ernesto
Wilson & Morgan Limited

Seth-Smith, William Jonathan Cory
Fixed Axis Ltd

Setterfield, Justine Laura
The Whitstable Distillery Ltd

Shackleton, Ian Alexander
Ian MacLeod Distillers Limited

Shalfrooshan, Mehdi
The Artisanal Spirits Co Ltd

Shand, Euan Coutts
Whisky Galore Limited

Shannon, Jack
Shannon & Thomas Limited

Sharman, Nicola Ann
Nibbs Spirits Limited

Sharman, Richard Michael
Nibbs Spirits Limited

Sharp, Steven Michael, Dr
Adnams PLC

Sharp, Susan
Harlequin Distillery Ltd

Sharrocks, Cheryl Anne
Stockport Gin Ltd

Sharrocks, Paul John
Stockport Gin Ltd

Shaw, Adam Dominic Bradley
Crossbill Distilling Limited
Crossbill Gin Limited

Shaw, Morven Fiona
Dulwich Gin Limited

Shaw-Browne, Guy
Sovereign Spirits Ltd.

Shaw-Browne, Luke
Sovereign Spirits Ltd.

Sheerin, Paul William
Flavour Premium Brands Limited

Shelbourne, James Clifford John
Spiritmen Limited
The Surrey Hills Whisky Co Ltd
Whiskymen Limited

Shenfield, Zak
Scotch Malt Distillers Ltd
Strathearn Distillery Ltd.

Sheriff, Gary
Sheffield Distillery Limited

Sherlock, Lianne
Distillers of Surrey Limited

Sherlock, Simon David
Distillers of Surrey Limited

Shevelev, Vladislav
KO Gin Limited

Shield, Darren James David
Fancy A Tipple Limited

Shoel, Graham Howard
William Grant & Sons Distillers Ltd

Shonpal, Jagdeep Singh
Csatrina Holdings Ltd

Short, Nigel Vernon
The Welsh Whisky Co Ltd

Showering, Jonathan
Brothers Drinks Co. Limited

Showering, Matthew Herbert
Brothers Drinks Co. Limited

Shubrook, Christine Anne
Elstead Village Distillers Ltd

Shubrook, Paul Richard
Elstead Village Distillers Ltd

Shuttleworth, Sean Anthony
Millom Distillery Limited

Siekierski, Alex
Tempus Gin Limited

Signolet, Lucie
Druid's Distillery Ltd

Signorello, Carmelo
Kafecal Global Co Ltd

Silva, Maria Joao Ferreira
Faith and Sons Limited

Sim, Alison Jane
Raven Spirits Limited

Sim, Callum Downie
Raven Spirits Limited

Sim, Peter Robert
Raven Spirits Limited

Sime, Kathryn Blanche
Blackford Craft Distillery Ltd

Sime, Katie Elizabeth
Blackford Craft Distillery Ltd

Sime, Keith Maurice
Blackford Craft Distillery Ltd

Sime, Neil Andrew
Blackford Craft Distillery Ltd

Simmonds, Carl Antony
Old Brenin Distillery Ltd

Simpson, Dylan Henry
The Cornish Distillery Co Ltd

Simpson, Neil Allan
Lone Wolf Spirits Limited

Singleton, Catherine
Brindle Distillery Limited

Singleton, Gerard Edmund John
Brindle Distillery Limited

Sirivadhanabhakdi, Panote
Blairmhor Distillers Limited
Blairmhor Limited

Sirivadhanabhakdi, Thapana
Blairmhor Distillers Limited
Blairmhor Limited
Inver House Distillers Limited

Skehan, James Anthony
Renegade Spirits Grenada Ltd

Skerratt, Karen Yvonne
Exeter Gin Ltd

Skerratt, Michael David Alexander
Exeter Gin Ltd

Skipworth, Paul Henry
The Artisanal Spirits Co Ltd
The Scotch Malt Whisky Society Ltd

Slater, Jessica Lucy
Whitby Distillery Limited

Slay, Benet Dunstan
Ncn'ean Distillery Limited

Sloan, David Alexander
CES Whisky Limited
John Fergus & Co Limited
MacDuff & Co Ltd
MacDuff (Scotch Whisky) Ltd
MacDuff International (Scotch Whisky)

Smallbane, Mathew
Fatman and Friends Ltd.

Smalley, Alexander David Strachan
Saddleworth Distillery Ltd

Smalley, Nicholas Geoffrey
The Teasmith Spirit Co Ltd

Smalley, Robert David Neil
Saddleworth Distillery Ltd

Smallwood, Mark
Alderman's Drinks Ltd.

Smart, Christopher Andrew, Dr
Smart Brewing and Distilling Solutions
The Surrey Copper Distillery Ltd

Smith, Alanna Naoimh
Beware Gin Brands Ltd.

Smith, Alison Joy
Nip from The Hip Limited

Smith, Andrew MacLeod
Escubac Limited
Sweetdram Limited

Smith, Andrew William, Dr
Little Brown Dog Spirits Ltd

Smith, Charles Monkton Lockhart
Unit Thirteen Limited

Smith, Charlotte
Riverside Spirits Ltd

Smith, Christopher Stephen
Distill8 Limited

Smith, Connor Jack
Commonwealth Gin Ltd

Smith, Craig
Parlay Drinks Ltd

Smith, Douglas Alexander
Hebridean Distillers Limited

Smith, Iain Stuart
Hebridean Distillers Limited

Smith, Inger Christine
Madame Jennifer Distillery Ltd

Smith, Ingrid Noel
Distinctively Orkney Drinks Ltd

Smith, Jamie Paul Vincent
The Jacobite Spirit Co Ltd

Smith, Jason McGuire MacKay
The Islay Boys Limited

Smith, Luke
Poetic License Distillery Ltd

Smith, Matthew Stephen
Beware Gin Brands Ltd.

Smith, Owen Oliver
Beware Gin Brands Ltd.

Smith, Patricia Elizabeth
The Smithies Gin Co Ltd

Smith, Paul William Cliburn
MWBH Bottling Co. Limited

Smith, Robert Scott
Distinctively Orkney Drinks Ltd

Smith, Simon Alexander
Lytham Distillery Co Ltd
Lytham Gin Co Ltd

Smith, Stephen Patrick, Dr
Beware Gin Brands Ltd.

Smith, Suzy
Matthew Gloag & Son Limited

Smith, Tye
Pryzm Cocktails Limited

Sneddon, Gail Marion
Gorgeous Gin Limited

Sokolov, Andrey
Global Premium Spirits Ltd

Sollom, Julian Wilfrid
Story Brands Limited

Sommerville, Judith Anne
William Grant & Sons Distillers Ltd

Sondur, Seshagiri
Annandale Distillery Co Ltd

Soora, Venkata Sainath
Conglomerate Spirits Ltd.

Sousa, Filipe Miguel Sequeira Rocha
Faith and Sons Limited

Southern, Howard
Moorland Spirit Co Ltd

Southworth, Tamara
Tickle Drinks Limited

Spackman, Anthony
Pronto Cocktails Limited

Sparks, Gregory
Hibernian Beverage Group Ltd

Speakman, Nick Paul
Kelpie Whisky Limited

Spears, James Allen
Azenja Limited

Spence, Ronald Thomas
Peedie Sea Distilling Limited

Spendlove, Lewis James
Bournemouth Distillers Limited

Spurrier, Barbara Joyce
Vijobar Ltd

Srikandan, Eric Satya Darshan
The Berkshire Distillery Ltd

Stancombe, Ann
Newbury Gin Limited

Stanforth, Andrew Colin Scott
Renaissance Vodka Limited

Stanforth, Andy
Renaissance Drinks Ltd

Staniland, Annette
Libaeration Limited

Staniland, Tim
Libaeration Limited

Stanley, Mark Arrowsmith
Cheshire Distilleries Limited

Stanley, Paul
Guilty Libations Limited

Stanta, Johannes Lukas, Dr
Horsforth Distillery Ltd

Stapleton, Anthony
The Jacobite Spirit Co Ltd

Stark, Richard
Eoforwic Distilling Co Ltd

Stefanuti, Ian
Buxton Distillery Limited

Stepanov, Nikita
Modern Botanicals Limited

Stephen, Mark James
Patient Wolf Limited

Stephens, Alex
The Churchill Distillery Ltd

Stephens, Nicholas William
Basil's Botanicals Limited

Stephenson, Carl Louis
The Bloomsbury Club UK Limited

Stephenson, Keith Caville
Alnwick Rum Co Ltd

Stephenson, Ruth Edith
Engin Yard Beverage Co Ltd

Stevenson, Alistair James Graham
The Glenallachie Distillers Co Ltd

Stevenson, Gilbert Buchanan, Dr
Islay Rum Co Ltd

Stewart, Alan Campbell
Rosebank Whisky Limited

Stewart, Donald John
Jorvik Distillery Limited
The Masham Distillery Co Ltd
Polaris Spirits Limited
Polestar Spirits Limited
York Distillery Limited

Stewart, Fiona Anne Campbell
Rosebank Whisky Limited

Stewart, George Danskin
Caperdonich Whisky Limited
Falkirk Gin Ltd
Falkirk Whisky Ltd
The Kelpies Whisky Limited
Rosebank Distillery Camelon Ltd

Stewart, Helen Avril
Badvo Distillery Limited

Stewart, Johnathan Charles
Bearded Lion Drinks Co Ltd

Stewart, Karen Margaret
The Kingsbarns Company of Distillers Ltd

Stewart, Matthew James Robertson
Rare Bird Distillery Limited

Stewart-Wood, Edward John Henry
Ten Bears Spirits Limited
Wood Brothers Distilling Co Ltd

Stibbe, Alan
Knockeen Hills Spirits Ltd

Stimson, James Peter
Curious Liquids Limited

Stirling, David William
Arbikie Distilling Limited

Stirling, Iain Anderson
Arbikie Distilling Limited
Arbikie X Limited

Stirling, John Alexander
Arbikie Distilling Limited
Arbikie X Limited

Stoddart, Timothy Dean
The Somerset Cider Brandy Co Ltd

Stokes, Stephen Harry
UK Distillers Limited

Stonex, Cato Henning
Westmorland Spirits Limited

Stow, Sarah
Portavadie Distillery Limited

Strachan, Craig Robert
The Start-Up Drinks Lab Ltd

Strang, Deborah Louise
The Shetland Distillery Co Ltd

Strang, Frank Allen
The Shetland Distillery Co Ltd

Stuart, MacNab
Coates & Co. (Plymouth) Ltd

Sudre, Guillaume
Ely's Cocktails Ltd

Sula, Serhat
Black Cat Distillery Limited

Sumner, Claire Louise
Tap End Brands Ltd

Sumner, Julie Anne
Rabakkan Ltd

Sumner, Robert Charles
Flavour Traders Limited

Sutcliffe, Jason Richard
Shotgun Limited
Wells Gin Limited

Sutherland, Alister John
South Loch Ltd

Sutherland, James Edward
South Loch Ltd

Sutherland, Richard Charles
South Loch Ltd

Sutherland, Susan
South Loch Ltd

Suttle, Graham Kenneth
Incognito Ltd

Swanson, George Allan
Leith Liqueur Co Ltd

Swinscoe, Jordan Karl
Batch88 Ltd

Symington, Andrew William
Dun Eideann Scotch Whisky Co Ltd
Edradour Distillery Co Ltd
Perthshire Whisky Co Ltd

Symington, Stephen Brian
Titanic Distillers Limited

Szor, Leon Daniel
The Cotswold Distilling Co Ltd

Tait, David
Goldings Distillery Ltd

Tait, Janet
Goldings Distillery Ltd

Tan, Andrew Chong Buan Lim, Dr
Whyte and MacKay Limited

Tantha-Obhas, Ueychai
Blairmhor Distillers Limited
Blairmhor Limited

Taplin, Chris Edward
Taplin & Mageean Ltd

Tapril, Stephen, Dr
Tappers Artisan Spirits Ltd.

Tardivel, Simon
Isle of Bute Gin Co Ltd

Tavener, Nicola Jane
Queen Cleo Rum Ltd

Tayburn, Lee Andrew
Liverpool Gin Distillery Ltd

Taylor, Douglas Adamson
The Botanist Limited
Lochindaal Distillery Limited
Port Charlotte Limited

Taylor, Graham
Crafty Scottish Distillers Ltd

Taylor, Graham Russell
Glasgow Whisky Limited

Taylor, James Geoffrey Bethune
180 East Limited

Taylor, Joanne
The Great Yorkshire Spirit Co Ltd

Taylor, Lynda
Union Distillers Ltd

Taylor, Mark
Long Walk Spirits Limited

Taylor, Victoria Jane
Glasgow Whisky Limited

Teeling, John James
Malcolm Browne Distillery Co Ltd

Telser, Marcel
Telser & Pauli Ltd

Temperley, Diana Elizabeth
The Somerset Cider Brandy Co Ltd

Temperley, Julian Harold Vazeille
The Somerset Cider Brandy Co Ltd

Temperley, Mary Clementine
The Somerset Cider Brandy Co Ltd

Temperley, Matilda Esmeralda Diana
The Somerset Cider Brandy Co Ltd

Tercero, Daniel Alejandro
Gower Distillery Ltd

Terrell, Lyndsey Ellen
Exeter Gin Ltd

Tesanovic, Filip
Spirit of Unicorn Ltd

Thapa, Bhai Raja
Amber Glen Scotch Whisky Co., Ltd

Thomas, Annabel Buick
Ncn'ean Distillery Limited

Thomas, Archelaus Joseph Harvey
Shannon & Thomas Limited

Thomas, Cerith James
NineTailsDistillery Ltd

Thomas, David
Garej Spirits Co Ltd

Thomas, Huw
The Welsh Whisky Co Ltd
Y Cwmni Chwisgi Cymraeg Newydd Cyf

Thomas, Joseph John
Penny Lane Gin Ltd

Thompson, Catherine Louise
Chivas Brothers Limited
The Gin Hub Limited

Thompson, David John Greenwood
Spirit of Yorkshire Limited

Thompson, George James
Dunbar Drinks Co Ltd

Thompson, Iain Christian
Azure Distilleries Limited

Thompson, Ian
Kettlesing Gin Limited

Thompson, Nathan Edward
The Clandestine Distillery Ltd

Thompson, Philip Duncan
Dornoch Distillery Co Ltd

Thompson, Rebecca Suzanne
Spirit of Yorkshire Limited

Thompson, Richard Ian
Kettlesing Gin Limited

Thompson, Sarah
The Boutique Cellar Limited
Windfall Wood Group Limited

Thompson, Simon Lowthian
Dornoch Distillery Co Ltd

Thomsen, Erik Pederson
CES Whisky Limited

Thomson, Benjamin John Paget
The Artisanal Spirits Co Ltd

Thomson, David Marshall Hall, Prof
Annandale Distillery Co Ltd

Thomson, Gregor McAulay
Still Shining Distillers Ltd

Thomson, Stuart Drysdale
Atlantic Distillery Ltd

Thongtheppairot, Prapakon
The Balblair Distillery Co Ltd
Blairmhor Distillers Limited
Blairmhor Limited
R. Carmichael & Sons Limited
James Catto & Co Ltd
Glen Calder Blenders Limited
Hankey Bannister & Co Ltd
Inver House Distillers Limited
The Knockdhu Distillery Co Ltd
J. MacArthur Jr. & Co. Limited
Mason & Summers Limited
Moffat & Towers Limited
The Pulteney Distillery Co Ltd
Speyburn-Glenlivet Distillery Co.
Wee Beastie Ltd.

Thornton, Fraser John
The Bunnahabhain Distillery Co Ltd
Burn Stewart (U.S. Holdings) Ltd
Distell International Holdings Ltd
Distell International Limited
Gordon Graham & Co Ltd
Hurlingham International Ltd

Thornton, Gary John
The Newcastle Whisky Distillery Co Ltd

Thorogood, John Laurence, Dr
Kilchoman Distillery Co Ltd.

Thorpe, Gabriella
LDN Spirits Limited

Thurlow-Begg, Richard
New Found Spirit Scotland Ltd

Thurston, Ashley Richard John
Sunfire Spirits Ltd

Thurston, Daniel Gary
Sunfire Spirits Ltd

Thurston, Sandra Jean
Sunfire Spirits Ltd

Tipler, George Michael, Captain
Lincoln Gin Ltd

Todd, Daniel
London Craft Distillers Ltd

Todd, Iain
The Kingston upon Hull Liqour Co Ltd

Toller, Alexandra
Henstone Distillery Limited

Toller, Christopher Ian
Henstone Distillery Limited

Tom Yew, Albert George
CL World Brands Limited

Tomlinson, Jessica Louise
Durham Gin Limited

Toms, Benjamin
Revelry Brewing & Distilling Ltd

Toms, Cassandra Jane
Revelry Brewing & Distilling Ltd

Toner, Regan
Distillery 96 Limited

Toomey, Aimee
Fox Gins Ltd

Toovey, Gwendolyn
Spirit of Captain Cook Limited

Torrance, Andrew
MacDuff & Co Ltd
MacDuff (Scotch Whisky) Ltd
MacDuff International (Scotch Whisky)

Torroella, Monica
Mezcal Reina Limited

Tough, Michael Stuart
Galldachd Na H-Alba Brewing Ltd

Townsend, Nicki Louise
Morant Bay Distillery Co Ltd

Townsend, Peter
Morant Bay Distillery Co Ltd

Townsend, Richard
Warwickshire Spirits Limited

Tran, James Douglas
JKM Spirits Limited

Traverso, Laurance
The Distinctly Different Spirits Co Ltd

Treadwell, Sean
Tready's Ltd

Trenchard, Rachel Elizabeth
Goosnargh Gin Ltd

Trenchard, Richard Ian
Goosnargh Gin Ltd

Trett, Samuel Joseph
Loca Beverages Ltd

Trevena, Michael
Snowdonia Spirit Co Ltd

Trimmer, Adan Anthony
Beaucroft Beverages Ltd

Trotter, Emily Charlotte
Little Rotters Limited

Tucci, Paolo Camillo
John Dewar and Sons Limited

Tucek, Hannah Eveline
Aberdeen Distillers Limited

Tucek, Robin Michael
Aberdeen Distillers Limited

Tucker, Harry
Sweetwater Distillery Limited

Tuddenham, Michelle
Raw Distilling Ltd

Turnage, William
180 East Limited

Turnbull, James Wilson
Food Development Co Ltd

Turnbull, Jonathan Michael
Kilchoman Distillery Co Ltd.

Turnbull, Simon March
Kilchoman Distillery Co Ltd.

Turner, Christopher Paul
Halton Turner Brewing Co Ltd

Turner, Eric Charles
Mossburn Distillers Limited

Turner, Kenneth John
Evolution Brewing Ltd

Turpin, Vincent
Chivas Brothers Limited
Chivas Brothers Pernod Ricard
Coates & Co. (Plymouth) Ltd
MacNab Distilleries Limited

Tutssel, Glenn Gifford
The Welsh Whisky Co Ltd

Tyler, Steven John
The Ecclefechan Whisky Co Ltd

Tyler-Street, William Gannel
Curio Spirits Co Ltd

Ubsdell, Mark
The Cuba Trading Co Ltd

Udale-Moseley, Isabel
Wrekin Spirit Limited

Uetsuji, Masumi
Tomatin Distillery Co Ltd,(The)

Unavane, Mukund, Dr
Linden and Lime Limited

Unsworth, Claire Elaine
Cartmel Gin Ltd

Urquhart, Neil Edward
Avonside Whisky Limited
The Benromach Distillery Co Ltd
Elgin Bonding Co Ltd
Glen Gordon Whisky Co Ltd
Gordon Bonding Co Ltd
James Gordon Whisky Co Ltd
Speymalt Whisky Distributors Ltd
Strathnairn Whisky Limited

Urquhart, Stuart David
Speymalt Whisky Distributors Ltd

Valius-Gilpin, Kristina Lisa
Westmorland Spirits Limited

Van Buuren, Martijn
Ginmeister Ltd

Van Schayk, Collin
VS Distillers Limited

Van Schayk, Emile Leonardus Josephus Maria
VS Distillers Limited

Van Zyl, Johan
Distell International Limited

Vaughan, Maxwell Lucas
The Peak District Distilling Co Ltd
White Peak Distillery Limited

Vaulkhard, Harry
Newcastle Gin Co. Limited

Vaulkhard, Oliver Tom
Newcastle Gin Co. Limited

Veitch, Graham Peter
45 West Distillers Limited
Urban Vodka Limited

Vig, Amandeep Kaur
Drinkology Limited

Vincent, Mary Anne
The Willow Tree Distilling Co Ltd

Vincenzo, Visone
The Still House Ltd

Visone, Vincenzo
1761 Limited
Thomas Dakin Artisan Distillers Ltd
Thomas Dakin Craft Distillers Ltd
Thomas Dakin Distiller Limited
Thomas Dakin Limited
G & J Distillers Ltd.
G & J Greenall Group Limited
G & J Limited
Gilbert and John Greenall Ltd
The London Dry Gin Co Ltd
Marblehead Brand Development Ltd
The Soho Shebeen Co Ltd

Volf, Michael Joseph
The Gibraltar Gin Co Ltd

Volschenk, Leonard Jacobus
Distell International Holdings Ltd

Wade, Katrina
The Brixham Gin Co Ltd.

Wadeson, Nick
Three Wrens Gin Limited

Wagner, George Jacob
American Beverage Marketers Ltd

Wainwright, Paul
Gaymens Gin Ltd

Waites, Rupert
Buck and Birch Ltd

Wakeham, Gemma Clare
Two Drifters Distillery Ltd

Wakeham, Russell Jon, Dr
Two Drifters Distillery Ltd

Wakelam, Ellen Catherine
In The Welsh Wind Distillery Ltd

Wakely, David
Cygnet Spirits Limited

Wakely, David Sidney
Cherry Drop Gin Ltd

Walford, Douglas
Afterthought Spirits Co Ltd

Walker, Andrew
New Galloway Inspired Ltd

Walker, Daniel Lee
Psychopomp Ltd

Walker, David Nathaniel
Cwmni Distyllfa Llanberis Cyf

Walker, Erika
The Spirit of Coalpit - Ysbryd y Pwll Glo

Walker, Laura Ann
Harrison Distillery Ltd

Walker, Matthew Mansell
UK Distillers Limited

Walker, Philip Lawrence John
The New Union Brewing Co Ltd

Walker, Stephen
The Spirit of Coalpit - Ysbryd y Pwll Glo

Walker, William James
The Glenallachie Distillers Co Ltd

Wallace, Derek Scott
The Ecclefechan Whisky Co Ltd

Wallace, Leanne
Wally Wonka Ltd

Wallace, Russell
Wally Wonka Ltd

Wallis, Adam John
Alcohols Limited

Wallwork, David Jonathan
Pure Wild Spirits Ltd

Walmsley, John
Lanty Slee Liquor Co Ltd

Walsh, Fiona Margaret
Redcastle Spirits Limited

Walsh, Neil
St Davids Gin Limited

Walsh, Ruth Louise
St Davids Gin Limited

Walters, John Anthony
JW Distillers Limited

Walton, Michael
Deer Island Distillery Limited

Walwyn-James, Christopher Darryl
Alnwick Rum Co Ltd

Warburton, Mark
Hawkshead Distillery Ltd
Hawkshead Gin and Spirit Co Ltd
Hawkshead Spirit Co Ltd
Ruskin Spirit Co Ltd

Ward, Emile
Gin Foundry Limited

Ward, Jeremy
Pin Fold Distillery Ltd

Ward, Kianne
Paradise Rum Limited

Ward, Matthew
Myperfectgin Ltd

Ward, Nicholas Howard
Irish Whiskey Co Ltd - The

Ward, Olivier
Gin Foundry Limited

Ward, Shaun Leslie
Shropshire Hills Distillery Ltd

Wardrop, Guy Thomas
Precision Spirits Ltd

Warke, Lauren Frances
Fourfolk Gin Co Ltd

Warner, Mark Douglas
Surrey Hills EBT Limited

Warner, Tom
Warner's Distillery Limited

Warner, Valentine Thomas
Moorland Spirit Co Ltd

Warren, Alice Faye
MK Drinks Co Ltd

Warren, Luke Anthony
Bitter Lemons Gin Ltd

Warren, Matthew James
Jim & Tonic Limited

Waters, Nagina Judge
Loch Ewe Spirits Limited

Waters, Patrick Rupert
Round Wood Distillery Ltd

Wates, Brian Michael
Scream Retail Limited

Watling, Richard Neil
The Cotswold Distilling Co Ltd

Watmough, George
Adventure Brands Ltd

Watmough, Jayne Margaret
Adventure Brands Ltd

Watson, Dorothy
Locksley Distilling Co Ltd

Watson, Gillian Anne McGregor
Speymalt Whisky Distributors Ltd

Watson, Jarlath Francis
Dunville & Co. Limited
Echlinville Distillery Limited

Watson, Scott McMurray
Ayrshire Craft Distillers Ltd
LDC Scotland Limited

Watt, Andrea
Orkney Spirits Limited

Watt, Gary David
Orkney Spirits Limited

Watt, Gordon Robert
The Edinburgh Distillery Co Ltd.
Edinburgh Whisky Ltd.

Watt, James Bruce
Lone Wolf Spirits Limited

Watts, Gary Stephen
Liquid Revolution Ltd

Watts, Stuart Henry
William Grant & Sons Distillers Ltd

Wear, Angus Robertson
El Pulpo Loco Ltd

Weatherall, Nicholas Mark
Weatheralls Distillery Limited

Weaver, Fawn
Uncle Nearest Ltd.

Welch, Jonathan David
Armadillo Spirits Limited

Weldon, Gary Owen
UK Distillers Limited

Weller, Sam
Conscious Collaborative Ltd

Wemyss, William John
The Kingsbarns Company of Distillers Ltd
Wemyss Distillery Limited

West, Fiona Colette Michelle
The Benriach Distillery Co Ltd
Glendronach Distillery Co Ltd
The Glenglassaugh Distillery Co Ltd

Weston, Simon John
Unit Thirteen Limited

Wharton, Stephen David James
Stargazey Spirits Ltd

Wheatley, Douglas Gordon George
Isle of Bute Gin Co Ltd

Wheeler, Attica
Waters of Deugh Limited

Wheeler, Martyn Gary
Waters of Deugh Limited

White, Charles Patrick Purcell
Cross Stream Distillery Ltd

White, Chloe Elizabeth
Cross Stream Distillery Ltd

White, Gerry
Jawbox Spirits Co Ltd

White, Phillip David
Conscious Collaborative Ltd

Whitehead, Caroline Mary
The Dartmouth Distillery Co Ltd

Whitehead, Lance James
The Dartmouth Distillery Co Ltd

Whitelock, Sian
The Welsh Whisky Co Ltd

Whiteside, Marc Andrew
Botanical Jack's Limited

Whiting, Andrew George
Crafted Beverages Limited

Whiting, Emma
Crafted Beverages Limited

Whiting, Francis
Stonehenge Distillery Limited

Whitley, Timothy John
Dartmoor Distillery Limited

Whitlock, Jennie Margaret
Braefoot Distillery Ltd

Whitlow, John Robert
Second Son Distillery Limited

Whitney, Hilary
EMS Corp Limited

Whittaker, Jane Suzanne
Harrogate Distillery Ltd

Whittaker, Toby Sam
Harrogate Distillery Ltd
Whittaker's Distillery Limited

Whittington, James
Glass Jigsaw Ltd.

Whitwell, Philip
Batch Brew Ltd

Wickman, Paul Nigel
The Bloomsbury Distillery Ltd

Wiggins, Jennie Louise
Curious Liquids Limited
Drinks of Manchester Limited
Spirit of Manchester Distillery Ltd

Wilczak, Barnaby Michael
Capreolus Distillery Ltd

Wild, James Anstey Preston
Incharvie Group Limited

Wilding, Joy Emily
Nip from The Hip Limited

Wilkins, Vincent James
Spirit of The Lakes Limited

Wilkinson, Alexander William Durham
Great Don Ltd

Wilkinson, Gary
The Suffolk Distillery Limited

Wilkinson, Gillian Margaret
Darlington Brewing and Distilling Co Ltd

Wilkinson, John Michael
4t's Brewery Ltd

Wilkinson, Melanie Mary
The Suffolk Distillery Limited

Wilkinson, Rachel Iona
Grey Dog of Meoble Limited

Wilkinson, Ralph English
Darlington Brewing and Distilling Co Ltd

Williams, Alan John
Hendre Distillery Ltd

Williams, Amanda Elisabeth
The Tiny Tipple Co Ltd

Williams, Anna May Iv
Second Son Distillery Limited

Williams, Antony James
Mezky Ltd

Williams, David Samuel Walter
Fifty-Nine Spirits Co Ltd

Williams, Harry
Great White Gin Limited
Liverpool Spring Gin Limited

Williams, Ian Edward
Desire Drinks Limited

Williams, Jack Peter
High Water Distilling Co Ltd

Williams, Jonathan
Barti Rum Ltd

Williams, Kay Maxine
New Forest Spirits Ltd

Williams, Mark Steven
New Forest Spirits Ltd

Williams, Richard John
Penrhos Spirits Ltd

Williams, Thomas Francis
Barcelona Spirit Brands UK Ltd

Williams, Timothy Lloyd
The Northlew Distillery Ltd

Williams, Victoria Nancy
Hendre Distillery Ltd

Williams-Silva, Linus Paul
H & S Distillers Ltd

Willis, Simon
Verset Vodka Holdings Limited

Willoughby, Helen
Rum To You Ltd

Wills, Anthony John Vernon
Kilchoman Distillery Co Ltd.

Wilson, Alistair MacCaskill
Isle of Skye Distillers Ltd

Wilson, Anthony Joseph
Alkemista Limited

Wilson, David Lloyd, Dr
Oxford Distillers Limited

Wilson, David William James
Beam Suntory UK Limited

Wilson, Gareth Malcolm
Crawford's Rock Ltd

Wilson, Matthew Philip
Yarm Gin Ltd
The Yarm Spirits Co Ltd

Wilson, Michelle
Crawford's Rock Ltd

Wilson, Nicola Louise
Oxford Distillers Limited

Wilson, Robert
Lamson Wine Co Ltd

Wilson, Ronald William Henry
Crawford's Rock Ltd

Wilson, Tessa Desanne
Crawford's Rock Ltd

Wilson-Laing, Scott Michael
WL Distillery Ltd

Wilton, Darren
The Whitstable Distillery Ltd

Winchester, Dale
D & M Winchester Ltd.

Winchester, Mark
D & M Winchester Ltd.

Winterbourne, Michelle
Fen Spirits Limited

Wirkner, Marina
Caribbean Drinks Ltd

Withers, Martyn Christopher
Lucent Drinks Ltd

Witter, Anita Beatrice
Jewel Isle Global Productions Ltd

Wodke, Maciej
Liquid Vision Enterprise Ltd

Wolens, Roger
Land's End Gin Limited

Wolpert, Alexander Michael Ramin
East London Liquor Co Ltd

Wolstencroft, Michael Graeme
Lytham Distillers Limited

Wood, Andrew Charles
Adnams PLC

Wood, Douglas
Kinrara Distillery Limited

Wood, James
The Gentlemen Distillers Ltd

Wood, Matthew
Conscious Collaborative Ltd

Wood, Stephen Ross
The New Forest Distillery Ltd

Woodburn, William
F.W Exports Ltd

Woodley, Adam Marc
Tickle Drinks Limited

Woods, Brian David
Ayrshire Craft Distillers Ltd
LDC Scotland Limited

Woodward, Geoffrey Dylan
The Honey Gin Co Ltd

Woodward, Nicholas Shaun
Armadillo Spirits Limited

Woodward, Nick
Jim & Tonic Limited

Woodyatt, Adam
Neat Distillery Ltd

Woodyatt, Beverley Anita
Neat Distillery Ltd

Woolgar-Norton, Michael Paul
Hoggnorton Limited

Woolhead, Rachel Margaret
R2 Distillers Ltd

Woolhead, Raymond Paul
R2 Distillers Ltd

Woolston, Gail Lesley Gina
The Really Brilliant Co Ltd

Woolston, Graham
The Really Brilliant Co Ltd

Worontschak, John Robert
The Ginking Co Ltd

Wratten, Kathryn Margaret Mary
Black Cat Brewery Limited

Wratten, Paul
Black Cat Brewery Limited

Wright, Alexander
Paradise Cocktails Ltd

Wright, Christopher James
Aber Falls Distillery Limited

Wrixon, Eric
Irish Whiskey Co Ltd - The

Wyatt-Nicole, Kieran David
KSSM International Limited

Yamaoka, Toshiya
Tomatin Distillery Co Ltd,(The)

Yeardley, Kane Steven
True North Brew Co Limited

Yeomans, Richard Spencer
The Glenmorangie Co Ltd
MacDonald & Muir Limited

Young, John, Dr
Ulster Distilleries Limited

Young, Jonathan David
20trees Gin Ltd

Young, Lorna Ann
20trees Gin Ltd

Young, Ronald William Grandison
Contract Bottlers Glasgow Ltd

Younger, Michael James
Edinburgh Gin Limited
Ian MacLeod Distillers Limited
Spencerfield Spirit Co Ltd

Yusen, Jonathan Mark
William Grant & Sons Limited

Zaum, Dan Lawrence
Greenwood Spirits Limited

Standard Industrial Classification
excluding
Distilling, rectifying and blending of spirits

01240 Growing of pome fruits and stone fruits
Damsons in Distress Limited
Liberty Orchards Limited

01270 Growing of beverage crops
Kiko Mezcal Ltd

01500 Mixed farming
Brindle Distillery Limited
McKerr Farming Ltd

01630 Post-harvest crop activities
Crawford's Rock Ltd
Damsons in Distress Limited

02300 Gathering of wild growing non-wood products
Mudlark Investments Ltd

10110 Processing and preserving of meat
Giorgio's Continental Ltd.

10320 Manufacture of fruit and vegetable juice
Food Development Co Ltd
Liberty Orchards Limited
Neptune SA Ltd
Spnet Ltd.
UK Dorset Ltd

10390 Other processing and preserving of fruit and vegetables
A Little Luxury Distillery Ltd
A Little Luxury Ltd
Food Development Co Ltd
Lincolnshire Gin Ltd

10512 Butter and cheese production
Giorgio's Continental Ltd.

10520 Manufacture of ice cream
Beaumonde Desserts Limited

10710 Manufacture of bread; manufacture of fresh pastry goods and cakes
Kafecal Global Co Ltd

10821 Manufacture of cocoa and chocolate confectionery
Linlithgow Distillery Limited

10831 Tea processing
Benjamin & Blum Limited

10840 Manufacture of condiments and seasonings
Hilary Blackford Associates Ltd
Caribbean Flaava Limited
Crawford's Rock Ltd
Riverside Spirits Ltd

10850 Manufacture of prepared meals and dishes
Caribbean Flaava Limited

10890 Manufacture of other food products n.e.c.
Azenja Limited
Equilibrium Food & Drink Ltd
London Spice Co Ltd
Wolftown Distillery Limited

11020 Manufacture of wine from grape [14]
Alko Vintages UK Ltd
Boutique Cellar Limited
Clandestine Distillery Limited
Cool Brew Dept Ltd
Michel Couvreur (Scotch Whiskies)
Devine Distillates Group (Manufacturing)
K1 Beer PLC
Ludlow Vineyard Limited
Luxbev Limited
Mastropasqua & Brothers Ltd.
Skinnybrands Ltd
Spirits Development & Management Company (SDMC)
Swift Half Collective Ltd
Universal Robo Innovations Ltd

11030 Manufacture of cider and other fruit wines [30]
A Little Luxury Distillery Ltd
Angola Beverages Holding Co Ltd
Boutique Cellar Limited
Brothers Drinks Co. Limited
Broughton Ales Limited
Clandestine Distillery Limited
Cool Brew Dept Ltd
Damsons in Distress Limited
Distell International Holdings Ltd
Ginsecco Ltd
Holler Brewery Limited
Kendal Brewery Ltd
Kingston upon Hull Liqour Co Ltd
Lamson Wine Co Ltd
Liberty Orchards Limited
Ludlow Vineyard Limited
Marron (Lincoln) Ltd
Neptune SA Ltd
New Union Brewing Co Ltd
One Swan Ltd
Penton Park Brewery Limited
Portsmouth Distillery Co Ltd
Rock Hill Cider Co Ltd
Saint Patricks Ltd
Salcombe Cider Co Ltd
Sky Pirate Ltd
Solway Spirits Ltd
Southey Brewing Co Ltd
Still Wild Limited
Zymurgorium Ltd

11040 Manufacture of other non-distilled fermented beverages [26]
Angola Beverages Holding Co Ltd
Animal Spirits Ltd
Brittains Beverages Ltd
Cool Brew Dept Ltd
Dirty Drinks Collective Ltd
Distell International Holdings Ltd
Dunbar Drinks Co Ltd
Ginsecco Ltd
Hawkshead Gin and Spirit Co Ltd
Kingston upon Hull Liqour Co Ltd
Lindsay's Still Room Ltd
Lochaber Craft Brewing and Distilling
London Botanical Drinks Ltd
Mastropasqua & Brothers Ltd.
Mulberry Distillery Limited
Norfolk Rum Co Ltd
One Swan Ltd
Originalsip Ltd
Rum Club Ltd
Saint Patricks Ltd
Sky Pirate Ltd
Thames Distillers Limited
Tiny Tipple Co Ltd
Tippling Tonic Limited
Universal Robo Innovations Ltd
Zymurgorium Ltd

11050 Manufacture of beer [51]
Adnams PLC
Batch Brew Ltd
Black Cat Brewery Limited
Boutique Cellar Limited
Branscombe Vale Brewery Ltd
Broughton Ales Limited
Clandestine Distillery Limited
Colonsay Beverages Ltd.
Darlington Brewing and Distilling Co Ltd
Droylsden Craft Limited
Duration Brewing Ltd
East Neuk Organic Brewing & Distilling
Etrusca Brewery & Distillery in St. Andrews
Evolution Brewing Ltd
Forth Bridge Brewery and Distillery
Galldachd Na H-Alba Brewing Ltd
Gleneagles Distillery Limited
Halton Turner Brewing Co Ltd
Holler Brewery Limited
K1 Beer PLC
Kendal Brewery Ltd
Kimbland Distillery Ltd
Liquid Revolution Ltd
Little Rotters Limited
Loch Earn Brewery Ltd
London Brewery Limited
Lost Roots Limited
Lough Neagh Distillers - 1837 Ltd
Luxbev Limited
Mersey Gin Co Ltd
Mousehole Brewery Limited
Mudlark Investments Ltd
New Union Brewing Co Ltd
One Swan Ltd
Penton Park Brewery Limited
Ramsbury Brewing and Distilling Co Ltd
Revelry Brewing & Distilling Ltd
Silvertown Brewery and Distilling Co Ltd
Skinnybrands Ltd
Sky Pirate Ltd
Solway Spirits Ltd
Southey Brewing Co Ltd
Square Street Distillery Ltd
St Andrews Brewers Limited
Steel River Drinks Ltd
Swift Half Collective Ltd
True North Brew Co Limited
Two Fathoms Distillery Ltd.
Universal Robo Innovations Ltd
Yarm Brewing and Distilling Co Ltd
Zymurgorium Ltd

11060 Manufacture of malt
Devine Distillates Group (Manufacturing)

The UK Spirits Industry

Glen Monarch Distillery Ltd
Justerini & Brooks, Limited
Scotch Malt Distillers Ltd

11070 Manufacture of soft drinks; production of mineral waters and other bottled waters [36]
Alko Vintages UK Ltd
Bitter Salvation Ltd
Botanical Alchemy Ltd
Caledonian Bottlers PLC
Country Garden Drinks Co Ltd
Diageo Great Britain Limited
Drinkology Limited
Equilibrium Food & Drink Ltd
Etoh Studio Limited
Gibraltar Gin Co Ltd
Ginsecco Ltd
Hawkshead Gin and Spirit Co Ltd
Hendre Distillery Ltd
Kendal Brewery Ltd
Kingston upon Hull Liqour Co Ltd
Koolvibes Limited
Liveras Limited
Loch Ness Drinks Ltd
London Botanical Drinks Ltd
Lough Neagh Distillers - 1837 Ltd
Luxbev Limited
Moores of Warwick Limited
Nele Drinks Limited
Neptune SA Ltd
Originalsip Ltd
Paradise Rum Limited
Portavadie Distillery Limited
Saint Patricks Ltd
Salcombe Cider Co Ltd
Sendivogius Limited
Start-Up Drinks Lab Limited
Strawhill Estate Spirits Co Ltd
Tea Rocks Ltd
UK Dorset Ltd
White Smoke Distillery Ltd
Willimott House Limited

15200 Manufacture of footwear
Soak Engineering Ltd

20140 Manufacture of other organic basic chemicals
Global Premium Spirits Ltd

20420 Manufacture of perfumes and toilet preparations
Linden and Lime Limited

20530 Manufacture of essential oils
Duckenfield Ltd
Linden and Lime Limited

20590 Manufacture of other chemical products n.e.c.
Alcohols Limited

21100 Manufacture of basic pharmaceutical products
St Andrews Botanics Limited

28990 Manufacture of other special-purpose machinery n.e.c.
EMS Corp Limited

32120 Manufacture of jewellery and related articles
Little Rotters Limited

32990 Other manufacturing n.e.c.
3D Shapie Limited
Jewel Isle Global Productions Ltd
Spirit of Yorkshire Limited
Whisky Galore Limited

41100 Development of building projects
AJC Homes Scotland Limited
K1 Beer PLC
Raer Scotch Whisky Ltd

41202 Construction of domestic buildings
AJC Homes Scotland Limited

46150 Agents involved in the sale of furniture, household goods, hardware and ironmongery
Todka Limited

46170 Agents involved in the sale of food, beverages and tobacco
Animal Spirits Ltd
Honey Spirits Co Ltd
Jervis Trading Limited
Lazy Drinks Ltd.
Luxury Trading Co Ltd
W & S Distillery Limited

46180 Agents specialised in the sale of other particular products
Vape Pure Ltd

46220 Wholesale of flowers and plants
Mudlark Investments Ltd

46341 Wholesale of fruit and vegetable juices, mineral water and soft drinks
Gibraltar Gin Co Ltd
Start-Up Drinks Lab Limited

46342 Wholesale of wine, beer, spirits and other alcoholic beverages [180]
180 East Limited
3 Lids Rum Ltd
55 Above Ltd
A Little Luxury Distillery Ltd
Adnams PLC
Adventure Brands Ltd
Afterthought Spirits Co Ltd
Alko Vintages UK Ltd
Angola Beverages Holding Co Ltd
Arisaig Distillers Ltd
Arundo Limited
Atom Brands Limited
Atom Cask Holdings Limited
Atom Drinks Limited
Atom Group Limited
Atom Scotland Limited
Atom Supplies Limited
Aztec Spirits Ltd
Be Rude Not To Ltd
Bearded Lion Drinks Co Ltd
Beeble Liquor Limited
Beets Incorporated Ltd
Benjamin & Blum Limited
Bitter Lemons Gin Ltd
Black Cat Brewery Limited
Bloomsbury Distillery Ltd
Bombay Spirits Co Ltd
Bonny Gin Ltd
Borders Distillers Limited
Borders Distilling Limited
Botan Grey Ltd
Brindle Distillery Limited
Broad Street Brands Limited
Brockmans Gin Limited
Broughton Ales Limited
Bunnahabhain Distillery Co Ltd
Burn Stewart (U.S. Holdings) Ltd
Chalk & Charcoal Limited
Clock Tower Distilleries Ltd
Cognac Growers' Collective Ltd
Coleburn Distillery Limited
Spencer Collings & Co Limited
Conscious Collaborative Ltd
Michel Couvreur (Scotch Whiskies)
Crafted Beverages Limited
Cuba Trading Co Ltd
De Facto Spirits Limited
Deco Spirits Limited
Delicious Drinks Limited
Demball Limited
Demon Vodka Limited
John Dewar and Sons Limited
Diageo Great Britain Limited
Dirty Drinks Collective Ltd
Distell International Holdings Ltd
Distell International Limited
Distillery 96 Limited
Doctor Bird Rum Ltd
Droylsden Craft Limited
Duchy Beverages Ltd
Edmunds Cocktails Ltd
Eight Vodka Limited
Ely's Cocktails Ltd
H.B. Evelyo Ltd.
Family of Hounds Limited
Foxhole Spirits Limited
GNR Distillery Limited
Galldachd Na H-Alba Brewing Ltd
Gibraltar Gin Co Ltd
Gin Dobry Gin Co Ltd

Ginkhana Limited
Glen Monarch Distillery Ltd
Glen Scotia Distillery Co Ltd
Glenallachie Distillers Co Ltd
Gleneagles Distillery Limited
Glenturret Limited
Matthew Gloag & Son Limited
Goldy Gin Limited
Good Life Gin Co Ltd
Good Spirits Ltd
Gordon & MacPhail Limited
Gordon Graham & Co Ltd
Greenwood Spirits Limited
Guilty Libations Limited
Halton Turner Brewing Co Ltd
Ian Hart Distilling Limited
Hidden Gem - Urban Artisan Spirit Ltd
Highland Distillers Limited
Hunter Douglas Scotch Whisky Ltd
Hurricane Rum Co Ltd
Irish Gin Co Ltd
Ironbridge Gorge Gin Co Ltd
Isle of Bute Gin Co Ltd
Jervis Trading Limited
Jivana Spirits Ltd.
Justerini & Brooks,Limited
Kimbland Distillery Ltd
Kirklee Scotch Whisky Limited
Kozuba & Sons Limited
LDC Scotland Limited
Andrew Laing & Co Ltd
Lamson Wine Co Ltd
Land's End Gin Limited
Lang Brothers Limited
Lanty Slee Liquor Co Ltd
Lazy Drinks Ltd.
Lincolnshire Gin Ltd
Liquid Lounge Drinks Co. Ltd
Liquid Vision Enterprise Ltd
Littlemill Distillery Co Ltd
Loaded Spirits Ltd
Loch Lomond Distillers Limited
Loch Lomond Distillery Co Ltd
Lombard Scotch Whisky Limited
Londinio Liqueurs Ltd.
London Spiced Dry Limited
Lough Neagh Distillers - 1837 Ltd
Ian MacLeod Distillers Ltd
Ian MacLeod and Co Ltd
Master of Malt Limited
Masters of Malt Limited
Maverick Brands Limited
Maverick Drinks Limited
Maverick Spirits Limited
Wm Maxwell (Scotch Whisky) Ltd
Mayfield Distilling Co Ltd
McLean's Gin Ltd
Mezcal Reina Limited
Modern Botanicals Limited
Molotov Brand Limited
Mr Kegz Ltd
My Nan's Favourite Ltd
Nele Drinks Limited
Nightrep Limited
NineTailsDistillery Ltd
Norfolk Rum Co Ltd
Old Brenin Distillery Ltd
Pant y Foel Gin Ltd
Perth Distillery Co Ltd
Pink Gin Co Ltd
Portavadie Distillery Limited
Portsmouth Gin Co Ltd

Pryzm Cocktails Limited
Psychopomp Ltd
Raer Scotch Whisky Ltd
Raven Spirits Limited
Red Door Gin Co Ltd
Maurice Richard Ltd
William Riddell & Sons Ltd
Row & Co Ltd
Rum Club Ltd
Peter J Russell & Co Ltd.
Russian Doll Vodka Limited
Sacred Spirits Holdings Ltd
Shieling Scotch Whisky Co Ltd
Solway Spirits Ltd
Somerset Craft Distillery Ltd
Speymalt Whisky Distributors Ltd
Speyside Distillers Co Ltd
Spirit of Glasgow Ltd
Spirits Development & Management Company (SDMC)
St Davids Gin Limited
Stockholm Distillers and Vintners
Stockport Gin Ltd
Sunderland Gin Limited
TBD Tipples Ltd
Telser & Pauli Ltd
Thames Distillers Limited
Three Stills Co Ltd
Tipo Loco Drinks Co. Limited
Titanic Distillers Limited
UK McLouis Liquor Co Ltd
Uncle Nearest Ltd.
West Spirits MCR Ltd
Whisky Galore Limited
Whitetail Spirits Limited
Whitley Neill Limited
Wild Foragin Ltd
Yarm Gin Ltd
Yarm Spirits Co Ltd

46370 Wholesale of coffee, tea, cocoa and spices

Botan Grey Ltd
British and Colonial Merchants of Jamaica

46390 Non-specialised wholesale of food, beverages and tobacco

Crafted Beverages Limited
Kafecal Global Co Ltd

46420 Wholesale of clothing and footwear

Maurice Richard Ltd

46900 Non-specialised wholesale trade

Dirty Drinks Collective Ltd
Jervis Trading Limited
Maurice Richard Ltd
Spnet Ltd.

47110 Retail sale in non-specialised stores with food, beverages or tobacco predominating

Cognac Growers' Collective Ltd
Paradise Cocktails Ltd
Rum Club Ltd
TBD Tipples Ltd

47190 Other retail sale in non-specialised stores

Hidden Gem - Urban Artisan Spirit Ltd

47250 Retail sale of beverages in specialised stores [49]

Adnams PLC
Artisan Brands Limited
Atom Brands Limited
Atom Cask Holdings Limited
Atom Drinks Limited
Atom Group Limited
Atom Scotland Limited
Atom Supplies Limited
Avinshaw Industries Limited
Blendworks Ltd
Bonny Gin Ltd
Break Line Brewing & Distilling Ltd
Bright Spirits Limited
British and Colonial Merchants of Jamaica
Club Rum Limited
Spencer Collings & Co Limited
De Facto Spirits Limited
Deco Spirits Limited
Dornoch Distillery Co Ltd
Eden Mill Distillers Ltd
Engin Yard Beverage Co Ltd
GNR Distillery Limited
Gin Dobry Gin Co Ltd
Good Spirits Ltd
Gordon & MacPhail Limited
HMS Spirits Co Ltd
Honey Gin Co Ltd
Hunter Douglas Scotch Whisky Ltd
Andrew Laing & Co Ltd
Lamson Wine Co Ltd
London Spiced Dry Limited
Master of Malt Limited
Masters of Malt Limited
Maverick Brands Limited
Maverick Drinks Limited
Maverick Spirits Limited
Oxford Gin Co Ltd
RWB Drinks Ltd
Red Door Gin Co Ltd
Sacred Spirits Holdings Ltd
Shieling Scotch Whisky Co Ltd
Shorts Boy Distillery Ltd
Somerset Craft Distillery Ltd
Speymalt Whisky Distributors Ltd
Spirit of Glasgow Ltd
Steel City Craft Spirits Boutique Ltd
TBD Tipples Ltd
Whitetail Spirits Limited
Yorkshire Gin Limited

47290 Other retail sale of food in specialised stores

Crawford's Rock Ltd

47810 Retail sale via stalls and markets of food, beverages and tobacco products [10]

Beaumonde Desserts Limited
Deco Spirits Limited
Engin Yard Beverage Co Ltd
Equilibrium Food & Drink Ltd
Good Spirits Ltd
Lincolnshire Gin Ltd
London Spiced Dry Limited
Modern Botanicals Limited
One Point Eight Bar Limited
Perth Distillery Co Ltd

The UK Spirits Industry

47910 Retail sale via mail order houses or via Internet [11]
Gin Foundry Limited
Gin Tales Ltd
Gleneagles Distillery Limited
Goldy Gin Limited
Hunter Douglas Scotch Whisky Ltd
Andrew Laing & Co Ltd
Perth Distillery Co Ltd
Portavadie Distillery Limited
Raven Spirits Limited
Shieling Scotch Whisky Co Ltd
Warwickshire Spirits Limited

47990 Other retail sale not in stores, stalls or markets
Hayter Divisions Limited
Hukleys Limited

50200 Sea and coastal freight water transport
New Dawn Traders Ltd

52103 Operation of warehousing and storage facilities for land transport activities [13]
Atom Brands Limited
Atom Cask Holdings Limited
Atom Drinks Limited
Atom Group Limited
Atom Scotland Limited
Broxburn Bottlers Limited
Coleburn Distillery Limited
Master of Malt Limited
Masters of Malt Limited
Maverick Brands Limited
Maverick Drinks Limited
Maverick Spirits Limited
Towiemore Distillery and Warehousing

55900 Other accommodation
Jo & Matt Ltd

56101 Licenced restaurants
78 Dbar Limited
Be Rude Not To Ltd
Duration Brewing Ltd
Incognito Ltd
Tres Amigos Limited

56103 Take-away food shops and mobile food stands
Kafecal Global Co Ltd
Spirit of Unicorn Ltd
Tres Amigos Limited

56210 Event catering activities
Alderman's Drinks Ltd.
Buck and Birch Ltd
Kammerling's Investment Holdings Ltd
Kammerlings Limited
Liquid Revolution Ltd
Modern Botanicals Limited
One Point Eight Bar Limited
Sloosh Limited

56290 Other food services
Beware Gin Brands Ltd.
Blend Experts Limited
London Spice Co Ltd
New Dawn Traders Ltd
Uncle Nearest Ltd.

56301 Licenced clubs
Beets Incorporated Ltd
Blend Experts Limited
Sloosh Limited

56302 Public houses and bars [14]
78 Dbar Limited
Barclay Distillery Limited
Be Rude Not To Ltd
Brindle Distillery Limited
Broken Wings Limited
Dr Eamers Emporium Limited
Duration Brewing Ltd
Dutch Courage Spirits Limited
Hackney Distillery Limited
Halton Turner Brewing Co Ltd
Libation Liberation Limited
Liquid Revolution Ltd
Sloosh Limited
True North Brew Co Limited

58190 Other publishing activities
Gin Foundry Limited

59111 Motion picture production activities
Cuba Trading Co Ltd

59113 Television programme production activities
Cuba Trading Co Ltd
Jo & Matt Ltd

61200 Wireless telecommunications activities
Spnet Ltd.

62012 Business and domestic software development
Luxury Trading Co Ltd

62020 Information technology consultancy activities
Knowcal Limited

62090 Other information technology service activities
Luxury Trading Co Ltd

63110 Data processing, hosting and related activities
Privacy Domains Limited

64202 Activities of production holding companies
HS (Distillers) Limited
LWD Holdings Limited

64209 Activities of other holding companies n.e.c.
CL World Brands Limited
Highland Distillers Group Ltd

68100 Buying and selling of own real estate
Castleheather Facilities Management Ltd
Soak Engineering Ltd

68209 Other letting and operating of own or leased real estate
Hinch Distillery Limited

70100 Activities of head offices
Burn Stewart (U.S. Holdings) Ltd
Diageo Great Britain Limited
Food Development Co Ltd

70210 Public relations and communications activities
Whisky Club Ltd

70229 Management consultancy activities other than financial management
Artisan Blending Limited
Hendre Distillery Ltd
Langs Consulting Ltd.
Mannequin Ltd.
Maxchater Ltd
Alastair McIntosh Management Services
Nightrep Limited
Rademon Estate Distillery Ltd
Whisky Club Ltd

71122 Engineering related scientific and technical consulting activities
Bros Distilling Ltd
Cloughmor Consulting Ltd
Nightrep Limited
Soak Engineering Ltd
Still Shining Distillers Ltd

72110 Research and experimental development on biotechnology
Animal Spirits Ltd

72190 Other research and experimental development on natural sciences and engineering
EMS Corp Limited
Libaeration Limited
Still Shining Distillers Ltd

73110 Advertising agencies
Beware Gin Brands Ltd.
Wicked Wolf Limited

73120 Media representation services
Old Chapel Brendon Limited

74100 Specialised design activities
Chalk & Charcoal Limited
Still Shining Distillers Ltd

74901 Environmental consulting activities
Caribbean Flaava Limited

74909 Other professional, scientific and technical activities n.e.c.
A.D.C. Halford & Co Ltd
Start-Up Drinks Lab Limited
YDC Ltd

74990 Non-trading company
Bunnahabhain Distillery Co Ltd
Gordon Graham & Co Ltd
Hurlingham International Ltd

77390 Renting and leasing of other machinery, equipment and tangible goods n.e.c.
Hooting Owl Distillery Ltd

77400 Leasing of intellectual property and similar products, except copyright works
Libaeration Limited
Whisky Club Ltd

79901 Activities of tourist guides
Sip Antics Limited

81300 Landscape service activities
Michel Couvreur (Scotch Whiskies)

82301 Activities of exhibition and fair organisers
Craft Distilling Expo Limited

82302 Activities of conference organisers
Craft Distilling Expo Limited

82920 Packaging activities
Broxburn Bottlers Limited
Contract Bottlers Glasgow Ltd
Distell International Limited
Gin Foundry Limited

82990 Other business support service activities n.e.c.
3R Whisky Limited
Aurora Brewing Limited
Bombay Spirits Co Ltd
Montrose Scotch Whisky Ltd.
Soul of The Spirit Limited

85520 Cultural education
Ginwimmin Ltd

85590 Other education n.e.c.
Belfast Gin and Spirits School Ltd
Belfast Whiskey School Limited

90020 Support activities to performing arts
Beets Incorporated Ltd
New Dawn Traders Ltd

90030 Artistic creation
Kiko Mezcal Ltd
Little Rotters Limited

91030 Operation of historical sites and buildings and similar visitor attractions
Glenturret Distillery Limited

96090 Other service activities n.e.c.
Belfast Gin and Spirits School Ltd
Belfast Whiskey School Limited
Exeter Gin Ltd
Holy Grail Beverages Limited
Kammerlings Limited
Lakeland Moon Limited
Whisky Galore Limited

99999 Dormant company
Coleburn Distillery Limited
Hidden Gem - Urban Artisan Spirit Ltd
Hurlingham International Ltd
Lime Street Distillery Limited
Towiemore Distillery and Warehousing

Printed in 8pt Nimbus Sans L

Designed by URW++ Design and Development GmbH

Dellam Publishing Limited

2 Heath Drive, Sutton, Surrey, SM2 5RP

Fax: 020 8770 7478   email: enquiries@dellam.com

SAN: 0177881   EAN/GLN: 5030670177882